INTERACTION DESIGN FOR COMPLEX PROBLEM SOLVING:
developing useful and usable software

Critical Acclaim for *Interaction Design for Complex Problem Solving*!

Barbara Mirel has spent years studying users for whom simple software solutions aren't sufficient. Interaction Design for Complex Problem Solving *is the first book to tackle the thorny problem of developing software that is both usable and useful for users who have complex problems to solve. With clear explanations, detailed case studies, and thoughtful ideas about how to proceed, this is an excellent resource for designers, developers, and usability specialists.*
Janice (Ginny) Redish, Redish & Associates, Inc.

At last we have a text to help interaction designers, technical communicators, and programmers understand (rather than defeat) the complexities of users engaged in knowledge work in real-world contexts. Barbara Mirel's Interaction Design for Complex Problem Solving *weaves theory and practice into a coherent, rich framework for thinking about, researching, and designing powerful and useful systems.*
Johndan Johnson-Eilola, Clarkson University

Barbara Mirel cracks open the problem of software usefulness with vigor and ambition. Her rich analysis of real-world problem-solving scenarios yields insight into previously neglected general and domain-specific aspects of complex problems. From these she generates much-needed advice for designing intelligently useful software.
T. R. Girill, University of California,
Lawrence Livermore National Laboratory

We are, in my view, faced with a new situation in design where the goal of software development is the facilitation of interaction and change. A reliance on process rather than upon static elements makes system design a challenging task: Barbara's contribution helps to inquire relevant elements, and arrange them for user- and work-relevant usage—a major breakthrough in contextual design.
Christian Stary, University of Linz, Austria

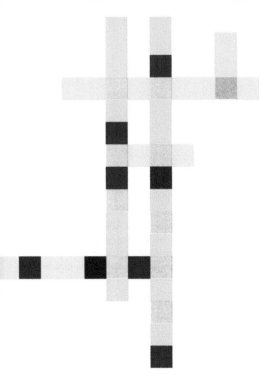

INTERACTION DESIGN FOR COMPLEX PROBLEM SOLVING:
developing useful and usable software

BARBARA MIREL

ELSEVIER

AMSTERDAM • BOSTON • HEIDELBERG • LONDON
NEW YORK • OXFORD • PARIS • SAN DIEGO
SAN FRANCISCO • SINGAPORE • SYDNEY • TOKYO

Morgan Kaufmann is an imprint of Elsevier

MORGAN KAUFMANN PUBLISHERS

Publishing Director: Diane D. Cerra
Senior Project Manager: Angela Dooley
Editorial Coordinator: Mona Buehler
Text Design: Graphic World Publishing Services
Composition: Cepha Imaging Pvt Ltd
Technical Illustration: Graphic World Illustration Studio
Copyeditor: Graphic World Publishing Services
Proofreader: Graphic World Publishing Services
Indexer: Graphic World Publishing Services

Morgan Kaufmann
An imprint of Elsevier
500 Sansome St., Suite 400
San Francisco, CA 94111
http://www.mkp.com

Printed and bound by CPI Group (UK) Ltd, Croydon, CR0 4YY
Transferred to Digital Print 2011

Library of Congress: Cataloging-in-Publication Data: A record for this book is available from the Library of Congress.

ISBN: 1-55860-831-1

This book is printed on acid-free paper.

The Morgan Kaufmann Series in Interactive Technologies

Series Editors:
- Stuart Card, PARC
- Jonathan Grudin, Microsoft
- Jakob Nielsen, Nielsen Norman Group

Interaction Design for Complex Problem Solving: Developing Useful and Usable Software
Barbara Mirel

The Craft of Information Visualization: Readings and Reflections
Written and edited by Ben Bederson and Ben Shneiderman

HCI Models, Theories, and Frameworks: Towards a Multidisciplinary Science
Edited by John M. Carroll

Web Bloopers: 60 Common Web Design Mistakes, and How to Avoid Them
Jeff Johnson

Observing the User Experience: A Practitioner's Guide to User Research
Mike Kuniavsky

Paper Prototyping: The Fast and Easy Way to Design and Refine User Interfaces
Carolyn Snyder

Persuasive Technology: Using Computers to Change What We Think and Do
B. J. Fogg

Coordinating User Interfaces for Consistency
Edited by Jakob Nielsen

Usability for the Web: Designing Web Sites that Work
Tom Brinck, Darren Gergle, and Scott D.Wood

Usability Engineering: Scenario-Based Development of Human-Computer Interaction
Mary Beth Rosson and John M. Carroll

Your Wish is My Command: Programming by Example
Edited by Henry Lieberman

GUI Bloopers: Don'ts and Dos for Software Developers and Web Designers
Jeff Johnson

Information Visualization: Perception for Design
Colin Ware

Robots for Kids: Exploring New Technologies for Learning
Edited by Allison Druin and James Hendler

Information Appliances and Beyond: Interaction Design for Consumer Products
Edited by Eric Bergman

Readings in Information Visualization: Using Vision to Think
Written and edited by Stuart K. Card, Jock D. Mackinlay, and Ben Shneiderman

The Design of Children's Technology
Edited by Allison Druin

Web Site Usability: A Designer's Guide
Jared M. Spool, Tara Scanlon, Will Schroeder, Carolyn Snyder, and Terri DeAngelo

The Usability Engineering Lifecycle: A Practitioner's Handbook for User Interface Design
Deborah J. Mayhew

Contextual Design: Defining Customer-Centered Systems
Hugh Beyer and Karen Holtzblatt

Human-Computer Interface Design: Success Stories, Emerging Methods, and Real World Context
Edited by Marianne Rudisill, Clayton Lewis, Peter P. Polson, and Timothy D. McKay

For Josh, Lisa, and Diana, who make complexity lovable.

TABLE OF CONTENTS

PREFACE

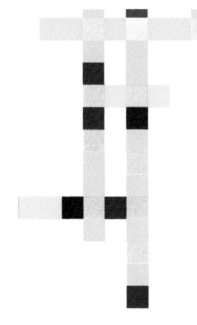

INTRODUCTORY QUOTATIONS

"Empty life of its incongruities... and [you impose a] simplification that coheres – and misapprehends everything" (Roth, 1998, 305).

"Context independencies and anytime-anywhere functionality are misguided...[I]n designing for real life, real contexts have to be part of the process" (Thackara, 2000, 12).

"It is very easy to be blinded to the essential uselessness of [products] by the sense of achievement you get from getting them to work at all. In other words...their fundamental design flaws are completely hidden by their superficial design flaws" (Adams, 1984, 177).

In describing computer interfaces and their potential to improve understanding, Nathan Shedroff (1997), an interaction design specialist, writes, "Certainly, we cannot say that computers have made us more 'wise,' but the interactions computers offer do give us more chances to communicate our thoughts and build wisdom if we only knew how to" (4). Similarly, this book envisions improved software that supports shared thoughts, discovery of knowledge, and wiser decisions, especially for complex problem solving. Yet, like Shedroff, I am concerned that we may not realize this vision because we do not know how to. Based on this concern, this book focuses on getting the work right when designing software for complex problem solving so that applications foster exploratory analysis, adapt to dynamic work, and extend knowledge and communication.

The book's vision centers on understanding and designing for the synergistic activities of users' dynamic work to ensure that applications for complex problem solving are truly useful. Getting users' work right involves capturing and accommodating users' emergent analytical activities, activities that are open-ended yet integrated and opportunistic yet coherent. In complex problem solving, users move through large volumes of data in problem spaces variably shaped by situational conditions, contingencies, and emergence. If application designers are to get users' work right, they must understand the contextual conditions shaping the intertwined regularities and idiosyncrasies of open-ended inquiries and create software that supports the right moves and degrees of freedom at the right times and places and for specific purposes.

In developing this useful support, human-computer interaction (HCI) specialists and others on a design team also need to get their own work right. Design thinking, methods, and choices must be in sync with the demands of complex problem solving. User-centered designing (UCD) is a start, but it is not enough. Designing for complex problem solving demands distinct approaches, as well.

In this book I explore in depth these two faces of "getting the work right:" (1) Understanding and aptly representing users' problem solving activities in which no one best path, no "true" answer, and no fixed rules for entry or stopping exists; and (2) following design approaches that lead to useful support for the structured openness of this problem solving. To examine both aspects of getting the work right, I present numerous extended scenarios of complex problem solving in context, which have been drawn from actual examples. For each, I examine approaches for designing for usefulness.

My own steps toward writing this book reflect these two aspects of "getting the work right," as well. First was the vision and understanding step. Initially with my dissertation and then for a decade after as a university professor, my research and teaching focused on discovering what people actually do when they conduct complex tasks in context and what support they need. I consulted in industry and conducted a good deal of user experience field studies and usability testing related to complex problem solving in numerous work settings. I gained insight into the behaviors and software interactions people performed as they carried out their complex analyses and decision-making in the midst of the diverse demands of their everyday work lives. I analyzed the support users received from their software for their open-ended inquiries, the support they needed, gaps between the two, and reasons for these gaps.

Initially, I focused on *instruction* as the critical factor for improving users' task performance—documentation and help. But I discovered from cumulative results of my studies and steadily advancing graphical user interfaces (GUIs) that this focus was misplaced. It became increasingly clear that even with more accessible interfaces and online help, problem solvers' most pressing difficulties with software for complex problem solving were not training issues. Rather they derived from inadequate representations of complex problem solving in the software and interfaces and insufficiently integrated program functions and features for users' contextually driven moves, strategies, and goals. I realized that for these deep-seated usefulness problems, instruction through online help and the like could not make up for ill-conceived designs; for complex tasks, presentation cannot be separated from application. During these years, my vision of users' complex problem solving evolved, and I came to understand that users need integrated support for the synergistic and integrated problem solving they do.

These "vision" years gave me a solid foundation in the experiences and needs of complex problem solvers and in the importance of treating software for complex problem solving as a distinct breed of design in order to make it useful. But my role as an academic researcher and consultant could only take me so far in understanding what is needed to develop useful support for complexity. At its heart, this question is one of implementation, and increasingly I wanted to explore it from the inside. I felt I needed to become part of a software team, a design team member, and a full-time user experience and usability specialist in a software company. Such an occasion presented itself in 1997, and with it the necessary next step toward writing this book: Experience in the design side of "getting the work right."

At an opportune moment, I was offered the lead human factors position in a software venture that was turning powerful, interactive data visualization technologies into commercial products for exploratory data analysis. I jumped at the chance to become part of the process of creating software for users' complex inquiries and to participate from the inside in what it takes, start to finish, to develop useful software for dynamic knowledge work. In the same way that I needed to see users' complex problem solving immersed in the context of their everyday work, I needed to see design efforts shaped by the day-to-day dynamics of production contexts. In industry, as in academia, I continued to analyze users' complex problem solving in context and the usability of software for it—always focusing on domain experts who are experienced in complex problem solving but are not power users. Now I also took part in the design process.

After a couple years with this visualization group, I moved to other lead usability positions in development organizations, each time working on software projects for users' complex tasks. This merging of vision and practice has been part of my work ever since. It runs throughout the book and is a strong motivation for writing the final chapter on the politics of usefulness—a chapter that looks ahead to what else besides appropriate design strategies and criteria we need to implement to ensure useful and integrated support for dynamic work. In terms of what else is needed, maneuvering politically to institute usefulness into the structures and practices of production contexts is just as important as adopting appropriate design practices.

WHAT IS IN THIS BOOK?

More than anything else, this book is an argument intended to help HCI specialists convince their managers and software teammates to pursue the design and development practices required for useful applications for complex problem solving. It is neither a how-to guide (although it offers many practical strategies and methods) nor an academic or theoretical treatment of software for complex problem solving (although it rests on and references numerous conceptual frameworks, principles, and research findings). Rather, this book makes a case for why we need to improve the design of applications for complex problem solving and suggests how to do so. It highlights the serious shortcomings in usefulness that occur in dynamic knowledge work when we do not adequately approach the design of these applications, and it elaborates on appropriate design assumptions, methods, and choices. It applies these approaches to specific areas of support that in actual work contexts prove to be crucial to achieving truly useful software for complex problem solving. Ideally, these arguments will help foster changes in development contexts and application designs.

Currently, HCI specialists address many issues contributing to the design of useful software for complex problem solving but, by and large, deal with them separately. For example, we variously specialize in understanding users' experiences in context; in applying interaction design patterns, scenarios of use and object-oriented designing; in supporting human cognition, problem solving and decision-making; in designing information visualizations and software agents for exploratory analysis; and in testing the usability of user interfaces. Unfortunately, in the field in general and in specific production contexts, very little "connective tissue" binds these distinct concentrations. A seamless path does not yet unite the interactive relationships among these critical dimensions of design. Consequently, we face a large gap with little direction for applying interconnected insights to the implementation of actual products. This book strives to unify all these issues–conceptually and practically–and does so by focusing on designing for complex problem solving as the binding force. Designing for usefulness can assume this unifying role, however, only if we see software for complex problem solving as a distinct brand of product development.

This book is the outcome of years of research into software-supported complex problem solving and extensive industry-based user observations, design experiences, and usability testing. In every chapter, I present and draw on scenarios of complex problem solving, all of them composites from my work observing and designing for more than 100 complex problem solvers in 30 work sites, primarily in three domains. As the scenarios in Part 2 depict, these domains are product marketing in retail, in-patient care and medication in hospitals, and advanced (tier-two and tier-three) troubleshooting in information technology (IT). I have conducted projects in other domains, as well, and other scenarios in the book relate to them.

Several themes structure the scenarios and design approaches I explore and develop throughout the book. Phrased as interrelated propositions for getting the work right in both senses of the meaning, they are as follows:

- Software teams need to treat applications for dynamic and exploratory analysis as a distinct breed of design, shaped by the dynamics and traits that distinguish complex problem solving from well-structured tasks.

- In this distinctive designing, teams must give usefulness top priority in usability engineering and bring software and usability engineering together in new ways by addressing usefulness requirements in the front-end of development.

- To ensure usefulness, HCI specialists must go to the field and watch and analyze users as they conduct their software-supported complex inquiries during their everyday jobs.

- In observing users and analyzing data, design teams must focus on users' high-level, integrated patterns of inquiry as they are shaped by interactivity, contexts, and variability (ICV).

- Because choices about *how* to represent users' dynamic work determine whether design teams create integrated or piece-by-piece support, teams must create models of users' coherent patterns of inquiry and turn them into conceptual designs before jumping to task and screen objects. They must represent how users move from indeterminacy to resolution based on interactive conditions and constraints, variable choice points, regularities, and idiosyncrasies, and how seemingly identical tasks, in fact, function differently for distinct goals and inquiry patterns.

- As they turn models of users' dynamic work into designs, interaction designers and their teammates must negotiate what, when, and how much adaptability, power, control, domain-specificity, and flexibility users need for seamlessly exploring problems and making valid judgments in uncertainty.

HOW IS THIS BOOK ORGANIZED?

In organizing the ideas and approaches of this book, I have sought to give readers many different ways into the material to suit their particular project needs and purposes. First, I have divided the book into three parts to highlight, respectively, the conceptual foundation for "getting the work right," the applied cases (three in-depth scenarios), and the politics of usefulness. Though organized into separate sections, these areas are inter-related. For example, readers interested in getting a high-level, practical overview may look at Chapter 3, methods relevant to designing for use-fulness for complex problem solving, and Chapter 9, a synthesis of the design strategies and choices covered in the in-depth scenarios.

Readers may also concentrate on supporting users' needs through interactive information visualizations or conventional GUIs by selectively reading certain scenarios. Scenarios in Chapters 1 and 4-7 focus on interactive visualizations; scenarios in Chapters 2 and 9 deal with standard GUI applications.

Moreover, in the three extended cases in Part 2, the diversity of scenarios is intended to meet the needs of readers who may be interested in just one specific type of problem and domain or in a variety of software-supported complex tasks. On one hand, each scenario offers an in-depth analysis of designing for an individual class of problem and domain: Troubleshooting, product mix, and in-patient drug dosage decisions. On the other hand, the diversity of cases enables readers to recognize both the generic and custom support that experienced problem solvers need across problem types and domains.

In addition to giving readers an opportunity to focus on classes of complex problems in specific domains, the variety of scenarios lets them look individually or combined at particular systems of work and degrees of problem complexity. Each scenario in Part 2 gives insight into a specific system of work and level of complexity, as follows:

Troubleshooting in highly sophisticated, multilayered technological systems—a "centrally scheduled" system of work: Problem solving is fairly complex due to entangled faults when a multi-tiered network is in crisis.

Optimal product mix decisions in volatile, adaptive social systems (markets)—an information service system of work, one in which analysts use software tools to explore market conditions: Deciding best assortments from many possible options is highly complex due to multivariate analysis, idiosyncratic conditions and constraints, and numerous contending criteria and priorities.

In-patient drug dosage decisions in complex social and technical systems that continuously adapt to and transform each other, with centralized record systems making this a flexible operations and administration system of work: Problem solving has a special brand of complexity due to users dynamically coordinating social processes of work across professional divisions and interacting with and interpreting data in a complex technical system of centrally computerized records.

Specifically, the issues emphasized in each chapter are as follows:

In Part One, Understanding the Work, **Chapter 1** defines the traits and uncertainty that distinguish complex problem solving from well-structured tasks. Through a scenario in which an analyst investigates whether to manufacture a new product, it exemplifies the distinct support people need for dynamic and emergent inquiries. This chapter also describes the interactive conditions within and across many contexts that combine with these distinguishing traits and uncertainty to shape the direction of people's open-ended inquiries.

Chapter 2 explains why, in usability engineering for complex problem solving software, concerns about usefulness must precede those related to ease of use and be given top priority in design. It describes the ways in which concentrating on usefulness requires software teams to focus on problem solvers' practical patterns of inquiry (often called application or socio-technical patterns), on the task landscapes problem solvers configure for these patterns, and on core activities within these landscapes. Through a scenario on risk assessment, this chapter exemplifies the software support a hospital team requires for its core activities in analyzing root causes of a medication error. The chapter establishes the main concepts and terms used throughout the book to discuss the activities of complex problem solving and requirements for usefulness.

Chapter 3 is the main methods chapter. It identifies current gaps in user-centered designing and in the interplay between usability and software engineering for the purposes of designing useful support for applications for complex problem solving. This chapter presents design assumptions and approaches for filling these gaps. It details why five assumptions conventionally applied to applications for well-structured tasks are counterproductive for complex problem solving software and offers alternatives. It discusses methods for user and task analysis, work modeling, and conceptual designing that extend or revise many current contextual design approaches to address the distinct demands of complexity more adequately and completely. This chapter examines such issues as the appropriate unit of analysis for field studies and processes for modeling and designing for patterns of inquiry before jumping to the design of task and screen objects.

Part Two, Solving Problems in Technical, Social, and Co-Emergent Systems, presents extensive case studies that embody the ideas and processes explored in the first three chapters. As mentioned earlier, the troubleshooting and product mix cases in Chapters 4 through 7 focus on the design of interactive data visualizations for usefulness as a technology well-suited to the demands of exploratory analysis. The medication dosage case in Chapter 8 is based on standard GUI designs.

Chapters 4 and **5** highlight useful support for IT troubleshooting—a complex problem in a complex technical system. **Chapter 4** presents a tier-two troubleshooter's software-supported activities and a design team's efforts to create a tool for them. It shows the serious usefulness flaws that occur in the team's prototype, largely due to the team not following many of the methods appropriate for complexity described in the first part of the book. **Chapter 5** follows the same team as it redesigns this data visualization troubleshooting tool, this time with the group concentrating positively on modeling the effects of interactive contextual conditions on users' possible moves and strategies and on turning them into designs for integrated support and optimal user control.

Chapters 6 and **7** explore the problem of choosing the best product mix—a complex problem in a complex social system. This optimizing decision involves multidimensional analysis, weightings, comparisons, and situationally determined priorities and choices. **Chapter 6** depicts the experiences of a domain expert as she strives to solve her product mix problem with the help of data visualization software. The discussion following her story abstracts her patterns of inquiry and visualizes their task landscapes. **Chapter 7** explores designs for usefulness and appropriate external representations for five problem solving activities crucial to this analyst's optimizing decisions but often inadequately supported by current software. These activities include: Drawing comparisons, figuring out the meanings of single and cumulative displays of information, getting "from here to there" in task landscapes, performing complex queries visually with uncomplicated program interactions, and composing notes and presentations in tandem with ongoing analysis.

Chapter 8 presents the case of a hospital nurse's dosage decision as she administers medications to patients on her floor—a complex problem in complex, co-emergent social and technical systems. This chapter illustrates and analyzes necessary design assumptions, methods, and choices beyond those explored in other cases. These additional approaches relate to the support users need for the joint and interactive social coordination and the integration of centralized data that occur in open dosage judgments. It introduces the politics of design and gives special emphasis to designing a place and not just a space for problem solving and to representing and integrating diverse data from many sources to create new knowledge.

Chapter 9 synthesizes the design approaches and choices of the three case studies, emphasizing issues, strategies, and conceptual designs shared across cases and specific to individual cases. This chapter categorizes support by problem solving objectives, and it references the places in the scenario chapters in which design choices for this support have been presented.

In Part Three, Thinking Strategically, **Chapter 10** extends the arguments developed about design approaches and outcomes into the political arena. It points to the next necessary steps for designing for usefulness for complex tasks, namely, politically instituting the ideas and practices developed in this book into the structures of production contexts and processes of development groups. It highlights four opportunities for strategically positioning designing for usefulness in a development organization, opportunities that are often overlooked in conventional discussions about the politics of usability. It concludes with an overall vision of achieving a breakthrough in software and interfaces for complex problem solving so they are truly useful for people's dynamic work.

WHO SHOULD READ THIS BOOK?

This book is aimed at HCI specialists, whether their roles are user-experience analysts, interaction designers, usability specialists, interface designers, content strategists, information architects, cognitive engineers, human factors specialists, consultants, instructional designers, documentation specialists, or performance-technology experts. Because of this lengthy list of possible roles, I "shorthand" my references to intended readers throughout the book and refer either to HCI specialists in general or to user-experience analysts, interaction designers, or usability specialists. These references are not intended to exclude any of the other roles. Basically, any HCI specialist who is involved in some aspect of UCD should read this book, bring its approaches to development and design groups, and encourage teammates and managers to build usefulness into applications for complex problem solving from start to finish.

Ideally, all members of design and software teams and their development, product, and project managers should understand and consider the ideas and practices in this book. Everyone needs to be involved in rethinking the ways usability and software engineering interact and in revising conventional approaches to software so that they better accommodate the demands of intellectually demanding inquiries and dynamic and emergent work. My hope is that, eventually, these other members of development groups will read and be receptive to these ideas and practices. Until then, I urge HCI specialists to draw on the book to convince their teammates of ways to "get the (complex) work right."

In instructional and research settings, the book can guide teachers and students in exploring ideas and practices necessary for making significant breakthroughs in the design of useful software and Web applications for complex problem solving. This training can help prepare students to become innovative leaders in their development groups. In addition, classes may use the cases as hands-on exercises, with students generating design possibilities beyond what any given case currently explores. The scenarios also provide wide-ranging opportunities to critically analyze the accompanying discussions about task modeling and design choices, thereby presenting a springboard for lively debates about open design questions.

ACKNOWLEDGEMENTS

Writing this book has been a journey covering a great deal of territory and time. Throughout it, more colleagues, co-workers, students, users, and friends have influenced my thoughts and projects than I am able to thank in these acknowledgements. To all of them, I extend much gratitude for their inspiring and supportive conversations, insights, debates, challenges, laughter, and collaborations.

Collaborations have been just as central to the writing of this book as they are to complex problem solving and software-development processes. For over a dozen years, I've collaborated on and off with Leif Allmendinger, an exceptional graphic designer, including our work together in this book on the visuals for modeling the interactive contexts and task landscapes of users' complex inquiries. Once, in an earlier project, Leif and I wrote about and contrasted "assembly-line" collaborations (hand-offs) with what we called "symphony" collaborations—a harmonizing of specialties (rather than hand-offs), practiced together over time, creating something greater than either specialty alone could achieve. Here I profoundly thank him for turning our many conversations about interactive contexts, patterns, and task landscapes into wonderful visual harmony.

Russell Borland has also been invaluable in getting this book written. His influence on my work is immense and has been throughout my career.

He inspired many of the ideas in this book, including the power of stories with their 365 views and deeply "running water" of human experience. He has spent hours with me critically talking about software improvements and usability. His comments and critiques of the entire manuscript were extremely helpful and perfectly pitched—keen and kind—a rare blend and perfect for keeping a writer going.

Along the way, some special colleagues sustained my writing in diverse ways, and I owe a great deal of thanks to them. They include David Arksey, Bob Bain, Ann Blakeslee, Mitchell Gass, Johndan Johnson-Eilola, Mary Jane Northrup, John Rury, and Roger Theodos. I've also been fortunate to have many exceptional teammates on software projects in industry, learning more from them than a world of books could offer. I hope they find the many Easter eggs I've left for them. In addition, clearing my head and coming back refreshed after a break was often just as important as the writing. For that, I owe many thanks to Mary and Maris Vinovskis, who regularly reminded me that pleasure trumps work.

I'm grateful to the people who reviewed individual chapters or discussed ideas in them with me, including James Gutierrez, Ed Israelski, Tim Jedlicka, Nick Petroff, Dwight Stevenson, Lisa Talman, and Scott Wood. I am also deeply indebted to the four reviewers who closely read and critiqued all the chapters for Morgan Kaufmann: Dave Farkas, Chris Nodder, Ginny Redish, and Karen Ziech. They provided me with outstanding suggestions and comments and helped me tremendously. In addition to their comments, I appreciate their gracious flexibility in what was a demanding review cycle.

I want to thank Diane Cerra, my managing editor, for her strong and perceptive support, her candid and always helpful suggestions, and her great enthusiasm throughout the project. Thanks also to Mona Buehler, editorial coordinator; Bruce Siebert, the copyediting manager; and Belinda Breyer, developmental editor. Belinda was available at just the right time for me and did a wonderful job shepherding this book.

Finally, I offer thanks beyond measure to my husband, Jeff. He has supported and encouraged me throughout the many years and territory of this project. He is a continuous source of insights. He has tirelessly explored and shared ideas, critiques, and challenges with me and has believed in the book unequivocally, at times more than I did when temporary blocks set in. In the midst of his own demanding career and scholarship, he has accommodated the serendipity and rearrangements the writing of this book has brought to our lives with grace, humor, and always love.

REFERENCES

Adams, Douglas. *So Long and Thanks for All the Fish*. New York: Crown/Harmony, 1984.

Roth, Philip. *I Married a Communist*. Boston: Houghton Mifflin, 1998.

Shedroff, Nathan. "Interfaces for Understanding." In *More than Screen Deep: Toward Every-Citizen Interfaces to the Nation's Information Infrastructure*. Technical Report of National Research Council, Nation's information Infrastructure Steering Committee, Washington, D.C.: National Academies Press, 1997, 252-259.

Thackara, John. "The Design Challenge of Pervasive Computing." Keynote speech, CHI Conference on Computer-Human Interaction, The Hague, The Netherlands: ACM, 2000. Available at www.doorsofperception.com

INTRODUCTION

Over the last decade, a lack of software that is truly useful for solving complex problems has become a pressing concern. Professionals who use such software vent their frustrations with increasing exasperation:

"My analysts need an application that helps them know what they're seeing in the numbers. They're overwhelmed by information and end up regurgitating data without analyzing it." (Director of Category Management in a nationally renowned super center)

"Our medication program doesn't intend to impede clinical judgment, but it certainly does. It limits what nurses can do and when and how they can do it. Nursing isn't that exacting. In a lot of ways, the program causes more problems than it solves." (nurse manager in a nationwide hospital conglomerate)

"My biggest problem is getting the data, which is more important than how they're presented. Even though we've asked the vendor repeatedly, the application doesn't have features to get all the data we need for really hard problems." (network analyst in an international telecommunications company)

"Data cubes are great for complicated analysis, but I haven't seen a program yet that keeps you from getting lost when you drill down in a cube, sometimes eight or ten levels." (analyst in a human resources consulting firm)

"The problem with the program's visualizations is that when I need to talk to someone remotely, we don't have a common frame of reference like we do when I say to them, 'Where are you in log messages?'" (troubleshooter in a major telecommunications firm)

These software problems have not gone unnoticed. Commentators who specialize in technology trends have leveled harsh criticism at these unsolved problems. Whether applications are for customer relationship management, business intelligence, medication processes, telecommunication networks, or other knowledge work, these commentators blanketly describe them as "hideously difficult to use" for complex problems and deem most usability improvements as no better than "putting makeup on a pig" (Dalton, 2002). The next big breakthrough in the software industry must be useful applications for dynamic, open-ended work that defies being formalized completely.

This book seeks to advance this breakthrough. It focuses on the question: What does it take to design applications that are truly useful for the complex problem solving domain specialists do everyday?

Answers to this question will develop only when interaction designers, usability specialists, and other software team members treat applications for complex problem solving as a distinct class of software with its own brand of usefulness demands. This is not to say that software for more routine problems or well-structured tasks does not share a number of the same usability concerns. It does, but dynamic work and the support it requires are distinct. Unfortunately, many applications today—such as those commentators denounce—are difficult to use precisely because software teams treat what is really dynamic work as if it were routine or well-structured.

Designing truly useful software for complex problem solving demands that development groups build usefulness into all aspects of a product, not only its user interfaces (UI). Toward this end, they need to restructure product development processes so usability and software engineering are more tightly coupled, with usefulness concerns taking on a prominent role in requirements planning.

Once development groups put this restructuring in place, they then need to shape assumptions and methods to the distinct demands of complex problem solving in their contextual inquiries, task analyses, modeling of users' work, and conceptual mock-ups and designs. This book provides suggestions for such approaches built around a series of case studies to guide human-computer interaction (HCI) specialists and their development teams. It also explores interactive data visualizations as an effective means for making applications more useful to knowledge workers.

These demands for creating useful applications for people's dynamic work are challenging but, as I strive to establish in this book, they are feasible. Important first steps have been taken in some production contexts and research and development groups. Now it is time to implement more dramatic improvements on a larger scale across the software industry.

WHAT IS COMPLEX PROBLEM SOLVING?

Complex problem solving always has been an intrinsic part of people's work lives. Even so, it is not easy to capture the diverse factors and forces that converge to make various inquiries and decisions complicated. In the novel *War and Peace* Leo Tolstoy provides a vivid example of entangled dilemmas in military decision-making that shows how we often mistakenly look at other people's problem solving and think obvious paths are much clearer than they really are.

The activity of a commander-in-chief does not at all resemble the activity we imagine to ourselves when we sit at ease in our study examining some campaign on the map, with a certain number of troops on this and that side in a certain known locality, and begin our plans from some given moment. A commander-in-chief is always in the midst of a series of shifting events and so he never can at any moment consider the whole import of an event that is occurring. Moment by moment the event is imperceptibly shaping itself, and at every moment of this continuous, uninterrupted shaping of events the commander-in-chief is in the midst of a most complex play of intrigues, worries, contingencies, authorities, projects, counsels, threats and deceptions, and is continually obliged to reply to innumerable questions addressed to him, which constantly conflict with one another.

[After the fact], learned military authorities quite seriously tell us that [General] Kutuzov should have moved his army [to retreat from Moscow] to the Kaluga road long before reaching Fili, and that somebody actually submitted such a proposal to him. But a commander-in-chief, especially at a difficult moment, has always before him not one proposal but dozens simultaneously. And all these proposals, based on strategies and tactics, contradict one another. A commander-in-chief's business, it would seem, is simply to choose one of these projects. But even that he cannot do. Events and time do not wait. ... And [an] order to retreat carries us past ... the Kaluga road. The chief of hospitals asks where the wounded are to go, and a courier from Petersburg brings a letter from the sovereign, which does not admit of the possibility of abandoning Moscow, and the commander-in-chief's rival... presents new projects diametrically opposed to that of ...the Kaluga road, and the commander-in-chief himself needs sleep and refreshment to maintain his energy, and ... the inhabitants of the region pray to be defended... and a spy, a prisoner, and a general who has been on reconnaissance, all describe the position of the enemy quite differently.

People accustomed to misunderstand or to forget these inevitable conditions of a commander-in-chief's actions...assume that the commander-in-chief could, on the 1st of September, quite freely decide whether to abandon Moscow or defend it. (Tolstoy, 1941, Book XI, 8-10)

Every day, people face problems on the job that have many of the same characteristics as those facing Tolstoy's commander-in-chief. For example, they often need to figure out how to decrease operating costs while increasing output or where to reallocate resources for the greatest gain and least amount of risk. As one HCI specialist describes these ill-structured problems, "Goals are not clear; what would constitute a solution is not known in advance; there is no reason to think that familiar methods will help; and if a solution is achieved, it may not be recognizable as such" (Casaday, 2003). Complex problems involve uncertainty, incomplete and diverse sources of information, multiple logical and situational factors, and competing demands from numerous stakeholders. Methods for solving them are not fully conceived at the outset and are often not covered by rules, even if they seem to be when analysts and designers reflect on them after the fact.

We can see from Tolstoy's description that the first challenge interaction designers and their software teammates face in creating applications for dynamic and open-ended problem solving is to understand the intricate complexity of users' work. They then need to inventively create useful support for work that eludes being captured in logical, rule-driven, or formulaic descriptions. Overall, in designing for exploratory and dynamic inquiries, HCI specialists must keep in mind that applying a closed-system paradigm to open-system problem solving is no more effective for software than it is for Tolstoy's commander-in-chief. Many design approaches used for well-structured tasks are too close-ended to lead to useful software for complex problem solving. Complex problem solving is a different beast.

In dynamic knowledge work, problem solvers need support deliberately shaped to the uncertainty and distinctive traits of complex problems and to the processes of emergent and opportunistic inquiries. They need to adapt the functionality of their applications to their situated patterns of work, patterns defined by idiosyncrasy and changing conditions. They need flexibility in program interactions so they can approach the same question at various times in different ways and can explore it within a single inquiry from multiple perspectives. They need power from the software that is approachable and forgiving (especially if they are not technically expert) so they can analyze large amounts of data with the intellectual sophistication that gives their work meaning. Furthermore, they require mechanisms for coordinating, collaborating, and communicating with stakeholders who influence the direction and meaning of their investigations. They also expect guidance in determining an appropriate entry point to a line of questioning when many are possible and a stopping point where none is apparent. To be valued as useful, applications must support all these aspects of complex problem solving.

DESIGNING FOR USEFULNESS IN THE WHOLE PRODUCT

Usefulness is a *value* users experience. They experience it when they know their work is better for having interacted with an application. Usefulness—doing better work—is not the same as using an application more easily. Operating a program easily may contribute to usefulness but in itself does not improve the quality of work (Thackara, 2000). When design teams focus on ease of use, they strive to build the product right. When they emphasize usefulness, they strive to build the right product (Notess, 2003).

For complex problem solving, a product is built right when it accommodates exploration and uncertainty for problems in which no fixed paths or single right answer can be anticipated. When users conduct such inquiries they commonly rethink their goals, alter strategies and methods on-the- fly, and vary their priorities according to evolving situational conditions. As the playwright Tom Stoppard (1993) puts it, "The unpredictable and the predetermined unfold together...Each [action] sets up the conditions for the next, [and] the smallest variation blows prediction apart" (47-48).

If applications are to be useful for such problem situations, all aspects of a program—its architecture, functionality, modules, and interfaces—must give problem solvers the power, adaptability, flexibility, control, and approachability they need for their multilayered and dynamic investigations. Usefulness applies to every component of an application.

Software architecture, for example, is the mediating factor for effective user adaptability, which is a vital requirement for dynamic work. Applications provide "user adaptability" when users can "adjust...processes [and configurations] to [their] own work approaches, personal best practices, and habits" (Sturm, 2001). If software architecture is not planned in advance to allow for this adaptability, later design attempts to support it through functionality and user interfaces will be restricted or, worse, impossible. Usefulness considerations from the start must supplement architects' more system-based concerns about extensibility and software adaptability (as opposed to *user* adaptability).

For these and other front-end decisions, usefulness criteria must be based on actual evidence, and interaction designers must be the source of this evidence. As Alan Cooper (Nelson, 2002) notes, interaction design is akin to requirements planning; designers need to influence the whole product from the development of a business case on. If they do not, "there [will be] a gap between the functionality of a technology and its perceived value, [and] sooner or later, the gap will be adversely reflected in the market (Thackara, 2000, 7).

Applications are not useful for dynamic and intellectually demanding work if they are structured largely around pre-supposed, generic procedural routines, controlled choices, and clear-cut roadmaps for task performance. Even if the interfaces in such applications are stellar—with exemplary ease of use, access, navigation, and transparency—usefulness will be low because the underlying model of problem solving is misconceived and misrepresented. To avoid a misfit of models, John Rheinfrank (1993), a leading experience analyst and interaction designer, urges development groups to design the context of use before the product itself.

These views are evident to many software architects, interaction designers, and developers (Coplein, 1996; Hackos and Redish, 1998; Johnson, 1998; Cooper, 1999; Furnas, 2000; Rosenberg et al., 2000; Bellotti and Edwards, 2001; Grudin, 2001; Bass et al., 2002; Albers 2003), but they are difficult to realize. In large part, this difficulty is tied to the conventional ways in which usability and software engineering interact in the product development cycle. A look at these conventions reveals why designing for usefulness frequently falls through the cracks.

PUTTING USEFULNESS IN THE CENTER OF USABILITY AND SOFTWARE ENGINEERING

Insights about usefulness depend on user and task analysis. In usability engineering, this analysis occurs early in the initial phase of analyzing requirements. The trouble is that in the overall product life cycle, this usability engineering phase commonly enters a software project *well after* the cycle has begun. In most development contexts, user and task analysis rarely occurs early enough or achieves a high enough organizational priority as a front-end process to influence all components of an application, starting with requirements planning. Instead, usability is a "downstream process," and software teams, consequently, do not have ample opportunity to apply insights about users' actual work in context to their decisions about data models, architecture, and functionality.

As one standard handbook on usability engineering describes, insights about actual work and software use in context, at best, come into the software engineering side of development during its later phase of analysis modeling (Mayhew, 1999). However, at this point, developers are in the midst of creating object-oriented models and functional requirements based on already determined higher-level requirements. Findings about user and task needs may shape these models, but earlier decisions about requirements are likely to have already unintentionally closed some opportunities for developing useful support. Moreover, in most development groups the prime function of user and task findings is to guide interface design, not the requirements of all aspects of the product.

In reality—especially the reality of complex inquiries that defy rule-based predictions or logical formalisms—findings about how people go about doing their work are crucial for determining *front-end, high-level requirements for an entire application*. They are not simply interface issues. Unfortunately, the conventional ways of running usability and software engineering in parallel result in a large gap in designing for usefulness.

The gap persists throughout the development process. Once usability engineers derive user-experience findings, they then model and re-engineer users' work and conceptualize design. Roughly at the same time, software engineers begin to design and construct modules for specific platforms and implementation approaches. Again a dynamic interplay occurs between usability and software engineering that does not merge the two in a unified process to ensure all parts of the software get the model of users' work right. Instead, during interface and program-module designing teams often skip the process of testing this fit to users' problem solving in context and move directly to assessing ease of use, accessibility, efficient navigation, learnability, and the like. The result is that application teams often end with a finished product that is "really well-constructed but doesn't solve the problem" (Nelson, 2002). In short, usefulness falls through the cracks because development groups do not quantitatively and qualitatively test whether all aspects of design—architecture, functionality, modules, and screens—get people's work right.

WHERE DOES INTERACTION DESIGN COME IN?

Interaction design seeks to remedy this problem. By definition, interaction design focuses on getting the work right in all aspects of product design before starting on "constructionary interface issues" (Nelson, 2002). Interaction designers keep usefulness primary by centering on how people desire to use a product for work-related goals, why, and with what patterns of behavior. Moreover, interaction designers strive to enhance intended users' work practices beyond what they currently are. From an interaction design perspective, when users interact with software for exploratory analysis they intermingle their internal knowledge with external conditions, constraints, and information in the environment, including interface displays. Control over problem solving activities flows between users and the software and internal and external information in different ways at different times. It changes as users' actions lead to new objectives and as they generate, often ad hoc, new information and relationships between tasks. Based on users' levels of expertise, complex problems, and goals, interaction designers need to address two critical open design questions: What external information, contextual conditions, and implicit inferences from them do users need for their task at-hand and how do they (and might they) relate these factors to the internal knowledge that they bring to the task and act on them (Wright et al., 2000)?

Instituting interaction design at the start of the development cycle and integrating contextually derived requirements for usefulness into all phases of software engineering are important for any software project. Nowhere, however, is its absence felt more deeply—and with a greater chance of undermining users' efforts to turn information into knowledge—than in software projects for complex problem solving. Currently, the HCI community rarely attends to the interaction-design approaches required distinctly for these dynamic, open-ended inquiries. This book aims to bridge that gulf. It presents both a vision and a practical approach for designing usefulness into software for complex problem solving.

HOW FAR ALONG ARE WE AND ARE USEFUL APPLICATIONS POSSIBLE?

A quick survey of the software field would seem to indicate that the era of useful software for complex problem solving should be well underway. Many groups in the development community are working already on different aspects of it. For example, decision-support system developers focus on aiding people in making discretionary decisions. Specialists in usability testing, interaction design, and other UCD areas have made headway in highlighting the need to create systems that work for users, not simply systems that work. Experts in computer-supported collaborative software and context-aware computing support coordinated and cooperative work processes and situated activities. Finally, designers of advanced technologies such as interactive data visualizations and intelligent agents support users in exploring huge amounts of data with reduced cognitive loads through perceptual encoding and built-in processes that reason probabilistically.

Despite all these relevant pieces, nothing adequately connects the progress made by specialists in these separate areas to answer the overall question of what it takes to create useful applications for complex problem solving (Barnard et al, 2000). As mentioned in the Preface, for so pressing a question we still have only partial and non-cohesive answers. Consequently, we risk being like the blind men and the elephant in the old story, each of whom defines the entire beast by describing just the part they touch.

With so much development activity going on around the problem of supporting dynamic work, without getting to the center of it, HCI specialists and their software teammates cannot help but wonder whether truly useful applications for such fluid work are possible. This book maintains that they are and that applications—for well-structured as well as ill-structured work—can be improved greatly if software teams place a high priority on designing for usefulness.

Fortunately, some complex problem solving applications are available to exemplify varying degrees of useful support, and in the book I cite many of them to illustrate design strategies and choices for various scenarios. Of these exemplary applications, the best go beyond providing piece-by-piece solutions to one or two discrete requirements at a time. The best focus on making open-ended inquiries coherent by providing integrated support for users' integrated moves and strategies in their dynamic work.

Most of the applications that I highlight as exemplary in the book use interactive data visualizations to support people's exploratory querying, data analysis, and related communications. Interactive, dynamically linked graphics are powerful for complex problem solving because they enable users to offload many cognitive demands to their perceptual system, a system attuned to discriminating groupings, patterns, distinctions, trends, and aberrations in data.

For complex problem solving, data visualization products and studies for a wide range of analytical purposes are steadily growing. Most of them, however, concentrate heavily on the technology—the features and capabilities of data visualizations—and then, starting there, look for suitable applications. Very few begin by concentrating on usefulness requirements for specific domains and problems. Some that do include Roth et al., 1997; Wilkinson, 1999; Bertin 1997; products from MAYA Viz (www.mayaviz.com), the SAGE Visualization group (www.2.cs.cmu.edu/Groups/sage/sage.html), Spotfire (www.spotfire.com), the Pacific Northwest National Laboratory's Spatial Paradigm for Information Retrieval and Exploration (SPIRE) group, the Advanced Interface Design Lab at the University of Toronto (sydewww.uwaterloo.ca/Research/AIDL/new/projects.htm); and some projects at XeroxPARC, the MIT Media Lab, the University of Maryland HCI Lab, IBM Watson Research, Microsoft Research, and the Distributed Cognition and HCI Laboratory at the University of California, San Diego. This book primarily seeks to build on and advance this work.

As good as many of these exemplary applications are, most still need to support users better in the full range of integrated requirements that problem solvers such as Tolstoy's commander-in-chief have for strategic choices, conditional moves, and discretionary judgments. Even some of the most useful examples, for instance, are powerful and robust but need to be more approachable or offer better access to prerequisite data structures. Other exemplary applications often trade necessary power or flexibility for approachability and forgiveness. Yet others provide effective ways for users to deal with huge amounts of data in exploratory analysis but fall short in usefulness because they do not adequately keep users oriented in their problem solving activities and information workspaces. Despite some successes, software for complex problem solving is still in its infancy in terms of attaining the right combinations of power, flexibility, approachability, wayfinding support, and forgiveness (Wiss and Carr, 1998). This book focuses on approaches for designing for this usefulness for specific types of problems and domains, including a final chapter on the political strategies for instituting these approaches.

SETTING THE STAGE

Returning to Tolstoy's commander-in-chief, but now with an eye on capturing his complex problem solving visually, a graphic of Napolean's Russian campaign of 1812 readily comes to mind. Created by the French engineer Charles Minard in 1861 and made famous by Edward Tufte (1983) this graphic, pictured in Figure F.1, was and still is groundbreaking. It visualizes relationships among six variables in an approachable way (troop size, time, rivers crossed, temperature, march direction, and cities passed) to emphatically show the high costs of Napolean's retreat from Moscow, Minard's intended anti-war message.

To visualize complexity, as Minard has done is a tremendous intellectual breakthrough. Later in this book we will consider other ways that design teams can model users' work and create visualization software designs for it. However, a big gap exists between Minard's multivariate representation and Tolstoy's description of similar moments in military events.

What gets lost in the graphic are the nonlinear deliberations at any crucial time, the backtracking or other indirect movements en route to the destination, and the anticipated versus unintended local effects of

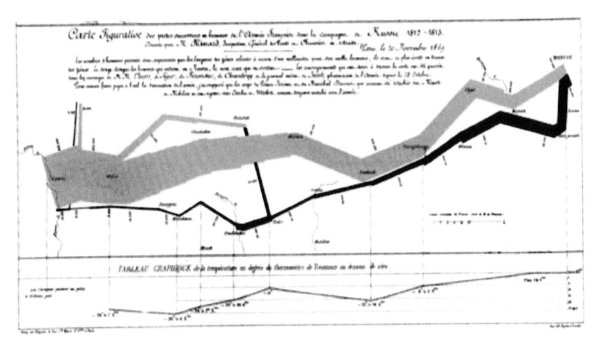

FIGURE F.1 Napoleon's retreat from Moscow. (Tufte, 1983)

choices. Missing in the graphic are the swirling tensions among competing interests and actors and contradictory priorities. Absent is the uncertainty surrounding various actors' actions and the subjective and contextual influences shaping choices, perspectives, and moves.

In other words, the advances of visualization come with a challenge, namely to show meanings through multivariate relationships as Minard does *and* to interweave them with the drama of users' experiences and choice points as Tolstoy does. Unfortunately, when design teams visually represent users' exploratory problem solving or create interactive visualization interfaces for it they often concentrate primarily on the data relationships part of the challenge dissociated from a problem solver's exploratory story. For a complex problem solver who is moving through uncertain and open terrain to clarify and resolve indeterminate problems, data meanings cannot be separated from the journey involved in deriving them. This journey is the problem solving narrative.

To be useful, applications for complex problem solving have to highlight both the narrative (the journey) and the arrival (the meanings). This intertwining needs to present a perspective (for example, placing users in a first, second or third person role in relation to the situation) and should not simply display "objective information." Perspective is intrinsic to narrative. It "bridges context to decision" and makes or breaks individuals' choices at uncertain but pivotal moments (Meadows, 2002, 17).

Applications for complex problem solving also have to reveal to users the structure or arc of their "investigative story," even though neither problem solvers nor designers can fully know the exact paths, methods, or judgments in advance. In addition, another way for HCI specialists to merge investigative stories with data meanings in applications is to give users ample interactivity to explore, set courses, shift perspectives, and configure investigative plots as needed. Toward these ends, analogies with other visual media such as movies and the interactive narratives of computer games can offer software teams guidance. Both genres have an overarching concern with visually presenting action and problem solving through the lens of story, context, and meaning.

Cinematic techniques and editing are relevant to the design of useful software for complex problem solving in the way they to assign each shot a meaning pertinent to the actions of the story *while at the same time* portraying the conditions and constraints of reality in ways that highlight potential meanings. The classic World War II film *Casablanca* offers an example.

In *Casablanca*, Victor Laszlo, an anti-Nazi leader, and his wife Ilsa, flee from the Gestapo and end up in Casablanca. They hope to obtain letters of transit for an escape to the United States from Rick, an American expatriate and, unbeknownst to Victor, Ilsa's former lover. Against this storyline, the film perpetually lingers on the setting and reveals indeterminate realities such as a crowded open-air bazaar in which everything is for sale, the legal as well as the illicit. Shadows dominate in almost every scene and draw viewers' attention variously to mysterious pasts, fears of being followed, hidden meanings, dual identities, and murky situations politically, socially, ethically, and romantically.

Software renditions of complex problem solving need to similarly advance actions while exposing the significance of contextual realities by presenting them from different perspectives. In movies and problem solving computing alike designers can suggest hidden provinces of relationships through such techniques as contrast, juxtaposition, close-ups, alternating shots, focal points, and framing. The final scene of *Casablanca* reveals the ways in which these techniques determine the success of presentation.

According to film historians, the first take of the final scene in *Casablanca* was a failure. In it was a frame of Rick shooting Strasser, a visiting Gestapo agent, to keep him from obstructing Victor and Ilsa's flight. It was followed directly by a frame of Louis, the French officer in charge of the territory, arriving on the scene and giving his men the famous order, "Round up the usual suspects." The original scene fell flat with preview audiences, and the writers and filmmakers had to redesign it. They added two new frames between Rick's shooting of Strasser and what became Louis's oft repeated line. The first was a close-up, dwelling on the complex emotions on Louis's face when he arrived; the second zoomed into Rick's face as he gazed back at Louis. It is this reflective pause with its juxtaposed details of the two men's facial expressions in relation to the actions that give Louis's order layers of meaning and a powerful emotional impact.

Like *Casablanca's* filmmakers, software designers need to pay attention to the drama that problem solvers experience as they investigate thorny questions, and designers need to structure this drama into the software through such spatial techniques as juxtaposition, arrangement, foreshadowing, and flashback. Another way for interaction designers to involve users in the drama of their complex investigations is to draw on the dynamic interplay between users' internal and external worlds and prompt problem solvers to invest their internal motives, knowledge, and intuitions into their software interactions at the right times and places. Finally, interaction designers for complex problem solving applications may borrow strategies from such cinematic examples as the camera work in the last scene of *Casablanca*. They need to help users linger, pause for reflection, find and fill in gaps, and zoom in and out of potentially significant data relationships and situational conditions.

Software designers, unfortunately, rarely put these techniques to work for dramatic effect. Yet without them complex problem solvers often find themselves struggling in frustrating ways to become situated in the concrete time, place, and set of circumstances that determine the meaning of their work. As a guiding metaphor, movies can inspire new strategies and techniques for complex problem solving software but in the end they are limited. They are not interactive like problem solving software has to be. For additional guidance, designers of complex problem solving applications can turn to software and web-based games. Specialists in this area have long paid attention to the requirements of designing interactive narratives.

Three principles from this area of computer games are especially relevant to designing useful software for complex problem solving. The first is that from the very start of a project designers must meticulously work out the structures or patterns of "players" investigative experiences and the content, type and degree of interactivity that users require to immerse themselves in the experiences. If, as an afterthought, designers try to slap different perspectives and greater user control over storylines and information onto pre-defined views, action sequences, functionality, and architecture, the outcome for users will be less than useful (Meadows, 2002). Users will be hamstrung in effecting their goals, and their interest and investment in the application will take a nosedive.

This need for sustained interest and investment is the second relevant interactive narrative principle. Users' interest and investment will increase the more they are drawn into interactive experiences, succeed with few interruptions, and find that the benefits outweigh the costs of their invested time, attention, and resources (Meadows, 2002). Although complex problem solvers do not need to be entertained as gamers do, they will abandon applications that are too cumbersome for getting their complex work done. In striving to engage users, interactive narrative specialists use many visual techniques that overlap with filmmaking and are relevant to the design of applications for complex problem solving, as well. To introduce such factors as opinions and perspective, thereby evoking roles for users verbally and visually, they mix textual cues and dialogues with varied camera shots (e.g., close, standard, far, and top views), background images and spatial configurations. They also build in freedom for users to explore different opinions and points of view. Other high-level techniques that capture users' interest, time, and energy relevant to interaction design for complex problem solving are ensuring that users clearly see their goal-oriented meanings in events and relationships and enabling users to readily acquire the means to solve problems and be recognized for having solved them.

Finally, a third relevant interactive narrative principle is the need to distribute control effectively between users and the software. In games as well as complex problem solving applications, a prime design objective must be to find the right balance between designers turning the "story" over to users and designers ensuring necessary guidance and constraints. On one hand, users' investment, interest, evolving knowledge, and success in goals depend on their being able to control investigative directions and choices based on situational factors and their own expertise and ingenuity. On the other hand, problem solvers and gamers alike need guidance and some linear sequencing at critical points to keep their investigative path intact. That is, they need an optimal balance of constraint and freedom in their explorations.

Striking this delicate balance for complex problem solving diverges from games insofar as game designers often make these decisions by relying heavily on their own imaginations. When design teams create applications for the complexities of real world problem solving, they must go into the field. They need to watch, understand, and model the patterns and flux that characterize users' complex work in context.

Insights from movies and interactive narratives can only go so far in guiding the design of software for complex problem solving because films and games differ from applications for knowledge work in a number of ways. Nonetheless, techniques and principles from them can help to set the stage as design teams embark on projects to support users' indeterminate problem solving. Borrowing from movies and interactive narratives can help us envision new possibilities that may lead to more useful software than commentators find in the field at present. We need to recognize and design for the experiential dramas of problem solvers like Tolstoy's commander-in-chief and interweave these experiences with support for deriving meaning from huge amounts and diverse types of data under various conditions. These combined aims may help us enrich our already effective user-centered design methods with the fresh approaches required for this novel breed of software. Exploring and detailing these fresh approaches and applying them to a variety of actual complex problem solving situations are the subject of this book.

REFERENCES

Albers, Michael. "Complex Problem Solving and Content Analysis." In *Content and Complexity,* edited by Michael Albers and Beth Mazur. Mahwah, NJ: Lawrence Erlbaum Associates, 2003, 263-283.

Barnard, Philip, Jon May, David Duke, and David Duce. "Systems, Interactions, and Macrotheory." *ACM Transactions on Computer-Human Interaction 7* no. 7 (2000), 222-262.

Bass, Lee, Bonnie John, and Jesse Kates. *Achieving Usability Through Software Architecture.* Technical Report. Pittsburgh: Software Engineering Institute, Carnegie Mellon University, 2002.

Bellotti, Victoria and Keith Edwards. "Intelligibility and Accountability: Human Considerations in Context-Aware Systems." *Human-Computer Interaction* 16, no. 2/4 (2001): 193-212.

Bertin, Jacques. *Graphics and Graphic Treatment of Information.* Berlin: Walter de Gruyter & Company, 1981.

Casaday, George. UTEST posting. January 24, 2003.

Cooper, Alan. *The Inmates are Running the Asylum.* Indianapolis: Sams, Macmillan Computing Publishing, 1999.

Coplein, James. *Software Patterns.* New York: SIGS Books and Multimedia, 1996.

Dalton, John. "Packaged Applications Fail the Usability Test." *Forrester Research Technology Strategy Report.* (April 2002), Streaming video/audio: *www.forrester.com/ Research/List/Date/1,3767,0,FF.html?selecteddatevalue=April:2002.*

Furnas, George. "Future Design Mindful of the MoRAS." *Human-Computer Interaction* 15, no. 2/3 (2000): 205-261.

Grudin, Jonathan. "De-situating Action: Digital Representation of Context." *Human-Computer Interaction* 16, no. 2/4 (2001): 269-286.

Hackos, JoAnn and Janice Redish. *User and Task Analysis for Interface Design.* New York: John Wiley & Sons, 1998.

Johnson, R. Robert. *User-centered Technology: A Rhetorical Theory for Computers and Other Mundane Artifacts.* Albany: State University of New York Press, 1998.

Mayhew, Deborah. *The Usability Engineering Lifecycle.* San Francisco: Morgan Kaufmann, 1999.

Nelson, Elden. "Extreme Programming vs. Interaction Design." Interview with Kent Beck and Alan Cooper. *FTPOnline.* January 15, 2000, *www.fawcette.com/interviews/beck_cooper.*

Notess, Mark. UTEST posting. January 24, 2003.

Rheinfrank, John. "The Technological Juggernaut: Objects and Their Transcendence." In *The Edge of the Millennium: An International Critique of Architecture, Urban Planning, Product and Communication Design,* edited by Susan Yelavich, 168-173. New York: Whitney Library of Design, 1993.

Rosenbaum, Stephanie, Janice Rohn, and Judee Humburg. "A Toolkit for Strategic Usability: Results From Workshops, Panels, and Surveys." In *Proceedings of CHI 00 Conference on Computer-Human Interaction,* 337-344. The Hague: ACM, 2000.

Roth, Steven, Mei Chuah, Stephen Kerpedjiev, John Kolohejchick, and Peter Lucas. "Toward an Information Visualization Workspace: Combining Multiple Means of Expression." *Human-Computer Interaction* 12, no. 1/2 (1997), 131-186.

Stoppard, Tom. *Arcadia.* London: Faber and Faber, 1993.

Sturm, Gretchen. "Moving From Adoptability to Adaptability." *Recruitsoft Knowledge* September 25, 2001, *www.recruitsoft.com/en/knowledge/discover/articles/20010925_GS.html .*

Thackara, John. "The Design Challenge of Pervasive Computing." Keynote speech, CHI 2000 Conference on Computer-Human Interaction, The Hague, 2000. Available at www.doors of perception.com.

Tolstoy, Leo, *War and Peace,* translated by Louise Maude and Aylmer Maude. Oxford, UK: Oxford University Press, 1941.

Tufte, Edward. *The Visual Display of Quantitative Information.* Cheshire, CT: Graphics Press, 1983.

Wilkinson, Leland. *The Grammar of Graphics.* New York: Springer-Verlag, 1999.

Wiss, Ulrika and David Carr. *A Cognitive Classification Framework for 3D Information Visualizations.* Technical Report, Computer Science and Electrical Engineering. Lulea, Sweden: Lulea University of Technology, 1998.

Wright, Peter, Robert Fields, and Michael Harrison. "Analysing Human-Computer Interaction as Distributed Cognition: The Resources Model." *Human-Computer Interaction* 5, no. 1 (2000), 1-41.

ABOUT THE AUTHOR

Barbara Mirel is a visiting associate professor and research investigator in the School of Information at the University of Michigan. She teaches information visualization and continues her research in projects related to complex problem solving. She has co-directed a joint academic degree program in Computer Science and Liberal Arts and has been a senior manager of human factors at a data visualization software company, a Member of the Technical Staff at Lucent Technologies, and Director of User Experience at Scient Corp. With teammates, she holds a patent for Visual Discovery design. Barbara is the recipient of numerous research grants for usability studies and has worked as a consultant to Fortune 500 companies across the country. She has co-edited a volume of essays, and has published numerous book chapters and articles on user and task analysis, data visualizations for exploratory analysis, and usability studies.

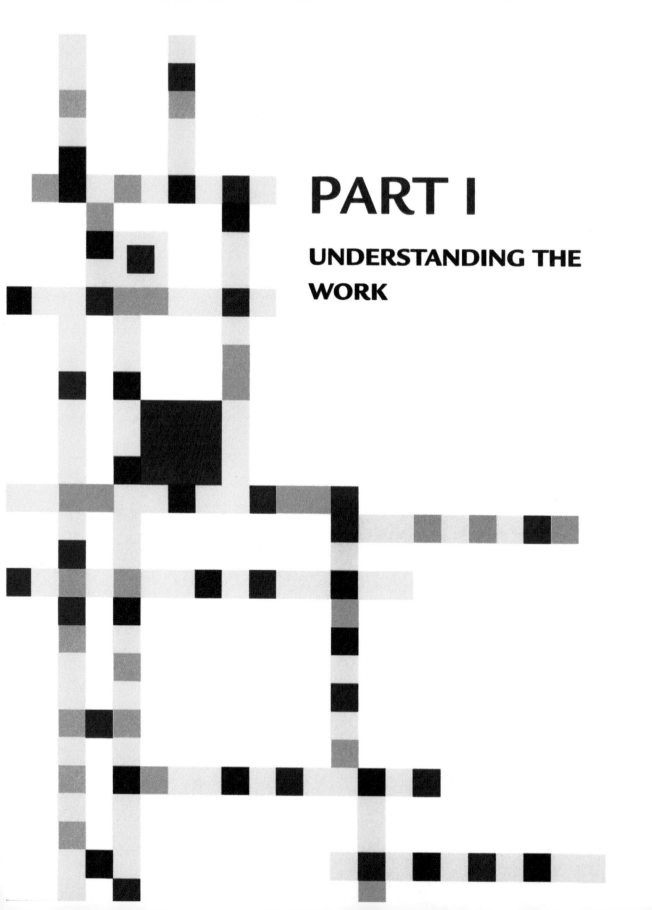

PART I

UNDERSTANDING THE WORK

1

What Makes Complex Problem Solving Complex?

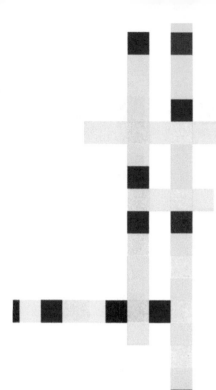

To an analyst swamped with data and struggling to stay afloat while solving complex problems, today's computerized work world seems a pretty unfriendly place. Massive amounts of data are available for everyday problem solvers and decision makers, but the resources for making strategic use of them are paltry. For example, to figure out who is buying what and how to cross-sell to them, analysts for an e-commerce Web site must integrate and interpret a sea of data on buyers' portal entries, click-through paths, transactions, and demographics. Similarly, hospital nurses determining dosages of medications have to work with huge amounts of medical data—often dispersed across systems—including information on patients' conditions, care plans, medication histories, allergies, laboratory tests, adverse drug interactions, prescription orders, and drug concentrations carried by the in-patient pharmacy. As the volume of data grows (and with it the expectation that problem solvers will become smarter in business and safer in operations), these problem solvers find it increasingly difficult to make decisions in indeterminate situations with confidence. From the eyes of a "drowning" analyst, with a lifetime of data passing before her eyes, problems seem to be complex mainly because of the sheer volume of information.

Enter advanced software for complex problem solving, which promises to make huge amounts of data manageable. Promoters of this software claim that with it, the people closest to the problems will get the tools they need to advantageously analyze available data and answer complex questions. Current data visualization applications for Web log analysis, for example, enable them to display and make sense of gigabytes of data in graphic presentations.

If only fixing the data volume problem was enough to facilitate complex problem solving through software support. Unfortunately, more is needed. Only part of the complexity of dynamic and emergent inquiries derives from large amounts of data. Complex problem solving is also complex because it requires reasoning in uncertainty and such higher-order analyses as cumulatively interpreting comparative relationships (sensemaking). It requires structuring your way from indeterminacy to resolution (wayfinding), integrating heterogeneous data from multiple sources, and relating multifaceted data relationships to situational conditions and fluctuating priorities (data ordeals) (Passini, 2000).

The distinguishing traits and dynamics of complex problem solving and the distinct support it requires warrant treating applications for open-ended inquiries as a separate area of software design and development. In many ways, complex inquiries are polar opposites of well-structured problems and tasks. They have vague or only broadly defined goals and inputs. They cannot be conducted through fixed rules, procedures, or algorithms. In fact, it is impossible to know all feasible solutions in advance. Moreover, unlike well-structured work, complex problem solving has no single correct answer.

Unfortunately, development groups often fail to recognize these distinctive demands and instead create applications based on assumptions and design methods used for well-structured tasks. The result is inadequate support for problem solvers' high-level sensemaking, wayfinding, and data ordeals, and therefore, applications that are not fully useful to the people who depend on them.

Part of the reason for this failure is that development groups rarely ask the two questions that will give them insight into the thinking, methods, strategies, and choices required for designing usefulness in applications for complex problem solving. These questions are as follows:

- What makes complex problem solving complex?
- What support is truly useful for the distinguishing demands of complexity?

In this chapter, I address the first question to lay a foundation for the second, which is discussed in subsequent chapters in greater detail. In this chapter I provide only broad and suggestive insights into the issue of optimal support.

This chapter describes the ways in which problem solvers' directions and possible actions in dynamic and emergent work invariably are shaped by interactive conditions within and across four main contexts: The technology and data context, work domain, problem space, and subjective context. I also identify the dynamics and traits of complex problem solving that make it complex, distinguishing it from well-structured work.

The implications are that complex problem solving requires unique support. Not only must this support address large and complicated information spaces, it also must help users configure, negotiate, and coordinate resources in landscapes of activity that are both patterned and variable. That is, software support must accommodate the structured openness of complex problem solving. Problem solvers follow certain regularities tied to professional practices, domain conventions, and business rules. However, they never fully foresee the routes and moves they will take because they organize their directions and choices around idiosyncratic situational factors, emergent insights, serendipity, and external flux.

To dramatize the challenges of complex problem solving, I start the chapter with a scenario about an ill-structured marketing problem and use it to frame the subsequent discussion about complexity and its support. The scenario reveals that a good deal of the support that problem solvers need, like Marty in the case study, is not currently built into their software. Marty's case is the first of many in this book. Altogether, the cases reveal support for core areas of complex problem solving that users need but currently lack, by and large, in software today.

Software teams and HCI specialists do not have to design marketing applications to find relevance in Marty's problem solving scenario. In terms of complexity, this story speaks to any team's efforts to understand and design for users' open-ended inquiries.

SCENARIO: SHOULD WE BREAK INTO A NEW MARKET NICHE?

For ten years, Marty has been a category manager at Quality Paper, a company that manufactures several brands of paper towels, tissues, and napkins. For years he has been solving complex problems, most of which involve figuring out how to gain greater market share for his company's brands. Currently, he manages the multibillion-dollar category of paper towels. To see if his company is manufacturing the right goods for market demand, Marty continuously assesses the paper towel market. He grapples each quarter with new sets of data on sales, profits, promotions, competition, customer demographics, buying patterns, and best practices. He uses complicated procedures to get data into the right format and to analyze relationships. Because markets are volatile and company objectives change, no two analyses Marty conducts are exactly the same.

What Is the Problem?

For the past several months, Marty has been paying close attention to a new premium-tier of paper towels whose sales are strong. He concedes that *premium* is fast becoming a profitable niche in the market. His company has no paper towel product in this niche, and without one, it could lose market share. It is time to figure out whether the company should break into this part of the market.

Marty's goals are no more concrete or specific than the previous sentence suggests. His goals will become clearer as the inquiry evolves.

Marty begins his inquiry with an hour-long meeting with his manager Nancy. They start by discussing how big a problem the lack of a premium product might be for the company. Even if results from Marty's proposed investigation suggest it is wise for Quality Paper to enter this niche, this will likely be a tough sell to corporate decision makers. If the inquiry is to address their bosses' greatest concerns, Nancy and Marty must turn the data he collects into persuasive communication.

The plan is for Marty to do a quick, first-run analysis at a high level and see what he discovers. He will meet with Nancy again to decide if what he finds confirms their theory. If it does, he will have to do a more thorough review and report. With that report, Nancy and Marty will create a presentation aimed at persuading decision makers to adopt the recommendation to produce a premium paper towel.

Verifying That the Problem Is a Problem

From the start, Marty's quick, first-run analysis is slowed by the volume and structure of the data. He uses syndicated data from a national subscription service. Like other analysts, Marty uses one set of syndicated data on product and market performance and another on customer behaviors and demographics. These datasets are huge and have far more information than Marty needs. The first thing he does is filter out all but the data of interest.

Ordeals in Accessing and Preparing Data

Ordinarily, filtering for a first-run inquiry is not arduous because the syndication service pre-processes a top-line dataset for such purposes. The top-line data include figures only for high-level subcategories, which, for paper towels, are the three tiers of products—premium, value, and economy. However, because the premium tier is new, some vendors have not yet adequately tagged their products for the syndicated service to include as premium in its dataset. Consequently, Marty dives into the mass of detailed data to select for himself the high-level data he needs.

From experience and domain expertise, he knows the profile of premium products and selects them. After filtering the syndicated data, Marty imports it into a spreadsheet. He now spends more than half a day formatting the fields and figures. He creates customized aggregations and some new fields and derived values for his purposes. One custom aggregate represents the major brands that informally belong in the premium tier. Marty goes through all the same processes of filtering, importing, formatting, and customizing with the customer data. Seventy-five percent of the time spent on this first-run analysis is devoted to data conditioning. When this tedious and mind-numbing task is finally finished, Marty is revived by actually beginning to explore the information.

Organizing Inquiry for Selectively Focused Analysis

For a first-run exploration, Marty aims for just a few salient descriptions to gauge whether his company's sales are hurting because of its lack of a premium product. Electronically he asks: How many people are buying "high end" paper towels? Are they brand loyalists? What has his company's household penetration with paper towels looked like since premium products began to appear?

Conducting these queries with his spreadsheet program is cumbersome, but Marty uses it instead of the other problem solving tool he has available—a new data exploration program with interactive information visualizations. The visualization program does not give him the same reporting capabilities that he gets from the spreadsheet suite, and he needs professional-looking reports to bring answers back to Nancy immediately. He works with two spreadsheets on the screen at once: One on product and market performance and the other on customer behavior.

He also flips back and forth between spreadsheet views of the data and charts. The charts are best for seeing the strength of relationships and trends; the tabular data let him see details to verify his interpretations. This flipping between textual and visual displays of the data and the cross-referencing of product and market performance and customer loyalty are supreme juggling acts. The graphics show that consumption of premium towels has increased, some customers' loyalties have changed, and the market penetration of Marty's company has remained stagnant.

Communicating Findings and Organizing In-depth Inquiry

Marty organizes the charts into a report and brings them to his meeting with Nancy. The two agree that a timely yet thorough analysis of the premium product situation is crucial. They spend most of the meeting discussing what their explanation will have to be to win over the decision makers. Nancy and Marty will need to turn details into a compelling story that addresses external conditions and internal resources. Marty has to make sure the ways he investigates questions represent these contextual dynamics. By projecting the convincing arguments with Nancy, Marty realizes the types of evidence he needs and the system or patterns of inquiry he should impose on the data to get them. This goal of persuasion will be present in each step of his investigation.

Inquiring Into the Problem and Managing Inquiry

To gather and prepare data for this comprehensive inquiry, Marty starts with the same processes but on a larger scale. Using the syndicated data program, he now selects considerably more data on product and market performance. He works across quarters with every level of data, from aggregated vendor data to detailed values for individual items by attributes (towel size, weight, texture, and so on). The volume of data he selects is much larger than his first-run analysis, and his manipulations of the data are more labor-intensive. When these data are ready for analysis, Marty uses his new, interactive information visualization program. With interactive visualizations, he can display tens of thousands of records and see patterns in five minutes that would take hours to discover in a spreadsheet.

Structuring Inquiry and Exploration

Marty's methods of analysis are different from his first-run overview. He organizes his inquiry around three basic yet complex questions: (1) What is happening in the market?; (2) Why is it happening; and (3) So what?

1. What is happening?

Marty wants to make sure the picture he puts together about the paper towel market is valid, so he asks a series of "what" and "how" questions:

- What vendors, brands, and products in the paper towel category are the most successful in different markets?

- Based on these products' performances, what is the baseline of success?

- What is the competition in the premium niche? Which products are doing best in the markets of most interest to his company?

- How do the premium products perform against this baseline?

- How do the other tiers perform against this baseline?

- How do his company's products perform against the baseline?

- How do his company's products perform compared to high-performing premium products?

By answering these questions, Marty will get a sense of the market strength of premium products, and he can gauge the competitive problem they pose to his company. However, he has retrieved more than 50,000 records and needs some systematic way to order them that will allow him to view, query, and manipulate them.

Marty uses an entry point and three subsequent patterns of inquiry that are standard practice for category managers, regardless of their company. He starts with top vendors in the product hierarchy and drills down (gets low-level details on performance) for each level of the hierarchy—vendors, brands, products, and product attributes. He then moves to the geography hierarchy (nation, region, market) and similarly analyzes each level, what category mangers call "working the funnel."

While working the funnel of the product and geography hierarchies, Marty follows another prototypical pattern. He creates a baseline for successful performance. To create this baseline, Marty singles out the overall dominant vendors, as well as those at each specific level of the product and geographic hierarchies. He calculates a baseline of success from these players' combined performance measures.

In a third pattern common to the industry, Marty runs a series of comparisons against the baseline. He judges the performance of his own company's products and those of competitors. He asks: Where are my company's products falling short of the market success factors? Where are they exceeding them? How are my main competitors doing against the same baseline? Analysts commonly set and use this bar to measure success, but they do not all derive the same baseline values from the same data. Baseline figures depend on how analysts interpret values and relationships, which in turn depends on their subjective biases, company priorities, and ability to interpret for competitive advantage.

These three patterns—working the funnel, deriving baseline measures for success, and comparing against this baseline—help Marty and other analysts like him arrange and order overwhelming amounts of data. Each new vendor or region Marty examines takes him down the same hierarchical path, so he continuously interacts with the same surrounding data. Successive comparisons against the baseline are similarly repetitive. An effect of these repetitions is that Marty grows increasingly familiar with the data and comes to know them well enough to think about the information in chunks.

In working the funnel, Marty uses interactive graphics in his visualization program—mostly in the form of pie charts and bar graphs—to view dollar sales; unit sales; growth; market share; and market penetration for vendors, brands, and products. Marty queries and arranges the data directly in the graphic display. From the display, Marty sees the top vendors in terms of dollar sales and wonders if these vendors also dominate in market share. Much to his surprise, he finds that they do not. This seems odd, and it causes Marty to question the data.

Marty diverts his attention from his graphic analysis to double check the integrity of the data. He moves out of the visualization program and back to his spreadsheet where he can more easily scrutinize the figures. His overriding concern at the moment is with the data in the spreadsheet. He sees that earlier he did not clean the data well enough. In some instances, brands are formatted as individual products, causing duplication in the data. He cleans the data and, when finished, pauses for a moment to remember where he left off in his analysis. He recalls, shuts down, and reopens the visualizations. He reconstructs the steps he took before interrupting the inquiry. The visualization program does not give him a way to save and automatically replay his commonly performed patterns. Eventually, Marty gets back to a view of the dominant vendors and their sales, this time with clean data. He sees now that, in fact, all three vendors have top sales as well as the largest market shares.

Marty moves along quickly, getting performance measures on these top vendors and their brands and products. He explores the brand strength of the vendors in the half-dozen markets that are of most concern to Quality Paper. He explores the top brands, looking across time periods, and identifies peaks and valleys for market share, growth, and sales. He often loses track of where he is in the data and how far along he is in accumulating figures for a baseline. He also has some trouble making transitions between details and overview, between the particulars of performance in a given quarter and overall figures for all quarters combined.

When Marty gets to the most detailed level of the product hierarchy—individual products and product attributes—he finds the product attributes that seem to contribute most to success. For example, eight-roll premiums do better than either four-rolls or twelve-rolls in most, but not all, cases. He begins to explore why products with the same attributes from different brands vary in profitability, but he stops himself from heading off on this tangent. Instead he scribbles a note to remind himself to look at these issues later when they are more directly relevant to his "why?" questions. For now, he resumes his measurements for a baseline. Marty would mark this view in his program, but the software offers no bookmarking capabilities.

Finally, Marty finishes collecting all the measures he needs, and now he creates the baseline of success measures from the combined performance values of the top vendors, brands, and products. To do so, he moves out of the visualization program and back into the spreadsheet display. He uses his spreadsheet program for this task because he can more easily and flexibly standardize values.

When he has the new baseline data ready, he returns to the visualization program and again creates graphic views of the product and market data, now including the baseline variables. He compares premium towels, the other two tiers, and his company's products against the baseline. Again the comparisons are performed by repeatedly funneling through the data.

Marty finds only three vendors produce premium towels, and, in general, this tier is steadily rising in sales, growth, and market penetration; the growth rates for premium towels, in fact, exceed the baseline growth rate for the paper towel category as a whole. This growth is reflected in increased market share among the three top premium tier vendors. From Marty's earlier first-run analysis, he knows that one of these vendor's success comes from customers who were previously loyal to Quality Paper's brand crossing over. Quality Paper's market share and sales have been flat, an unhealthy sign when other companies are capitalizing on opportunities for growth.

2. Why is it happening?

These results raise questions that need explanations. Why are Quality Paper's sales persistently flat? What is the relationship between its weak sales and its lack of products in the premium market? Why have premium paper towels become successful? Who is buying them and why? How likely is it that premium towel sales will continue to grow and for how long? Why are some brands growing faster than others? Answers to these questions will help Marty derive strategies for improving his company's market position.

Compared to Marty's earlier "what?" analysis, the methods and structures for discovering causes are only loosely defined. To ask "why?" questions, Marty draws on his expertise and sets boundaries on the content and range of relationships that he will examine. He knows that certain questions and data relationships best explain product performance, market trends, and customer buying patterns. But within these bounds, his inquiries are fairly fluid. He follows where the data lead him.

Based on his knowledge of the paper towel category, Marty examines various influences on the market. His pattern is to discover insights from the customer data, then switch to the product and market data, repeatedly analyzing how preferences and loyalty play out in particular markets. Keeping track of where he is at any given point becomes difficult, and he continuously jots down notes. Marty finds that some market data run counter to the customer data. He digs into these discrepancies and examines details. To his relief, he finds that the markets in which Quality Paper is most interested accurately reflect customer preferences and buying patterns. He decides not to be too concerned about contrary instances in other markets.

Sometimes he backtracks; sometimes he pursues two parallel streams of thought. He plays with various combinations, holds some constant, and looks at changes over time. Before he shuts down the visualization program for analyzing data, Marty captures the last screen display he has been working on, prints it, and on a pad of paper writes extensive notes. He will open to this display the next day and will check it against the print-out to be sure of its accuracy.

The next day Marty finds that one of the hardest aspects of this "why?" analysis is knowing when to stop. He wants to make sure he has gathered enough data to draw valid conclusions and make a convincing case. He finally decides he is ready to move to the last phase of his inquiry.

3. So what?

In the third phase Marty explores data for persuasive purposes. He interprets what he has found and what it means to his company's future. He is driven directly by decision makers' likely questions and concerns. "So what if premium towels are on the rise?" they will ask. "What does it mean to the bottom line, and what should we do about it?" Marty gathers evidence to answer these "so what?" questions.

Marty first has to figure out the meanings and draw preliminary conclusions from them. Later he and Nancy will jointly review the data and draw final conclusions. At this point, he determines his own initial interpretation. He gets a sense of what he and Nancy are likely to recommend and how decision makers may respond.

Marty structures this part of the analysis differently. He analyzes his findings on paper, away from the computer. He prints the data and graphics he has captured. He brings in other market reports. He jots down notes and highlights important figures and relationships. After completing this offline analysis, he goes to his spreadsheet program and filters to data critical to his interpretation. This further look at these data reinforces Marty's conclusion that the company must enter the premium niche. Drawing on results from his "why?" analysis, he concludes that the company should introduce premium towels in its brand that has the greatest customer loyalty, and it should launch promotional campaigns tailored to high-end customer segments in select Great Lakes and Northeast stores. Based on his analysis he predicts that after just three months, Quality Paper will see marked increases in sales.

Marty now goes back to the visualization program to support these conclusions with evidence geared toward decision makers' likely concerns. Decision makers in his division are usually wary about producing new products. One of Marty's main "so what?" strategies is to analyze less risky choices that decision makers might prefer and to compare these possible alternatives to the option of entering the premium market. Marty looks at a number of existing underdeveloped opportunities and digs into details once again to explore these options. Marty calls up another software program, one his company has developed specifically for integrating relevant product and customer data. With it, he calculates traffic opportunities and turns them into dollar figures.

Working with multiple programs makes this analysis protracted. It is difficult for Marty to compare and capture options with data across software programs. He needs to integrate the data, but the programs do not interact. At one point, he is ready to give up because the data manipulations and mental strain are so challenging. But he sticks to it, knowing that this analysis is crucial. Finally, Marty finds that even if Quality Paper tried to promote these underdeveloped opportunities, they do not have the potential to generate as much traffic and profit as premium towels.

Marty also explores other scenarios to respond to decision makers' "so what?" questions, but they are less taxing. Marty finds little to change his conclusions. The most compelling argument he can make to improve the company's position is still to enter the premium niche. Premium is the only area that offers room for the growth that Quality Paper needs to compete in the paper towel category overall. Altogether, Marty has spent a week and a half analyzing this problem. Now the challenge is to put the data together for persuasive proof.

Marty writes his report to Nancy. The range and depth of this week and a half's worth of materials is large and complicated. He spends the rest of the week writing his report, mixing graphics and data into prose descriptions and explanations. He submits the report, and he and Nancy meet to discuss the investigation and create their presentation.

Communicating Results: Composing a Convincing Story

Nancy and Marty spend long hours turning their conclusions into recommended actions. They have to rank different possibilities for action and create a persuasive story for the decision makers. To build a case, they focus on market forces and competition, resource allocation, and costs. Often they return to the data and visualizations to double check interpretations.

They also re-create and modify views that Marty had captured to make them accessible for persuasive purposes and incorporate them into their presentation. None of this work is done in one sitting. Other projects and responsibilities cause them to continuously suspend their lines of thought and mark their places in the data to resume later on. Finally, their presentation is ready, and they feel pleased at having put together a case they can stand behind.

DESCRIBING CONTEXTS AND CONDITIONS SHAPING COMPLEX PROBLEM SOLVING

Marty's problem solving experiences raise an important question: What do software teams need to do to create a program that would make his work more productive and more efficient? Typically, software teams give their immediate attention to Marty's actions and the data he accesses and analyzes in such patterns as working the funnel, or they seek to automate some of the data preparation processes. But in targeting these issues, software teams leap too quickly to design choices without first establishing and agreeing on the most appropriate *criteria* for design choices that will be useful for the full range of problem solving needs that users have. Marty's situation and problem solving experiences reveal that design teams need to know much more about such experiences to determine these fundamental criteria.

A starting point is a shared understanding of what makes users' problem solving complex. Some usability designs pertain to complex and well-structured work alike, but beyond this common ground, the two classes of work have different demands for *useful* support. Jumping to fixes for evident obstacles without an understanding of this difference will very likely result in less-than-useful fixes. Marty's case demonstrates that he needs software support that differs in kind, not just degree, from support for well-structured tasks.

At a basic level, Marty's situation shows that complex problems are defined by the difficulties people experience in their *interactions* with events and values in their worlds. Complexity does not reside as a property in the data, in an external situation, or in a problem solver's cognitive profile alone. It is impossible to talk about complex problem solving separate from the interchanges that go on between problem solvers and their environments. To Marty, the increased sales of premium towels is a problem because it signals that Quality Paper's interactions with the market are out of joint with the company's goals. Marty's sensitivity to the competition convinces him that his company has to take immediate steps to better align its market interactions and goals. The rise of a premium market is a problem for Marty because it threatens his company's standing, a development that could affect every dimension of his company's organizational life.

It is common in user-centered design to focus on people's activities in context. But this singular use of the term "context" is misleading. In real world activities, people act in a large number of contexts—contexts that are social, technological, organizational, physical, cultural, intellectual, perceptual, informational, and environmental. User- or human-centered methodologies usually refer to a singular, all service, generic context. Many HCI specialists, such as those in context-aware computing, strive to find an inclusive definition of context that can direct designers' attention to a wide range of prominent influential factors. But they too refer primarily to context in the singular. This singular reference is inadequate when designing software for complex problem solving.

For complex problem solving, software teams need to refer to and design for plural contexts. Because complex problem solvers' explorations are open-ended, people are continuously faced with many possible and equally legitimate moves and strategies. To choose, they rely on cues and signs about multi-contextual conditions and the actions these contextual forces structure for them. They also project how these contextual conditions are likely to change, based on one choice rather than another, and how the changes may affect subsequent strategies. For example, in pursuing his "so what?" analysis, Marty is cued by organization-based biases; he seeks analytical paths that aptly address these concerns. For design teams to build the analytical frameworks that problem solvers like Marty need for such situational criteria, they have to understand the influences of many contexts. Moreover, they need to talk about multiple contexts with a shared language relevant to usefulness.

Some contextual designers have catalogued more than 80 situational and subjective factors that influence computer-supported work (Bevan and McLeod, 1994). Even the most well-intentioned design teams, however, can become paralyzed by trying to account for so many factors at once in analyzing, modeling, and designing for users' work. To make these contextual influences more manageable, I group them into four categories or contexts.

As seen in Figure 1.1, each of the four contexts involves numerous conditions that affect the ways in which problem solvers, such as Marty, approach their inquiries. I will discuss each set of contextual conditions and their effects in turn.

- **Problem:** Its severity and complexity, triggers that initiate problem solving, and patterns of inquiry relevant to a given type of problem.

- **Technology and data:** Infrastructure constraints; available information and its content and format; database structures, content, and access mechanisms; and opportunities and limitations of user interfaces, software tools, and architectures.

- **Work domain:** Workplace culture, organizational structures and processes, social roles and relationships, professional practices, physical layouts and arrangements, external/environmental conditions, and time pressures.

- **Subjective:** Cognitive abilities, knowledge, and commonsense know-how; perceptual abilities and knowledge; experiential knowledge; personal preferences; and motivation and incentives.

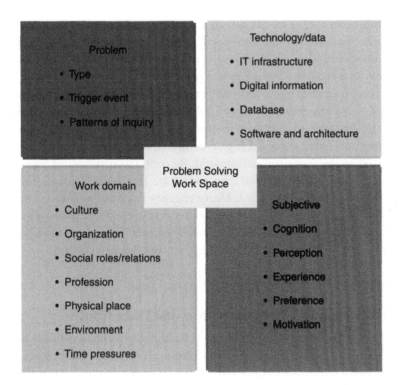

FIGURE 1.1
Contexts and conditions influencing complex problem-solving.

 Describing the Problem Context

Marty reacts to his problem situation by defining it as a certain *type*—namely, the problem of entering a new market to stay competitive. This problem definition strongly directs Marty's choices in organizing his inquiry and in drawing interpretations. If he had given more weight to Quality Paper's culture and its aversion to risk, he might have alternately defined the problem as figuring out ways to compensate for a new niche that his bosses might see as too costly to enter. If so, Marty would have made different inquiry choices and taken alternate directions.

Marty's choices are also affected by *trigger events* that set the investigation in motion. Different triggers push inquiries and methods in distinct directions. Investigations may be self-initiated, prompted by other people through directives, or triggered by alarming conditions demanding immediate attention. In this case, Marty surveyed the state of the market and saw a problem in need of a solution. This self-initiated trigger directs Marty's investigation differently from the ways other triggers might direct it. It gives him a great deal of leeway in posing and answering strategic questions, but it also means he and Nancy have to convince the decision makers. Because they need to put together a convincing story, Marty examines some data that he might not have analyzed if the decision makers were the ones initiating change.

Also as part of the problem context, Marty uses *patterns of inquiry* that he and other professionals in his field regard as effective methods for solving this type of problem in this domain. Some of these inquiry patterns are fairly structured (e.g., cycling repeatedly through the data to find and characterize top performers). By contrast, patterns for investigating "why?" and "so what?" questions are far looser. Because these patterns are more open-ended, Marty engages in extemporaneous backtracking; shifting in scale; and cross-referencing of product, demographic, and traffic opportunity data. Moreover, he adjusts his patterns of inquiry to constraints of time as established by his work domain context.

 Describing the Technology and Data Context

At almost every step, Marty's inquiry is structured by the availability and usability of relevant information and tools. In his first-run analysis he asks a limited number of questions, partly because the analysis is preliminary but also because the data preparation takes up almost three-fourths of the time he has for the inquiry.

During Marty's comprehensive, exploratory analysis, data and tools similarly constrain his investigative strategies. His problem solving involves two sets of data—demographics and data on product and market performance—and interactions with four different programs—the syndicated data program, the spreadsheet, the interactive visualizations, and the traffic opportunity application. Combined, these data and tools shape the depth and breadth of his inquiry. The extent to which Marty can relate differently formatted data depends on the integration capabilities of the tools. Similarly, in putting together data relationships to shed light on reasons for his company's current standing, Marty can follow his inclinations to explore or backtrack only to the extent that his programs allow. The effectiveness of reporting also depends on the structure of the data, the functionality of the tools, and the goals of problem solving.

Finally, the volume of data—50,000 records—affects Marty's reliance on certain methods of inquiry. In part, he repeatedly funnels through the data to familiarize himself with the vast number of variables so he can analyze his "what?" questions without external memory aids. Clearly, interdependencies exist across technological and cognitive (subjective) conditions.

Describing the Subjective Context

Marty's inquiry is intellectually arduous and limits his analysis. He is only able to do as much as he can keep track of. He must keep track of where he is in formatting the data, a process requiring many steps. He also needs to remember how he arrived at various points in his inquiry. Whenever the software helps with these mental efforts, Marty is free to pursue more analytical steps. When it does not, Marty finds himself needing to remember moves and insights and to figure out how to synthesize piecemeal displays of findings into a bigger picture.

Cognitive load and the software-based support Marty requires both depend on the particular demands of the inquiry. Marty may benefit from support that lets him replay some of the funneling moves for some circumstances, but he will not benefit from support that automatically performs the tasks and presents their outcomes. This automation would diminish his knowledge, situational awareness, and understanding of the data.

For some activities, Marty uses external memory aids such as capturing views and jotting down notes. Marty's physical acts, such as the motor activity of writing, may help him remember important insights. As artifacts, however, these written reminders introduce new cognitive demands, which, in turn, call up technological demands—namely the need for a problem solving workspace that accommodates coordination efforts. Aside from cognitive load, Marty's inquiry is taxed by his need to cognitively interpret visual cues in interactive graphics in relation to questions. The costs of sensemaking affect what, how, and how much Marty is willing to investigate.

Finally, on an intellectual level, Marty's expertise directs him toward the problem definitions and strategies he pursues. This knowledge also cues him as to when to capture views. Marty's expertise extends to being savvy organizationally. Previous encounters with decision makers have heightened his ability to project "so what?" scenarios. Less experienced analysts may work with the same situations but take different paths in their inquiries.

 Describing the Work Domain Context

Conditions in the work context affect Marty's inquiry processes. In the external environment, market forces converge to place Quality Paper in a precarious position that Marty believes can be improved through deliberate product innovation. Also, the time Marty spends on these issues is affected by a sluggish economy, one that has prompted his company to increase analysts' workloads. These external conditions intersect with conditions in the problem context, interactively cueing Marty to name the situation in certain ways and follow patterns of inquiry associated with this type of problem situation.

Within the category-management profession, analysts share conventions for classifying problem situations, and they commonly follow the same patterns of inquiry for particular types of problems. Professionally, as well, Marty is socialized to know which data are relevant for specific types of problems and which custom aggregations are necessary. Marty's strategies for finding a way through the problem space arise from a network of interdependencies among professional conventions, data conditions, and market forces.

Marty's joint efforts with Nancy and his projections about decision makers' attitudes affect his selection of relevant data. Analytically, he examines data that explain the problem situation. Socially, he considers data to be relevant when they reflect other people's notions of what can be counted as valid and persuasive findings. Keeping the company's culture of risk aversion in mind, Marty tailors the type and amount of evidence that he collects.

Finally, organizational conditions, such as the autonomous role Marty assumes, shape his inquiries. He has the freedom to initiate analysis and the responsibility to provide Nancy with high quality recommendations that she can promote to higher-ups. Practices for running a market analysis are structured to maintain Marty's autonomy. Were the organization more hierarchical, the patterns of inquiry and resulting knowledge might have been far less integrated. Marty might not have been able to continuously bring his expertise to bear on the resolution, as much of the data were stored in his head alone.

As Marty's case reveals, organizational structures interact with a constellation of other contextual forces to direct the course of inquiry. Organizational structures assure Marty's autonomy in pursing his own directions; constraints in the technology and information context bound the power he has in analyzing data; and professional standards establish the patterns of inquiry he uses. Inquiry proceeds most smoothly when all interactive contextual forces are in sync in supporting problem solvers' purposes.

Complex problem solving cannot be separated from the conditions within and across *many* contexts that interactively shape investigators' possible directions. Conditions within any given context make some problem solving actions possible and rule out others. As problem solvers face these contexts and the resulting array of possible actions, they adapt to available options and surrounding contexts. In designing for complex problem solving, software teams cannot presuppose that a fixed set of steps can satisfy users' needs. Such design strategies may work for formulaic tasks, but they do not hold for complex problem solving.

Taken alone, contextual conditions and constraints do not define complex problem solving. But when contextual influences combine with dynamics of uncertainty and other distinguishing traits of complexity, this array of characteristics defines a class of activity that is different from other workplace tasks. Understanding these attributes provides a vocabulary for supporting this kind of work. Software teams can check whether their prospective designs for complex inquiries hold up to these implied attributes and, in doing so, gauge the design's usefulness.

IDENTIFYING DYNAMICS AND TRAITS OF COMPLEXITY

Conversations about supporting complex problem solving go back several decades. In the 1970s, specialists in design and engineering began to speak of "wicked problems" in their fields—problems that had no readily available answers and could not be solved through rule-based methodologies. In the 1980s and 1990s, software engineers also adopted this phrase to characterize projects with evolving requirements and iterative methods of development. They contrasted these projects with "tame problems," those for which linear, waterfall phases seemed to suffice. Wicked problems in design, engineering, and software development involve the same situational and intellectual complexities as knowledge work today (Rittel and Webber, 1973; DeGrace and Hulet Stahl, 1990; Conklin, 2001). When Marty tackles the question, "Should we break into a new market?" he is exploring a wicked problem. I use *wicked* and *complex* problem solving interchangeably.

Examining the Dynamics of Uncertainty

Multi-contextual influences on the direction of inquiry are one aspect of wicked problem solving. Inescapable uncertainties are another. Uncertainties that make problem solving complex rather than tame include huge amounts of information, incomplete data, or insufficient access to information. In addition, uncertainty confounds problem solving when relevant factors change with emerging insights; when goals shift with evolving conditions; and when unexpected findings arise and cast doubt on earlier assumptions. Furthermore, in dynamic inquiries, problem solvers often are unsure about the implications of their choices. Overall, in complex problem solving uncertainty prevails; in one area after another gaps occur between the information that problem solvers possess and the information required to resolve the problem.

These uncertainties imply that complex inquiries involve both unique interactions with data and a distinct open-endedness in methods. These qualities deserve explicit attention because they are crucial to design efforts. They mark where well-structured tasks leave off and complex problem solving begins.

Deciding if Problem Solving Is Complex: Unique Traits of Complex Inquiries

Perhaps no issue is more important for software teams to determine at the start of a project than whether they are designing for complex or well-structured tasks. Teams often wrongly assume that users' work is well structured because they ignore many of the defining traits of dynamic inquiries. As a result, software teams minimize the complexities for which they design and consequently build inadequate support. They develop the right support for the wrong activities.

Horst Rittel (1972) is best known for identifying the traits that distinguish complex from well-structured activities. I adapt his definitions to designing useful software support. These traits are listed in the following box and will be explained more fully later in this section.

Well-structured tasks have none of these traits. For example, these traits do not occur in routine data entry or in the retrieval of fact answers to such questions as, "How many defective parts were returned to the plant this quarter?" or "What is the percentage increase in returns since

---

TRAITS OF COMPLEX PROBLEM SOLVING

Ill-defined situation and goals

Tied to the interests of diverse stakeholders

Complex information from many sources

Dynamic and emergent

No pre-set entry points or stopping points

Iterative and opportunistic with socially based patterns of inquiry

"Good enough" solutions with no one right answer

---

last quarter?" As a rule, people do not perform complex tasks or solve wicked problems when their work requires little interpretation or when it is shaped by expected standards of practice or automated processes with little reason for varying the routines. Complex problem solving may involve some standardization or automated processes, but at some point in complex inquiries, people have to bring their intentions and ingenuity to bear, and they must have leeway to shape the methods, strategies, priorities, content, and arrangements that they use. Some problems may have fairly systematic methods and "right answers" but be complex largely because they involve massive amounts of data, because time is short and exploratory possibilities are large, or because they involve working within a complicated system. Others may have much higher degrees of complexity because they embody all the distinguishing traits of wicked problems.

These distinguishing traits are embedded in the multiple contexts discussed previously and contribute to the strategies that problem solvers can possibly pursue. They are the underlying aspects of open-ended inquiry that shape the software support that users need. What follows is a brief description of each.

- **Ill-defined situation and goals:** In complex problem solving situations, problem solvers cannot definitively name the problem. In Marty's case, other analysts might have addressed the premium tier problem differently. Problem solvers spend a good deal of time and effort looking for an acceptable definition from among many possibilities. Like Marty, they may do first-run explorations and re-formulate the problem throughout inquiry. They try to find an optimal level of abstraction for defining a problem and correspondingly adjust their perspectives. Ill-defined problem situations give rise to goals that are broad or vague. Complex problem solvers clarify their goals as inquiry progresses.

- **Tied to the interests of diverse stakeholders:** Wicked problems are embedded in larger organizational arenas so that numerous stakeholders contribute to defining the problem and its solution. Marty's choices are influenced by Nancy's biases and those of the decision makers. He also keeps in mind customer behavior, competitors' strategies, and manufacturing feasibility. Additional considerations, though not previously mentioned explicitly, are other analysts' endeavors in his own company and their demands on resources. Stakeholders' demands often change; they are apt to conflict; and new stakeholders may arise at any time. Their diverse and often competing agendas make it necessary for problem solvers to search for alternatives and weigh tradeoffs.

- **Complex information from many sources:** Complex problems involve complicated webs of information. Problem solvers cannot know all the information needed for understanding and solving a problem. Moreover, they need to examine numerous interconnected issues, many of which are not easy to untangle or discover. To comprehensively explore a situation, problem solvers often have to obtain information from diverse sources that are difficult to integrate. They often encounter infrastructure obstacles and software inadequacies for data integration. Moreover, problem solvers often have to arrange data on-the-fly and derive new values for needs that cannot be projected ahead of time. Information that problem solvers need to consider is usually voluminous and multidimensional.

- **Dynamic and emergent:** Changes occur over time because contextual conditions, constraints, and goals emerge with inquiry and independently of it. The result is that problem solvers constantly adjust their inquiries. Changes are unavoidable. Environments relevant to a problem situation are in flux; allocated time and resources and new demands from stakeholders surface unexpectedly. The more dynamic the situation, the more uncertain the inquiry.

- **No pre-set entry points or stopping points:** When confronting wicked problems, people may start at any number of entry points, depending on how they formulate the problem, how they socially orient themselves to problem solving, and what data they have available. The entry points that problem solvers construct set them on a given course. As insights emerge and contextual conditions exert new influences, problem solvers often redirect their investigations. When they do, they have to decide all over again on new entry points. People often "enter" inquiry anew many times during the course of a single investigation. Similarly, problem solvers have no fixed, formulaic stopping point. Problem solvers often harbor some doubt as to whether they have explored enough to stop. Given the contextual dependencies of where to start and stop, problem solvers have to structure the ways into and out of a problem for themselves, relying a good deal on situational awareness. In fact, this self-directed wayfinding occurs throughout inquiry.

- **Iterative and opportunistic with socially based patterns of inquiry:** In open-ended inquiries, problem solvers like Marty move through indeterminacy by progressively making sense of data, reducing data complexity, and incrementally staking out stable boundaries. They structure their way through problem solving, as Marty does with his three-part organizing scheme of "what?," "why?," and "so what?" But these problem solvers have no context-free formula for proceeding step-by-step to a solution. How problem solvers structure inquiries depends, in part, on the ways in which their professions tackle certain types of problems. A defining trait of complexity is that the means emerge and become more specified as exploration continues. What problem solvers do as they progress through their inquiries depends on earlier choices for selecting, arranging, coordinating, and relating relevant factors. Many renditions are possible, and the ones that problem solvers decide to compose depend on contextual demands. Marty works in very structured ways when working the funnel, creating a baseline, and comparing products. By contrast, when questioning "why?" and "so what?" his organizing scheme is more flexible—a set of heuristic strategies about salient relationships worth examining. The less systematic a problem solver's wayfinding patterns are, the more dynamic the processes of inquiry will be.

- **"Good enough" solutions with no one right answer:** Emergent and dynamic inquiries allow for several possible outcomes. In a wicked problem, no perfect solution exists. The rightness of a solution depends on its fit with the situation at hand. Marty's problem of whether to venture into a new niche involves many fact questions but no one right answer. If venturing into a new market niche is the right solution for Marty's company, it is right because, given the circumstances, it is better than others. It is better, for example, when addressing a number of interrelated sub-problems, such as declines in market share, customer retention, and market visibility. Yet the solution will introduce new problems, such as conflicts over resources. Complex problem solving requires investigators to understand the consequences of their potential solutions for other problems. Marty gathers objective evidence to support the merits of his solution, but this does not guarantee acceptance. A wicked problem like Marty's does not get eliminated. Marty finds an optimal solution, but solving complex problems is paradoxical. In the process of working through and reducing the uncertainty of an immediate problem to find a solution, problem solvers often grow increasingly aware of interlocking conditions that create large and *persistent* uncertainties. They recognize the tentative nature of their solutions. In Marty's company, the need for a similar inquiry will re-surface, but each time it will be different.

In summary, complex problems arise from people experiencing difficulty and uncertainty in their world with no easy definition or pat resolution.

Formulating what the real problem is and clarifying goals are ongoing processes. Throughout problem solving, people tackle these questions by continuously shifting perspective and attempting to find the right level of detail for their analysis. Complex problem solving in general is nonlinear. Open-ended inquiry involves an evolving set of interlocking issues in constantly changing contexts. It requires knowledge from many different sources, and solutions require working in several disparate problem spaces. Answers are provisional and emergent; various legitimate options exist to satisfy goals; and optimal choices depend on contextual circumstances.

CONCLUSION: REVISITING MARTY AND THE SOFTWARE SUPPORT HE NEEDS

Software design teams play a large role in determining the technology constraints that problem solvers encounter. Therefore, they need to build for the traits of complexity, striving to permit software users to carry out their inquiries in accordance with their contextually shaped goals. The next two chapters, and the cases in Part Two, explain various user experiences and inquiry patterns that software designers need to support to create useful products. To conclude this chapter, I return to Marty's case for a glimpse into some of these user needs and design criteria that application designers need to address.

Marty's complex problem solving is shaped inescapably by his software interactions. His computing experiences reveal positive aspects of software support, such as efficiency in querying, the ability to conduct both broad and deep analyses, the capacity to derive values for such relationships as traffic opportunities, and the ability to pick up where he left off due to persistent views.

His computing experiences, however, also reveal many unnecessary difficulties. His visualization and traffic opportunity programs offer basic functions but do not interact to give him access to their combined data. Nor do they support such core problem solving activities as finding and organizing paths for inquiry amidst many contending possibilities, drawing meaning from *cumulative* queries, and managing knowledge in relation to contextually defined goals. As Marty uses generic features to select and drill down into data, he concurrently needs to interpret what the graphic display means in relation to his goals and keep track of how close he is to achieving a resolution. Support for such sensemaking and wayfinding is especially vital when Marty has to interrupt his investigation and resume later.

The available programs do not adequately help Marty prepare and condition data, create custom aggregates, or calculate values and derive new fields on-the-fly. The costs of these inadequacies are high. He has no support for creating the custom aggregates common to his trade, despite his program being designed specifically for his profession. Overall, his programs sorely underestimate complex problem solvers' needs. Problem solvers need to have the right data in the right form, with enough flexibility to accommodate unforeseen questions, new values, and unintentional oversights in data conditioning.

Marty also needs far more support than he gets from his tools for integrating diverse data. Complex information from many sources is a fact of life in Marty's world. Yet he cannot work easily with data nor bring data from his in-house program into his visualization displays. When he heads down parallel paths to compare possible "what-if" projections, his tools give him no single electronic workspace in which to process multiple views for comparison. Instead, he has to rely on eyeballing data across multiple windows.

Marty experiences even greater gaps between what he needs and what he receives when it comes to organizing investigations with many legitimate paths and outcomes. Marty organizes his multi-pronged analyses by naming the problem and structuring it into phases: "what?," "why?," and "so what?" Yet the software provides few cues in classifying the problem. Nor does it structure its virtual workspace into an organization similar to his patterns of problem solving (e.g., working the funnel, comparing against a baseline). Part of the problem is that the program lacks adequate domain content to guide Marty in putting together patterns of inquiry conventional to types of problems in his field. Neither does it have any built-in adaptation to notice recurrent patterns and, in response, support and improve users' related behaviors (e.g., through replay options).

In addition, in organizing paths through his inquiry, Marty lacks support for setting up new entry points as his explorations unfold. For example, during his "why?" analysis, he drills down into store-level detail to see if customer patterns held in stores that were of interest to Quality Paper. He then completes this line of questioning and moves to look anew at other explanatory relationships. The software does not provide mechanisms for discovering and comparing possible consequences of various scenarios in the "so what?" analysis; therefore it offers little aid for determining whether findings are complete enough to conclude these appraisals.

The application lacks support for yet another aspect of Marty's wayfinding, namely help in monitoring where he is and what he knows as he organizes and moves through his inquiry. Instead, he has to depend on handwritten notes randomly strewn across his desk and attached to his computer monitor.

The software is no better at supporting Marty's higher-order reasoning as he strives to make sense of emergent insights and relate them to the goals of his problem. Marty works in parallel to logically analyze data and socially assess its relevance for corporate decision makers. Yet he has little software support for drawing *parallel* interpretations or for capturing them and their distinct implications. The visualization program may help Marty make sense of discrete pieces of information in individual graphic views, but it does not enhance sensemaking that is cognitively complex, such as interpreting views in relation to each other, understanding displays in relation to pragmatic questions, or cumulatively developing insights. In the same vein, Marty's programs do not help him gauge the validity of his judgments or the pragmatic implications of choices he makes.

Finally, Marty has to find makeshift ways to write notes and communicate insights to others. He constantly has to capture views and write comments on print-outs because of shortcomings in his visualization program. The software provides only rudimentary reporting, history, and save capabilities with little user control to enter explanatory notes, re-label, or add call-outs and the like, all of which are as crucial to Marty's problem solving as filtering and selecting data.

These unmet needs for complex problem solving differ dramatically from demands of context-free, rule-based tasks—tasks that have known methods and *a priori* right outcomes. As the distinguishing dynamics and traits of complex problem solving reveal, users face complexities that have no exact analogues in well-structured work. The usefulness of software is directly related to the extent to which it addresses these complexities as an integrated whole. The next chapter examines what usefulness for complex problem solving means and how and why designing for it requires HCI specialists to focus on the patterns of inquiry, malleable task landscapes, and core activities that arise from qualities of complexity.

REFERENCES

Bevan, Nigen and Miles McLeod, "Usability Measurement in Context," *Behaviour and Information Technology* 13, nos. 1 and 2 (1994): 132-145.

Conklin, E. Jeffrey, "Wicked Problems and Fragmentation." Cognexus White Paper. 2001. Available at: *cognexus.org/wpf/wickedproblems.pdf*.

DeGrace, Peter and Leslie Hulet Stahl. *Wicked Problems: Righteous Solutions*. Upper Saddle River, NJ: Yourdon Press, 1990.

Passini, Romedi, "Sign-Posting Information Design." In *Information Design*, edited by Robert Jacobson, 83-98. Cambridge, MA: MIT Press, 2000.

Rittel, Horst, "Second Generation Design Methods." In *Design Methods Group 5th Anniversary Report: DMG Occasional Paper* 1 (1972): 5-10. Reprinted in *Developments in Design Methodology*, edited by N. Cross, 317-327. Chichester: Wiley & Sons, 1984.

Rittel, Horst and Melvin Webber, "Dilemmas in a General Theory of Planning," *Policy Sciences* 4 (June 1973): 155-169.

2

Usefulness: Focusing on Inquiry Patterns, Task Landscapes, and Core Activities

O nce HCI specialists and their design teammates survey the uncertain territory of complex problem solving, they encounter formidable challenges. Users have broad goals, incomplete and heterogeneous information, and competing situational priorities. Moreover, problem solvers need flexible software support that gives them optimal control over their critical investigative moves and choices. Where exactly should user-experience researchers, interaction designers, usability specialists, and their teammates focus their attention to create truly useful software?

As long ago as 1985, John Gould and Clayton Lewis described usable systems as those that are "easy to learn (and remember), useful ... contain functions people really need in their work, and ... [are] easy and pleasant to use" (Gould and Lewis, 1985, 300) Then as now, the ideal for usable systems is to be "useful" by supporting the right model of people's work and "easy to use" by disclosing an application's logic and operations. Useful and easy to use are both necessary. They are not either-or design objectives. Unfortunately, software teams frequently treat them as if they are.

When software projects face time and budget constraints, development groups often respond by focusing almost exclusively on ease of use. Design teams give top priority to crafting interfaces that reveal how a system works and that make its features and functions apparent, readily accessible, and simple to use. Usefulness often falls by the wayside. Usefulness is harder to design for, requiring teams to decide in the first place on the *right* features, functions, and screens for users' actual approaches to situated and dynamic work. The result is an application that supports users in knowing how its operations work but not how to operate it for the purposes and complexities of their real world tasks (Ziech, 2001). Separating usefulness from ease of use and focusing primarily on the latter produces a product with incomplete usability. In any situation, an easy to use application that lacks useful support is no more acceptable to users than is partial system performance. But lack of useful support is particularly detrimental in software for dynamic work. This chapter stresses that applications for uncertain and variable problem solving demand designs in which usefulness is primary, with ease of use efforts flowing from there. Focusing on usefulness gives design teams the starting point they need for charting the indeterminate terrain of users' inquiries. This focus is also the bridge for unifying development groups' usability and software engineering processes, leading developers to consider user experiences in all aspects of an application, from start to finish in a project.

In this chapter, I define usefulness and examine why, in designing for usefulness, software teams must focus on users' dynamic work at a *practical* level of detail—their situated or socio-technical patterns of inquiry. Before leaping to low-level object-oriented design, software teams need to model and conceptualize mock-ups and designs for users' practical patterns of inquiry. This chapter defines and explores these patterns of inquiry. It highlights the recurrent landscape of tasks that problem solvers configure in these patterns for particular types of problems to tackle ordeals with data, make sense of multidimensional information, and find their way through indeterminacy. I examine the core data ordeals, sense-making, and wayfinding activities of complex problem solving and describe the functions they serve for different problem solving objectives. Altogether, to assure usefulness these structures of people's dynamic work—their practical patterns of inquiry, associated task landscapes, and core activities for various problem solving processes—need to be the focus of design teams' observations, analysis, modeling, and conceptual designs.

After describing patterns of inquiry and task landscapes, I present a complex problem solving case in which a team of medical experts use software to figure out the root causes of a close-call medication error in their hospital. The scenario illustrates these medical experts' inquiry patterns, task landscapes, and core activities for various problem solving objectives. It also shows shortcomings in the software they use for their root cause analysis. These shortcomings typify many applications for complex problem solving. This chapter emphasizes that the first step toward producing truly useful software and overcoming such shortcomings is focusing on the right level of detail.

DEFINING USEFULNESS

Making usefulness a high priority does not diminish the importance of ease of use. Ease of use is a layer of support that applies equally to software for well-structured tasks and complex inquiries. Giving priority to usefulness simply directs software teams toward first getting people's dynamic work right in models and conceptual designs, and only then making sure the designs are easy to use, access, navigate, and learn. This process is an established concept in user-centered design, but it is not always a followed practice. For complex problem solving, it must be. If experienced problem solvers cannot work through the complexities of their inquiries according to situational and professional demands, even the easiest-to-use application is not useful and, ultimately, not usable.

The relationship between ease of use and usefulness is best seen by watching complex problem solvers conduct their everyday software-supported dynamic inquiries. After observing more than 100 problem solvers doing this work, I have seen that ease of use is vital at first but is not enough to keep analysts going effectively. Problem solvers need ease of use to get started: To understand their applications, what they offer, and how to move around in them. After that—often as soon as 10 minutes into an inquiry—problem solvers expect and look for useful support in their software. If that is missing, their work discernibly slows down. Worse, they find they cannot conduct their work thoroughly, coherently, and accurately, and they give up on the application. Ease of use alone does not keep them motivated. Only after programs usefully help problem solvers resolve open-ended and emergent inquiries in ways they value professionally and organizationally will users look for further ease of use. Then they will be ready to operate what they now perceive to be a valuable application.

Usefulness in software for complex problem solving means designing for dynamic work that cannot fit into the formalisms of usual software engineering. Typically, software teams design for discrete, low-level tasks, such as "sort," "select," and "save." Describing aspects of users' work in terms of such unit tasks is a handy way to turn task descriptions into notations, formal requirements, and coding. Unit tasks require no control structure and represent the simplest actions users can handle without going into problem solving mode (Green et al., 1988). In dynamic, open-ended inquiries, however, people regularly handle work at a higher level because they are very much in "problem solving mode."

Higher-order processes give coherence to the synergy of open-ended investigations. If users' software focuses only on actions for unit tasks without unifying them into these higher-order processes, problem solvers will not be able to shape to their own ends the emergence, serendipity, idiosyncrasy, and uncertainty that come with solving perplexing problems. In carrying out productive, coherent, and complete inquiries, problem solvers by necessity think about and perform their tasks at this higher level of integrated processes. Support is useful, therefore, when it helps users integrate moves and strategies into the advanced reasoning and social coordination inherent in complex problem solving (Viller and Sommerville, 1998). Support is useful when it lets problem solvers improvise in their open-ended inquiries, yet work within recognizable structures, a tricky yet crucial balance for HCI specialists to achieve.

FOCUSING ON COMPLEX PROBLEM SOLVING AT A PRACTICAL LEVEL

The underlying recognizable structures that organize problem solvers' complex investigations are their practical-level patterns of inquiry. For various types of complex problems, experienced analysts in a specific domain by and large structure their inquiries into similar patterns. For these patterns, they configure task landscapes that let them move through the stable and variable aspects of dynamic and emergent inquiries to reach a conclusion. The following sections describe these patterns of inquiry and task landscapes in detail.

Examining Patterns of Inquiry

Patterns of inquiry for complex problem solving are recurring sets of actions and strategies that have a successful record in resolving particular types of problems. Patterns are the stable parts of dynamic problem solving onto which problem solvers latch the improvisational strategies they use in response to emergent insights, conditions, and other idiosyncratic influences. In pattern-based explorations, stability and serendipity freely intermingle. When something unexpected enters the process, problem solvers reconfigure patterns of tasks and often start down an alternate path.

In Marty's case in Chapter 1, an example of tasks in a pattern of inquiry is "comparing contending solutions," which he carries out when he examines whether he should enter the new niche of premium towels or focus on existing underdeveloped opportunities. Figure 2.1 identifies one of his sub-goals and its sub-pattern of inquiry:

This partial description of Marty's investigation cannot be isolated from his other investigative patterns. Patterns connect to each other with feedback constantly flowing across the connections. If design teams look only at the context-free tasks in Figure 2.1, they are likely to decompose them into generic actions. They may, for example, target Marty's task, "relate opportunity dollars to product performance data," assume that it requires the same support in all circumstances, and create features and user interface (UI) controls to support it. In Marty's practical work, however, when he relates these variables during other phases of his investigation, he uses different moves because the task of relating these same variables functions in distinct ways for each purpose.

Inquiry patterns revolve around relationships among parts, arranged according to how each part addresses a specific problem and purpose in context. Arrangements within and across patterns make a difference for achieving a complete analysis. For complex inquiries, composite patterns do not add up to the whole of a problem solving experience. Rather they are iterative and synergistic. Interactions between the patterns making up a problem solver's inquiry often give rise to unpredictable results, leading the problem solvers to put together unforeseen task landscapes and solutions on-the-fly. This free-flowing inventiveness often endures in later inquiries as the problem solver incorporates it into his or her regular approach to resolving this type of problem. In Chapter 3, the section,

FIGURE 2.1
Pattern of inquiry for
investigating whether to
introduce a new product.

Comparing Contending Solutions

Subpattern—Preferred Vs. Less Risky Solution

Context and goal: After analyzing data and finding a solution, problem solvers compare it to other solutions that may be preferred by decision makers.

Example: A category manager finds a solution (e.g., entering a new niche) but decision makers may want a less risky one.

Tasks
- Access data on less risky alternatives, such as ratcheting up sales in other channels. Validate.
- Calculate opportunity dollars. Validate data integrity.
- Relate opportunity dollars and product performance data. Verify.
- Structure a workspace for running many scenarios at once and making comparisons.
- Display data appropriately for scenarios and projected results. Run the scenarios.
- Capture outcomes for comparison with the preferred solution.
- Identify similarities/differences between solution options.
- Transform data into compatible formats for comparing outcomes of the scenarios to outcomes related to the preferred solution (entering a new niche).
- Accumulate judgments. Relate to decisionmakers' biases. Create reminders about important factors. Figure out next moves.
- Structure a workspace for comparing the costs and benefits of each solution according to company priorities.
- Call up prior data and outcomes. Display appropriately for comparisons. Validate. Select and compare.

"Analyzing Patterns of Inquiry and their Conditions and Constrants" identifies traits to focus on to analyze patterns of inquiry.

Clearly, patterns of inquiry cannot be captured as procedures. They are, at once, loose and pliable and fundamental and recurrent. They pertain to specific classes of problems and describe "the core of the solution to that problem in such a way that you can use this solution a million times over, without ever doing it the same way twice" (Alexander et al., 1977). In open-ended problem solving, everything affects everything else and evolves in new ways each time.

Inquiry patterns describe work from a user's point of view. Users consolidate actions, knowledge, resources, and strategies at a practical (application) level and structure them according to work-related goals. They "chunk" various groups of actions into what to them is a "basic" task in their problem solving, a much higher level "task" than programming notions of low-level unit actions. Users unify and configure chunked tasks into a landscape: An integrated field of moves and strategies that they navigate to get "from here to there" through indeterminacy to resolution.

Examining Task Landscapes in Patterns of Inquiry

Task landscapes are the "spaces users interactively construct out of the resources they find when trying to accomplish a task" (Kirsch, 2001).

Putting together the right task landscapes for the right problem is vital to the success of open-ended inquiries. It is the fundamental means by which experienced problem solvers impose their expertise on their problem space to diminish uncertainty and streamline their plans (Kirsch, 1995).

In software-supported complex problem solving, when experienced analysts structure their inquiries into task landscapes they join chunked tasks into "tracts" and integrate the tracts according to their goals, the effects of various tasks on program states, contextual conditions, and available next steps. For opportunistic inquiries, users need the freedom to configure their task landscapes for these considerations. Therefore, design teams must create software that gives complex problem solvers ample discretion to choose what moves to integrate with others.

In addition to structuring problem solving spaces into landscapes relevant to their complex work, problem solvers "seed" these spaces to make complex inquiries more manageable. As needed, they highlight and structurally manipulate the landscapes of their work to flag and remind themselves about unfolding events and local circumstances that are relevant. This "seeding" of information in problem solving environments includes leaving markers as reminders or cues about aspects of an inquiry that problem solvers know will be important later in their investigation. It includes hiding irrelevant data to unclutter the workspace and to minimize the number of items competing for attention. Seeding the terrain of a workspace also involves writing notes about relevant choices and paths to explore further, leaving them in opportune spots, and saving important aspects of an investigation-in-progress for presentations or collaborations. In these ways, problem solvers increase their situational awareness, a critical need in contextually determined, dynamic work. Through these space-arranging activities, problem solvers strive to structure information and desktop displays so everything they need for an immediate question lies directly at hand.

As this description of seeding activities suggests, a good number of problem solvers' wayfinding and sensemaking "seeding" activities are not "mainline" analytical tasks. Mainline tasks are the procedures that users perform to manipulate information or objects for a work goal by changing the content of a data display (e.g., the task of filtering to data of interest) (Denley and Whitefield, 1998). By contrast, seeding activities and many other inquiry interactions do not change the content and structure of the data for analytical purposes but are nonetheless essential to success. They make it possible for users to perform their mainline tasks. These actions are "enabling tasks," tasks tightly integrated with mainline actions and instrumental in their conduct (Denley and Whitefield, 1998).

Users configure task landscapes by putting together the mainline *and* enabling tasks necessary for reaching their goals, based on contextual conditions and constraints.

This practical-level focus on patterns of inquiry and task landscapes is at a higher level than the patterns many development groups commonly discuss and target in their applications. Commonly, application teams focus on software patterns and interface or interaction patterns. It is important not to mistake a practical pattern of inquiry for these other patterns relevant to software development and design or to substitute these other patterns for it.

WHAT IS THE DIFFERENCE BETWEEN INQUIRY PATTERNS AND DESIGN PATTERNS?

Patterns of inquiry focus on users' work at an application or job level and are a function of people's purposes, contexts, and problems. HCI specialists variously call them socio-technical, application, or task patterns, with a related offshoot in computer supported collaborative work (CSCW) called patterns of cooperative interaction (Erikson, 2000; Martin et al., 2002). Practical-level patterns differ from the programming orientation of software patterns, such as the "composite" pattern that guides developers in "compos[ing] objects into tree structures to represent part-whole hierarchies" (Gamma et al., 1995) They are also unlike UI patterns that capture design strategies for screen layouts, formats, widgets, and controls (Tidwell, 2000; Borchers, 2001). Software and UI patterns are lower than the level at which users think about the task landscapes of open-ended exploration. Combinations of UI patterns may provide design strategies to support users' patterns of inquiry, but they must not be mistaken for them.

A small group of pattern advocates have begun to examine and describe higher-level application patterns, but so far their results neither adequately capture the mixed regularity and variability of complex problem solving nor portray its rich contextual interactions (Lafreniere and Granlund, 2001). Instead, most current application patterns focus principally on summing low-level mainline tasks for work-related activities.

One example of this type of current application pattern is "patient record review," which represents a physician reading a patient's record before consulting with the patient to break the news of a serious disease (Lafreniere and Granlund, 2001). In this pattern, the doctor's record review includes numerous actions: Filtering to only the data of interest, zooming in on details, viewing data about the patient's condition over time, and relating details to the big picture. To its credit, the pattern underscores the combined actions that make up the review of the patient's record. But it focuses only on mainline analytical moves for generic circumstances, precisely the ones that user interface designers can translate in one-to-one fashion into interactions with screen controls.

The application pattern does not capture the diverse tasks that enable mainline actions and that, at a practical level, cannot be severed from these actions. Some of these enabling tasks include examining details from another source for important relationships; recalling information views, such as allergies and medication history; verifying the accuracy of the records; and validating conclusions. Other tasks vital to reviewing a patient record include determining data of prime interest, accumulating and mentally integrating impressions into provisional judgments, and writing notes.

The "patient record review" pattern fails to give insight into the full array of mainline and enabling tasks that complex problem solvers configure into landscapes. For different doctors, landscapes will vary depending on a patient's disease, needs, closeness to the doctor, and other issues. For example, the most important issue to one doctor may be reviewing hidden causes of an illness to infer a prognosis with confidence. To another, it may be bringing in other specialists' opinions and integrating them into the "patient record review." Landscapes that doctors configure will be dissimilar for each distinct priority.

For useful software, design teams need different practical patterns of inquiry from those modeled by "patient record review," a point reinforced by the scenario on medication decisions in Chapter 8. HCI specialists and their teammates need to focus on inquiry patterns and highlight the "structured freedom" that users need for configuring combined mainline and enable moves for complex problem solving. Because problem solvers are constrained by domain-based conventions, such as shared patterns of inquiry and business rules, the options they choose from when constructing task landscapes may vary but they are bounded. To illustrate this "structured freedom" and the software support that users require for it, I turn to an actual case of medical experts uncovering the causes of a medication error.

SCENARIO: ANALYZING THE ROOT CAUSES OF A DRUG OVERDOSE

Fatal medical errors or near misses are a major problem in healthcare. To prevent these calamities, hospitals devote enormous amounts of resources to analyzing adverse events. Hospital risk managers assemble internal teams of medical and other healthcare specialists who delve deeply into the causes and recommend improvements to guard against future occurrences. Teams look at contexts and systems in a hospital rather than blaming the individuals who were immediately involved in the accident.

For example, teams may trace a life-threatening delay in administering medication to the obvious source: The nurse on duty. But they push farther to uncover systemic issues. These issues may include a resident who entered the electronic prescription incorrectly, which traces to his just having started his rotation in this hospital, which uses a dissimilar electronic ordering system from his prior place of residency without providing training in the differences. In addition, the computerized ordering system may play a role in the incident for lacking fail-safe mechanisms to guard against common errors. Other hospital divisions and processes may be involved, as well. Pharmacists may have failed to catch the error because their pharmacy software packages, incompatible with the ordering system, have not been upgraded to display all the fields included in the ordering system. Information technology (IT) analysts may have planned to upgrade the pharmacy package but were forced to postpone it due to budget cuts mandated by hospital administrators.

Currently, the prime hospital accrediting agency—the Joint Commission on Accreditation of Healthcare Organizations (JCAHO)—along with reports such as the Institute of Medicine's *To Err is Human: Building a Safer Health System* (Kohn et al., 1999) strive to implement such systemic approaches in all hospitals nationwide. JCAHO officials have found that blaming individuals has had little effect in lowering the number of adverse medical incidents. Therefore, they have charged hospitals with assembling teams of medical experts to investigate and correct deep-rooted systemic causes.

The process for examining causes is lengthy and abstract. It has been carefully defined by JCAHO and other agencies to ensure uniform approaches and categories of causes across hospital teams. Increasingly, commercial software is incorporating these methods into root cause analysis (RCA) programs, and many medical centers are implementing them. The software supports teams in all aspects of an RCA: From reconstructing the events that led to an error, to analyzing relationships, determining likely causes, proposing and delegating responsibility for improvements, and reporting results. The software also collects data generated from a team's inquiry and stores it in a central database along with data from other teams' analyses. Hospital managers and other authorized analysts can then examine aggregated cases to gain insights into patterns that may help in devising further preventive measures.

Prelude to a Story: Inquiry Activities and Incidents Under Investigation

In this case, a hospital risk manager has organized a five-person RCA team to examine a close-call medication incident. In addition to the risk manager, the team consists of a nursing informatics specialist, a pharmacist, a doctor, an IT analyst. Team members are all experienced in conducting RCAs, because they have served on at least five RCA teams in this hospital, though never before together. They are familiar with the standard RCA methodology endorsed by JCAHO and followed by their medical center. This methodology structures root cause inquiries into the following phases:

1. **Preliminary work:** Team members, on their own, read information about the incident, then convene to decide on and gather additional data. This phase assures the team that they have the right data for an informed analysis.

2. **Integrated analysis:** The team investigates incident events and causes.

3. **Proposed solutions:** Solutions are recommended by team members as ways to guard against recurrences.

4. **Report:** Final findings are presented to hospital officials. This report is composed by the risk manager to document the team's processes, findings, and recommendations for sign-off and implementation.

Focus of the RCA Team's Investigation

This scenario narrates only the activities in the second phase of the RCA methodology: The integrated analysis. During this phase, the team focuses on the following investigative activities:

- Reconstructing the events leading to the incident

- Identifying factors contributing to each event

- Grouping factors to discover root causes

The incident under investigation is a medication error in which a patient received a double dose of a pain medication while hospitalized for back surgery. Prior to meeting today, the team has already read the incident report. The report details the adverse event as follows.

Incident Narrative

A 26-year-old female underwent back surgery and was supposed to spend the standard 24 hours recuperating in the intensive care unit (ICU).

After 20 hours, however, the patient was transferred to the acute medicine ward because the ICU was overcrowded, and the patient seemed to be recuperating nicely. In the acute care ward, she was to continue with the same schedule and dose of pain medication.

A half-hour before the patient transferred from the ICU to acute medicine, at 11:00 AM, the nurse in the ICU started the ICU's second medication pass of the day. At this time, the patient, as scheduled, received her second dose of painkillers. Soon after, at 11:30 AM, the ICU clerk checked the patient out, noting in the patient's computerized record that she was a transfer patient.

Hospital procedures and computerized processes for transfer patients dictate that before a patient moves from one ward to another, the attending physician must electronically order new medications that will follow the patient to the new ward. When a patient checks out of the old ward, the previous orders for medication get cancelled automatically through the linked patient record and medication administration systems. Then, upon checking into the new ward, the patient becomes "active" again in the systems. Accordingly, the systems automatically update the patient's records with the new drug orders and read the patient's medication history from the old orders into an archived history portion of the patient's electronic medication administration record (MAR). During their scheduled medication passes, nurses use the electronic MAR to identify what drugs a patient should receive, when, and how much. The MAR notes, for example, whether a patient is to get medication once a day, at every scheduled pass, or every other day. Few nurses have the time to check the archive screen to see a patient's medication history when they do their medication passes. It is only a keystroke away, but it cannot be viewed alongside the current medication administration screen for easy and quick comparisons. Nurses primarily look only at the default screen showing what medications each patient receives and how many times a day.

In this case, the transfer patient checked into acute medicine at 11:35 AM. Once the ward clerk finished admitting her, and after her MAR was automatically updated, she was wheeled to her room. At noon, the medication nurse on this floor began her scheduled medication pass. Nurses in acute medicine and the ICU follow different schedules for administering medication. In acute medicine, the noon administration was the third medication pass of the day, only an hour later than the ICU's second medication pass. The acute medicine nurse saw the patient's second dose checked off on her electronic MAR and assumed that the patient was ready for her third dose of the day. The nurse was unaware that ICU and acute medicine medication times differed. Therefore, she never thought to look closely at the MAR screen where, buried amidst other details, the exact time of the patient's second dose of morphine (administered in the ICU) was displayed. The nurse, believing she was keeping the patient on schedule, administered the drug. Soon after, the patient became violently ill. Her spasmodic reaction to the double dose of the painkiller threatened to damage the still-delicate setting of her spine. Fortunately, the doctor averted the damage, but it required hospitalizing the patient for five extra days.

At first glance, it may seem that the cause of this overdose incident is obvious: The acute medicine nurse messed up. But in this hospital RCA team members have been trained in JCAHO's alternate systemic approach and conduct their analysis from its perspective.

Reconstructing the Events Leading to the Incident

Before today's session, the RCA team met earlier in the week for a preliminary discussion about any gaps in the incident information that needed to be filled before the group began its analysis. Various members volunteered to gather the additional data the team decided it wanted, and they circulated the information to everyone before today's meeting. They filled in the gaps in the information and now believe they have a complete and accurate picture of the double-dose incident. At today's meeting, the team begins to analyze events and find root causes.

Methods Built into the Program

The first step is to reconstruct the chain of events leading to the error. The pharmacist volunteers to be the recorder. He opens the RCA application to the flowchart screen and displays it on the wall so the group can work collaboratively.

In this flowchart module, the program is designed for users to investigate linearly. This assumed approach—and the program's associated support—structures users' work first into a process of brainstorming important events and putting them in a workspace. Then, users are supposed to discuss the events and move peripheral items to a "parking lot," which is a cordoned-off area on the screen for events that may become relevant later. From the relevant items (those left in the workspace), analysts are supposed to structure a flowchart of events. As it is built into the program, flowcharting is assumed to be a series of fairly systematic, sequential steps. RCA teams are expected to create each entity, link it to other entities in the diagram, then move each event to the right spot in the diagram.

The Team's Practical Approaches

The RCA team's approach does not conform to this linear model. They mention an event without writing it down in the workspace. They swiftly decide its importance and never use the parking lot. They write important items directly into the flowchart without first listing all possibilities in the workspace. They rapidly add events to the flowchart—events such as checking the patient in and out of the wards, the doctor writing orders, pharmacists sending the medication, and combined patient record and medication systems' handling of information. With this almost single-step process of brainstorming and charting, the group relates events instantly and not always at the same level of detail. The flowchart is the workspace, demanding a lot of on-the-fly manipulations and revisions that are not presupposed in the software's task model.

The team also creates many flowchart versions, not just the one the program presumes. Team members' approaches clearly are growing messier than the application's built-in process assumes. These healthcare professionals continuously assess and change the level of detail with which they describe an occurrence, sometimes examining minutiae, such as the clicks the nurse must have made on the MAR screen, and sometimes focusing on broader events, such as how long the nurse spent at various patients' bedsides during this medication pass. They create different versions that highlight distinct perspectives—the nurses' activities, the patient's experiences, and the uses of computerized records. Working around the RCA software constraints, the team finds a way to save flowchart versions and then experiment with other renditions. They aim to compare "top versions" at the end of the process and make a final choice.

The group consistently discusses its rationales for ordering events in certain ways and for deciding a version is complete enough to move on. They talk about the cues that prompt them to rethink the scope and level of detail in events and revise accordingly. Unfortunately, the program has limited flexibility for their approach. Teammates spend longer than they want figuring out how to work the program. For example, it has no easy mechanisms for copying and revising portions of flowcharts or for saving, bookmarking, and later displaying multiple versions.

The final rendition they create brings together the multiple streams of parallel events that reflect all the perspectives they diagrammed separately. For this version they need to do a lot of program manipulation, frequently repositioning items on the flowchart. They assess this new version as they go and consider additional, noteworthy events, such as ICU nurses' reference to policy about overcrowding and technicians in the pharmacy labeling drugs. All the while, the teammates manipulate the RCA program as best as they can, given the software's failure to antici-pate or offer much adaptivity for such constant changes in flowchart events.

Members unanimously agree that the best version is the flowchart that covers all perspectives, and they move on.

Identifying Factors Contributing to Each Event

The RCA team is ready to identify the factors that contributed to each event portrayed in the flowchart. The pharmacist moves to the corre-sponding analysis module in the RCA software.

Methods Built into the Program

The analysis screen is split into three sections: One displays the flowchart that the team selected as its final version, another shows the parking lot of peripheral ideas (it is empty), and a third provides a workspace for creating links, one by one, between an event in the flowchart and its contributing factors. This workspace provides access to the categories JCAHO has devised for analyzing adverse medical events. RCA teams are urged to use this controlled vocabulary so risk managers and other researchers have uniform data that they can aggregate to analyze trends.

As in the flowchart, this module presupposes certain methods for users' analysis. It assumes that RCA teams will pick a flowchart event, access the program-provided JCAHO listing, and go through each category to identify factors relevant to the flowchart event. For example, the "rules, policies, and procedures" category includes such items as no overall management policy for addressing risk, a lack of clarity in policies and procedures related to work processes, and an everyday disregard of relevant policies and procedures. When a team selects one of these factors, the software automatically links it to the event.

The Team's Practical Approaches

As logical as this approach is, the RCA team follows it only when its members are not familiar with the conditions of an event. When team-mates have expertise in an aspect of the incident, they delve right into an analysis without referring to the JCAHO categories. Most of the team's work on this case involves this "delving in" approach.

The team's inquiry is structured by progressively asking "why?" and diving deeper into each factor it considers. They look at the computerized processing related to patient care and transfer, drug ordering, fulfillment, and administration times. They ask why these multiple systems do not cross-check or give warnings of discrepancies between the medication administration times in the two wards. They also ask why, in the absence of warnings about medication schedule differences, people never update a transfer patient's record with this discrepancy when they write and process the new medication order and check a patient into the ward. The team similarly delves into factors related to training, workload, and cross-functional communications between the parties involved.

Teammates are never certain where their questioning will lead. They find their way through these "why?" questions with complementary sub-strategies. For each "why?" question they methodically examine whether motivating behaviors are a matter of some social, cultural, technical, or environmental condition, or caused by an omission. Then they turn the inquiry around and ask, "why not; why were things not done differently?" As they probe, they carefully keep track of what they know so far, given their accumulation of information. The recorder works the program and also writes notes longhand, monitoring the group's knowledge and progress.

The program offers little support for users to generate their own factors instead of employing those built into the controlled vocabulary for the JCAHO categories. The program offers a notepad on which to jot down factors, but no mechanisms for easily structuring them hierarchically, matching them to the JCAHO lexicon, or connecting them to an associated event. These omissions hamper the team's efforts. Without a hierarchy of factors, for example, team members cannot readily judge whether they have yet looked deeply enough into causes. They begin to use the whiteboard in the meeting room to supplement the screen, sketching freehand some of these hierarchies of factors.

Drawing Preliminary Conclusions

Despite the program's rigidity and thanks to the team's decision to plot some relationships on the whiteboard, the group ends up focusing on several important factors leading to critical events. They find that two different development teams built each software system, each at different sites. Neither communicated much with the other, and both competed for scarce IT resources. Moreover, the development teams were composed mostly of off-site contractors who had little interaction with frontline healthcare staff. The medication administration system developers were halfway through the project before they realized medication schedules varied across wards and that this posed a considerable risk for transfer patients.

A group of contractors addressed this issue as best they could, given that requirements were set already and development was well underway. They produced, as a "Band-aid," a small program strictly for checking in transfer patients to be used by ward clerks instead of the computerized record system. Had the different development teams communicated and integrated their projects better, this small program could have at least been incorporated into the larger computerized patient record system. Because it was not, ward clerks often forgot about the program, and some were never trained on it. Training was also neglected for other reasons. For months, nursing shortages coupled with performance reviews that rewarded efficiency made managers reluctant to spare any nurses for training.

Further Program Obstacles in the Wrap-Up

The RCA team completes this "factor-finding" phase of the analysis by matching its own terms for factors (generated during its exploratory analysis) with terms from the JCAHO vocabulary and categories. Because the team's approach is not modeled adequately in the program, this step is an ordeal. However, the alternative—following the model of work built into the program—was even more unacceptable. Had the team's domain experts adapted to the program model, they never would have uncovered important factors, such as the isolated software development teams, the makeshift program for transfer patients, and ward clerk accountability. These factors all came to light because of the team members' combined expertise. In fact, the JCAHO list does not include some of these contributing factors as options.

Most of the team's factors do have JCAHO matches. Yet in some cases, no adequate term exists in the controlled vocabulary, especially in relation to the computerized patient record, medication, ordering, and pharmacy systems. The JCAHO categories and factors are not altogether up to date with technological advances in this hospital. For these technical contributing factors, the team has to invent and enter its own terms. Once again, the program does not readily accommodate this need. The team spends a lot of time figuring out how to enter its own terms and how to flag terms that are non-standard. They end up using a comment field intended for other purposes but, fairly exasperated at this point, they decide it is "good enough" for their immediate objectives.

Finally, now that they have finished the first and second phases of analysis, the teammates take a break. They save their work, once again expecting support the software does not provide. They want to add comments to capture the decisions that led them to their selection of factors, but the program lacks these capabilities. The pharmacist uses a word-processing program to electronically record these and other comments he has written longhand for use later in the team's final report.

Grouping Factors to Discover Root Causes

After a short break, team members reconvene, review their progress, and head into the last part of the analysis: Synthesizing factors into systemic root causes. This root cause analysis requires them to reorganize all the contributing factors identified for events into networks of associations. Closely linked items in the network will reflect shortcomings in particular structures and processes, and these will indicate root causes of the error.

Methods Built into the Program

The RCA software offers a special workspace for creating network diagrams in this phase. The network-diagram function lets users link factors and place them in ways that reveal groupings. Users can also link factors across groupings.

The Team's Practical Approaches

No one right method exists for classifying similarities between factors or for linking them to one another. The team discusses how to proceed and agrees on criteria and methods for grouping factors. Team members start by associating factors that relate to the hospital's processes for developing computerized systems. The team, for example, links together the following factors: The hospital lacks formal means for communication among different project developers; no routines exist for basing system design on actual end-user experiences in context; and management processes for identifying the results of system changes before they are implemented are missing.

Often team members disagree about associations and links among factors. On one occasion, these debates raise issues that prompt the team to reevaluate the very factors they are considering. Looking closely, team members wonder whether they may have been mistaken in their earlier "factor-finding" phase of analysis. One term they chose for a technical factor relates to three different events. Now that the teammates' perspectives have shifted from events to root causes, they realize that nuances of difference distinguish this factor across the three events, and it should not be represented by a single term. Backtracking, they set about reexamining and revising their prior work in naming this contributing factor.

They return to the earlier RCA screen used to identify contributing factors for each event. On this screen, they revise the terms they used earlier. These changes update the network diagram they are constructing in their current phase of analysis. At present, this diagram is not visible, as it has been minimized to do this backtracking.

When the team resumes its grouping of factors into root causes and reopens the minimized network screen, its members spend several minutes reorienting themselves to the now updated diagram. They remind each other about how the screen looked before they momentarily left it to puzzle over possible new meanings implied by the revised factors.

Adding to the intellectual challenge of grouping factors, the layout of the network diagram causes difficulties. Links between factors are becoming increasingly crisscrossed, and associations are hard for teammates to sort out. About three-quarters of the way through the analysis, the team reaches its limit with the tangled networks. Team members cannot tell if they have created duplicate groupings or not. They want to structure the information into a hybrid network-and-cluster view to see relationships more clearly, but the program constrains them.

Frustrated, the pharmacist goes to the whiteboard, sketches the groupings, and draws a hybrid diagram. The team finishes its analysis with colored markers on the whiteboard. Time pressures, combined with the analysts' limited facility in getting the RCA program to disentangle networks, prompt the team to opt for this more expedient analysis.

Drawing Conclusions and Getting Closure

Finally, the RCA team identifies important root causes. The most important are the organizational processes that allow incompatible electronic systems to be implemented without checks and balances and the hospital's reliance on a makeshift transfer-patient program. Other system-based causes include ambiguously written policies for overcrowded units and overworked staff; a workplace culture that does not encourage communication between front line staff across units because of rigid adherence to communication channels; and, in computerized systems, insufficient design of relevant information, integrated as users need it.

Later in the week at a follow-up meeting, the group completes all phases of the JCAHO-sanctioned methodology. Team members discuss ways to correct or prevent root cause conditions and write recommendations. The risk manager composes the final report to hospital administrators using templates built into the RCA program. As good as the templates are, the risk manager still needs to add explanatory text. In adding this text, she laboriously sorts through her disorganized notes from the meeting to remember the important ideas. She also refers to the notes the recorder wrote regarding the team's ideas and rationales in their analysis. Had the program offered annotation capabilities, she could have avoided this final data ordeal.

SUMMARIZING PATTERNS OF INQUIRY AND TASK LANDSCAPES IN THE RCA CASE

The RCA scenario describes the team's problem solving activities—online and off—at a practical level of detail. The medical experts structure their patterns of inquiry around the three phases of analysis sanctioned by JCAHO: Reconstructing the events leading to the incident; identifying for each event factors contributing to its occurrence; and grouping factors to discover root causes. Certain sets of moves and strategies—the task landscapes—characterize these patterns, for example, the subpatterns of brainstorming and charting in one fell swoop for reconstructing events. In brainstorming and charting, team members iteratively and dynamically generate ideas about possible events to include, structure events into an evolving flowchart without listing them elsewhere first, and rearrange them in relation to other events that they continuously add. Team members combine these mainline tasks with indispensable enabling tasks, such as remembering and writing longhand what teammates previously thought and rationalized based on domain expertise, turning data into multiple versions of the reconstructed incident, and revising levels of detail in named events, in turn triggering the need for more rearranging.

Most importantly, at a practical level of configuring task landscapes and workspaces, the team thinks about their "basic tasks" at a chunked level, such as backtracking to assure valid conclusions about root causes when they group factors to discover root causes. They do not think about this "task" either as a series of low-level mouse clicks or as program operations such as minimizing the current window and opening the event and factors chart window. At a practical level, strategic and tactical approaches converge in problem solvers' choices, decisions, and actions. Janus-like, practical patterns of inquiry point problem solvers toward step-by-step procedures for an immediate inquiry action and toward heuristic strategies for realizing broad analytic aims and outcomes.

FOCUSING ON CORE ACTIVITIES WITHIN TASK LANDSCAPES

Many tasks in practical patterns of inquiry are structured by domain-specific goals, needs, and practices. Later case studies highlight this domain specificity. Here the focus is on activities that can be generalized. They are the foundation for the actions that software for complex problem solving must support to be useful. These tasks generalize across problems and domains because they derive from the distinguishing traits of complex problem solving detailed in the previous chapter. In complex problem solving, people undertake three core activities (Figure 2.2):

- **Data ordeals:** Dealing with large volumes of multidimensional, multi-scaled data.

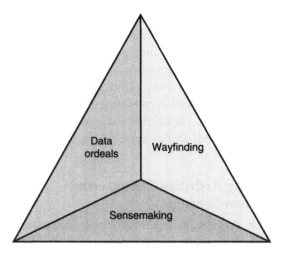

FIGURE 2.2
Core activities of complex
problem solving.

- **Wayfinding:** Organizing and finding a way through dynamic explorations and analyses.

- **Sensemaking:** Understanding and finding meaning in multifaceted data relationships seen from many perspectives.

What Data Ordeals Characterize Complex Problem Solving?

Data ordeals involve grappling with large volumes of data. Some data ordeals involve filtering out irrelevant data and validating data accuracy. Others include integrating, arranging, and relating data to find answers. Problem solvers face further ordeals when they try to construct complex queries and verify results. Finally, they become immersed in data ordeals when they attempt to retrieve information from diverse sources and try to format and scale it compatibly so they can display it at the right level of detail for their purposes.

Data ordeals the RCA team members face include continuous revisions to flowcharts-in-progress as they add events, change event positions, and adjust levels of detail. Teammates collaboratively work through data ordeals in creating multiple flowcharts and comparing them. They also struggle with data when they create networks with crossed links and when they try to enter their own local terms for contributing factors (new data) into the system.

Of the three core activities of complex problem solving, programs most often address data ordeals. Usually software supports these ordeals, aiming to ease users' interactions in selecting data, filtering, sorting, calculating, rotating, panning, and zooming. However, few programs offer adequate support for many of the other data ordeals, such as retrieving, integrating, arranging, and analyzing diverse data from different sources. Few sufficiently support users in deriving values on-the-fly, querying data across hierarchies at disparate levels of detail, or customizing the range of colors in color-coded displays. The scenarios on product-mix decisions and medication judgments in Chapters 7 and 8 concentrate on users' needs and design options for these less-supported data ordeals.

What Wayfinding Activities Characterize Complex Problem Solving?

If data ordeals are the most designed-for activity in software for complex problem solving, wayfinding is the least (despite the fact that without adequate wayfinding support, problem solvers often cannot complete their tasks). Wayfinding helps problem solvers organize their complex inquiries. It involves setting the right paths for the right purposes within a problem space. It also involves determining when and where to take actions. Wayfinding is woven into every stitch of an open-ended inquiry. Wayfinding strategies move problem solvers from indeterminacy to resolution and largely occur on an *ad hoc* basis. In conducting complex inquiries, people work in multiple problem spaces and create paths as they go. They work through numerous choices, crossroads, tangents, parallel streams of thought, backtracking, and the like. As new information and insights emerge, problem solvers follow the "scent" of potentially important insights. When they analyze data in familiar ways and encounter expected results, the scent for what to do next is strong. When unprecedented methods are neccessary, such as finding an effective means for disentangling complicated networks of relationships, the scent is weak, and organizing a path is far more difficult and uncertain. In wayfinding, problem solvers read cues and manage their inquiries accordingly. Many wayfinding activities for managing inquiry involve collaborating or coordinating with co-workers.

To wend a way through their investigation and stay oriented, members of the RCA team give rationales for their flowchart choices as they go. They go to the whiteboard and sketch displays that will keep them oriented as they work through complicated data relationships. The risk manager wayfinds when she sorts through her notes to remember ideas relevant to the final report. Other wayfinding activities include deciding whether a chosen flowchart version is good enough to warrant moving on and where to head next after taking a short break. Chapter 5's scenario about troubleshooting in corporate networks goes into depth about wayfinding requirements for saving, commenting, recalling, and managing data displays of interest and for finding entry points into an inquiry.

WHAT SENSEMAKING ACTIVITIES CHARACTERIZE COMPLEX PROBLEM SOLVING?

Sensemaking refers to knowing the data and their implications for a given situation. During sensemaking, problem solvers mentally process data displayed on a screen, draw relationships and inferences, and construct meanings relevant to their purposes. Sensemaking occurs in various forms throughout problem solving. People make sense of a situation by viewing information about it and figuring out what they see in the display. They assure themselves that what they think they see in a display is really what the display is showing. At a higher level of processing, problem solvers make sense by relating what they see in data displays to their own problem and intentions, and they strive to understand linked displays and synthesize cumulative findings.

Additionally, sensemaking includes analyzing and interpreting information of interest. Problem solvers conduct comparisons and analyze frequencies, distributions, correlations, trends, affinities, and aberrations. In these analyses, sensemaking includes many higher-order reasoning processes. Problem solvers bring assorted factors together, take multiple perspectives on the same data, discern patterns, and from patterns create explanations that are valid for a specific purpose. Sensemaking occurs as problem solvers draw inferences and continuously relate them to their goals and situations; and it occurs as they determine what they know so far and what they do not know but need to. Finally, sensemaking extends to analyzing and making meaning socially. Problem solvers pore over screens with co-workers during the process of inquiry. They also create persuasive meanings from data that "speak" to others during presentations or briefings.

To problem solvers, sensemaking is one of the costliest activities of complex inquiry. The RCA team's time and effort in puzzling over the meaning of revised factors in the network diagram is one case. Their difficulty sorting out associations in the entangled network is another. The members also engage in sensemaking when they see they have named a factor wrong and backtrack to correct it. In addition, sensemaking includes their constant questioning about why an event happened, as well as naming their non-standard terms for the technological factors contributing to various events. The problem solving scenarios for product-mix decisions in Chapter 7 and for medication judgments in

Chapter 8 highlight a number of users' specific needs for sensemaking and the support they require.

Data ordeals, wayfinding, and sensemaking interact throughout problem solving. They unite as a means to achieve various objectives in problem solving, and their form within the distinct processes of complex problem solving is shaped by these objectives.

FOCUSING ON COMPLEX PROBLEM SOLVING OBJECTIVES FOR CORE ACTIVITIES

Up to this point, the discussion about focusing analysis and design at a practical level has rested on a hierarchical view of the activities for design teams to examine. These activities are pictured as a landscape in Figure 2.3. As the figure shows, the mountain range is a user's patterns of inquiry for a particular problem. For subgoals of various inquiry patterns, problem solvers construct and move through variable and stable task landscapes—mountainsides and ridges. These landscapes are made up of combined mainline and enabling tasks, each of which moves problem solvers along in conducting the core data ordeals, wayfinding, and sensemaking activities associated with open-ended inquiry.

One more dimension of this practical-level view of users' work needs to be included: The interactions between core data ordeals, sensemaking, and wayfinding activities and complex problem solving objectives and processes. Problem solving objectives and processes shape the form and content of users' core activities.

Six problem solving objectives (processes) shape data ordeals, sensemaking, and wayfinding (Figure 2.4). Descriptions of each are presented with examples from the RCA scenario that illustrate the relation between problem solving processes and core activities in complex inquiries. The examples are structured into charts that "open up" sections of the diagram in Figure 2.4. They show specific data ordeals and sensemaking and wayfinding activities that pertain to each problem solving objective.

Preparing Data for Inquiry and Its Core Activities

For data preparation, problem solvers concentrate on knowing the content of available data and the analyses they can support. Problem solvers also identify the sources and structures of data. Problem solvers condition and transform data to assure accurate and complete analysis. The chart on page 56 identifies data ordeals, wayfinding, and sensemaking occurring in general during data preparation and exemplifies them based on the RCA scenario.

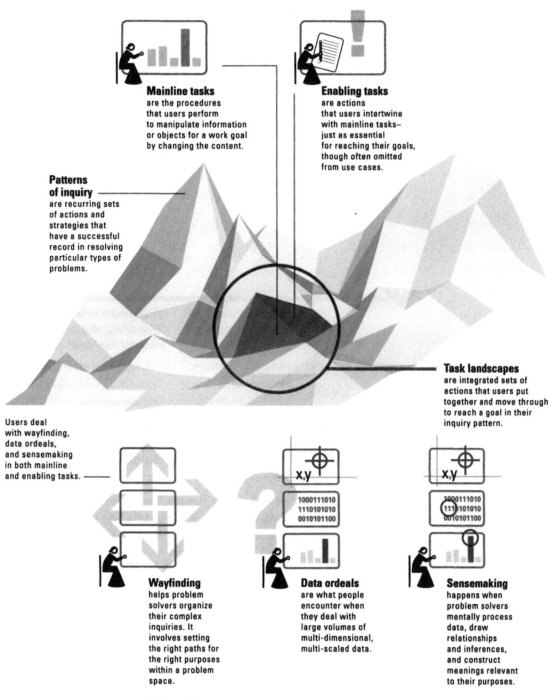

Mainline tasks
are the procedures
that users perform
to manipulate information
or objects for a work goal
by changing the content.

Enabling tasks
are actions
that users intertwine
with mainline tasks—
just as essential
for reaching their goals,
though often omitted
from use cases.

**Patterns
of inquiry**
are recurring sets
of actions and
strategies that
have a successful
record in resolving
particular types of
problems.

Task landscapes
are integrated sets of
actions that users put
together and move through
to reach a goal in their
inquiry pattern.

Users deal
with wayfinding,
data ordeals,
and sensemaking
in both mainline
and enabling tasks.

Wayfinding
helps problem
solvers organize
their complex
inquiries. It
involves setting
the right paths for
the right purposes
within a problem
space.

Data ordeals
are what people
encounter when
they deal with
large volumes of
multi-dimensional,
multi-scaled data.

Sensemaking
happens when
problem solvers
mentally process
data, draw
relationships
and inferences,
and construct
meanings relevant
to their purposes.

FIGURE 2.3 Levels of a practical focus on patterns of inquiry.

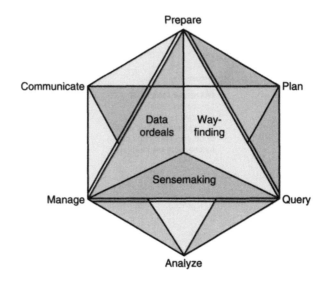

FIGURE 2.4
Interplay of core activities and general problem solving processes.

	Preparing data for inquiry, in general	**RCA team experiences: Preparing the contributing factors for later analysis**
Data ordeals	Arrange, transform and filter data to suit intended analysis.	The team repeatedly scrolls through JCAHO factors to find synonyms.
Wayfinding	Survey available data and data structures in relation to analysis goals.	Teammates know when to stop looking for synonyms that do not exist. In addition, the team seeks workarounds.
Sensemaking	Know the data, their condition, and their relevance.	The team relates its own generated terms to JCAHO terms.

Planning and Defining Goals and Its Core Activities

Planning involves choosing the best displays of information for given goals. In planning, problem solvers structure, lay out, and derive new values and fields on-the-fly. They assure themselves that data of interest are the focal point without losing the larger context of the information space. In general, and in the RCA case specifically, planning and defining goals include the following core activities.

	Planning and defining goals, in general	RCA team experiences: Planning for complicated root cause relationships
Data ordeals	Select or set up the right displays.	Team members create networks with the least number of crossed links possible.
Wayfinding	Map the analysts' model of the problem and its issues to the right view of the data.	The team determines whether tangled networks are losing their clarity and whether manual analysis is needed.
Sensemaking	Know what the view shows in relation to the goals of analysis.	The group analyzes networks and interprets each part in relation to the whole to avoid duplicates.

Querying and Verifying and Its Core Activities

Development groups often lump querying and analyzing into a single process that includes selecting, hiding, and deleting data; drilling down to detail; and rolling up to overviews. These activities reflect querying but not analyzing and higher-order reasoning. To problem solvers, analyzing is a different process from querying. To them, querying involves identifying, retrieving, and verifying data of interest. Querying also includes organizing and highlighting retrieved data to facilitate verification. Core activities in general and in the RCA search take the following shapes.

	Querying and verifying, in general	RCA team experiences: Querying contributing factors to the electronic patient transfer processes
Data ordeals	Select data of interest, and hide or delete the rest; drill down, roll up, and integrate data from different sources; rearrange it to verify.	The team selects the events of interest and lists detailed factors for each.

Wayfinding	Determine that intended questions are right for the circumstances; determine which query best serves analysis purposes.	Due to analysts' expertise, they choose to "delve in" instead of using JCAHO prompts. They also structure inquiry around "why" questions.
Sensemaking	Know how to frame the query to represent intended questions and verify retrieval results.	Team members know how to ask about conditions, constraints, omissions, and barriers; the team decides if answers are systemic enough.

Analyzing and Judging and Its Core Activities

Analyzing and judging applies causal, conditional, and predictive logic and analogy to understand relationships, trends, and anomalies. In analyzing, problem solvers weigh factors and construe meaning. For example, they relate findings to their situation, judge importance, evaluate tradeoffs, and draw conclusions for further action. Generally, and in the RCA case, analyzing and judging call for the following activities.

	Analyzing and judging, in general	**RCA team experiences: Analyzing and judging flowchart versions**
Data ordeals	Interact with data to see labels; values; indications about visible, hidden, and deleted data; and coding.	The team calls up multiple versions, arranges them side-by-side, and brings differences into focus.
Wayfinding	Plot the next move and determine when knowledge and conclusions are "good enough" to stop.	The team decides if versions are good enough to stop creating more.

Sensemaking	Interpret and infer meanings from single and cumulative queries and findings.	The group judges versions against each other to decide on the most thorough with the best detail and greatest validity.

Managing Inquiry and Its Core Activities

Throughout problem solving, people keep track of what they know, how they know it, and what they need to know next. They figure out how to find the additional information they need and monitor their progress in relation to their job-related goals. They determine when courses of actions, goals, or both need to be revised. Core activities in managing inquiry are as follows.

	Managing inquiry, in general	**RCA team experiences: Managing inquiry**
Data ordeals	Navigate within and across views, return to prior steps, and transform data on the fly.	Teammates return to an earlier screen to revise the naming of contributing factors.
Wayfinding	Coordinate many views of the data, stay oriented in the workspace, know when to backtrack, and resume after interruptions.	The medical analysts resume work by reviewing current insights and next moves.
Sensemaking	Assess knowledge gathered so far and the knowledge still needed for intended goals.	The team assesses evolving networks of factors to agree on implied systemic causes so far.

Communicating and Reporting and Its Core Activities

Communicating involves presenting information to others. Informally, as problem solvers proceed, they communicate by writing notes to themselves and to others. They capture displays for exploration, create call-outs, relabel axes, highlight items, or otherwise articulate points of interest. They create reports that variously stress arguments, information, or creativity. They integrate their analysis and reporting software. To communicate and report, problem solvers conduct the following core activities.

	Communicating and reporting, in general	RCA team experiences: Writing the recommendation report for hospital officials
Data ordeals	Write comments or annotate views. Capture, save, print, and comment on views; change labels, titles, and the like, as needed.	The risk manager searches meeting notes and writes explanatory text for the diagrams. She cuts and pastes from the recorder's document that details the team's decisions.
Wayfinding	Mark critical points for later review; maintain a line of thought despite interruptions.	She figures out where to turn to remember ideas to include in the explanatory text.
Sensemaking	Know the views that are critical to share and how to present them.	She determines what to include in the report.

Overall, this multidimensional array of activities in complex problem solvers' inquiry has implications for how designers approach design, in addition to what they design. By structuring users' work into patterns of inquiry, composed of landscapes of mainline and enabling tasks, and by envisioning these landscapes as core activities shaped by the function they serve for problem solving objectives, design teams have a number of options for how they organize their analysis of users' dynamic problem solving. Part of designing for usefulness involves deciding the best way to slice and dice users' practical work during design discussions. From my experiences, I have found that highlighting and organizing by the complex problem solving processes described previously creates the most productive bridge with software engineers and others on a team who want to create useful software but are not sure where to start. Problem solving processes serve as a good meeting ground for usefulness advocates and these software engineers.

CONCLUSIONS: HIGHER-ORDER NEEDS VERSUS SUPPORT DELIVERED

"Getting the work right" for complex problem solving requires software teams to focus on users' work at a practical level rather than immediately jumping to its composite, low-level unit tasks. In many development contexts, this focus on complex tasks is poorly understood and inadequately implemented. As exemplified by the RCA analysts in data ordeals, sensemaking, and wayfinding, complex problem solving involves higher-order reasoning, judgments, and collaboration. Problem solvers draw conclusions about relationships, weigh factors circumstantially, decide on acceptable trade-offs, and socially negotiate meanings and courses of action. One of the most serious shortcomings in software support for complex problem solving is its neglect of these higher-order needs.

Higher-order practical work requires support that differs from the support needed for the processes associated with formulaic procedures, on the one hand, or with macro-level generic activities, on the other. To support tasks at a pattern of inquiry level, programs have to call forth the contexts, cues, analytical perspectives, and possibilities for action that frame problem solvers' actual goals and practices. Problem solvers need to know how contextual conditions fit together and what this fit implies for pragmatic inquiry choices. Programs can support these user needs by providing the flexibility and user control that allow a seamless recognition and pursuit of effective and efficient approaches.

Traditionally, software has not done a good job of supporting higher-level social and cognitive processing. The RCA software in the scenario is a case in point. At a macro-level, it provides a generic module for analyzing factors contributing to an adverse event. At a micro-level, it models scripted procedural methods that end up constraining the users in the scenario. In between, at a practical level, it neglects many of the actual integrated strategies and approaches that the team values and wants to apply.

Why are such practical-level tasks and needs for open-ended inquiry overlooked by software for complex problem solving? It cannot be because context-of-use studies are foreign to software development teams. To the contrary, contextual inquiry and other situated methods are very familiar to development groups today. Yet many teams still do not design for problem solvers' complex activities at a practical level. More contextual analysis alone is not the answer. Contextual analysis without the right lens for analyzing and modeling complex problem solving will not produce useful software. HCI specialists' lens must focus on the distinctive dynamics of complex problem solving.

As this chapter argues, software teams need to set their lens on patterns of inquiry, associated task landscapes, and users' various needs for "structured freedom." Field studies and user requirements need to center on these patterns and their combined mainline and enabling tasks. Interaction designers and usability specialists must capture the interplay of core activities and problem solving processes described in this chapter to ensure complete enough descriptions of pattern-based task landscapes.

Moreover, software teams need to reconsider assumptions about task support so these beliefs are in sync with the demands of complex problem solving. Many current assumptions that designers apply actually run counter to these demands. Holding the wrong assumptions about support is enough to keep a team from building for complexity, adaptability, flexibility, and opportunism. Changes in assumptions will yield important new approaches to task analysis, modeling, and conceptual design, approaches more appropriate for supporting dynamic work.

Dealing directly with counterproductive assumptions early in a software project is vital to design efforts. Assumptions and their implied design methods can make or break a team's commitment to usefulness. The next chapter examines conventional assumptions that undercut designing for usefulness in complex work and proposes alternatives and the design directions they imply. It also analyzes methods for gathering and analyzing data and modeling users' work associated with these alternatives. The methods build on current contextual and user-centered approaches but extend them to address the dynamics and demands of open-ended inquiry. All combined, these alternative assumptions, methods, strategies, and choices for conceptual designs will help software team members steer clear of prematurely breaking down users' practical patterns of inquiry into low-level tasks.

REFERENCES

Alexander, Christopher, Sara Ishikawa, and Murray Silverstein. *A Pattern Language.* New York: Oxford University Press, 1977.

Borchers, Jan. *A Pattern Approach to Interaction Design.* New York: John Wiley & Sons, 2001.

Denley, Ian and Andy Whitefield. "A Case History in Applying Task Analysis in the Design of a Multimedia Cooperative Document Production System." *Journal of the American Society for Information Science (JASIS)* 49(9): 817-831.

Erikson, Thomas. "*Lingua Francas* for Design: Sacred Places and Pattern Languages." In *Proceedings of Designing Interactive Systems: Processes, Practices, Methods, and Techniques.* August 17-19, 2000, Brooklyn, New York, 357-368.

Gamma, Erich, Richard Helm, Ralph Johnson, and John Vlissides. *Design Patterns: Elements of Reusable Object-Oriented Software.* Reading, MA: Addison-Wesley, 1995.

Gould, John and Clayton Lewis. "Design for Usability: Key Principles and What Designers Think." *Communications of the ACM* (28, 3) (1985): 300-311.

Green, Thomas, Franz Sciele, and Stephen Payne. "Formalisable Models of User Knowledge." In *Working with Computers: Theory vs. Outcome,* edited by G. Vanderveer, T. Green, J. M. Hoc, and D. Murray, 3-41. London: Academic Press, 1988.

Kirsch, David. "The Intelligent Use of Space." *Artificial Intelligence* 73 Issue 1-2 (1995): 31-68.

Kirsch, David. "The Context of Work." *Human-Computer Interaction* 16 Issue 2-4 (2001): 305-332.

Kohn, Linda, Janet M. Corrigan, and Molla S. Donaldson, eds. *To Err is Human: Building a Safer Health System.* Washington D.C.: National Academies Press, 1999.

Lafreniere, Daniel and Asa Granland. "Pattern Supported Approach to User Interface Design." Tutorial at meeting of the Usability Professional Association, Las Vegas, NV, June 25-29, 2001.

Martin, David, Mark Rouncefeld, and Ian Sommerville. "Applying Patterns of Cooperative Interaction to Work (Re)Design: E-Government and Planning." *Proceedings of CHI 2002.*

Tidwell, Jennifer. "Common Ground: A Pattern Language for Human-Computer Interface Design." Available at: www.mit.edu/~jtidwell/interaction_patterns.html, 1999.

Viller, Stephen and Ian Sommerville. *Coherence: Social Analysis for Software Engineers.* Cooperative Systems Engineering Group Technical Report CSEG/15/1998. Lancaster, UK: Lancaster University, 1998.

Ziech, Karen. Personal communication. 2001.

3

Filling in the Gaps: Integrating Usefulness Into User-Centered Design

After years of researching and developing applications for complex problem solving, Kim Vincente (2002) concludes that the usual approaches to software and interfaces are woefully wrong for this breed of application. These approaches, he says, are the "low-hanging fruit" that developers eagerly grab as solutions, but for dynamic inquiries they do not work. Emphasizing the points of the previous chapters, Vincente argues that to create support for complex problems software teams must refrain from following conventional approaches, those typically used to support well-structured work.

As we have seen, dynamic inquiries are distinct. Problem solvers' moves are often unplanned—adapting to changes in conditions and constraints—and built-in software procedures can never fully anticipate or contain them. Problem solvers follow identifiable patterns of inquiry, but their exact actions are rarely the same twice. Consequently, users need software that enables them to put together task landscapes adaptively without complicated interactions and without a reduction in the intellectual sophistication of their investigations.

For these needs, conventional approaches for designing and developing applications are not so much wrong as decidedly incomplete. As I noted in the introduction to this book, gaps in the relationship between usability and software engineering processes severely undercut usefulness. Software teams typically skip crucial aspects of interaction design in their software and usability engineering. They pass over the processes of modeling users' dynamic work at the practical level of integrated patterns of inquiry. These perspectives on users' work, therefore, do not adequately inform requirements planning or the conceptual design of functionality, data modeling, application architecture, program modules, and user interfaces (UI).

Most software teams do positively concentrate on ease of use issues for UI designs and detailed screen concepts. They often heuristically evaluate test prototypes for programmatic usability. What they do not do, however, is test whether the concept of work informing interfaces, functionality, data structures, architecture, and program modules is, in fact, the right concept of work from problem solvers' situated points of view.

Because of these omissions, software teams commonly fail to design for issues that are critical to providing useful support for complex problem solving. The issues they should address and the conventional orientations they take instead often differ, as the chart on the following page shows.

To address usefulness and its associated issues, software teams need to start with contextual perspectives on users' work and analyze tasks and needs through context of use studies, ethnographies, and other activity-based and participatory design methodologies. But numerous software teams already take these orientations, and they still do not adequately

Design Orientations to Complex Problem Solving	
What software teams should address	**What they conventionally address instead**
Synergies of complex problem solving	Work as the sum of its component tasks
Mainline *and* enabling tasks	Mostly mainline tasks
Structural and spatial support for orienteering task landscapes and adapting to idiosyncratic conditions	Primarily procedural support for generic unit tasks
Users' needs for ample control over variable aspects of inquiry	Presupposed user moves with pre-defined support for them
Support for domain–specific aspects of users' patterns of inquiry	Abstracted and generic, reusable support
Automated processes that ease investigative burdens without simplifying the intellectual complexity of the work	Automated processes that streamline users' choices and simplify work

carry out the interaction design work required for usefulness. Even with user-centered design (UCD) practices, many teams do not create integrated models of users' patterns of inquiry. Nor do they apply them to high-level requirements program-wide or test prototypes specifically to validate models of work in context.

This chapter answers the question of what to do differently beyond common contextual orientations. Contextual orientations are not a panacea. They do not ensure that designers adopt the assumptions, methods, and design strategies necessary for usefully supporting users who reason in uncertainty and make judgments dynamically and opportunistically. This chapter explores these necessary orientations and approaches for designing for usefulness—with the aim of filling in the gaps that currently exist in many development groups. The focus for various aspects of this designing includes the following:

- **Understanding and rethinking assumptions:** Adopting assumptions appropriate for the demands of complex problems and using them as frameworks for defining and creating support for complex problem solving.

- **Gathering data about users and their work:** In user-experience studies, capturing holistic problem situations and inquiry activities when identifying targeted users, setting the project scope, defining the unit of analysis for user studies, and observing users doing their work in context.

- **Analyzing and synthesizing data:** Highlighting issues and data in task analyses, user personal, and scenarios that are attuned to the traits of open-ended inquiries and domain-specific influences.

- **Modeling users' work:** Representing practical, integrated patterns of dynamic problem solving as shaped by three conditions—interactivity, contexts, and variability (ICV).

- **Conceptualizing design:** Applying design strategies and choices for conceptual designs that are sensitive to users' needs for control, adaptability, and power and that highlight users' often-neglected core problem solving activities.

These approaches correspond to early phases in development projects, sequentially spanning requirements analysis and planning, the modeling of users' work, and the conceptual designs of programs and interfaces (Mayhew, 1999). The first approach, understanding and rethinking assumptions, however, comes before any of these phases. Software teams must start development projects for complex problem solving by critically examining their assumptions.

UNDERSTANDING AND RETHINKING ASSUMPTIONS

Software teams rarely examine their assumptions. In fact, many development groups may go years without believing they have reason to reflect on them. However, when teams apply assumptions about well-structured tasks to applications for users' complex analytical investigations these assumptions often undercut usefulness.

In many ways, teams' unexamined assumptions—those appropriate for users' well-structured work—trace back to software engineering principles that shape usability engineering practices. Software engineering directs design thinking toward formalizing tasks into programmable interactions, revealing functionality and object relations in interfaces, and defining system states and allowable actions. Software engineering also influences the ways in which designers think about data relationships, various types of navigation, and consistency. User-centeredness wraps the cloak of user experience around these basic programming orientations and concerns. Design teams for example, often draw on software-engineering influences to translate user experience findings and descriptions into interface designs. User-centered teams turn models of users and situated work into formalized task and interface objects. For complex problem solving however, this leap comes too quickly. In between their modeling and object-oriented designing, teams do not pause to create practical level representations of coherent and integrated patterns of inquiry. These representations are vital because they guard against losing the synergies, contexts, and variability of users' dynamic problem solving in a conceptual design.

Conceptions of all aspects of a program must capture users' experiences and needs completely, coherently, and appropriately. For usefulness, these conceptions must support problem solvers' needs for emergence, opportunism, idiosyncratic priorities, situational conditions, and many contending "good enough" solutions. When design teams for complex problem solving software leap over the interaction design processes that ensure valid models of users, situated problems, and actual approaches to problem solving, they often produce the right design for the wrong problem.

Underlying assumptions—whether examined or not—drive all methods of design. To design useful applications for open-ended inquiries some assumptions are more appropriate than others. In adopting these more appropriate assumptions, software teams often have to rethink their conventional beliefs and refrain from a tendency to jump prematurely over the interaction design processes required for "getting the work right" in all components of an application. New assumptions that need to replace the old include the following:

Parts to whole
New: Complex work is synergistic.
Old: The whole of users' work is equal to the sum of its parts.

Who leads and who follows
New: Programs have to move closer to users and adapt to them.
Old: Users must adapt to the logic of a program to improve their task performance.

Customized tools, yes or no?
New: Support is more adaptable when it is domain specific.
Old: Support is more versatile when it is generic.

Keep it simple and smart (KISS)
New: Support should be simple to operate but promote intellectual nuance and sophistication.
Old: Support should simplify work.

Dramatic interaction

New: Problem solvers are extemporaneous actors in an open
and unfolding plot.

Old: Problem solvers are fairly predictable rational agents.

Most importantly, these new assumptions and, as we see in later sections, the methods they imply affect more than interfaces. They also shape front-end decisions about the program scope and the engineering of architecture, features, and data structures. This piece in usability engineering—that is applying the insights about "getting the work right" to front-end decisions—is often missing in product development yet it is crucial for usefulness. When software teams embrace the assumptions appropriate for complex problem solving, they implicitly take up new directions in designing for the whole application.

Tying Assumptions to a Complex Problem Solving Example: Managing Projects

The following discussions of each new and old set of assumptions draw on the stories about Marty and the root cause analysis (RCA) team from Chapters 1 and 2. The discussions also refer to the following scenario as a more immediate and fresh example of users' needs for complex problem solving.

SCENARIO: MANAGING PROJECTS
Why is this consulting project losing money?

Carlos is a business manager in a systems integration firm that helps other companies implement large enterprise computing systems. In his unit, human resource systems, Carlos is in charge of evaluating the profitability of implementation projects in the North, South, East, and West regions. Carlos's own performance as a manager is judged by the revenue and margins that his unit's projects bring in.

To assess the profits and losses of human resource system projects, Carlos examines at least 250,000 transaction records every quarter. He usually spends a full week arranging the quarter of a million rows of data into just four pages (screens) of cross-tabulation charts.

Carlos then conducts his analyses with spreadsheets and graphs. He looks at trends across quarters for each practice area overall and for each project within a practice area. Within projects, he examines gross revenues, discounts, labor costs, compensation time, billed and non-billed travel,

---

and operating incomes. He compares projects in different regions against each other and against a baseline of acceptable performance. He calculates values as he goes, including projects' shares of the total revenue, labor costs, travel and comp time, as well as percent changes from one quarter to the next.

In today's analysis, Carlos sees by the trends that one region, the West, has dipped considerably this quarter. He discovers that the loss is huge: $2.4 million. Where is the problem? he wonders. Is it one project or many? Might it be due to the ways the West is handling certain costs such as billed and non-billed travel? The practice of traveling gratis even for premier customers has lately become a company-wide taboo.

Carlos looks at the aggregated profits and losses for each project in the West. Some projects are immediately seen as clear losses, but Carlos knows healthy-looking aggregates may mask some problems in non-billed travel. In fact, none of the problem projects—alone or combined—looks bad enough to explain the $2.4 million loss.

Carlos works on his hunch that non-billed travel is bringing this area down. He looks at the costs incurred in all projects, both the healthy and unhealthy ones. He sees a week-by-week breakdown of costs by type, labor, billed and non-billed travel, and comp time, but this display does not show Carlos what he is looking for. Labor overwhelms the cost displays, which is not a surprise because labor typically makes up 80 percent of most project costs. What Carlos cannot tell from the display is whether the West is using non-billed travel in ways that are resulting in major losses. Project by project, abuses with non-billed travel may not readily show up graphically because this cost constitutes only about 5 percent of a project's costs. Across projects, however, these abuses could mushroom and explain why the West did so badly.

At this point Carlos realizes he has to derive standardized values to draw comparisons across types of costs. He has to manipulate and rearrange data extensively to do these calculations. In the process, Carlos loses track of how he had planned to evaluate non-billed travel.

Adopting Assumptions About Parts to Whole

New assumption   Complex work is synergistic.
Old assumption   The whole of users' work is equal to the sum of its parts.

Even without a story like Carlos's, many software teams today are wary of logically breaking users' work down into its smallest set of tasks (unit tasks), and they shun the notion of formal decomposition. Contextually oriented, these teams strive instead to depict tasks from many different angles, such as workflows, task sequences and goals, uses of artifacts, cultural dynamics, physical layouts of a work environment, user or persona descriptions, decision trees, and "quick maps" of business processes. They value and compose rich and varied descriptions, but something goes awry in the move from these descriptions to conceptual designs. When designers turn findings into scenarios, use cases, task formulations, and screen objects, aspects of users' work, such as external influences and high-level conditional interdependencies, frequently get lost. UCD teams often end up focusing conceptual design on separate elements of users' work rather than on integrated patterns of inquiry.

Defining Users' Situated Work as Objects

It is not that UCD teams do not strive to embody the multiple functions and roles of users' contextual actions and experiences in use cases and to design task objects and corresponding screen objects accordingly. But, when users' experiences relate to complex problem solving, this process for bridging situated work to object technology often fails to capture holistically the ways in which users, through their patterns of inquiry, handle variability and emergence to give their open-ended inquiries coherence and integration. Instead, teams narrow their vision too soon to a low-level focus on unit tasks and map these tasks one-to-one to interface objects. The unintentional result is the same unit task-level focus that occurs in formal decomposition, and the software similarly expresses the assumption that the whole of users' work is no greater than the sum of its parts.

Objects are especially attractive to human-computer interaction specialists during design. HCI specialists often use such object-oriented methods as usage-centered design; object, views and interaction design (OVID); logical user-centered interaction design (LUCID); the Bridge; and other informal Unified Modeling Language (UML) methods (Rosenberg and Scott, 1999; Kreitzberg, 1999; Hudson, 2001; Constantine and Lockwood, 1999; Dayton et al., 1998; Krutcheon, 2000; Kulek and Guiney, 2000). An object orientation involves attributing property elements, actions, and message passing to low-level objects. Unquestionably, a low-level task orientation is needed once product development moves to specifications and programming. Moreover, object technology does not mean that software teams have to design principally for low-level operations. In fact, object-orientation emphasizes giving users support for taking whatever actions they want while focusing on the primary task. Implicit in object technology is the need for carefully constructing classes and appropriate relationships. For software for complex problem solving, object technology per se is not a problem. Prematurely jumping to objects, however, is. It is a problem to focus too quickly on individual aspects of inquiries and monolithic solutions to the exclusion of the integrated frameworks that help users move from "here to there" as they explore uncertain territory.

Examining Inquiry Patterns as the Building Blocks of Complex Problem Solving

In UCD for complex problem solving, teams can guard against too quickly leaping to object design if they do not start with the assumptions that the whole of a user's dynamic inquiry is equal to the sum of its parts. Complex problem solving, like other tasks, does have building blocks. These building blocks are the recurring patterns that people use to work through uncertainty and open possibilities. For problem solvers, the *parts* of their inquiry experienced *together* are more basic than any individual portion. To Carlos, a "basic task" is to find differences between types of costs, first within a project and then across projects. This two-phase task has many related interpretive parts. Problem solvers like Carlos unify actions and strategies through high-level organizing for data ordeals, sensemaking, and wayfinding. They draw complex relationships, coordinate findings, and make judgments based on such idiosyncratic criteria as corporate cutbacks on non-billed travel. The synergy of these and other similar processes cannot be formalized into steps and rules.

To support complex problem solving, teams must assume and highlight these synergies and design for them. Designing for them involves integrating software and interface components so that each augments the value of the others. It means revealing to problem solvers the structure of their problem situations and patterns of inquiry. Design teams must not prematurely sever related patterns from one another or examine sole actions in task landscapes in isolation. Relationships—the connections between procedural, spatial, and structural elements—are what give users' work coherence. Typically, software falls short in supporting this coherence. Applications often offer all-purpose features representing the generic actions but not the connections. Rarely, for example, do programs provide problem solvers like Carlos with capabilities for moving seamlessly from answering fact questions to integrating correlated factors across projects into judgments about causes.

If software teams assume that complex problem solving is no greater than the sum of its parts, they may unintentionally undermine the integrity of problem solvers' open-ended inquires. The software may over-constrain users' actions, underestimate the scope of their work, under-represent important contextual dynamics, and underdevelop the strategies and interactions people use for "getting from here to there."

Adopting Assumptions About Who Leads and Who Follows

New assumption Programs have to move closer to users and adapt to them.

Old assumption Users must adapt to the logic of a program to improve their task performance.

In Carlos's case, he arranges data from a quarter of a million records in one workspace. In other workspaces—graphics and spreadsheets—he analyzes the data and transforms their values on-the-fly as he delves deeper into questions. To find answers to questions that depend on how costs are spread in his particular region, he has to manipulate data values and graphic views extensively.

"It's a Training Issue"

What is wrong with this picture of Carlos's inquiry? Many software team members would answer, "Nothing." From a workflow perspective, Carlos has steps in the program that let him do all the data interactions he needs. But observing Carlos at work shows that this "can do" support makes for a choppy and imprecise analysis. Too often the response to such user findings on the development side of a project is, "It's a training issue. The program has the functionality. The user just needs to learn the program." This response fails to recognize that "being able to do it" and "being willing to do it" are often 180 degrees apart.

Carlos's disorientation in analysis is not due to his lack of skill with the program. Rather, the program's preset routines do not give his inquiry the fluidity he needs. Trying to work the program to get the arrangements he needs makes Carlos lose track of his line of reasoning. The same issue occurs in the RCA scenario in Chapter 2. The lockstep approach the RCA program assumes—selecting Joint Commission.on Accreditation of Healthcare Organizations (JCAHO) terms and evaluating their relevance for an event—neglects the hospital team's preferred method of "delving in." As is the case with most complex problem solvers, the RCA team does not change its approach to fit the program's model. But team members do experience a great deal of frustration, and they know their method is better than the program model.

Experts engaged in complicated searches expect programs to be responsive to their needs and the way they use resources to comprehend a problem, explore relationships, and generate solutions. The issue centers on user adaptability, which is different from software adaptability, or what IBM calls autonomic computing, a primary concern in adaptive computing. Software adaptability refers to the system, with a focus on its underlying structures and coding and on developers using application frameworks, software design patterns, and reusability to build programs that can learn and respond to the wishes and desires of users. The ability of software to automatically customize and alter its behaviors in response to changes in runtime environments can be an important means for achieving user adaptability. But software adaptability is not always put toward this end; nor is it the only means for getting there.

In contrast to software adaptability, user adaptability is the prime emphasis in this assumption about whether the user leads or follows. User adaptability means that users have a reasonable way in an application to initiate any kind of intelligent user support; decide on its type, amount, and point in time of initiation; and refine and adjust it (Encarnação, 1997). As one business analyst notes, "The degree to which a user can successfully combine all these elements, as well as the degree to which the technology can meet and conform to user needs, will influence the adaptability of the system" (Sturm, 2001).

Consciously or not, the design choices software teams make embody biases about whether programs should adapt to users or users should adapt to programs. Design teams tend to believe the latter. They like to believe they have captured users' task models in the program so well that if users have to assimilate to the program's workings, it is just a matter of them doing their everyday work. This is hardly the case in the scenarios presented in this book, which are based on real world user experiences. The result of these design biases is that users end up doing the lion's share of the work adjusting to the software.

Some business situations call for standardized practices and software interactions, and in these cases, having users conform to the dictates of program routines is positive and efficient (e.g., data entry, invoicing, record management, and canned reporting). In other cases, such as generic statistical, spreadsheet, and database applications, the application is open to diverse user-defined purposes and functions, and professionals often use it for dynamic inquiries. Yet many of these programs do not "adapt to the user." Rather, the dominant assumption behind them is that users will learn the program logic, then apply its power to their complex work. Users must "think like the application" to shape its rich and powerful capabilities to their work-related intentions. They must become power users and learn how to exploit available, though often hidden, features and functions for their particular purposes.

In business computing, few programs move closer to and adapt to users and their wide variations in solving an indeterminate problem, but those that do have distinct traits.

Letting the User Lead

Programs that adapt to users enable them to shape software interactions to their locales, adjust inquiry patterns for particular types of problems, and configure displays to suit their needs. They do not require users to become power users or technical experts. CoMotion 2.1 by MAYA Viz, for example, lets users collaboratively exchange and manipulate data remotely without having to understand what goes on beneath the hood *(www.mayaviz.com)*. This adaptability can take many forms, including seamless methods for integrating and relating data from diverse sources, cues that tie multidimensional data displays to business and inquiry goals, and mechanisms for thematically clustering data as needed without having to write macros or dig deeply for relevant functions. Adaptable systems also may signal to users the existence of other relevant data and, through "smart" algorithms or built-in intelligence, bring these data to the desktop. In these and other ways, adaptable applications modify themselves and let problem solvers modify them based on evolving or emerging conditions and requirements.

In business computing, relatively few programs are deliberately designed to adapt to users and their varying approaches to indeterminate problems. Building software and user adaptability into an application involves fitting the program to the needs of its intended users. Software and user adaptability are strategies that reach beyond the "low-hanging fruit" of usual software approaches. Semantic browse-and-retrieve applications in information retrieval systems, such as Galaxy of News or the Pacific Northwest National Laboratory's (PNNL) correlation tool (www.pnl.gov/inforiz/index.html), exhibit this innovative reach (Rennison, 1994). These semantic browse-and-retrieve tools dynamically cluster retrieved items by user-defined themes and let users interactively group, regroup, sort, and nest items around the attributes of their choice. The PNNL's correlation tool also lets users correlate themes and sources of interest. With these systems, users tailor their browsing to the associations that make sense to their immediate work. These applications anticipate user initiatives and take their cues from users' leads. They bring into view items similar to what users have in focus at the moment.

The habitual assumption in development groups that "if you build it, users will come" fails to take into account the improvisation that structures problem solvers' searches for "good enough" solutions. Assuming that users can or will follow a program's lead—even a very usable lead—badly misjudges what open-ended explorations are all about.

Adopting Assumptions About Customized Tools, Yes or No?

New assumption Support is more adaptable when it is domain specific.

Old assumption Support is more versatile when it is generic.

As seen with the previous assumptions, problem solvers need adaptable software that accommodates their choices and directions without over- or under-determining their interactions. They do not want discrete adaptability solely in the form of user-preference parameters they have to set for every analysis and reset for every alteration (Raskin, 2000). Rather, they want programs that can adapt to the prevailing and recurring issues, actions, and strategies that characterize their expert approaches to solving complex problems. These expert approaches are determined by domain-based conventions, business rules, and professional practices. Building for domain specificity goes hand-in-hand with designing for optimal adaptability.

What Is the Controversy About Domain Specificity?

A domain is "a class of work activities that bears similar aspects on the workers' situation and performance regarding interaction with customers'... decision making, information processing, and so on" (Gulliksen and Sandblad, 1995). Domains discussed so far in this book include Marty's field of category management (see Chapter 1), the healthcare experts' specific domains of nursing, pharmacy, risk management, and information technology (see Chapter 2), and Carlos's area of project management. In software design, debates often arise over how generic or local and domain specific applications should be.

For a number of reasons, software firms often prefer to produce generic applications. Product managers and marketing directors argue that horizontal applications capture a larger, more diverse, and, therefore, more lucrative market than silo- or domain-based products. Many production departments have structures and processes that are well-suited to creating and selling generic products for end-users; whether the products are commercial off-the-shelf software (COTS); toolkits for original equipment manufacturers (OEMs); or programs that buyers and their IT specialists subsequently customize for end users.

However, business strategists increasingly counsel software companies to focus on domain-specific products rather than generic ones. Users are clamoring for products that are better attuned to their domains so they can more effectively conduct the business intelligence that is central to their competitive advantage. Creating such applications will help development organizations establish their reputations and become prime players in the industry.

Domain specificity is a contentious issue from many angles: Organizational practices, market economics, technical feasibility, reusability, and usefulness. In deciding how to address domain specificity for complex problem solving projects, user-experience researchers, interaction designers, and usability specialists must have an influential voice representing concerns tied to usefulness.

Why Does Domain Specificity Matter for Usefulness?

From a usefulness point of view, generic applications for complex problem solving—even powerful ones—are often less than useful for anyone other than power users. In addition, generic applications presume that, in any given field, the software-supported processes of knowledge work can be separated from the content and problem solving patterns of the domain without significantly damaging the quality of the work. Domain specificity, by contrast, rests on demonstrated evidence that different domains have distinct ways of knowing and doing (even for the same problem) and that the effectiveness and efficiency of problem solving are improved when structured by domain-based cues and patterns (Gulliksen and Sandblad, 1995; Berg, 1997; Siy and Mockus, 1999; Weiss and Lai, 1999; John and Bass, 2000; Bass et al., 2001).

Domain-specific software represents professionals' patterns of inquiry and helps them maintain a connection between their goals and available actions. Moreover, such software is sensitive to interactive contextual conditions relevant to particular problems and domains. In this way, designs connect with domain expertise and help users make sense of their work. For example, because unequally distributed classes of project costs are common to project management, Carlos would greatly prefer that his program generate and, in one keystroke, display standardized values formatted in comparative views. This would save him from executing numerous keystrokes and moving between screens and modes to standardize data and redisplay them. Domain-based applications for complex problem solving also know when to leave the way open to provide optimal user control and adaptability.

In addition, designs centered on domains rely on a familiar, domain-based vocabulary. The designs also structure ideas around relevant domain content for specific types of problems. Finally, they evoke scripts, patterns, and roles that are common to an industry. Domain-specific designs help ease users' burdens without constraining them as they work. These designs maintain the intellectual integrity of problem solving with minimal program complications.

Adopting Assumptions About Keeping It Simple and Smart (KISS)

New assumption Support should be simple to operate but promote intellectual nuance and sophistication.

Old assumption Support should simplify work.

Software teams continuously make decisions about the extent to which a program should pre-define views and control methods for conducting tasks. When designers' choices weigh heavily toward program control and pre-scripting, they do so, in part, for the sake of making programs simpler for users to use.

Offering Simplicity Versus Power
Simplicity involves giving users an almost foolproof set of interactions to follow for their various tasks. The software minimizes the functions, modes, and commands users need to know to get their work done, and it makes the needed ones easy to learn and use. Programs also work simpler by assuming the portion of users' efforts that automation does best, such as tedious calculations, routine and repetitive sorting, and rule-driven information transfer and processing. Simplicity in programs may curtail some of users' activities, but it assures that whatever they do, they do it easily.

To investigate indeterminate situations, users need uncomplicated program interactions, but they also need to retain a good amount of autonomy in choosing their data displays, methods, and paths. Programs provide power when they support users' methods for investigating the full scope of a problem in all of its richness with functions necessary for conducting their patterns of inquiry. Users need flexible access to this power so that, given changing conditions, they have several means to choose from in reaching their goals. Ideally, interfaces make this power and flexibility approachable by aptly representing relevant constraints, roles, and relationships that influence choices and consequences.

Envisioning a Different Kind of Simplicity for Complex Problem Solving

Problem solvers' needs for power and flexibility do not mean that design teams should disregard simplicity. But simplicity for complex problem solving assumes a different meaning from simplicity for well-structured work. For complex problem solving simplicity means a program eases users' investigative burdens without reducing the layering and nuances of their work. Unfortunately, in many development contexts, easing burdens and simplifying work get equated.

Distinguishing between these two concepts in applications for complex problem solving is crucial. To maintain the integrity of intellectual complexities but make them simpler to conduct, design teams need to target problem solvers' integrated and strategic needs, not only their isolated and tactical actions. Like software for well-structured tasks, complex problem solving applications should assume the processing of tedious calculations. But the computations they offer users in a keystroke must aim at the right, high-level, recurrent, pattern-based questions to avoid piecemeal analysis. For example, complex problem solving programs should let users readily derive values on-the-fly, such as standardized costs, and automatically update datasets accordingly if users signal them to do so. Moreover, these programs should alleviate users' work without oversimplifying it when their displays help users find the best paths in uncertain situations and make sense of data amidst incomplete knowledge. In addition, without making problem solving simple, programs need to ease the burden of progressing through intellectual complexities by showing users the *structure* of their problem spaces, the paths and landmarks in their ongoing efforts, and the meaning of relevant information. They need to give users ample freedom to apply their expertise as they see fit. This kind of support requires software designers to know a good deal about user domains and expertise, business rules, and collaborations used for specific types of problems.

Adopting Assumptions About Dramatic Interactions

New assumption   Problem solvers are extemporaneous actors in an open and unfolding plot.

Old assumption   Problem solvers are fairly predictable rational agents.

Finally, software teams must examine their suppositions about users as they create user profiles and personae and design for them. These user descriptions must come from observed cases. If HCI specialists simply hypothesize personae, they are likely to do little more than "humanize" users as rational agents, still emphasizing the logic driving users' mainline activities. By contrast, if designers hope to capture the nuances of people (like Tolstoy's commander-in-chief mentioned in the book's introduction) who tackle perplexing problems in their jobs amidst uncertain conditions and competing interests, they must actually see these people at work. Users are rational and goal-oriented, but they are also extemporaneous and opportunistic. An open-ended and emergent inquiry is a story that starts with uncertainty and progresses through changes. These inquiries are structured by drama as much as by logic, and the best way for designers to get the drama right is to witness or be part of it.

Extemporaneously Exploring Problems

Because goals are often vague, broad, and perpetually up for revision, problem solvers engage in emerging events, which are partly scripted and partly improvised. Actions and analytical strategies vary by circumstance, point of view, and representations of relevant factors. Problem solvers deal with conflicts that have unpredictable outcomes, and they encounter impasses that have no ready answers. Moreover, they actually seek out these events and deliberately explore uncharted territory as a way to shed light on vital issues for effective solutions.

Problem solvers explore a world of elusive truths. As they work to find answers to their problems, accidents and serendipity are prominent. Strategic methods of inquiry—the stock in trade of expert explorers—help users "tame" uncertainties, and clues shed light on aspects of a situation viewed up close, far away, and in diverse relationships. Evidence is incomplete and has multiple potential meanings. Different contending stories about a problem arise depending on how investigators arrange "the facts." Problem solvers put the same events and items together over and over again in different versions, much as Marty does in "working the funnel" (see Chapter 1) and as the RCA team does first in identifying factors and then looking at them as networks of systemic associations (see Chapter 2). Far from being bored by the repetition, problem solvers are absorbed by it, finding and registering all the differences and similarities between versions. In fact, explorers' successes depend on being able to put into action productive investigative repetitions and patterns and being skilled in adapting them to the inevitable variability they encounter.

Interaction Designers as Playwrights

Solutions, per se, compose a small part of a problem solving drama. Most complex problem solving episodes involve investigators trying to turn an indeterminate problem into a more structured one to resolve it. As with any tale, the telling shapes what listeners believe to be true and important. As the "storytellers," interaction designers and usability specialists influence how design teammates see users' complex problem solving, and ultimately, how teammates determine what mockups they design and requirements they write.

Coming around full circle, the designs that software teams create retell problem solvers' stories back to them. The model of work on which a design rests, therefore, must have a dramatic sense of scene, setting, characters, and perspective so that problem solvers recognize it as their own. These models include the information, tools, conditions, fortuity, co-workers, identities, and points of view that problem solvers use. The stories are bounded, but it is up for grabs how various forces and features will release their meanings and what paths problem solvers will take to make sense of them.

In summary, at the start of a software project, design team members need to discuss underlying assumptions about task support. They need to agree to apply new assumptions that truly serve the processes and purposes of complex problem solving. These assumptions highlight the following:

- Synergy

- Adaptability

- Simplicity *and* smartness

- Domain specificity

- Drama

Integrating these new assumptions into software design often calls for teammates to change their common beliefs about well-structured tasks because they run counter to designing for complex problem solving.

To put these assumptions into effect, software teams need to draw on many current contextual methodologies, including contextual inquiry and design, interaction design, participatory design, ethnography, and various use case and scenario approaches. However, as these methodologies stand now in the literature and in practice, none concentrates specifically on designing for complex problem solving, with its indeterminacy, flux, multiplicity, and decision complexities.

For open-ended inquiries, many aspects of current contextual methodologies are appropriate, but others need to be modified. These modifications, along with some new approaches, are described in the remaining sections of this chapter. These sections do not detail the processes of current user-centered design methodologies because other human-computer interaction specialists have ably described them. Rather, my focus is on methods specific to complex problem solving and crucial to designing for usefulness.

GATHERING DATA ABOUT USERS AND THEIR WORK

Design methods begin with needs gathering. Various methodologies for context of use studies advocate collecting similar data, even though they often differ in technique. Ethnography, participatory design, contextual inquiry, scenario-based design, interaction design, and contextually oriented (usage-centered) software engineering methods all collect data on workflows; business rules; workers' core competencies, roles, and relationships; collaborations; and social practices. They also identify cultural norms intrinsic to users' activities, physical layouts of a workplace, the uses of various tools and other resources, and the channels and content of communications. However, they assign different degrees of importance to specific types of data, to the uses of interviews and observations, and to the importance of observing simulations, reenacted or real-time work (Beyer and Holtzblatt, 1998; Hackos and Redish, 1998; Constantine and Lockwood, 1999; Rosenbaum, 2000; Rosson and Carroll, 2002).

This section does not promote any particular methodology for determining needs, but it does advocate three approaches that should be included in any methodology. These three approaches are as follows:

- Setting a project scope for complexity

- Defining a unit of analysis as part of the inquiry focus

- Gathering sufficient data through field observations to gain insight into patterns of inquiry and problem solving synergies

Setting a Project Scope for Complexity

Project scope identifies the business problem that software helps solve. It defines the type and range of activities that an application will support based on the significance of the work in relation to some larger related enterprise, the problems ("pain points") people experience when doing this work, and the intended users and customers. Setting a scope for a new product in an undefined market is far more difficult than setting it for a sixth or seventh version of a program in a well-established market segment.

Because a project scope rests on three connected dimensions—best market (for the program), best people (to put it to use), and best uses (to put it to)—user experience analysts, interaction designers, and usability specialists must be involved in setting this focus. They are the experts on the *uses* of a program, and not just the *customer* requirements. In any software project, whether for well- or ill-structured tasks, it is risky to follow a project scope that does not have substantial input about actual users. Project scope may change during the course of development, but if its initial focus is ill conceived, changes will not correct this basic flaw.

Setting an appropriate project scope for complex problem solving software involves distinguishing users from customers and deciding who the intended users are. Who they are depends on whether a software team envisions that it is designing a generic problem solving application for lay users (including power users), a generic or core product that information technology (IT) specialists or other engineers will customize for end-users, or a domain-specific application for end-users. If software team members do not adequately discuss such product visions and primary users from the start, they may end up focusing design and development on functions rather than actual uses-in-context. They may build generic and rich functionality and slice and package it differently to claim two markets at once, for example, end-users and the OEMs who will customize the application for domain-specific end-users. Such software often has relevant functions for problem solving but is not necessarily useful, and this insufficient usefulness may not become apparent until after a number of irrevocable design choices are in place. For example, without an appropriate scope, functionality built for reading and writing data within and across applications may be too limited and constrain problem solvers from integrating data as they need to for their inquiries (John and Bass, 2000).

In addition to defining primary users when setting a project scope, software teams need to understand users' problem solving space and set valid and manageable boundaries for what the application can and will support. For example, will the program support preparing and conditioning data? How about reporting? If these aspects of problem solving are too costly to support in a first version but will be slated for later releases, the project scope needs to ensure that the architecture will adapt to needed functions later on. Design teams have to make decisions about many such aspects of open-ended inquiries. Table 3.1 indicates some of them. The scenarios in Part One elaborate on many of these complex problem solving activities that software teams need to consider when defining a project scope.

In deciding whether or not to exclude any of these activities and support for them from the program scope, software teams must base their

TABLE 3.1
Project scope
considerations for complex
problem solving.

Project Scope:
Will the Application Support These Aspects of
Problem Solving?

Preparing data

Reporting and communicating: Generic and customized, informal
and formal

Annotating and commenting on views of data

Saving and being able to "replay" effective paths

Backtracking and returning to departure points

Conducting *ad hoc* analyses

Integrating and manipulating diverse data from many sources

Seamlessly accessing data sources

Dynamically updating data sources with the results of data
manipulations

Resuming work at the exact point of interruption

Collaborating face-to-face and remotely

Conducting domain-specific practices, calculations, and
interpretations in a keystroke

judgments on real-world data about users and their work. User-experience researchers and interaction designers need to conduct naturalistic observations and make these data available early in a project. Such data ensure that decisions about scope will not be based solely on market requirements and technical feasibility.

Should software teams choose to omit support for some of the aspects of problem solving listed previously, their statements about the project focus need to justify the omissions convincingly. A carefully crafted statement of focus ensures that a team will gather, analyze, and represent the right data for usefulness and leave a record to guide future releases.

Defining a Unit of Analysis as Part of the Contextual Inquiry Focus

Software teams commonly set an inquiry focus to identify targeted users and tasks, but they do not always go on to specify the unit of analysis for their user-experience study. A unit of analysis is the "basic entity about which observations and generalizations are made and for which data are collected" *(datalib.library.ualberta.ca/accoleds/workshops/units.ppt)*. It identifies the type of actor, social unit, setting, or relationships that field teams study and characterize. Often it includes many combined areas of interest, such as specific groups, transactions with software, and activities of interest.

Instead of defining a unit of analysis, software teams often agree that their project is user-centered and leave it at that. The trouble is, user-centeredness encompasses many possible units of analysis, among them activity systems, tasks, collaborations, individual users, and information. If field teams set too narrow a unit of analysis for complex problem solving—such as a focus on programmatic tasks—they may fail to collect the contextually rich data on practical-level work and goals required for designing for usefulness. Too broad a unit of analysis, such as a work activity system with ever-expanding boundaries, threatens to overwhelm field investigators and overload them with data past the point of manageable inquiry. A subjective unit of analysis, such as individual problem solvers, is too idiosyncratic.

For users' open-ended inquiries, field teams should define their unit of analysis as the *problem situation*. Setting a problem situation as the unit of analysis keeps user experience analysts focused on the interactions between people, conditions in the situation that spurred them to investigate matters, and conditions and resources shaping this investigation. Such an approach narrows the scale of an activity system as the specified unit of analysis while still maintaining its emphasis on distributed work.

Using the problem situation as the unit of analysis involves examining behaviors and knowledge related to users, teams, computer interactions, collaborations, and information flows within the problem-based relationships specified in Table 3.2. Discussions in upcoming sections in this chapter—Analyzing and Synthesizing Data and Modeling Users' Work—expand on what to examine in these targeted areas when collecting and analyzing data and representing consolidated and integrated models of users' work.

Conducting Observations of Everyday Work

For complex problem solving, user-experience analysts and, if possible, others on the design team, must go to users' work sites and watch them conduct their inquiries during the course of their daily activities. As fruitful as other methods may be, no amount of interviewing, card sorting, or cognitive walk-throughs can substitute for actually seeing people deal with the complexities of their problems in their everyday settings. Open-ended inquiries are too fluid to grasp in any other way. No other means illuminates the points at which either a genuine "ah-ha" or

TABLE 3.2
Inquiry activities and a
problem situation as the
unit of analysis.

Unit of Analysis:
Problem-Based Relationships to Examine

Events and methods related to composing the problem. When and how problem solvers clarify a problem and how this clarity helps them draw closer to resolution. Intertwined problems that analysts deal with in relation to one another.

Interactions and interdependencies between multi-contextual conditions affecting problem solving moves and strategies.

Problem solvers' task landscapes and patterns of inquiry as shaped by their goals, roles, priorities, and biases. In addition, problem solvers' mainline and enabling tasks, the choices they make, and the extent to which choices open or close opportunities for action.

Problem solvers' uses of explicit reasoning and tacit or commonsense knowledge. How they combine the two, when they use each, and how.

Problem solvers' uses of situational and subjective criteria to make decisions, determine relevance, and arrive at judgments in uncertainty.

The language of a problem situation in relation to organizationally shared practices, cues, and resources.

The relationship between breakdowns, impasses, missteps, and paths not taken and problem solvers' successes and confidence in results.

frustrated "aargh" sets in, and the reasons and responses for it. Observations reveal the cultural values and knowledge triggered by a problem, prompting users to proceed in one way rather than another.

Some types of data about complex problem solving that are important for field groups to gather through observations are detailed in Figure 3.1 and categorized by context. In actual observations or ethnographic analyses, however, contexts overlap, and field teams cannot so neatly divide data into contextual boxes. User-experience analysts and others on the field team need to be more attuned to the spirit than the letter of the contextual divisions.

Observations are paramount but are not an exclusive means for gathering crucial data. Alone they cannot provide a full picture of complex problem solving. When necessary, user-experience researchers should combine (or triangulate) them with other methods such as interviews, problem solving

FIGURE 3.1
Data to gather relevant to
complex problem solving.

Problem

How people compose their problem, e.g.,
the cues, feedback, knowledge, social
interactions, and timing used to define
goals and constraints

Triggers that make people aware of a
problem and that prompt them to take it
on as their own

Characteristic patterns of inquiry

How people change and improve their
inquiries as they gain insight into the
problem

Technology/data

Roles of tools in problem solving

Effects of problem solving on systems,
infrastructure, data integration,
database structure

Information needed and used for various
intents (what it is, where it comes from,
who can and can't access it, what
formats, who decides what counts as
relevant, what it is used for).

Various manipulations of data and why
Shortcuts/workarounds with tools

Problem Solving
Work Space

Work domain

People's "qualifiers" of work and when
used
People's language for talking about a
problem
Changes in one aspect of work and their
effects
Physical layouts and effects of proximity

How people's behaviors and knowledge
are affected by: social relations, power
relations, company missions and goals,
cultural norms, policies and procedures,
performance measures, external
events, costs of information, daily work
loads and habits, role clarity

Effects of corporate culture on behaviors

Subjective

Effects of prior knowledge and computing
experience on problem solving.

Ah-ha's and Aargh's—when and why
Reliance on tacit scripts or other
commonsense strategies and
knowledge

How people's behaviors and knowledge
adapt to and shape goals, motives,
cognitive demands

When and why problem solvers need
cognitive/perceptual aids for wayfinding
and sensemaking and what exactly they
need

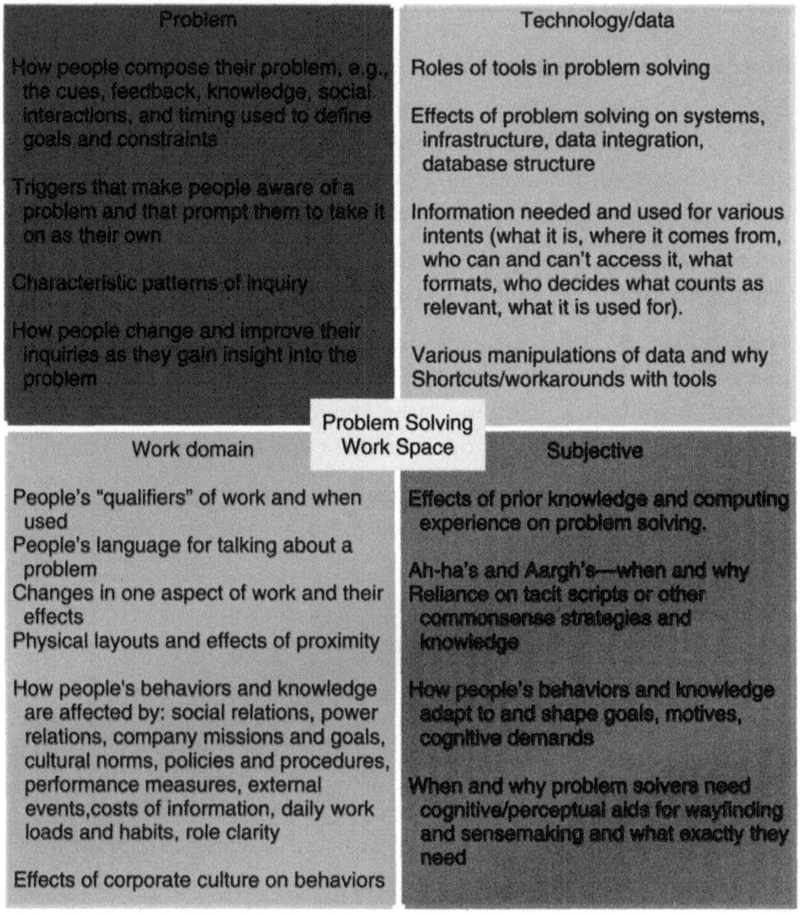

skills inventories, card sorting, simulations, and software logs, all of which
help to uncover problem solvers' methods. Depending on the situation,
user-experience researchers may need many or all of these techniques.

ANALYZING AND SYNTHESIZING DATA

Because of the many distinguishing traits of open-ended inquiries, user
experience researchers and interaction designers need to highlight
relevant issues when they analyze field data on users and tasks. In their
methods of analysis, they need to derive findings about issues specific to
the demands of complex problem solving, which are as follows:

- Analyzing patterns of inquiry and their conditions and constraints

- Capturing users' language of problem solving

- Re-engineering work for enhanced problem solving

- Highlighting users' needs for analytical control

Analyzing Patterns of Inquiry and Their Conditions and Constraints

Every pattern of inquiry has a purpose, strategies, knowledge, actions, context, and feedback. For example, Carlos, in exploring his hunch about non-billed travel, uses the pattern "identify small multiple costs causing losses," which involves comparing project costs, standardizing data, applying knowledge about billing practices, and working with data. User researchers can identify such problem solving patterns by concentrating on the following resources, interactions, and events:

- The information, goals, objectives, strategies, actions, and conditions that interactively constitute a "chunk" of users' practical-level work, given their roles, domains, and workplaces

- Ways problem solvers think in this "chunk" of inquiry, such as how they organize the inquiry, what strategies and rules they use, what models they create before taking action, what cues they monitor, and what assumptions they apply

- Decision points and their interrelationships, conditions, choices and available information; factors affecting decisions; the scope of problem solvers' considerations; and information relevant to decisions, as well as criteria for validating solutions and assessing "good enough"

- Changes that threaten the stability of a pattern, their indicators, and users' responses

- Relationships between patterns of inquiry

- Anomalies and variability and the conditions under which they occur

- Aspects of users' current technologies that mesh with or obstruct their patterns of inquiry

Capturing Users' Language of Problem Solving

Overtly or subtly, problem solvers' language expresses their notions of work and the level of detail at which they think about what, to them, is a basic task. In addition, their language communicates areas of social agreement about their analytical work and the components of a problem that rate consideration. They express these things through category names, chosen terms, shifts in jargon when discussing business goals versus interactions with technologies, and the framing of intentions.

User-experience researchers and interaction designers do not need to be linguists to pay attention to these aspects of problem solvers' communications. What they do need is to capture users' exact words and verbal constructs. For example, field teams may hear category managers, such as Marty in Chapter 1, talk about "working the funnel" to find "top movers" in sales and separating "winners" from "losers." Such language shapes these product analysts' thoughts about their work and can suggest to designers strategies for structuring electronic workspaces. In this case, workspaces should reflect that positionally high is better (winning is up; losing is down), competitive comparisons are essential, and analysis is a spiraling process. Category managers' language gives a sense of the frameworks that tacitly shape their complex inquiries and that UI designs could call forth spatially and structurally.

When user-experience researchers, interaction designers, and others on a software team analyze problem solvers' language, they should pay special attention to how problem solvers qualify their work when they talk about it. Qualifications, for example, include comments about a network running "too slowly" or profit margins being "uncompetitive." These distinctions reveal aspects of users' complex work in which some standard is in play. The use of qualifications, because they are relative judgments, indicates that these aspects of work and their surrounding and supporting environments may be open to reassessment. Users socially and intellectually negotiate criteria about what is variable and standard throughout problem solving. Software teams need to create conceptual designs that evoke support for these pivotal distinctions. Finally, by analyzing conversations, such as when and how problem solvers indicate their objectives, request help, and seek or give explanations, user-experience researchers and their teammates can distinguish plans, beliefs, and intentions that workmates either take for granted or question.

Re-engineering Work for Enhanced Problem Solving

Introducing software into users' problem solving situations changes their work. To change it for the better, software teams need to design for work improvements. Problem solvers' demonstrated ways of investigating problems might not be the most effective ones. Their current practices may not be optimal once their inquiries have an electronic dimension to them. Field observations reflect the inquiry boundaries and criteria that problem solvers value and that applications need to respect. However, observed problem solving behaviors do not necessarily demonstrate the most productive approaches. Therefore, software field teams need to look for opportunities for improving (re-engineering) users' work when analyzing and modeling it.

In part, identifying these opportunities involves finding indications of lapses in experts' problem solving and decision-making. Many of these lapses are common to experts across domains (Salomon and Perkins, 1989; Kitajima and Polson, 1992; Johnson et al., 1993; Prietula et al., 2000). In collecting and interpreting data on observed work, user-experience analysts should pose the following questions that highlight these common lapses:

- Where do users fall back on "default" strategies and give them more weight than they deserve for a given situation?

- Where do users founder in attempts to integrate and synthesize multiple factors?

- Where do they neglect mundane information that seems trivial in light of a single case but is important for many cases combined?

- Where do they focus on the wrong level of detail for a given purpose?

- Where do they factor the idiosyncrasies of a particular case into a solution and lose track of other variables?

- Where do they decide on a solution without justification?

- Where do they fail to transfer relevant abstract rules, principles, strategies, or "automatic" procedures from one situation to another?

- Where do they encounter obstructions that keep them from verifying their intuitions and instead force them into making complex inferences?

Software solutions that address these lapses—depending on why they occur—may take the form of feedback, cues, workspace structures, reminders, more integrated functions, and easy access to data from divergent sources.

Highlighting Users' Needs for Problem Solving Control

Implicit in the preceding areas of analysis are issues related to user control. Figuring out how to distribute control between software and users is one of the thorniest design problems that teams confront in any software project, and it is an issue I will return to in many subsequent chapters. For example, problem solvers invariably need to integrate and relate diverse data, but it is an open question whether designers should give users the bulk of the control through a range of options for integrating data or whether they should rely more on program control through some kind of "intelligent manager" to automate the process.

One of the most important groups of findings field studies can provide is insights into this issue of control. Findings can reveal how much control users need analytically, for what purpose, and when. Findings from observations need to highlight the points at which user freedom is pivotal to the success of complex problem solving and when it is not.

Many software specialists strive to create an all-purpose model aimed at helping design teams know what interactions users should control and with what degrees of freedom. These specialists, however, are the first to acknowledge that such modeling "is not an exact science" (Parasuraman et al., 2000). Perhaps their greatest contributions have been the frameworks they have produced that categorize different types of control. User-experience researchers and interaction designers can use these frameworks to analyze users' needs for control and to evaluate, later during conceptual design, how to distribute control between users and the program. One such framework points field teams toward analyzing users' required degrees of freedom by structuring these requirements around four problem solving processes:

- Preparing data and planning inquiry

- Querying and analyzing information

- Deciding on and selecting action

- Implementing action (Parasuraman et al., 2000)

Within each problem solving process, users have different needs, and user-experience analysts need to highlight them distinctively. They also need to assess the costs and benefits of having users or a program control a given instance in terms of the effects on users' cognitive load, situational awareness, skill degradation, and intellectual engagement. Safety and software reliability also factor into decisions about distributing control.

Importantly, automation designers have found that programs with too much automated control may be associated with reduced situational awareness, intellectual disengagement and complacency, and skill degradation. By analyzing these issues and bringing findings to the design table, user-experience researchers and interaction designers will contribute immeasurably to software usefulness. I discuss these issues in more detail in Chapter 9, Designing for Usefulness Across Cases.

These methods for gathering and analyzing data on complex problem solvers and their work lead design teams to the point of turning findings into models of users' complex problem solving. I now turn to methods for creating models that foster designing for usefulness. How interaction designers and their teammates represent users' dynamic inquiries plays a vital role in usefulness. These representations shape requirements and conceptual designs.

MODELING USERS' WORK

As stressed earlier, interaction designers, usability specialists, and other design team members must create models of users' complex work that do not encourage a premature breakdown into smaller and smaller constituent tasks. Holistically, they need to capture the "structured openness" of complex problem solving.

Because complex problem solving is emergent, models need to structure in openness so they give rise to conceptual designs that are suggestive rather than imitative of users' complex work. They need to represent the divergent insights, judgments, paths, and outcomes that result from problem solvers manipulating problem solving resources differently. Carlos's hunch about non-billed travel, for example, directs him to distinct paths. If he unexpectedly discovers abuses in the company's billing system, he will respond by digging deeper and perhaps uncovering other unforeseen issues. Certain events, information, and conditions incite Carlos and other problem solvers like him to linger at certain spots, to magnify them until they show unsuspected meanings, or to pull various pieces together so that patterns gel or significant boundaries between past and present trends emerge. Models of problem solving need to show these hidden meanings and significant elements.

In creating models of users' work, design teams need to do the following:

- Orient their model-building toward capturing "structured openness"

- Create models of users' problem solving that represent interactivity, contexts, and variability

Capturing "Structured Openness" in Models of Users' Work

When interaction designers, usability specialists, and other design team members view complex problem solving as an emergent, improvised drama, they realize that they should not try to represent *all* the possibilities in an open-ended problem situation. No one can articulate a complete account of problem solvers' potential actions. Designers can model users' patterns of inquiry, but they cannot anticipate within these patterns the exact task landscapes and choices that users will configure in practice. Nor can they neatly define all the attributes, roles, and functional relationships that resources in problem solving may assume. As tempting as it is for teams to specify in semantic networks or concept maps every move and use of information in a type of problem solving experience—something that is commonly attempted by knowledge engineering—complex problem solving eludes this "packaging." Interaction designers' efforts to understand and model the uses of problem solving resources and problem solvers' actions and knowledge will be forever partial because of chance and change. Variability often leads problem solvers to put together enabling and mainline tasks in unexpected ways to accomplish a goal.

During the 1990s, Kim Vincente (1999, 2002) and Jens Rasmussen, Annelise Pejtersen, and L.P. Goodman (1994) proposed ecological interface design (EID) models for capturing the bounded interactivity that frames users' open-ended inquiries. EID takes an interactivity-based approach to representing complex work and is just as relevant today for complex problem solving as it was when first proposed. However, commercial software teams often cannot easily use the modeling templates. The templates are too complicated, not particularly visual, and tied more to theory than practice.

The modeling approach and diagrams I will advance as alternatives draw on many of the same ideas as EID, while modifying some, adding others, and making them generally more accessible. I propose models that represent the structure of domain-based patterns for inquiry and task landscapes and that leave enough freedom and flexibility for users to handle situations differently for given circumstances. Such models emphasize interactivity, contexts, and variability.

Creating Models That Represent Interactivity, Contexts, and Variability

The approach to modeling complex work that I propose is not a substitute for methods used by contextual designers, such as scenarios or consolidated workflow models. Rather it extends and supplements them by highlighting and visualizing the interactive forces of users' practical problem solving activities.

Methods for Creating Interactivity, Contexts, and Variability Models

Approaches to modeling users' complex problem solving focus on capturing the many directions their patterns of inquiry may take as shaped by interactivity, contexts, and variability (ICV). Design teams' methods need to ensure they create models that highlight the incompatibilities across contextual conditions and the constraints that block problem solvers from seamlessly carrying out effective inquiries. These models also need to distinguish elements of the problem environment and information workspace that are open to being rearticulated from those that are not. They must capture places and ways in which problem solvers continue to have the leeway they need to perform their work when dynamic changes occur.

TABLE 3.3
General approaches to
modeling patterns of
inquiry based on ICV.

Modeling Approaches

- **Represent a best-case scenario of unhindered performance:** Identify the conditions and constraints that need to line up compatibility (in the problem, technology and data, work domain, and subjective contexts) to make possible the actions needed for this best case.

- **Represent numerous less-than-best-cases (practical, real cases):** Highlight the incompatible interactive conditions across numerous contexts that obstruct users from pursuing the patterns of work they value.

- **Describe the task landscapes users construct for their patterns of inquiry and subgoals**: Use these practical cases for reference.

- **Represent the relations between mainline and enabling tasks that make up pattern-based task landscapes:** Also describe the choice points and variable and stable factors influencing problem solvers' decisions at these crossroads.

- **Identify the core activities problem solvers must perform in an integrated way to solve this type of problem:** Use task landscapes to identify core activities for various conditions.

- **Identify criteria for usefulness related to these core activities:** Consider the function of various core activities in relation to the surrounding task landscape and task landscapes of other subgoals.

- **Show interconnections and dependencies between this pattern of inquiry and others. Identify the integrated support that is needed for elegant, useful designs.**

A general summary of methods to use to create such models is presented in Table 3.3. I apply this modeling framework to the cases presented in Part Two.

The ideas underlying these methods for modeling users' complex problem solving revolve around evoking and supporting the dynamics and effects of interactivity, contexts, and variability. The following sections expand on each of these aspects of modeling:

- **Modeling for interactivity:** Includes diagrams of interactions among many contextual conditions and constraints that open or close actions that users may take in their patterns of inquiry.

- **Representing contexts:** Includes diagrams of task landscapes for specific patterns of inquiry as shaped by contextual interactions.

- **Capturing variability:** Includes choice points and variable and stable factors affecting decisions in close-up views of pattern-based actions and shows overall views of integrated landscapes across patterns.

Modeling for Interactivity

In complex problem solving, insights, important relationships, and new interactive conditions emerge continuously. Such emergence occurs because, in indeterminate problem spaces, constant interactions among actors, objects, and events lead to unpredictable outcomes. Problem solvers may approach a complex investigation with a small number of analytical rules and guiding principles, but no sooner do they get underway than the situation expands and new lines of questioning lead to unexpected implications. Individuals' choices, in turn, affect the options that are subsequently available, and the shifting contexts impact their work even further. This dynamic interactivity leaves a large, but bounded, range of possible moves.

Problem solvers' original methods often get transformed into different courses of action due to emerging insights and unforeseen opportunities. Problem definitions, goals, methods, and routes evolve and progressively reveal uncharted territory for problem solvers to explore. Problem solving is intrinsically experimental because uncertainties leave space for interactive conditions to introduce unanticipated possibilities and restraints.

A number of interactions affect the ways in which users conduct patterns of inquiry to resolve their problems. Software designers need to represent complex problem solving in ways that capture, for example, interactions *among* the following:

- Goals, constraints, and contingencies that bind a problem solving workspace

- Information, tools, collaborations, and other forces that shape actions and relationships between people, things, and ideas in specific patterns of inquiry

- Dynamic changes within the bounds of a workspace

Representing Contexts

Contexts provide designers with a means for structuring the interactivity of complex inquiries. Design team members, for example, can represent complex inquiries as the interplay of conditions and constraints within and across the problem, technology, work domain, and subjective contexts. Such representations will account for the interactions among such influential elements as available data and their formats (technology context), accepted standards of practice in a given workplace (work domain context), users' prior knowledge (subjective context), and patterns of inquiry (problem context).

A visual representation of interactive contexts is shown for the troubleshooting case in Chapter 5, Figure 5.1. The diagram in this figure captures the ways in which interactions occur across multiple contextual conditions (blue and yellow balls) and the effects of these interactions on the course of users' inquiry action. As Figure 5.1 shows, when an inquiry action courses through the buffeting of interactive conditions, this interplay leaves some opportunities open but closes others. Some contextual conditions may interact compatibly in ways that keep paths for users' desired actions open. Others may not be compatible, and problem solvers hit impasses; the "dotted lines" get deflected, and individuals scramble for workarounds, or worse, they curtail their intentions to suit prevailing conditions and settle for diminished achievements. Interactions are incompatible, for example, when remote collaborators cannot quickly exchange information due to interactions between rigid communication channels in the work domain and a painfully slow network.

Capturing Variability

In addition to interactive contextual conditions, representations of complex work must capture variability. In open-ended inquiries, stability always mixes with inconstancy, so problem solving inevitably has an element of unpredictability. Conventions that impart stability include patterns of inquiry, business rules, and rules of thumb. Variability derives from situational idiosyncrasies such as currently available resources, stakeholders' biases, and shifting priorities. It also derives from time pressures, norms in the organizational culture, and environmental contingencies.

Variability shapes users' choices in configuring task landscapes and contributes to the criteria they use for decisions at critical points. Diagrams for modeling task landscapes are shown in the product mix case in Chapter 6. The first model, the task landscape and its connected "tracts" and complex routes, is depicted in Figures 6.17 and 6.18. These two figures show that some landscapes (Figure 6.18) are more complex to configure and traverse than others (Figure 6.17). Models of work need to capture these task landscapes: The options available and those relevant to particular variable conditions and problem-based goals.

Models of complex problem solving also need to capture users' choices within these task landscapes. Figure 6.19 in the product mix case in Chapter 6 depicts a close-in view of a "task chunk" in a landscape to show the decision points and multiple choices for paths that checker the terrain at any given moment in a problem solvers' inquiry.

Choice points are the conceptual crossroads problem solvers encounter when they face equally legitimate next steps. To decide, they consider a mixture of variable and stable factors. The following example illustrates a choice point and the influences that shape a user's decision.

CHOICE POINT: WHAT DO I DO NEXT?

[◊ indicates stable influences; ■ indicates variable influences]

◊ Conventional patterns and other domain practices and heuristic strategies

◊ Logical criteria for solution

■ Personal preferences and motives

■ Company policy

■ Role-related responsibilities

■ Stakeholder pressures

■ Incentive system

■ Company priorities

■ Available information scents

■ Signposts and other indicators of means for jumping elsewhere

Finally, a last diagram captures different task landscapes within a pattern to represent the relationships and integrated connections across current and prior patterns that give problem solvers' dynamic work coherence and completeness (see Figure 6.20). When design teams model patterns of inquiry, task landscapes, and relationships between contextual conditions and users' actions in ways that aptly capture ICV, they create integrated *and* consolidated representations of work. These representations, moreover, do not lend themselves to premature decomposition. They help teams conceptualize integrated support for users' integrated work in a design that ideally offers users maximum investigative support in minimum structures and procedures.

CONCEPTUALIZING DESIGNS

At present, the overriding influence on designs for complex problem solving comes from advanced technology groups in research and development (R&D) organizations. Some of these groups concentrate on supporting ill-structured activities through adaptive computing: Software agents, non-linear probabilistic modeling, and natural language interfaces. Others advocate domain-specific software architecture and smart algorithms to ensure deep support for the problems and patterns of particular areas. Yet another group lauds interactive data visualizations as the best technical solution for open-ended data exploration. Regardless of their orientation, all these groups have great concern for the social and cognitive demands of complex problems. Yet when they design, they primarily conceive of support in terms of application structures, features, and functionality, not the interactive and integrated demands of situated complex problems and pattern-based inquiries.

Therefore, in the majority of the efforts currently devoted to designing for complexity, users are not truly at the center—neither in the language of design principles nor in the practices of conceptual designing. Fortunately, things are beginning to change.

Adopting Design Strategies for Usefulness

In some recent advances groups have begun to frame design principles so the resulting systems represent contextual aspects users need to know. These design principles include the following:

1. Inform the user of current contextual system capabilities and understandings.

2. Provide feedback including "feed forward" (what will happen if I do this?) and confirmation (what am I doing and what have I done).

3. Disclose identity and action, particularly in sharing restricted information: Who is that, what are they doing, and what have they done?

4. Defer control to the user over system, and other user actions that impact him or her, especially in cases of conflict of interest (Bellotti and Edwards, 2001).

Interaction designers and their teammates need to urge their development groups to follow these promising leads. They need to supplement the four previously mentioned strategies with others that are targeted specifically to complex inquiries and not just to contextual cuing.

Developed in greater detail in the scenarios in Chapters 4 through 8, these design strategies include the following:

STRATEGIES FOR CONCEPTUALIZING DESIGNS

- Enable users to seed their information workspaces for sensemaking and wayfinding purposes through structural cues, markers, highlights, and reminders
- Optimally distribute control between users and programs, with appropriate opportunities for user-defined views and interactions
- Build in domain specificity through such strategies as domain-specific architectures, smart algorithms, intelligent agents, dynamic interface components, non-technical end-user customizing, analysis in a keystroke, and domain-specific entry points
- Provide dynamically linked interactive data visualizations and perceptual encoding to help users manage and make sense of large amounts of data and understand the structure of their problem and solution spaces
- Provide single workspaces for retrieving, integrating, and exploring diverse data from different sources
- Integrate support for mainline and enabling tasks so users move coherently and completely from "here to there" within and across patterns of inquiries
- Give users capabilities to adapt data and views to the demands of situational constraints
- Give users the optimal mix of standardized terminology and free-text entries for their purposes
- Turn workspaces into places by evoking users' roles, responsibilities, and values
- Design elegantly by ensuring that numerous tasks integrate most efficiently before jumping to final design decisions
- Target support for core problem solving activities that are currently neglected in many applications, including support for integrating heterogeneous data from diverse sources; saving and noting important insights of interest; composing in tandem with analysis; controlling the meaning of data displays for desired lines of questioning; conducting complex queries visually; seeing and setting cues, signposts, or flags for situated issues that influence problem solving choices; navigating through many programs or modules for a single pattern of inquiry; and collaborating

Conceptually Designing With an Eye on Classes of Program Interactions

In conceptual design, HCI specialists and their teammates need to highlight *classes* of program interactions before jumping to individual features or low-level operations. These classes directly relate to the types or chunks of tasks characterizing problem solvers' patterns of inquiry—the tracts in task landscapes. Focusing on classes of program interactions enables designers to connect design to the aspects of users' work for which users need adaptability and the aspects that are fairly well-structured. For example, for task chunks that involve different moves and directions for distinct purposes, such as saving views of data for later reference, designers can make sure this type of program interaction (saving for later use) is *ready* for adaptability, even though they cannot predict users' exact moves.

This focus on open-endedness and adaptability ensures that users will be able to fit the program to their needs. Looking at classes of program interactions shifts the focus from features to program-based trajectories of activity that are governed by users' initiatives (Barnard et al., 2000). Programs need to provide support that is tied to users taking the lead, for example, users' initiatives to explore a tangent or to multitask. Design deliberations at first should not be about specific features and their properties. Rather they should focus on identifying the *types* and trajectory of program actions that fit users' patterns of inquiry. Then designers should decide which types of action need to be ready for users' adaptive moves (e.g., reactivating a saved view) and what designs best foster this adaptability.

Adopting Design Choices Based on Usefulness Criteria

In creating designs for usefulness, design teams have numerous options from which to choose. These options, however, trigger thorny design questions. Because complex problem solving requires support for structured openness and stability *and* variability, interaction designers and their teammates need to determine, for example, what support should be domain specific and when generic is better. Many other similar decisions confront designers, and it benefits usefulness for teams to seriously engage these open design questions. In fact, as checkpoints for designing for usefulness, interaction designers, usability specialists, and their teammates should consciously ask each other whether they have adequately considered "when" and "how much" questions when it comes to including and balancing the following choices:

- Power versus simplicity

- Standardized terminology versus free text entries

- Unstructured flexibility versus goal-specific restrictions

- End-user programming/scripting for adaptability versus anticipated adaptive functionality versus user preferences

- Data visualizations versus intelligent agents

- Procedural versus structural support

- Consistency with conventions versus outside-the-box inventions

As interaction designers and their teammates choose from options and create designs, they must integrate their choices into elegant solutions based on all aspects of support that users will require from their specific product. In Part Two, I explore such design choices for specific types of problems and domains.

Designing for complex problem solving is in its infancy. The development community as a whole still needs to put together a better understanding of domain specialists' integrative patterns of complex problem solving and get a stronger grasp of how to conceptually design holistic support for these patterns. Across the industry, teams need to widely disseminate applications deliberately designed for usefulness, evaluate their effects, and share their findings with the larger development community. Only in this way can we evolve effective standards and guidelines for supporting problem solvers' complicated task landscapes for exploratory analysis and decision-making.

CONCLUSIONS: PUTTING IT TOGETHER

Overall, assumptions and methods for designing for open-ended inquiries need to be in sync with users' choices in open-ended work and the extenuating circumstances that affect these choices. Representations of users' work must highlight the structure of problem solvers' search for a solution and the dynamic interactions that bind unanticipated possibilities.

Teams have to use these models to inform their conceptual designs so that programs offer the power, cues, interactivity, and shifting frames of reference that users need for exploring and solving complex problems.

Scenarios in Part Two show how these assumptions, design directions, and methods apply to actual problem solving situations through three extended case studies. Each case focuses on software for a specific domain-based problem. Included in the cases are ICV representations and diagrams of users' complex inquiry patterns. The cases also present evolving designs and prototypes that strive to provide useful support.

The upcoming scenarios reveal actions, arrangements, and cues about contextual realities that are crucial for coherent and successful problem solving but that persistently are under-supported by software for complex problems. Discussions of the cases explore improvements and methods for achieving them. Each case represents a specific class of complex problem situated within a distinct system of work, as follows:

- Troubleshooting faults in a complex technological system in the IT domain

- Deciding on optimal product mixes in a complex adaptive-market system in the field of merchandising

- Making judgments about drug dosages for hospital patients in a complex and co-emerging technological and social system of work

REFERENCES

Barnard, Philip, Jon May, David Duke and David Duce. "Systems, Interactions, and Macrotheory." *ACM Transactions on Computer-Human Interaction* 7, no. 2 (2000): 222-262.

Bass, Len, Bonnie John and Jesse Kates. *Achieving Usability Through Software Architecture*, Technical Report 005. Pittsburgh, PA: Software Engineering Institute, Carnegie Mellon University, 2001.

Bellotti, Victoria and Keith Edwards. "Intelligibility and Accountability: Human Considerations in Context Aware Systems." *Human-Computer Interaction* 16 (2001): 193-212.

Berg, Mark. *Rationalizing Medical Work: Decision Support Techniques and Medical Practices*. Cambridge, MA: MIT Press, 1997.

Beyer, Hugh and Karen Holtzblatt. *Contextual Design: Defining Customer-Centered Systems*. San Francisco: Morgan Kaufmann, 1998.

Constantine, Larry and Lucy Lockwood. *Software for Use*. Reading, MA: Addison-Wesley, 1999.

Dayton, Tom, Al McFarland, and Joseph Kramer. "Bridging User Needs to Object-Oriented GUI Prototype Via Task Object Design." In *User Interface Design*, edited by Larry Wood, 15-55, Boca Raton: CRC Press, 1998.

Encarnação, L. Miguel. "Concept and Realization of Intelligent User Support in Interactive Graphics Applications." Ph.D. diss., der Fakultat fur Informatik, der Eberhard-Karis-Universitate zu Tubingen, 1997.

Gulliksen, Jan and Bengt Sandblad. "Domain-Specific Design of User Interfaces." *International Journal of Human-Computer Interaction* 7, no. 2 (1995): 135-151.

Hackos, Joann and Janice Redish. *User and Task Analysis for Interface Design*. New York: John Wiley and Sons, 1998.

Hudson, William. "Toward Unified Models in User-Centered and Object-Oriented Design." In *Object Modeling and User Interface Design*, edited by Mark Van Harmelen, 212-362, Boston: Addison-Wesley, 2001.

John, Bonnie and Len Bass. "Usability and Software Architecture." *Behaviour and Information Technology* 20, no. 5 (2001): 329-338.

Johnson, Paul, Imran Zualkernan, and David Tukey. "Types of Expertise: An Invariant of Problem Solving." *International Journal of Man-Machine Studies* 39 (1993): 641-665.

Kitajima, Muneo and Peter Polson. "A Computational Model of Skilled Use of a Graphical User Interface." *Proceedings of CHI 92* Monterey, CA, 1992: 241-249.

Kreitzberg, Charles. The LUCID Design Framework. Described on the Cognetics Corporation website at http://www.cognetics.com/lucid/index.html.

Kulak, Daryl and Eamonn Guiney. *Use Cases: Requirements in Context*. Boston: Addison-Wesley, 2000.

Mayhew, Deborah. *The Usability Engineering Lifecycle: A Practitioner's Handbook for User Interface Design*. San Francisco: Morgan Kaufmann, 1999.

Parasuraman, Raja, Thomas Sheridan, and Christopher Wicken. "A Model for Types and Levels of Human Interaction With Automation." *IEEE Transactions on Systems, Man, and Cybernetics* 30, no. 3 (2000): 286-297.

Prietula, Michael, Paul Feltovich, and Frank Marchak. "Factors Influencing Analysis of Complex Cognitive Tasks: A Framework and Example from Industrial Process Control." *Human Factors* 42, no. 1 (Spring 2000): 56-74.

Raskin, Jef. *The Humane Interface: New Directions for Designing Interactive Systems*. Reading, MA: Addison-Wesley, 2000.

Rasmussen, Jens, Annelise Mark Pejtersen, and L.P. Goodstein. *Cognitive Systems Engineering*. New York: John Wiley and Sons, 1994.

Rennison, Earl. "Galaxy of News: An Approach to Visualizing and Understanding Expansive News Landscapes." *Proceedings of UIST 94, ACM Symposium on User Interface Software and Technology*. 3-12. New York: ACM, 1994.

Rosenbaum, Stephanie. "Not Just a Hammer: When and How to Employ Multiple Methods in Usability Programs." *Proceedings of the 2000 UPA*, Section 19, 2000.

Rosson, Mary Beth and John M. Carroll. *Usability Engineering: Scenario-based Development of Human-Computer Interaction*. San Francisco: Morgan Kaufmann, 2002.

Salomon, Gavriel and David Perkins. "Rocky Roads to Transfer: Rethinking Mechanisms of a Neglected Phenomenon." *Educational Psychologist* 24, no. 2 (1989): 113-142.

Siy, Harvey and Audris Mockus. "Measuring Domain Engineering Effects on Software Coding Cost." *Metrics 99: Sixth International Symposium on Software Metrics*. Boca Raton, FL, 1999: 304-311.

Sturm, Gretchen. "Moving from Adoptability to Adaptability." Electronic Recruiting Exchange (April 11, 2003) Available at: http://www.erexchange.com/articles/db/467D03458219471B9BBADD3F05386DEF.asp

Vincente, Kim. *Cognitive Work Analysis*. Mahwah, NJ: Lawrence Erlbaum Associates, 1999.

Vincente, Kim. "Ecological Interface Design: Progress and Challenges." *Human Factors* 44, no. 1 (2002): 62-78.

Vincente, Kim and Jens Rasmussen. "Ecological Interface Design: Theoretical Foundations." *Transactions on Systems, Man, and Cybernetics* 22, no. 4 (1992): 589-606.

Weiss, David and Chi Tau Robert Lai. *Software Product Line Engineering: A Family Based Software Development Process*. Boston: Addison-Wesley, 1999.

PART II

SOLVING PROBLEMS IN TECHNICAL, SOCIAL, AND CO-EMERGENT SYSTEMS

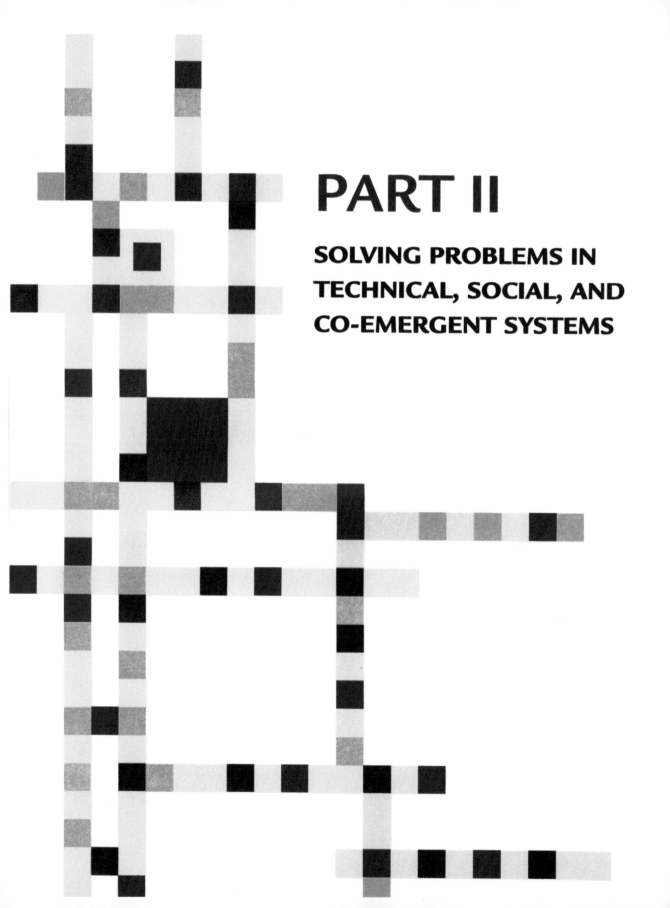

4

Keeping the System Up
and Running

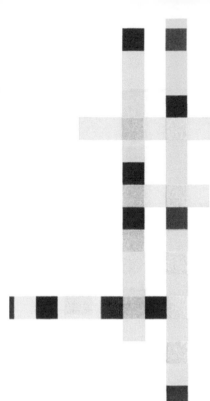

System analysts, database administrators, and technical support specialists make their living by keeping complex systems running smoothly. Working in information technology (IT), they monitor and troubleshoot distributed computing environments, telecommunication networks, process control systems, and the like. They assure that critical applications run effectively, reliably, and efficiently by preventing and fixing problems, planning and managing capacity, maintaining databases, and tuning applications.

These professionals perform work that is technical but still understandable by non-IT software design teams. In many ways, an IT professional's work resembles managing a store. Store managers monitor and analyze customer traffic between departments and correlate customer transactions with other events going on in the store. Technical specialists do the same. They monitor traffic patterns flowing across a network and find and fix causes of poor performance so electronic transactions move efficiently across the network. Their monitoring assures that customers (the end-users) have the right resources available when they need them.

With today's monitoring tools and network "sniffers," it is possible to have data on just about every transaction in a network. Such wide-ranging data enable technical specialists to shift views and understand system performance, usage, and traffic patterns from several perspectives: From an irate end-user's point of view, as well as from the vantage point of a hard-hit database, a memory-deficient application server, or a blocked signal-connection gateway.

This chapter examines the needs of tier-two and tier-three IT specialists for troubleshooting, preventing faults, and analyzing root causes. These are the analysts who deal with the complex problems that help-desk teams (tier-one support) cannot solve. Their goal is to keep end-users satisfied by assuring acceptable response times, resources, and connectivity. In this chapter, I present the case of a tier-two database administrator (DBA) who strives to restore order to his company's severely overloaded client-server network. He investigates entangled problems in the network that are causing response times to grind to a halt. These problems have been triggered by a batch job that ran over at the start of the business day.

In this chapter and the next, the case of this DBA, Benkei, offers HCI specialists and design teams insight into what is needed to design for usefulness and has implications beyond the immediate case. Benkei's troubleshooting practices and needs are indicative of a wide range of investigations. They pertain to any troubleshooting inquiries in which analysts, through a process of elimination, strive to solve complicated or intermittent problems that disrupt their complex technical systems or networks.

Benkei, for example, demonstrates the same needs for software support that other analysts have when they troubleshoot Internet sites, detect and fix faulty components in software systems, diagnose sources of aberrations in Internet call diversion telecommunication systems, or locate and repair errors in power plants or electronic scheduling systems. This case represents a wide range of situations in which analysts solve complex problems in the workings of complex automated systems. In these centrally scheduled systems, problem solvers serve the purpose of keeping the system up and running.

Following Benkei's scenario is the story of a design team and its first attempt to create a data visualization tool to help Benkei and other IT specialists like him troubleshoot corporate intranet problems. Benkei and the design team's stories reflect real problem solving and design situations. They are composites of actual cases, drawn from my design team experiences and my multisite field work and modeling of IT troubleshooting in corporate intranets and telecommunication networks.

In the design team story found later in this chapter, teammates analyze data about IT troubleshooting from their contextual inquiry, turn findings into a conceptual design, and create a working prototype. However, when they field test the prototype with users, they find that troubleshooters are exceedingly frustrated by its lack of usefulness. This chapter closes with an analysis of why the prototype falls short.

Fortunately, the design team has more success when we meet them again in Chapter 5. There they regroup for a second go at designing the troubleshooting tool. First, however, Benkei's case, combined with the team's first efforts, shows how designing for complex problem solving goes awry when software team members do not initially apply the design thinking, methods, and strategies discussed in prior chapters.

Specifically, team members, in their initial design efforts, overlook the following:

- They do not set the unit of analysis for their user-centered studies and design activities as the problem situation, but instead they focus on troubleshooters' questions and related data.

- They do not create consolidated *and* integrated models of users' work.

- Because of these two orientations, they fail to highlight and design for many of the effects that interactions between multi-contextual conditions have on IT troubleshooters' moves and choices and the support that troubleshooters need for them even in familiar problems.

These omissions neglect areas of support discussed in earlier chapters, such as:

■ Domain-specific patterns of inquiry	■ Mainline and enabling tasks in task landscapes	■ Task synergy
■ Analytical power	■ Integration of data within and across tools	■ User control
■ Adaptability	■ *Ad hoc* data transformations	■ Multitasking and interruptions
■ Collaboration to negotiate meanings socially	■ Screen captures and reminder notes for later uses	■ Reliance on structural signposts and situational cues

As Benkei's case shows, troubleshooting investigations are complex but do not have all the traits of complexity. Troubleshooting problems reside in a complex technical system that is governed by the dynamics of electrical engineering. At some level, a right solution exists, even if Benkei and others like him struggle with the complications of the system to find it. In this chapter, I focus on a type of problem solving that is not at the highest end of complexity to emphasize two points: (1) Useful support is just as necessary in moderately complex cases of problem solving and (2) it is just as elusive if design teams' mindsets and methods are not attuned to the requirements of dynamic work.

SCENARIO: CRISIS IN A CORPORATE INTRANET

Benkei is one of several DBAs in a multinational corporation with 60 branch locations. The corporation operates 150 NT servers and 14 databases and has more than 3,000 users worldwide. Its computing environment is built on a three-tiered architecture, which does not yet include Web-based applications. This environment constitutes the problem space for IT troubleshooters' and analysts' inquiries. The distributed nature of this architecture, combined with the large size of the network and its heterogeneity, plays notable roles in making troubleshooting, fault prevention, and root cause analysis (RCA) complex. It may be helpful to fill in a general background on distributed and networked environments.

How Complicated Is the Technical System That Gives Rise to the Problems?

In a many-tiered architecture, computing resources and processing are spread across several independent layers instead of residing in one place, such as only on an end-user's personal computer (PC), which is otherwise known as a *client*. In the top tier of a three-tiered environment, users interact with an application or Web browser from their PCs. Their query leaves their desktop to get processed. In the middle tier it travels over a network, possibly to a Web-based server, and then to an application server where function and logic reside. IT environments vary widely in how they split functionality and services between clients and servers. In any configuration, middleware components (messaging software) route client transactions to the appropriate server. Once transactions are in an application server, they often hop, again via middleware, to further destinations in the bottom tier such as servers for databases or printers. In the database server, a database processes transaction requests and sends responses back through the application server to the users' machines (Figure 4.1).

Technical specialists investigate problems such as slow response time first by getting a full picture of system performance and of all the hops that transactions make. They look at routers and traffic, uses of system resources, the availability of resources, and transaction sizes and times in and out of every stop along the way. Then technical specialists pinpoint causes of slow response time from possibilities within and across the tiers of the network. This multilayered dispersion makes it difficult for IT analysts to diagnose problems.

In addition to the complexities of this architecture, two other technological conditions make network- and system-performance problems vexing. First, networks are large and diverse. Tracing the path of transactions is difficult when they go through local area networks (LANs) that connect operations (some enterprises have scores of LANs), wide area networks (WANs) that link distant locations, and the Internet. Telecommunications has comparably intricate paths, especially new Internet call diversion architectures. Starting in a circuit world, calls often are routed through intricate paths across the country to arrive at the gateways, components, and Internet carriers that transform them into digital packets and connect them to their destinations.

Second, infrastructure equipment is varied, manufactured by diverse vendors, and often composed of old and new systems. Systems frequently run on a mix of operating systems, and various parts are apt to interpret standards differently. Processing usually is interoperable across disparate

FIGURE 4.1
Multi-tier architecture of
distributed computing.
(Evans and Bomigli, 1998)

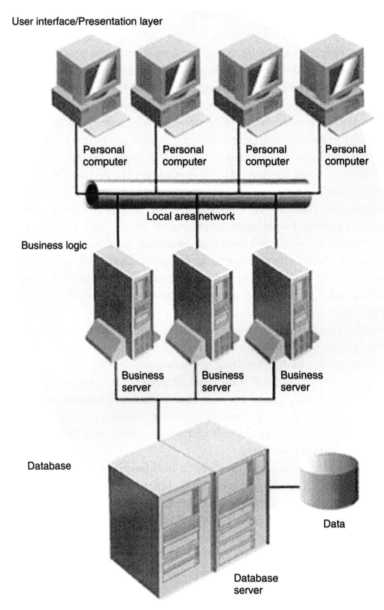

User interface/Presentation layer

Personal computer

Personal computer

Personal computer

Personal computer

Local area network

Business logic

Business server

Business server

Business server

Database

Data

Database server

equipment and platforms, but when technical specialists have to gather data about traffic, system performance, and availability of resources to solve problems, this heterogeneity can make life difficult. Often old and new systems are stitched together without the messaging that monitoring tools need to gather and relate transaction data. Alternately, heterogeneous servers, operating systems, and middleware purchased from different vendors may leave unexpected gaps in the network—"black holes"—that cannot be monitored by "sniffers" or tested by diagnostics. In these cases, network and system administrators cannot get comprehensive data or a complete picture of performance.

What Does Benkei Do as a Tier-Two DBA in This Distributed Computing Environment?

Benkei, as an advanced, second-tier analyst, confronts these system challenges daily. He works in the data center operations office. Benkei maintains and troubleshoots the performance of everything that goes on with a Citrix server and software and with a production server. Citrix is a software interface between users with old PCs and applications that require more computing power than these old PCs can handle. It resides on a separate UNIX server, uses proprietary protocols, and emulates the Microsoft Windows operating system for hundreds of old PCs. Because of these protocols, "sniffers" from application performance management tools cannot collect data on traffic flowing between Citrix and the old PCs, and this causes Benkei problems. Without these data, he never can form a full picture of the network. He always must infer missing data from other measures.

Benkei also manages a production server, its relational enterprise database, and business applications such as payroll, accounts/receivable, inventory, and ordering. On this server the traffic is constant and intense. It is not uncommon for more than 250 end-users to send requests concurrently from the accounts/receivable application alone. In managing this portion of the network, Benkei shares responsibility with different IT application specialists. They usually collaborate remotely.

Benkei works with two 24-inch monitors on his desk. These monitors display data and visuals from the numerous tools Benkei uses for monitoring, troubleshooting, and analysis. As is common in the systems-administration world, each tool monitors only a fragment of the ongoing transactions and available resources. Individually, none of these tools is more important than the others. For investigating end-users' slow responses from their applications, Benkei, like most IT specialists, particularly values the application performance-manager tool.

Problems and the Goal of Getting Relief Through Temporary Quick Fixes

When Benkei comes into the office today he finds the system in crisis because of a batch job that is running five hours behind schedule and has overlapped with the start of this workday. Compounding matters, early in the morning, unaware of the batch job, a user launched a major file transfer. Combined, the batch job and file transfer are hogging most of the system's resources, and every user is having response problems. Users are complaining that screen changes take seven minutes or longer. Benkei's beeper, set to go off every time an alarm fires, has been beeping so furiously that he has turned it off.

Benkei cannot abort the file transfer, but he can find places in the system to temporarily cancel other processes, such as end-users' print jobs, data processing requests, or warehouse scanners. If Benkei fixes some of these other problems, he might free the system enough for users to get at least their most important computing work done. The first thing Benkei needs is a good picture of what is going on with the file transfer and batch job combined. This perspective will help him gauge how bad things are and how much relief he has to provide. He can get the best overall picture from his UNIX tools, but, as luck would have it, he cannot open these tools. Before anything else, he has to free the system enough to get to them.

Thankfully, his database tools are functioning fine. Referring to them, he finds a large but inconsequential session and cancels it. In the bottom corner of his screen he glances at a 3D line graph of real-time performance measures that he always leaves displayed for ready access (3D makes it more noticeable). He sees that his action brought some relief. He worries a little, though, about the effect on Citrix users, which he cannot monitor directly. He writes a note and sticks it on his monitor to remind himself to check on Citrix clients as soon as he can. He tries his UNIX tools again and finally succeeds in opening three of them. He minimizes the database tool he just used. Benkei searches through the performance summary data to answer a number of questions: Is the production server saturated? He sees it is—100%. What else is going on in the network? Which servers are running? What is running on each server? What are users experiencing? Who has the highest central processing unit (CPU) utilization? He can envision what is going on in portions of the network and within individual components, but he has no tool that captures all the links.

Benkei gets a good enough picture and turns to creating some relief. He keeps defining problems, now with a new set of questions: What jobs are running that take long to process? When did they start and how much CPU usage have they accumulated? Are applications getting hung up somewhere in the LAN or WAN before they ever reach the database? He sees that network connectivity is fine and eliminates it as the source of the problem.

DETECTING PROBLEMS AND MAKING REPAIRS FOR IMMEDIATE RELIEF

Benkei identifies the longest, heaviest jobs and traces two of them to production reports issued on a regular basis. He wants to delay these reports until after the batch job ends. He closes all but one UNIX tool and intends to drill down for more details in another tool so he can infer the effects of delaying the reports. He could get these details from the UNIX tools, but he prefers to go to his enterprise manager tool because it details the same second-by-second performance measures more vividly through real-time graphics and tabular displays. Working with the summary data in UNIX and the details in the enterprise manager tool, Benkei continuously cross-references the two. He adds one more window to this workspace by recalling his minimized database manager screen. Combining perspectives from all three tools, he mentally estimates the effects that the two production reports are having on the system and projects what will happen if he postpones them for system relief. He sees that postponing them is the obvious answer and takes the necessary actions. Then he turns around to the whiteboard behind his desk and writes on his to-do list that he needs to create a script to restrict the work times for system-generated reports when certain thresholds are exceeded.

Encountering Unexpected Divergences While Trying to Analyze Alarms

Benkei checks the remedy in the real-time graph and sees positive results. Now he is ready to provide more relief by fixing the severe alarms. Leaving all the other windows open (four now in all, counting the always-open line graph), Benkei calls up the alarm screen of his application performance-manager tool. He sees that there have been no new alarms on this screen during the past 40 minutes, but this is not good news. Because the system is still congested, several alarms should be appearing on the screen every few seconds. Benkei grimaces, realizing he has more tool troubles. The batch job and file transfer must be blocking alarms from coming through. Unfortunately, nothing on the application performance manager screen alerts him that any alarm information is missing—neither what the information is, how much, nor where the missing alarms are occurring. As a result, Benkei will have to go to each system component log and examine the alarms accumulating for each one.

Before moving to the log of the first component, Benkei prepares for the fixes he anticipates making. These remedies will bring about minor improvements, so he needs a more nuanced reading from the real-time line graph to see the effects of his actions. He wants to change the unit of measurement on the x-axis from per-second counts to every half-second. He right-clicks on the x-axis of the graph, figuring that this keystroke will bring up a feature for changing axis measures. Nothing useful appears. He turns the graph from 3D to 2D and tries again, but he still gets nothing he wants. He swivels to his other monitor and calls up the CD-ROM help files. He scans the index until he locates what he wants and learns that he has to write a script for the changes he intends to make. Frustrated with having to spend more time on this modification than he wanted, he first minimizes unused windows to clear the clutter on his screen and then writes a script. It works, and Benkei begins his component-by-component look at current alarms.

Benkei starts by looking at alarms for the relational enterprise database, accessing them from the enterprise manager tool. He sorts the alarms by time and severity and moves this display so it is sitting directly next to the application performance-manager alarm window. By looking at both views together, he identifies when the application performance-manager stopped registering alarms. This estimate is imprecise because the two tools' timestamps are not in sync. Benkei marks the estimated time on a slip of paper and wishes he could verify it by replaying his real-time graph to validate whether a big spike occurred.

Analyzing Alarms and Carrying Out Another Detection and Quick Repair

Benkei now turns to the enterprise manager tool. He sorts the alarm table by alarm type, which is coded by a number and text description. The table displays well over 100 alarms, making it almost unusable for his needs. He cannot begin to find areas for relief until he filters out the unimportant alarms. When this filtering is finally completed, Benkei has a display of relevant alarms, and he sorts it once again, this time grouping them by severity and, nested within severity, by types. The alarms are also color-coded by severity, with red being the most severe, yellow moderate, and green just barely over the threshold.

He focuses on a severe deadlock alarm and drills down to get details on it by double-clicking on the alarm line in the table. It shows a pie chart of buffer-to-cache ratios that indicates a lock is happening, and it displays a real-time graph that climbs as more users enter the queue for the database. Neither graphic is interactive. The tool shows that many people are locked up, and it highlights the tables that are locked. As he moves through the data, Benkei prints screen shots. Later, when he is trying to correct the underlying cause, he will use these shots. This tool does not show which users and applications are experiencing the locks, but for now Benkei does not need this information. The tool satisfies Benkei's immediate goal of finding a quick remedy for relief. He has identified a severe problem and can correct it. In one last move before fixing the lock, he validates its severity by opening and checking data about it in his lock manager tool. Once validated, he makes the fix. He looks at his real-time graphic to assess the effects and sees some improvement.

Making a Preliminary Diagnosis and Then Moving on to More Detections

Before moving on to find more remedies, Benkei wants a quick assessment of why the lock occurred so he can later correct the problem at its source. He needs the names of the clients and applications involved in the locked threads. For this information, he has to look at historical data on events occurring before the alarm fired so he can determine what may have contributed to it. He can only access this information from his application performance-manager tool. Once again, he must juggle tools.

Alarms may not be registering right now in the application performance-manager tool, but it can display the historical and user data that Benkei needs. These data are processed differently from alarms. Unfortunately, the application performance-manager tool is fairly restrictive. As it now stands, it gives Benkei access to the data only through pre-defined reports. He picks a report most likely to cover the transactions relevant to this lock but, due to software constraints, he cannot filter the report information to see only the server and database of interest. He can, at least, select the time period of the problem. The tool returns a summary report of the slowest transactions throughout the network for the specified time period and identifies the applications and clients to which they belong. Because the report details only the top 50% of the worst transactions network-wide, Benkei is not sure if he is working with all the transactions relevant to his database problem. He shrugs, knowing it is the best he can do given the tools he has. He quickly scans the report to see if any company vice presidents have outrageously high times because IT gives highest priority to executives' services. None does.

Working now with the reports from the application performance-monitoring tool, Benkei continues by sorting and deleting rows of data for the servers and databases he does not need. From the streamlined report, Benkei selects different transactions and drills down to detailed table views. From the tables, Benkei sees how long a transaction spent in the network, how long it spent in the server, the number of rows returned from a query right before multiple locks occurred, and the type of transaction statements. By default, the data are color-coded by the amount of time a transaction spends in the server. The color-coding progresses through the spectrum. Lowest transaction times are in blue and as the amount of time increases the spectrum progresses through green, yellow, orange, and peaks with red, which indicates the highest transaction times. As Benkei looks at this display, something grates on him. If he remembers correctly, a transaction that appears here in red was not coded red for severity in his other tool. He checks by reopening that other tool—the enterprise manager alarm screen—and sees that he is right. But he has no time now to look into this issue further. It would involve figuring out the binning algorithm for each of the color schemes, and this information is not readily available in either tool. He prints shots of the contradictory screens for later reference, makes notes on the black and white printouts indicating how the data are colored, and continues.

Benkei correlates response times to the number of rows returned for each transaction and compares differences between transactions. Working with large amounts of tabular data, Benkei spends a long time on these analyses. Results confirm what he already suspects. Because network times are relatively low and server times are high, the network is not the problem.

Now Benkei focuses on relating query statements (application code) to server response times, and he finds some very questionable statements. Again, he prints screen shots for later reference and grows confident that he is homing in on the cause. He sees many offending statements, such as updates that typically run into locks, and from various statements he infers what users are doing. He drills down to specific users and sees what other applications and transactions they are running. At this point, he needs to view the data with the query statements as the focal point, not the transactions. Unfortunately, this tool does not allow him to rearrange data in these ways. Therefore, he resorts to pencil and paper. He copies, arranges, and analyzes relationships between problem statements, records the users who issued them, and writes down other statements these users ran before them.

Getting Interrupted in the Midst of a Detailed Analysis and Then Resuming

As he is doing this analysis, a fellow DBA steps into his office to ask Benkei about an unrelated issue, and the two talk for about five minutes. After his co-worker leaves, Benkei returns to his troubleshooting, but he has momentarily lost his place. He retraces his steps and familiarizes himself once more with the transaction-centric screen display and relates it to his statement-centric pencil-and-paper analysis. It does not take him long to get back into his stream of thought. At this point, he needs to see details of statement coding, so he brings up another tool, namely one of the enterprise manager tools he has not yet used today. He runs query statements and gets feedback on their execution plans and database tracing statistics. As he runs these simulations, he also prints screen shots of important findings and insights.

This analysis leads Benkei to single out the statement causing the heavily threaded lock and the client issuing the transaction. However, even after this exploration, he is not sure why this statement is bad. He has examined it as far as his expertise with indices, fragmentation, and the like can take him, but to no avail. He will forward the problem to the application specialist. Together, they will work on it later. Benkei assembles the various screen shots he has printed, organizes them for this later analysis, and jots comments on them to ensure that he will not forget their context and his current thoughts. He also writes himself a reminder for this later analysis to look into the history of this query statement over the past week: How many times it was executed, who executed it, and with what effects. Benkei then shrinks the windows of the tools he is using.

Benkei is almost ready to return to the task of creating additional relief in what is fast becoming a full-morning effort. First, however, he goes to his administrative tools to readjust the alarm thresholds. This readjustment is a common IT strategy that he uses to prompt the system to alert him automatically when the file transfer is almost done. This way, he will know when it is safe to return stopgap remedies to normal. Once the system is out of crisis, he also will set the alarm thresholds back to normal.

Detecting and Repairing More Problems

Returning now to troubleshooting, Benkei spends the rest of his morning looking at alarm logs in the database, the database server, the Citrix server, and, when the system finally unfreezes enough, on the alarm screen of the application performance-manager tool. His investigations into each trouble spot follow the same pattern. Benkei finds a fixable problem, validates it, implements a fix, verifies its effects, and looks for the cause to guide him later when he has time to make more lasting repairs. He works through interruptions and surprises, and later in the morning he brings in another DBA for help. His desk increasingly is strewn with notes, and his whiteboard to-do list is growing. He continuously loads his short-term memory with a running tally of things to check on, such as effects on Citrix users, and actions to take, such as setting threshold adjustments back to normal. His screen workspace is cluttered with open windows and his desk with printed screen shots and yellow sticky notes. In isolation, these windows and notes provide only partial information, and in combination they have no cues to help him remember how they relate to one another and for what purposes.

Summary of the Complexities of Benkei's Problem Solving

Benkei's troubleshooting and analysis of faults embody a number of complex problem solving traits and themes. These include the following:

- **Domain-specific patterns of inquiry:** Benkei frames his process of elimination around domain-specific questions and patterns of inquiry to detect aberrations, define problems, explore possible causes, and execute quick repairs. By examining certain correlations for example, he knows whether he can eliminate network connectivity as the problem.

- **Mainline and enabling tasks:** He interweaves mainline actions, such as calling up summary data in UNIX and details in the enterprise manager tool, with enabling tasks, such as creating mental estimates and writing reminders to himself based on what the data show.

- **Task synergy:** Combined tasks lead to unforeseen actions and insights that are greater than their separate contributions. When Benkei finds that alarms stopped registering on the application-monitoring tool, he has to alternately and unexpectedly analyze alarmed troubles by taking a combined look at component logs and the enterprise manager tool. From these combined tasks, he learns more about the historical progress of the system problems than he expects or would have had he pursued his original intentions.

- **Analytical power, data integration, and synchronization:** To get an accurate and complete picture of what is going on in the system, Benkei needs to cross-reference and analytically interpret data across tools, at times in different formats (tabular and graphic). Regularly, he works with two, three, or more windows of data at once to define and locate problems and validate his hunches. Moreover, to judge severity, he has to interact with color-coding displayed by different tools that, at times, are not in sync with each other.

- **Optimal user control and adaptability:** When Benkei makes a brief diagnosis of the deadlock problem, he wants to retrieve only the data of interest from the application performance-manager tool. Yet the tool gives him access solely to data contained in pre-defined reports. In another instance, he needs to rearrange data to highlight query statements, and he cannot. He has to go offline to conduct the analysis properly.

- *Ad hoc* **data transformations:** Benkei anticipates his future moves and recalibrates the alarms accordingly. But when he does, he has to change data measurements in the process, both real-time spans and alarm thresholds. The former turns out to require scripting (which Benkei does grudgingly).

- **Multitasking and interruptions, collaborations, and screen captures and reminders:** Benkei conducts his diagnosis of the deadlock problem with the application specialist in mind. He interprets, captures screen shots, and writes reminders for himself *and* for his applications colleague at once. He also fixes tools at the same time as detecting and repairing problems.

- **Reliance on structural signposts and situational cues:** Structurally, Benkei repeats the same patterns and subpatterns, which are detecting, validating, quick fixing, and minimally diagnosing problems. He also regularly calls up certain tools together for specific purposes. Benkei would like to move seamlessly through these structures, having tools give him, for instance, a system for managing windows of regularly joined tools to avoid window clutter.

For this complex inquiry, Benkei cannot conduct his work without multiple monitoring and problem solving tools, but these tools often contribute to investigative uncertainties. Therefore, problem solvers such as Benkei are always eager for better software. They especially value tools that can give them expanded perspectives on system traffic and performance and enhance their abilities to access, prepare, integrate, arrange, and analyze diverse, multidimensional data often scaled differently in detail and time. They also value any advances that remind them about what they have done, what they know, and where they are heading.

For troubleshooting and analyzing poor response times in business-critical applications, one of the most important tools is application performance-manager software. This software dates back to about 1996. It is the best tool for seeing and analyzing the infrastructure as users experience it. As we now turn to the work of the design team, we find that it is this tool that team members seek to improve. They hope to improve it, in part, by building in interactive data visualizations.

DESIGN TEAM SCENARIO: ANALYZING AND MODELING CONTEXTUAL DATA

The design team works in a company that has been researching and designing interactive data visualizations for more than a decade. The development group in this visualization company has many teams. It has a core development team made up of visualization experts who create interactive visualizations as Active-X components. These include interactive bar graphs, line graphs, histograms, pie charts, scatterplots, coordinate boxplots, time series, network graphs, and data tables. Application teams in the same development group take these core graphs, build platforms to house them, and provide domain-specific features to create commercial products. The VizAppManager is one of several such commercial projects. Its team is working with a product group from another company that develops the network monitoring engine and repository for data on infrastructure performance. The visualizations will hook into this repository and display data from its various tables in interactive graphics.

Why Application Manager Software and Why Data Visualizations

The visualization software company has decided to implement its interactive graphics in commercial applications for managing the network performance of business applications. This type of software gathers huge amounts of data on system performance, traffic, resource use, and availability by means of "sniffers" placed throughout a network. It collects these data in a vast repository, summarizes them, calculates values, such as percent of transactions exceeding threshold values, and provides technical specialists with data details and summaries. Application performance-monitoring tools provide vital end-user and application views of the world. No other monitoring program enables IT problem solvers to see the integrated connection between end-users, applications, databases, query statement coding, and traits of a problem. No other tool relates collected traffic and performance data to alarm thresholds. As we saw, Benkei needs this tool and uses it as much as his troubled system allows.

The visualization company's market research shows that IT customers are primed for a new application performance-monitoring product that can improve upon current versions in the marketplace. As Benkei's experiences show, current versions often are structured by pre-defined reports, which do not give users enough flexibility in their analysis or enough access to all the data that may be relevant. Ideally, IT specialists want to work with as much information as they see fit based on their purposes and contexts.

The design team for VizAppManager is a sub-group of the larger VizAppManager development team. This smaller group includes a project manager, interaction designer, usability specialist, product manager, and documentation developer. It also includes a system engineer, a software architect, and a programmer. All of the technical members of the team have extensive experience creating interactive visualizations. This team is confident that the VizAppManager tool will give users a workspace expansive enough to handle large amounts of data interactively, a great improvement over static reports and charts.

The VizAppManager design team has at its fingertips numerous interactive graphics, which it intends to combine into a troubleshooting tool. Linked interactive graphics mean that when users conduct an operation on one graphic, such as selecting data or color-coding, all the other displayed graphs automatically update as well. In this way, users can see different views of the same data and change each simultaneously.

As IT analysts troubleshoot with data visualizations, the analysts will be able to interact directly with the graphically displayed data by dragging, clicking on, or sweeping across them to arrange, select, delete, or hide the information. Also, users will be able to zoom in and out, pan, rotate, and bring details into focus. Through interactive color-coding, IT troubleshooters will have the ability to bring in and analyze more dimensions than those charted in a graph. They will have power to do other query-related interactions too—though not always easily—including accessing and filtering data from a variety of sources such as flat files or relational databases, drilling down into details and rolling up to aggregates, navigating through and across graphics, calculating data, creating new views from scratch, and capturing graphic displays. All of these capabilities turn the graphics themselves into a workspace for users to explore and manipulate freely. Unlike static graphics, problem solvers interpret meanings from visually displayed data and dig right into the visualization to find out more in many possible directions.

Outcomes from Gathering Data on Users and Tasks

At the start of the VizAppManager project, the team sets a focus for its analysis of users and tasks and conducts contextual inquiries. A field team observes and interviews 20 IT specialists in four different settings, each with a different infrastructure configuration. The team's focus is narrow, namely IT specialists' logical processes for analyzing data to solve problems. As a result, during contextual inquiry, field team members concentrate largely on discovering the questions that drive troubleshooting for different fault situations. They also focus on the information and relationships that IT troubleshooters examine, the methods they use for analysis, their choices and interpretations, and the basis for these choices and interpretations. The field team looks, as well, at IT specialists' uses of current tools and methods for determining and implementing solutions.

Guided by the team's inquiry focus, the field group finds some important conditions that shape IT problem solving in the technology and data, work domain, problem, and subjective contexts. However, the inquiry focus is narrow; and team members do not realize until later, after prototype testing, that these findings omit many important issues that do not fall neatly within the bounds of users' logical reasoning. As we will see, the VizApp Manager team pays too little attention to some critical tasks and contexts that affect IT analysts' practical patterns of troubleshooting.

Findings from the contextual inquiries do show that IT users' current tools for managing application performance (without visualizations) do not sufficiently support them for three main analytical needs. These inadequacies , which we saw Benkei's experience, as well, include the following:

- The current tabular forms make it difficult to arrange data for analysis, especially because they do not dynamically link to relevant graphic displays.

- Current tools do not facilitate drilling down, rolling up, and staying oriented in large volumes of data within and across tools.

- Current discrete data views make it mentally taxing for users to see and interpret data from multiple perspectives and difficult to keep window clutter to a minimum.

The design team believes that interactive visualizations will address all of these needs effectively.

Analyzing and Consolidating Data: What Do Tier-Two Troubleshooters Do?

After conducting its contextual inquiries, the team categorizes and profiles IT specialists and analyzes their activities into task hierarchies and interdependencies. The design team strives to be user-centered, and they follow many contextual inquiry and design practices. But their overarching concern in user-centered data analysis is to figure out what the visualizations can do for users, not what users have to be able to do with visualizations for complete and coherent inquiries.

As the team's data-gathering reveals, its unit of analysis (though never formally set) is the troubleshooters' analytical questions, the data relevant to these questions, and the tasks involved in working with the data to answer the questions. The unit of analysis is not the problem situation. As is common in many software projects, the team's user-centeredness is heavily slanted toward data and information processing. As we will see in the rest of the story, this bias frames team members' data gathering, analysis, work modeling, and design strategies and choices.

The team's data analysis focuses on consolidating findings in relation to the following questions about problems, tasks and data, workflows, users, and artifacts.

- What fault-management problems do users have and how complex are they?

- What analytical perspectives, questions, and data guide users' problem solving?

- What organizational structures and workflows shape users' inquiry roles and activities?

- What high-level patterns of inquiry characterize users' task sequences?

- What knowledge and reasoning do users bring to their problem solving?

- What artifacts do IT specialists use in their investigations?

What Fault-Management Problems Do Users Have and How Complex Are They?

The design team finds that the same prototypical problems plague IT specialists across organizations. The team lists these problem types on a new section of the whiteboard, as shown in Table 4.1.

TABLE 4.1
Tasks within the scope of the VizAppManager.

- **Troubleshooting poor performance, availability of resources, overload, and congestion**

  Performed in reaction to some alert (e.g., user complaint, trouble ticket, alarm going off)

- **Assuring acceptable performance, availability, and capacity before problems arise**

  Conducted to detect and prevent deteriorating conditions

- **Managing unexpected consequences of new deployments**

  Carried out in anticipation of problems by monitoring, analyzing, and troubleshooting new factors in the system—a re-engineered network, new system hardware, newly deployed applications, or software updates. Probably the situation with the highest incidence of system problems

Positively, the team limits the scope of its tool to solving just these problems. Findings from contextual interviews show that technical specialists also manage and prevent faults for reliability purposes. For example, they tune applications and other components (performed to improve system components and software code), and they determine health-of-the-system metrics (conducted to identify baseline measures for alarm thresholds). But these situations are handled by a different group of specialists, not those in charge of assuring functionality. Because reliability specialists are not the VizAppManager team's targeted users, design team members decide that support for tuning, optimizing, and other reliability activities are outside the scope of the program.

The design team characterizes the conditions of the fault-management problems that tier-two and tier-three analysts confront as follows:

- Systems and networks have highly sophisticated functions, structural relations, and multilayered architectures that users cannot adequately represent to themselves in any one model.

- Real-time systems are in perpetual flux due to human interactions and internal dependencies.

- Relevant data are dispersed across numerous sources and tools.

- A vast number of data elements are required for investigations.

- Continuously changing workplace situations influence users' interpretations of overall performance.

- Infrastructure problems ultimately have solutions that are not provisional. "Good enough" is not acceptable; in some cases goals are clear, and problems, once effectively formulated (not always an easy task), have fairly well-structured solutions.

Notably, as this list shows, design team members frame these traits of complexity as *system conditions, information elements,* and *data demands.* They do not phrase them in ways that put the focus on users' *experiences.* Subtly, this verbal presentation lends itself to a ready breakdown into task and graphic objects.

The traits the team identifies are common across situations and work sites. Degrees of complexity, however, vary from one troubleshooting situation to the next. Sometimes, IT analysts encounter common or familiar problems, and through experience, they have assimilated standard methods and fixes for investigating and repairing them.

In other cases, however, entangled infrastructure conditions or unapparent chain reactions confound analysts. Problems elude a clear definition and are difficult to trace to a source. One example is an intermittent slowdown with no obvious cause, and another is Benkei's entangled faults. The VizAppManager team realizes that its single application-monitoring tool must support all these degrees of complexity.

From contextual inquiry findings, the team estimates that roughly 80% of tier-two and tier-three troubleshooting involves common problems. The other 20% are abnormal, often intermittent, and may take days or weeks to solve. As we see later, because of this distribution, the team devotes most of its efforts to creating support for the 80%. Unfortunately, team members fail to realize that a good deal of complexity still resides in solving these familiar problems, and this complexity is shared by the other 20%, as well.

What Analytical Perspectives, Questions, and Data Guide Users' Problem Solving?

The team's observations and interviews reveal that for these problems, IT troubleshooters across industries and intranet systems take the same points of view to investigate conditions and generate fixes. In the simplest three-tiered architectures, IT problem solvers attend to one of four elements to enter into problem solving, often shifting between perspectives as they proceed. They begin by looking either at the performance of user workstations, applications, databases, or an overall view.

These entry points launch IT analysts on their problem solving, which, across the board, follows a process of elimination. Tier-two and tier-three analysts first interrogate one area thoroughly to confirm that it is *not* the source of a problem, then move to disqualify the next potential source and so on until they find the culprit. Ultimately, by exploring each vantage point—users, applications, databases, and overall—they relate performance data and data relationships; for each type of data, they examine snapshots of real-time occurrences, historic data, and trends over time. They also examine details, aggregates, and such derived values as the number and percent of transactions exceeding thresholds.

To model users' work and create a conceptual design, the VizAppManager team writes a description of IT troubleshooters' inquiries into each vantage point on the whiteboard, which is partially captured in Figure 4.2. A fuller set of questions is presented later in this chapter in the Design Team Story: Conceptualizing Design (p. 131).

What Organizational Structures and Workflows Shape Users' Inquiry Roles and Activities?

In addition to the questions IT troubleshooters pose to each element of the system, the design team describes users' workplace structures

FIGURE 4.2
IT analytical perspectives, questions, and data for troubleshooting.

User Workstation View of the World	Application View of the World
Is a user experiencing poor performance? What is going on at his or her desktop?	Is an application functioning? How well is it performing? Are its transactions coded properly? What other applications is it running into?
<u>Relevant data:</u> Applications open, processes running on the user's workstation	<u>Relevant data:</u> Contentions between applications for the same resources
Configuration of the desktop and other workstation information—e.g., memory, CPU type and usage, IP address, I/O usage	Statements executed by a user and code
Other users using the same application and their workstation experiences	Server performance—# and size of packets sent and received, # of processes running, response times in, through, and out
History of trouble tickets and currently open trouble tickets	Server configuration
	Network latency (time from tier-to-tier)

Database View of the World	Overall/Integrated View of the World
Is a database performing up to speed? Are deteriorating conditions causing problems?	What is going on with a transaction throughout the network, end to end?
<u>Relevant data:</u> User response time and processes running at the workstation	<u>Relevant data:</u> Length of time a process runs on a PC
Database performance measures	Network route that a transaction takes
Uses of indices, amount of data in tables, fragmentation, locks	Network utilization during the time of a problem
Bytes per second (time to move data)	Length of time a transaction spends at each server
Network latency (time from tier-to-tier)	Availability of resources, success of connections

and workflows. Responsibilities for overseeing the technical infrastructure are distributed across many organizational departments. Two large divisions are networking and systems. The networking group is responsible for the backbone of the infrastructure, including LANs, WANs, routers, and other hardware. The systems division—a group of database administrators, application specialists, UNIX specialists, and help-desk support—oversees critical systems, applications, and servers. These departments and divisions of authority vary widely across companies. In each of the groups, people have specialties. For example, tier-two and tier-three analysts are separate from less specialized technical support staff.

These structural divisions affect the flow of work. Typically, tier-two specialists get pulled into troubleshooting and fault management through several means: An escalated request to the help desk, a set of intertwined alarms that signal trouble in the specialists' areas of expertise, a call from high-ranking end-users in the organization, a directive from the head of IT, or findings from their own reviews of system performance reports. If a trouble ticket exists on a problem that tier-two specialists tackle, they claim the ticket, and from then on are accountable until they either solve the problem or hand it off to another specialist.

IT specialists commonly work alone on familiar problems. They may bring in collaborators mid-stream if evolving situations trigger the need for another pair of expert eyes, or they may hand a problem off if it proves to be outside their specialization. For intermittent problems and other highly complex investigations, IT specialists are more likely to collaborate from the start. During these collaborations, tier-two analysts often branch out to other IT groups, asking a group, for example, about its interventions in the system. IT troubleshooters also keep in touch with select end-users affected by the system problems.

The VizAppManager team targets only database administrators and application specialists as its primary users. Design team members combine their descriptions of questions and information that DBAs and application specialists, respectively, need based on their points of view of the infrastructure.

What High-level Patterns of Inquiry Characterize Users' Task Sequences?

In consolidating observations about IT troubleshooters' approaches to fixing problems, team members draw on the ways IT specialists themselves name their patterns of investigation, categorizing them as detection, diagnosis, and repair. For each of these three patterns, team members describe a high-level consolidated task sequence. These task models capture mainline tasks but few enabling tasks (Figure 4.3).

Detection starts with IT specialists becoming alerted to conditions of concern. They then formulate the problem. For many problems, this chunk of inquiry—especially activities dedicated to bounding and formulating the real problem—takes the most time and effort.

Subpattern: Getting alerted

Context and goal: Problem solvers want to discover potential problems before they occur or early enough to avert disaster.

Example: A manager in the financial department sees from daily reports on Accounts Receivable that an order payment is one of the top 10 worst performers. She calls IT to get it under control.

Tasks
- Field alerts from diverse sources.
- Sort, filter, and prioritize alerts.

Subpattern: Validating an alert

Context and goal: Problem solvers check that an alert is truly a concern and begin to typify it.

Example: After a call about a problem transaction, IT specialists check that it is not a false alarm.

Tasks
- Eliminate one-by-one all sources of a false alarm (network problems, instrumentation, thresholds).
- Refer to reports and consult with end-users, as needed.

Detection (continued)

Subpattern: Bounding and formulating a problem

Context and goal: Problem solvers describe a problem by locating its source and gauging its severity and complexity, usually taking a breadth-first approach.

Example: IT specialists trace events in a slice of time and over time and compare troublesome and trouble-free components to bound the problem's duration, affected users, magnitude, and traits.

Tasks
- Decide on an entry point—the best views of the infrastructure of the situation.
- Survey different views: Snapshot, over time, good versus bad processes, parts to whole.
- Locate the problem based on surveying and analyzing views of the infrastructure.

FIGURE 4.3
IT detection, diagnosis, and repair patterns.

In *diagnosis,* IT specialists search for the root causes of a problem. IT analysts often combine diagnosis and prognosis but refer to it singularly as diagnosis. Their approaches to diagnosis characteristically follow a process of elimination, which is often referred to as "pruning the search tree." After having conducted their "breadth-first" survey, IT analysts systematically look at various parts of the system. They usually move from the top down through each part of the network. They find problems and project the consequences of possible fixes. In a prognosis, they often anticipate and evaluate the implications of repairs by running what-if scenarios. To make a diagnosis and prognosis concurrently is intellectually challenging. It requires IT specialists to hold together two different modes of reasoning at once: Reactive and proactive. In diagnosis, they react to system conditions locally and globally and deduce and induce causes. In prognosis, by contrast, they anticipate system states by speculating about what may evolve if they do or do not make certain repairs. The two types of analysis are unified, and prognosis often sheds further light on the cause of a disturbance.

Diagnosis

Subpattern: Isolating a Problem/Generating and Testing Hunches

Context and goal: Problem solvers want to understand contributing factors and dynamics and narrow in on a cause and explanation for a problem.

Example: For a problem transaction, a DBA knows from earlier detection work that something is going wrong in the database but is not sure if the cause is the database, the server, or the code of the statement making requests of the database. He finally isolates the problem to the code and calls in the application specialist. Together but remotely they run tests until they find the bad code.

Diagnosis (continued)

Tasks
- Drill down into possible causes focusing on: Deviations from normal behaviors; familiar symptoms, matching them to common associated problems (e.g. if X is occurring, look at Y); event in time preceding the start of the trouble that could have led to it.
- Relate findings from different parts to infer interactive factors contributing to the problem.
- Generate hypotheses, run simulated scenarios, and project implications.
- Run diagnostic tests to verify hunches.
- Collaborate with co-workers including specialists from other areas; get them up to speed on an ongoing analysis as needed.

FIGURE 4.3 Continued

In *repair*, IT analysts identify an appropriate solution: A quick fix as well as a long-term correction to root causes. They choose the best resolution, implement it, and confirm that it works, often by seeing if it passes diagnostic tests. If it fails, technical specialists return to detection and diagnosis.

Repair

Subpattern: Identifying a Fix or Correction

Context and goal: Problem solvers want to select the best fix.

Example: A telecommunications technician traces a problem to a specific port and circuit card.

Tasks
- Infer the right remedy for a given diagnosis and prognosis.
- Run simulated scenarios to evaluate if the fix will work.
- When several options are possible, compare simulated scenarios.

Subpattern: Implementing and Confirming a Fix

Context and goal: Problem solvers want to follow procedures for fixing a problem and evaluate if they have resolved it as expected.

Repair (continued)

Example: The IT specialist replaces a faulty card, and sees from a diagnostic test that the card is still failing. Another test show that the unit does not even "see" the card. She speculates that the cable is the problem and begins diagnosis anew.

Tasks
- Take appropriate steps to remove or otherwise repair faulty components, processes, or code.
- Select and run diagnostics to confirm if an implementation results in positive outcomes.
- As a diagnostic runs, read and interpret real-time log results.
- If a diagnostic fails, access/interpret test results to determine why.
- Run repeated tests when necessary.
- Create backups and other recovery measures.

FIGURE 4.3 Continued

What Knowledge and Reasoning Do Users Bring to Their Tasks?

For these patterns of inquiry, IT specialists bring to bear their expert domain knowledge. Results the VizAppManager team brings back from the field show that, procedurally, IT analysts know the steps for recognizing and controlling recurrent disturbances, for exploring unfamiliar ones, for maintaining their systems, and for monitoring performance against a baseline. When they deal with fairly standard system problems—those that signal well-structured means for analysis and resolution—they apply their expert knowledge as rule- and skill-based methods, diagnostic tests, and a recognition of network performance patterns. When problems grow wicked, IT specialists rely on knowledge- and judgment-based methods.

Conceptually, IT specialists' knowledge includes well-developed mental models of the structures and functions of the system. They use structural models of the system to detect errors, isolate relevant subsystems, and find and implement fixes. They call forth functional models when they hypothesize causes, plan investigations, and make projections during prognosis. Based on these models, they know how parts of the system combine to produce various ends, including side effects of these combinations and different configurations that bring about the same result.

The visualization team realizes that neither structural nor functional mental models alone can capture everything about a system that problem solvers need to know. Problems rarely relate to a single cause but rather to interactions among components. Technical specialists need many representations of part-to-whole relationships and causality at different levels of abstraction. The design team aims to use multiple graphic perspectives for such representations.

The team identifies users' expert reasoning, as well. As with expert problem solvers in any domain, IT specialists know what to look for, how to manage cognitive demands, how to define problems by constructing subproblems, and how to shift from one level of detail to another as needed (Agre, 1997; Salomon and Perkins, 1989).

They also have a good deal of domain-specific advanced reasoning, which allows them to catch early malfunctions before breakdowns occur. IT experts reason about system interactions by relating huge amounts of disparate data. They typically draw meanings from data gleaned from numerous tools at once. They heuristically relate certain variables to disqualify one component after another as the source of a problem. They set thresholds to test certain hypotheses. In addition, when data are missing, IT experts know which relationships to examine to draw inferences.

Finally, IT specialists are well versed in organizational knowledge. They know enough about their workmates' specialties to collaborate productively, and they know the channels of communication to follow, the hierarchies for escalating problems, and the priorities in their service obligations.

What Artifacts Do IT Specialists Use in Their Investigations?

The design team describes the printouts, notes, and customized screen displays that aid IT problem solvers in wayfinding, sensemaking, and data ordeals. Troubleshooters often run printouts at the start of their day for updates on system conditions. They read notes left by others, and they frequently print screen shots of real-time performance against a baseline and later compare these shots to a current state. They print findings and share them with co-workers. Moreover, they make notes and to-do items to remind themselves, for example, to check certain variables that they do not typically monitor.

As an alternative to written reminders, some technical specialists customize displays in their monitoring and problem solving tools. Specialists are far more likely to customize if the tools are easy to adapt to their local needs. If not, IT specialists—despite being technically astute—usually write notes instead.

Finally, IT specialists consult an array of tools for examining response times. Technical specialists often leave as many as 15 tools active on their desktops to view the health and responsiveness of a system from multiple vantage points. For any one inquiry, IT problem solvers may display windows for five or six tools. These tools include, but are not limited to, an enterprise manager, application-performance manager, real-time traffic monitor, UNIX tools, and reporting tools.

Modeling Users' Work

After analyzing these contextually based aspects of users' work, the design team creates user profiles and consolidated models of task sequences, artifacts, and workflows. They follow templates suggested by leading proponents of contextual inquiry (Beyer and Holtzblatt, 1998). When finished, the team is ready to create a conceptual design. Its user experience findings and various models of work frame its approach to designing the VizAppManager tool.

What Is Missing for Usefulness in the Team's Analysis and Modeling?

Despite the design team's intention to concentrate on users and situated work, it leaves unfilled many of the gaps in analyzing data and modeling users' work that commonly keep many teams from designing for usefulness.

Some of the most important approaches that they leave out are listed in the "What is missing" on this page (Vincent, 2001).

Because the design team members do not implement these approaches, they move to the next phase of conceptualizing design with little to stop them from misjudging users' work and the support needed for complexity.

DESIGN TEAM STORY: CONCEPTUALIZING DESIGN

Right before VizAppManager design team members are ready to move from their user and work models to conceptual designing, the sales and marketing groups prevail on them to create a demo for potential customers with big accounts. Taking a quick divergence, a few design teammates work with developers from the larger VizAppManager team to create it. The demo has two screens. Each displays three to four pre-scripted interactive graphics arranged in different panes of the window, what this visualization software company calls a "perspective." Each perspective answers several interrelated questions, such as "Who are the heaviest users? What are the most heavily used applications? Which heavy users have slow response times, and why?" (The later prototype perspectives are similar. See Figure 4.4A).

The demo is a tremendous success. Prospective customers are delighted that they can visually query data in half the time it takes in current application performance-manager programs. They call the demo "revolutionary" and heartily endorse it. With such acclaims, the design team enthusiastically turns to transforming the demo into a conceptual design for a commercial product.

Matching Users' Tasks to Interactive Data Visualizations

Prospective customers' wholehearted approval of the demo motivates design team members to apply the same assumptions and approaches to creating the product. This orientation involves designing for answers to distinct questions. What goes unnoticed by teammates is that because they use a demo design—not intended for practical use—to direct them in conceptually designing the actual tool, they tacitly relegate support for improvisation, *ad hoc* analysis, and emergent methods to the background. They mistakenly assume that for familiar problems, troubleshooters do not experience these aspects of open-endedness but instead follow standard questioning that can be answered by rule-based procedures.

The team selects IT users' core questions in troubleshooting and analysis and composes perspectives for them. They make sure the graphics in each perspective present overviews and details. They color-code for what they believe are the important questions each perspective addresses.

In composing graphic perspectives for IT problem solving, team members use their visualization expertise to brainstorm appropriate graphics. They logically fit data types relevant to specific questions to the representational strengths of particular graphics. For example, they use bar charts to display distributions of categorical data ("What are the total or average response times for each application?"). They use time-series graphs to investigate alarms and patterns ("Is response time high for this server every day between 3:00 and 5:00 PM?"); and they display network graphs to depict connections between users, applications, and servers ("How many applications is this user running on her desktop?").

Team members are pleased with how readily graphic displays map onto users' questions and performance data. This emphasis on mapping graphics to discrete questions and data focuses on only a narrow set of contextual influences. The team concentrates solely on conditions in problem solvers' technological and subjective contexts, namely on the data of interest, the setup of IT infrastructures, and users' generic cognitive processes, both analytical and perceptual. Team members pay little heed to the triggers that lead IT users down different paths of investigation and decision-making. Nor do they acknowledge the open-endedness of problems and the control IT specialists need. Regarding conditions in the workplace, they create no deliberate support for collaborations, interruptions, and meanings in relation to stakeholders' demands.

In the design team's defense, even if teammates had emphasized these conditions, support would be hard to build. The interactive visualizations lack some of the functionality and adaptability necessary to support many of these variable contextual conditions and constraints. To put a high priority on getting such capabilities built quickly by the core development team would require a great deal of organizational politicking and support at the executive-leadership level.

One more piece remains for the team in mapping users' tasks to the screen design. The data visualizations reside in a "container" (platform) that, through menus, toolbars, and the like, provides functionality such as color-coding, saving, sorting, opening and closing views, and getting help. Teammates agree to use standard Microsoft Windows conventions in designing this platform. They presume that the interactive visualizations will give users plenty of novelty to get used to so that, for the platform, standard user interface (UI) objects and controls are best.

Acquiring Richer Data and Designing More Visualization Possibilities

So far, in graphic perspectives, the VizAppManager team has limited its choices to the visualization views that can be created from the available data. The partner company's data repository constrains what these data are. When the team reviews its initial design concepts, it worries that the visualizations do not adequately support users' questions. Therefore, it decides to overcome data constraints by restructuring the repository. A couple of the design team members work for days on this task and, thanks to their exceptional skills, the VizAppManager team now has a much richer source of data with which to work.

Immediately, team members begin to conceptualize new visualization designs. Certain individuals campaign for distinct graphics and screen layouts. Some push their own pet graphics. Others, especially the programmer and architect, who restructured the repository tables, want graphic displays to show as much data as possible at once so IT users see all the information they now have available for visual querying. These personal biases and associated graphic experiments increasingly propel the team toward the latest-and-greatest designing at each daily meeting. After a week and a half, the usability specialist, systems engineer, and interaction designer raise a red flag.

The team, they warn, is becoming too data-driven. First, it is losing track of the central objective of the application performance-manager tool, namely to show system performance and traffic from an end-user's point of view. The team has experimented with designs for dozens of perspectives but in the process has neglected to compose one that represents this end-user view as an entry into IT analysts' troubleshooting. Second, the team now is designing perspectives and individual graphics that are not based on what IT users *need* to have represented. After these warnings, the team reviews its design goals, IT users' problem solving questions, and analytical actions. Teammates pare down their efforts to the basics of users' inquiries, as represented in findings from contextual inquiry. The team proceeds to finalize six pre-scripted, pre-color-coded perspectives, each consisting of a multiple-pane window filled with four to six graphs. In addition, each perspective presents both an overview and details. The first four perspectives provide a snapshot of performance, drawing attention to an end-user point of view. The remaining two perspectives show trends over time.

Each perspective is structured to answer a specific set of questions. The team confirms the validity of these questions and perspectives with IT specialists. The specialists uphold that, taken together, the six sets of questions strike at the heart of troubleshooting, root cause analysis, and fault prevention. The questions for each perspective include the following:

Entry point   What alarms have fired against what machines, applications, and servers?

2.   Which end-user machines show poor performance and how are the applications and servers behaving that are connected to them? (see Figure 4.4A)

3.   What correlations between conditions explain performance (e.g., response times in relation to number of rows in a transaction or number of requests issued by a machine)?

4.   What are other machines, applications, and servers doing while this problem is occurring?

5.   What machines, applications, and servers have been experiencing high response time for a long time (See Figure 4.4B)?

6.   For intermittent alarms, what patterns have occurred over time for as long as data are available for all types of alarms (i.e., do certain alarms recur at the same time for specific machines or are certain alarms universal problems)?

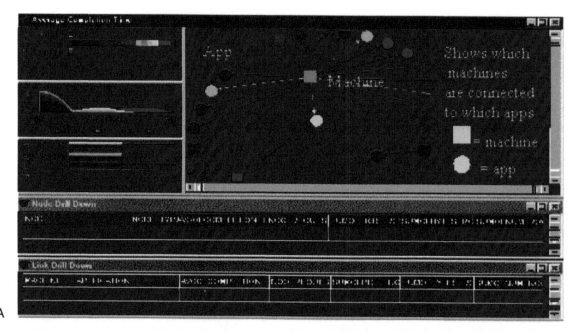

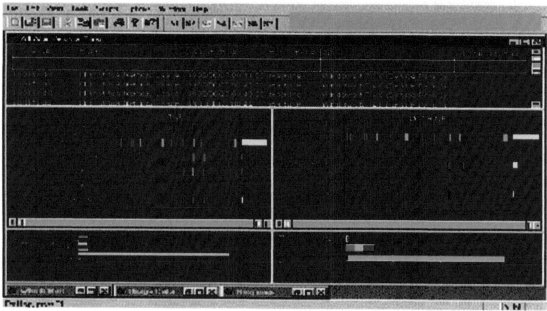

FIGURE 4.4

Sample screen shots from the VizAppManager prototype.

(A) Prototype view to answer the questions of which end-user machines show poor performance and how the applications and servers connected to them are behaving. End-user PCs are squares and are linked to the applications running on them, which are circles. Color-coding indicates response time. Red circles, squares, and links are performing most poorly.

(B) Prototype view to answer the question of what machines, applications, and servers have been experiencing high response time for a long time. The two top graphs show usage over time (the x axis is hours of day and each "tick" is a use). Color-coding reflects response time, with red showing the highest response time.

Finally Getting Around to Unstructured Aspects of Complex Problem Solving

Not until after all this discussion and mocking up of perspectives is completed does the VizAppManager team turn its attention to the vexing 20% of troubleshooting problems with uncharted and unpredictable approaches. The team decides that for this minority of inquiries, the program should offer IT users access to the somewhat obscure mechanisms the core team has built into the graphics for original equipment manufacturer (OEM) developers. These mechanisms let users create a new perspective from scratch, transform data, bring in new data, and join and link tables. However, they require interactions with source code. Such support may not be very accessible, the team reasons, but at least it is present.

The design team also assesses and records user needs that cannot be supported by their existing visualizations, such as comparing different snapshots of performance to each other and to user-defined baselines for specific performance measures. For these task interactions, the team submits enhancement requests to the graphics team. Modifying the core graphics is a slow process because many project teams in the company vie at once for improvements relevant to their projects.

After three weeks of discussion, mockups, use-case walkthroughs, and continuous tweaking, the team composes its high-level requirements for the interactions supported by the VizAppManager tool. The following two examples of the team's high-level requirements give an idea of some fundamental interactions they specify.

Views of the infrastructure world: In a user-workstation view of the world, the ability to display the right data and graphs for identifying an end-user experience of poor performance, the business applications the user is running, their processing speeds, a response time in seconds correlated with a user's complaint of poor response time, and the full range of resource activity on the desktop system.

Drill down: The ability to right-click on a link between an application and user machine or application and database server in a network graph and get the following data: Internet protocol (IP) addresses of the link endpoints; the network path between the links; details on a network, LAN or WAN; and its physical structure (e.g., T1 or Ethernet).

For the rest of the design process, the VizAppManager team focuses on ease of use, access, and navigation. Team members decide on defaults for color-coding, time scales, behaviors of child windows, and the units of measure displayed on graph axes. They determine the best UI designs for various interactions, for example, choosing toolbar buttons as a means for moving between different pre-scripted screens and providing pull-down lists on the graphs: In addition, they work on naming labels in ways that match users' terminology. They ensure that users see relevant information flowing from the screen through legible labels, indicators of over-plotting, and informative legends. The team also develops UI indicators to show that the program is busy.

Perhaps the biggest struggles involve finding a means—besides online help—to explain what the graphics in a perspective show. Teammates experiment with various legends. In addition, they try to build cues that tell users whether the aggregates represent averages, totals, or sums of averages.

At this point, the design team unites with the rest of the VizAppManager development team to create a prototype they can field test with actual IT problem solvers. Some screens from this trial prototype are presented in Figure 4.4.

Conducting Trials in IT Sites: What Support Do Users Need and What Do They Get?

Six IT fault analysts put the visualization prototype to the test for actual problem solving purposes. At their work sites, they read their own data into it and work with it in conjunction with their other monitoring tools. The VizAppManager usability specialist and interaction designer observe these IT users working with the tool during the course of their everyday work.

Like the customers in the demo audience, these trial users are "wowed" by the graphics, especially by the ways they are aided in quickly seeing patterns in huge amounts of data. The interactive visualizations demonstrably improve upon current application performance-manager tools in the three ways the team had hoped for: The visualizations ease the data ordeals of arranging and relating large volumes of data in table formats; they enhance sensemaking by enabling users to take in, at a glance, a view of details and aggregates and a focus on particular machines or transactions against trends in the entire network; and they aid wayfinding by making it easier to stay oriented when taking multiple perspectives or relating differently scaled data.

But not everything in the trial provides such positive results. Unlike demo customers, IT users in actual work contexts are determined to find, diagnose, and resolve real faults. They expect the prototype to accommodate their patterns of inquiry. The IT specialists in the field test do not get very far into their problem solving processes before it becomes evident to the observers that these inquiry processes exceed the design team's narrow focus on analyzing and moving through data. The interactive graphics and visual querying may be an advance analytically, but the tool falls short in supporting the full reality of troubleshooting in context. The scope of the prototype is too shortsighted. It does not support trial users in the following ways:

- Data preparation

- *Ad hoc* analysis

- Data integration

- Comparisons

- Saving and commenting

- Iterative analysis

- New perceptual perplexities, as follows:

  - Understanding the meaning of the color-coding

  - Being able to override the program algorithm for distributing colors across variables

  - Ensuring that remote collaborators have the same color shades to make accurate joint interpretations

  - Understanding at a glance why timestamps and colors are out of sync and whether it matters

  - Understanding the meanings of perceptual cues in densely plotted, multidimensional graphs

  - Having adequate signposts for maneuvering in a visual information landscape and for resuming interrupted work within it

  - Managing the size, position, and clutter of multiple-graph perspectives

The usability specialist and interaction designer write a report elaborating on the trial findings. The report identifies prototype flaws for users' specific interactions and provides quantitative and qualitative evidence of users' performances. The usability report also recommends improvements. For example, to support users in resuming inquiries after an interruption or diversion, the report proposes enhancements for recalling a prior display and for seeing and interacting with a history of interactions.

What Is Missing for Usefulness in the Team's Conceptual Designing?

Why did the design team miss many of IT users' needs and fail to support them in the conceptual design and prototype? A number of reasons explain the shortcomings. Some are related to organizational processes and politics within the production-team context, such as methods for handling modification and enhancement requests and setting priorities. These issues are the focus of Chapter 10, Next Steps: The Politics and Positioning of Usefulness. Other reasons pertain to unavailable technological capabilities, which, in part, trace back to inadequate development processes that do not ensure that usefulness gets built into all parts of the technology. But, in terms of the aspects of conceptual design that do fall within the immediate control of the team, VizAppManager designers worked from models of users' work that underrepresented complexity, especially for troubleshooters' more familiar problem situations.

In their conceptual designing, team members substituted discrete, pre-determined views that answered a set of low-level fact questions for the more fluid and emergent lines of questioning that typify IT analysts' actual explorations. The team spent more time on logically mapping data to graphs than on practically mapping actual work intentions and activities to classes of interactions, functions, and graphic malleability. They emphasized data at the expense of other structures and areas of user control that problem solvers rely on to conduct complete inquiries. For example, IT specialists need to keep track of evolving insights as they eliminate one suspected cause and then another. They also need optimal entry points into data when analyzing troubled systems.

Two overarching shortcomings are apparent in this initial phase of the design team's story, and they are instructive for how software teams should design differently.

- The team created consolidated, but not integrated, models of work, which directed them to conceptualize displays that underplayed the support users need for the dynamics and demands of complexity.

- The team's design concept underrepresented the support IT specialists need to ensure that multi-contextual conditions do not close possibilities for actions critical to their dynamic work. I will examine each of these issues in turn.

DESIGNING DIFFERENTLY BY CREATING INTEGRATED *AND* CONSOLIDATED MODELS

For complex problems, a contextual orientation alone is not enough to direct analysis, modeling, and conceptual designing toward usefulness. The VizAppManager team developed contextually based, consolidated models of task sequences, workflows, artifacts, physical arrangements, and the like. If they had developed more extensive contextual descriptions, it would have helped but still would not have been a sufficient solution. Regardless of contextual richness, teams do not achieve integrated representations of users' work by developing consolidated, but not integrated, models of it.

Beyer and Holtzblatt's seminal book on contextual design (1998) describes consolidated work models and gives examples from the IT domain. Its consolidated IT task-sequence model describes tasks as "Look at process log, look at the time of the crash, and call experts and explain the problem." As with the VizAppManager's task-sequence model, these tasks are generic and logical, not integrated with such related activities as noting insights to later pass on to experts, resuming after interruptions, making *ad hoc* inquiries into alarms failing to register, or coherently moving "from here to there" when recursively interweaving different patterns of inquiry. The contextual design book's consolidated IT cultural model highlights such themes as end-users' attitudes toward help desk staff ("Lose my data, lose your job"). These cultural themes are rendered separately from other representations of work. Yet as the realities of tier-two and tier-three troubleshooting demonstrate, actions for detections, diagnoses, and repair are intricately tied to these cultural biases, so workflow and cultural models are all of one piece.

Importantly, the Beyer and Holtzblatt examples do not pertain to complex IT problem solving. They target the by-the-book methods that help-desk staff use to address straightforward end-user questions and problems. For the "different animal" of complex problem solving—by definition the work of tier-two and tier-three analysts—and for the sake of usefulness, design teams must create integrated *and* consolidated models.

One brief example from the VizAppManager case reveals how usefulness was shortchanged by failing to integrate consolidated models of work. In its artifact model, the VizAppManager team described troubleshooters' uses of sticky notes, print-outs of screen shots, and other written notes. But team members did not highlight integral connections and interactions between this artifact model and other aspects of problem solving conditions and actions. Therefore, the team designed for mainline, unit tasks representing artifact-related interactions (e.g., "save a screen view" or "print log data"), but it skipped over many of the higher-order sensemaking and wayfinding activities associated with IT analysts' varied uses of artifacts. The design did not, for example, highlight IT users' needs to strategically arrange and comment on saved views in ways that bring collaborators quickly up to speed when they join the troubleshooting midstream. We saw this same outcome in Chapter 2 when application-level patterns for reviewing a patient record did not look at integrated support for integrated work that varied by circumstance, purpose, and subjective biases.

To highlight integrated activities and needs, design teams must carefully analyze and model the interactive conditions within and across multiple contexts that shape whether or not users can pursue actions relevant to their goals.

DESIGNING DIFFERENTLY: CAPTURING CONTEXTUAL INFLUENCES

Benkei's scenario exemplifies many of the contextual conditions that typically shape IT specialists' moves in troubleshooting and fault management, whether for familiar or baffling problems. The VizAppManager team did not fully account for the interactive conditions across contexts that shape what troubleshooters can and cannot do. Nor did team members frame design around how the troubleshooting tool could help to keep possibilities open.

The charts below highlight these conditions and the software support that users need in regard to them. The charts focus on conditions in each of the four contexts—technology and data, workplace domain, problem, and subjective—that are based on a fuller profile of IT problem solving across workplaces than Benkei's case alone provides. The design team in the story should have addressed these conditions to design for usefulness. The support associated with each condition helps ensure that IT specialists have the actions available to them that are critical for achieving their troubleshooting goals with the professional approaches they value.

 Technology and Data Context

Influential Contextual Conditions	Support for Keeping Relevant Actions Open
Multiple tools: Required for a complete and accurate view of the network	Give users a means to coordinate tools and integrate data across them.
Multiple views, many monitors: Used to display different views of the system (several monitors in control rooms)	Work out how visualization perspectives should look and behave to help users create connections between them and real-time log data.

Technology and Data Context—Continued

Influential Contextual Conditions	Support for Keeping Relevant Actions Open
	Assure compatibility between different program displays for color-coding, timestamps, and units of measure.
"Black holes" in the system: Creates uncertainty about the effects of problems or repairs	Give users ways to seed their workspaces so they can flag important conditions to note or return to.
"Broken" tools in "hung" systems: Unexpectedly triggers the need for work-arounds and the use of alternate problem solving tools	Make sure of compatibilities between tools across the problem solving environment, including back-ups in a crisis.
Multiple open windows: Disorients users in terms of where they are in problem solving	Provide a means for users to manage the windows of commonly joined tools in ways that reduce clutter.
Data preparation: Sometimes occupies 60-70% of problem solving, either in advance or on-the-fly	Include support for preparing, transforming, and pre-filtering data as an intrinsic part of troubleshooting.
Multipurpose alarm data: Used in different ways for many purposes, with the need to relate details and overviews and validate alarms in the context of other system events	Provide perspectives that combine views of alarms with other performance measures and trends and give users choices about what views to display and how. Give in-a-keystroke access to alarm thresholds.

Work Domain Context

Influential Contextual Conditions	Support for Keeping Relevant Actions Open
Collaborations: Initiated at the start of an inquiry, mid-stream, or as a hand-off, either face-to-face or remotely	Give users a way to save screen shots and create communications for collaborators while they are conducting their inquiry. Ensure that collaborators can synchronize their separate displays to show exactly the same thing.
Interventions by other IT groups: May set off an alarm for a fault when there is not one	Give users ways to cue and build situational signposts that show the work other groups are doing that could trigger "false alarms."
Multitasking and interruptions: Causes disorientation at resumption	Provide ample ways for users to leave and resume a line of questioning without losing their places or trains of thought.
Time pressures: Affects the breadth and depth of inquiry and creates the need for quick fixes	Give users ways to flag their provisional quick fixes, especially those that need to be dismantled later on.
Reliance on domain conventions and patterns: Used to structure and sequence processes of investigation	Signal the domain knowledge and patterns that organize users' work, with ample freedom for them to configure associated task landscapes, as needed.

Problem Context

Influential Contextual Conditions	Support for Keeping Relevant Actions Open
Entry point: Used as the best choice out of many to start investigating a line of questioning or hunch	Ensure that users have cues for where to begin based on their priorities and historic situations.
Core activities in patterns of inquiry: Used to get from here to there when exploring many possibilities	Ensure ample and integrated support and user control for such core activities as saving and commenting on data displays, cross-referencing and interpreting data from two monitors, understanding contradictory color-coding across tools, going off on tangents, and returning.
Complexity of familiar problems: Causes the use of different procedures and strategies despite the application of general, standard methods and insights	In light of provisional conditions, give users ample control without pre-defining all views, data displays, and procedures. Display indications of familiar aspects of a problem situation *and* cues about the flux going on in the larger problem space, making moves open-ended.

 **Subjective Context**

Influential Contextual Conditions	Support for Keeping Relevant Actions Open
Domain and problem solving expertise: Affects strategies and choices based on its application to practical realities	Provide situational cues, leeway for choice, and flexibility for arranging and transforming data in ways that allow users to apply their knowledge to the demands of a situation.

CONCLUSIONS

In the design story, the visualization team initially approached conceptual design by highlighting the contextual forces related to logical aspects of troubleshooting and fault analysis. They took a "rational agent" view of problem solving with little sense of its full drama. This view led them to a design that was too narrowly focused.

The VizAppManager team did not intend to be narrowly focused. In fact, team members assumed that they were user-centered and contextually oriented. They consciously shaped their design choices around users in terms of users' role-related views of the infrastructure; their demonstrated, in-context task sequences; their selection of important information for problem-based questions and goals; and many of their processes for working with large amounts of data and visual displays of them. Unfortunately, this user-in-context orientation was incomplete. The design team overlooked many data ordeals, sensemaking, and wayfinding activities equally related to, and just as much a core part of, IT specialists' investigations as logical problem solving and information and visual processing.

To address these other ordeals and activities, the design team needed a more extensive view of multi-contextual interactive conditions and actions. They needed to refrain from basing their design on a demo intended to "wow" customers and instead concentrate on practically supporting troubleshooting in context. They needed to highlight aspects of complex problem solving that occur in familiar fault situations as well as vexing ones; and they needed to realize that professionals—even technical professionals—do not want to dig deeply into the workings of their problem solving tools nor go through elaborate steps to customize them when they are in the midst of investigating a complex problem.

It is far easier to pinpoint where design goes awry in retrospect than during design time. To ensure that such insights do not occur too late in the design and development processes, software teams rely on prototypes, which are good catalysts for recognizing alternate, more effective design strategies. Prototypes, by definition, are meant to reveal problems, incite revisions, and point design teams toward necessary improvements. Getting it wrong in a prototype is hardly a grievous error. In fact, to the design team's credit in the story, the team members used the VizAppManager prototype to see if they had gotten the work right, not just to test the ease of use and clarity of the interfaces.

Even with rapid and iterative prototyping, the question of how to move effectively toward usefulness remains. For the purpose of greater usefulness, design teams need to couple the use of a more inclusive contextual framework with strategies that ensure integrated designs for integrated activities. For specialized IT analysts and their complex investigations, relevant findings about users and tasks must be consolidated *and* integrated. Because IT problem solvers make open-ended choices based on integrated considerations of various dimensions of work and because they integrate parts differently for distinct situations, they need software to represent their choices and work in integrated ways.

In Chapter 5, the visualization team returns to the design table with these more far-reaching and interactive multi-contextual conditions and actions in mind. This time the team more deliberately gives top priority to designing for usefulness. In its second go at design, team members strive to understand the integrated support IT specialists need for their integrated work. They focus on IT specialists' patterns of inquiry at a practical level with an eye on interactivity, context, and variability. Drawing on such models of IT users' work, they narrow in on two areas of support vital to effective troubleshooting and fault management. For each, they pursue design strategies and explore possible design choices that stay true to the requirements of usefulness.

REFERENCES

Agre, Philip. *Computation and Human Experience*. Cambridge: Cambridge University Press, 1997.

Beyer, Hugh and Karen Holzblatt. *Contextual Design: Defining Customer-Centered Systems*. San Francisco: Morgan Kaufmann, 1998.

Evans, Shara and Richard Bonugli. "How to Build an Intranet." *AAPT-Network Magazine*. 1998. Available at: www.net.aapt.com.au/ netmag/article3.htm

Salomon, Gavriel and David Perkins. "Rocky Road to Transfer: Rethinking Mechanisms of a Neglected Phenomenon." *Educational Psychologist* 24, no. 2 (1989): 113-142.

Vincente, Kin. "How do Operators Monitor a Complex, Dynamic Work Domain? The Impact of Control Room Technology." *International Journal of Human-Computer Studies* 54, no. 6 (2001): 831-856.

5

Getting IT Right

Following on the heels of the design experiences in the last chapter, we now find the VizAppManager team ready to create a better tool for information technology (IT) troubleshooters and their practical patterns of inquiry. After finding severe usefulness flaws in its original prototype, the visualization team has decided to structure this second round of conceptual designing according to the following two objectives:

- Provide *integrated* support for users' *integrated* strategies
- Adequately support data ordeals, wayfinding, and sensemaking with strategies and conceptual designs targeted to criteria for usefulness

With these objectives in mind, the visualization team starts revising their models of detection patterns. This chapter's redesign scenario shows the revised models the team creates to capture the interactivity, contexts, and variability (ICV) in IT specialists' familiar as well as wicked problem solving. Based on these models, VizAppManager team members then identify how the troubleshooting tool should behave for aspects of IT specialists' integrated patterns of inquiry. The team concentrates specifically on two wayfinding needs and conceptualizes designs for supporting them. In the process, team members realize additional high-level design strategies crucial for usefulness. The team's objectives and strategies inspire designs for holistic and useful support for IT problem solvers' inquiries.

In the software and web application world, creating useful support for the areas the VizAppManager team tackles is very much an open design question. For applications for complex problem solving, conventions and standards for a wide range of necessary and useful support are still formative. Innovative technologies crucial for advancing usefulness are developing rapidly and are changing the options software teams have for effective design choices. Therefore, not unlike other design teams' efforts, the VizAppManager team's choices are experimental and provisional. As I emphasize in the introduction to this book, interaction designers and usability specialists should not take them to be definitive solutions.

The VizAppManager team's design story may not offer definitive solutions but it is, nonetheless, instructive, and the entire chapter is devoted to it. The design choices the team favors for usefulness are exemplary and are more attuned to users' practical problem solving in context than the alternatives the team considers and rejects. Moreover, the team's second go at designing highlights fundamental usefulness criteria relevant to many design projects.

PRELUDE TO A STORY: LOOKING AT ONLY SELECT PARTS OF THE TEAM'S EFFORTS

The scenario in this chapter presents only a small part of the VizAppManager team members' work as they try once again to design an effective troubleshooting tool as follows:

- **Limited Patterns of Inquiry:** The VizAppManager case covers only two subpatterns in IT troubleshooting, both of which are part of users' larger pattern of detecting a problem. The first is "validating a problem," an activity relatively low in complexity with fairly standard methods and little variability. During detection, validation serves only the complex problem solving objective of preparing for inquiry. To validate a problem, IT specialists look into the trigger signaling the problem and examine conditions indicating whether it is a false alarm. In the VizAppManager team's return to the drawing board, team members purposely emphasize this relatively well-structured subpattern as a way to be sure they discover aspects of dynamic inquiry in need of support, even in a seemingly clear-cut set of actions.

    The second subpattern in the scenario is "bounding and formulating a problem," an activity that is considerably more complex. Within this single subpattern, troubleshooters wrangle with all the problem solving objectives and processes of complex problem solving: Preparing for inquiry, planning, querying data, analyzing data, managing inquiry, and communicating. Their main goals are to trace the source of abnormalities to a location and judge their complexity and severity.

- **Select Models of Users' Work:** The scenario describes only the VizAppManager team's models of the interactive contextual conditions affecting troubleshooters' available actions. In reality, the VizAppManager team constructs other models of IT specialists' pattern-based task landscapes and choice points, but I do not present them here. These other types of models are developed and illustrated in detail in relation to the product mix assessment scenario in Chapters 6 and 7.

- **Design Strategies, Criteria, and Choices for Two Activities:** In the team's conceptual designing, the scenario highlights design strategies, criteria, and choices for two wayfinding activities in IT users' patterns of inquiry. These activities are saving, commenting on, and recalling views of interest and finding an entry point for lines of questioning in which appropriate entries vary by circumstance.

INTRODUCTION: REGROUPING AND DECIDING HOW TO REDESIGN

The VizAppManager team members find the original prototype wanting and regroup for redesign. They now orient themselves differently to users' work and support. Team members decide to center design on what users can do with the visualizations, rather than on what the visualizations can do for users. The team strives to bring the software closer to users with greater flexibility and adaptability. Ideally, IT specialists should be able to integrate the revised VizAppManager so seamlessly into their work that they will wonder how they ever got along without it.

When the VizAppManager team reconvenes to redesign the trouble-shooting tool, teammates begin by reviewing the usability report on the prototype trials. The group is split on how to go about improving the design. Several individuals want to immediately turn the report's findings and recommendations into lists of features, functions, and requirements. Once that is done, developers can build for the recommendations that are feasible based on time and resources and slate the rest for a later version of the tool. The usability report, structured into discrete recommendations, tacitly suggests this course of action.

Others on the team resist. They contend that the problem with this list—and with the usability report recommendations—is that the fixes are dissociated. They are not based on how IT users actually *put together* investigations for a given purpose in the midst of uncertainty and changing conditions. Moreover, given the development group's modification request process, many recommendations are likely to get tabled. The "feature list" approach, the dissenters acknowledge, is logical and represents the usual course of events in their company. But, they argue, it will keep the visualization team from getting to the heart of the usefulness flaws.

Their alternative is to construct models of users' troubleshooting different from those the team originally created—models that will now make criteria for usefulness more apparent and guide conceptual design. Any other approach is likely to perpetuate the same piece-by-piece designing that led to the prototype's inadequacies. Specifically, this faction urges the group to begin redesign by modeling IT analysts' fault management activities as they are shaped by *interactivity* among conditions across various *contexts*: The contexts of troubleshooters' technologies and data, work domains, problems, and subjectivity. The models must also capture the *variability* and regularity of users' patterns of inquiry and task landscapes. Proponents of this strategy particularly urge their teammates to visually sketch the conditions and constraints that open and close opportunities for troubleshooters' desired approaches so the team may conceptualize designs that are compatible with users' needs and situated conditions. Basically, this faction promotes an ICV framework for modeling users' work.

After much debate, this proposed approach is adopted, and the team begins by representing IT users' practical patterns of inquiry based on an ICV approach. The VizAppManager team's earlier designing focused on describing IT specialists' work as detection, diagnosis, and repair, but within these patterns, they looked only at the questions IT users ask during each activity. Now the VizAppManager team intends to describe these patterns of inquiry more practically and fully by detailing and analyzing the interactive contextual conditions that determine how easily problem solvers can conduct these activities.

ANALYZING WHAT TROUBLESHOOTERS DO TO VALIDATE A PROBLEM

The design team looks first at troubleshooters' activities for validating a problem. Validation is the users' first step in detecting a problem and initiates their investigations into faults and fixes.

Describing Practical Validation Activities: Methods and Results

This time, as the VizAppManager team models IT specialists' problem solving, teammates move beyond the use cases that are standard methods in their development organization. Use cases generate best cases ("simple correct paths") and address practical realities peripherally through descriptions of alternate paths or "exception paths" (Kulak and Guiney, 43-44, 2000). However, teammates' initial design and prototype experiences lead them to judge these techniques as unrealistically optimistic. Tier-two analysts hardly ever experience best cases as the "basic course of events." Instead they regularly embark on alternate paths and not simply as idiosyncratic choices or pursuits of curiosity. They frequently *have to* take roundabout means, even for straightforward problem validation because contextual conditions, especially technological ones, often block their preferred courses of action. The VizAppManager team wants to capture with equal weight best cases and more typical alternate paths, what the team terms *practical cases*. By capturing both equally, the designers seek to identify the compatibilities needed to foster users' efforts to validate a problem and the incompatibilities that spur workarounds.

After reaching this consensus on methods, the team describes "validating a problem." IT specialists validate a problem by looking for and eliminating possible indicators of false alarms one-by-one. If they find evidence of a false alarm, they stop their inquiry. Otherwise, they proceed. When problems are real, IT specialists learn about the type of abnormality that confronts them from this validation and apply this knowledge to the rest of their trouble-shooting efforts. As the VizAppManager team sees it, in the best of all worlds, IT troubleshooters are able to move smoothly and straightforwardly through the following actions of validation:

- Confirming that a trouble ticket has been issued for an alert

- Inspecting alarm screens for an alerted condition

- Checking alarm threshold settings to be sure they are valid

- Examining calibrations of instruments to ensure they are not askew

- Confirming that intervention situations are not causing false positives

- Double-checking with the people who alerted them to the problem to be sure the report is not a mistake

- Returning to the alarm screen once a real problem is confirmed and examining correlated alarms to better define the problem

Numerous enabling tasks surround these mainline validation tasks. In a best-case vision, troubleshooters easily interweave enabling and mainline actions and sail through them. Enabling tasks for validation include the following:

- Examining various indicators recursively

- Writing notes

- Storing information and views for later reference

- Navigating to and managing various views of the infrastructure

- Consulting reports and users who are suffering from a slow or frozen system

- Communicating with co-workers about interventions elsewhere in the system

To conduct interwoven enabling and mainline actions without obstruction, IT specialists need multi-contextual conditions to interact compatibly. For example, troubleshooters need the technology tools and infrastructure to afford efficient navigation, querying, and analysis so they can fit their inquiry into workplace-driven time constraints for fixing problems. At the same time, in the subjective context they need to have expert enough domain knowledge to know where to look and what patterns to look for to detect false alarms. In the work domain, their roles as "service center" specialists and their relations of power with the divisions they serve must ensure sufficient autonomy in applying their knowledge, methods, and timing as they see fit.

The number of compatible interactive conditions troubleshooters need—even for this well-structured validating pattern—make best-case situations rare. Benkei, for example in the scenario in Chapter 4, runs into blocks when he cannot get to the alarm screen because his system is so bogged down. In his case, conditions within the technology obstruct what should be a simple and smooth process. The VizAppManager team explores the many incompatible conditions in everyday practice that bar troubleshooters like Benkei from taking the best course of action and begins to describe them.

The team notes that, as with Benkei's difficulty in accessing the alarm screen, the technology itself is often a prime impediment to validation actions. Incompatibilities within and across other contexts block trouble-shooters' desired actions, as well. For example, in the prototype trials, one IT analyst found suspicious settings in instrumentation that she knew to look for because her company had a history of instrumentation glitches. Organizationally, she also needed to collaborate with a specialist to be sure these glitches were not giving a false alarm about the problem. Unfortunately, based on technology conditions, she could not follow through on the demands of these complementary subjective and organizational conditions. The screens on which she viewed instrumentation could not be copied and annotated adequately to share with her co-worker for joint consultation.

After describing a good number of such incompatibilities in practical cases, the VizAppManager team creates models of users' work, starting with charts and diagrams of interactive contextual conditions.

Creating Models of Users' Work

In its work models, the design team represents interactive conditions and constraints within and across many contexts that shape the actions troubleshooters can and cannot take. The team captures these interactive contextual conditions and their effects on troubleshooters' actions in a chart and diagram (Table 5.1 and Figure 5.1).

Figure 5.1 shows the ways one action, validating alarm thresholds, gets buffeted by numerous contextual conditions, at times sending users to unanticipated places. For example, when the technological condition of a drastically slowed system constrains Benkei from accessing the tool that unifies all the alarms on one screen, he has to hassle with going to the individual logs of each component to see alarms.

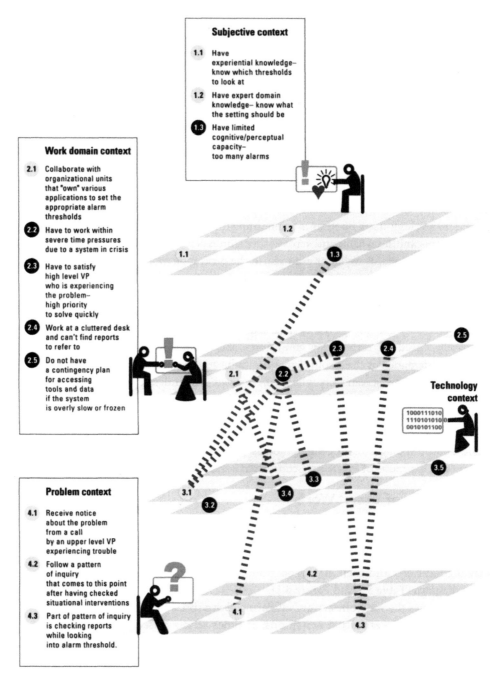

Subjective context

1.1 Have experiential knowledge– know which thresholds to look at

1.2 Have expert domain knowledge– know what the setting should be

1.3 Have limited cognitive/perceptual capacity– too many alarms

Work domain context

2.1 Collaborate with organizational units that "own" various applications to set the appropriate alarm thresholds

2.2 Have to work within severe time pressures due to a system in crisis

2.3 Have to satisfy high level VP who is experiencing the problem– high priority to solve quickly

2.4 Work at a cluttered desk and can't find reports to refer to

2.5 Do not have a contingency plan for accessing tools and data if the system is overly slow or frozen

Technology context

1000111010
1110101010100
0010101100

Problem context

4.1 Receive notice about the problem from a call by an upper level VP experiencing trouble

4.2 Follow a pattern of inquiry that comes to this point after having checked situational interventions

4.3 Part of pattern of inquiry is checking reports while looking into alarm threshold.

FIGURE 5.1
Interactive contextual conditions affecting validating alarm thresholds.

A VP calls a troubleshooter. VP's get top priority. The troubleshooter leaves the reports he is analyzing strewn across his desk and starts to validate the problem.

In the diagram, he is at the validation point of checking alarm thresholds to ensure they are not the problem. In the dotted lines we see all his obstructed moves because of surrounding conditions. They include the following attempts:

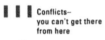

	Conflicts– you can't get there from here
1.1	Positive conditions
1.3	Threatening conditions

He has just finished validating that no situational interventions were going on. The programs for checking interventions and checking thresholds are different. He is slowed down, though not blocked, because he moves from one program to another.

Time is a constant force. To speed things up he wants to check with the IT financial application folks to see if they changed the threshold settings. No direct access to them exists in the troubleshooter's tools. Conscious of time, he abandons the idea and does the threshold check through the alarm screen.

Technology context

3.1 Can access the threshold settings through the tools

3.2 Cannot easily correlate alarms because tool lacks the functionality to do it automatically– inefficient and mentally burdensome

3.3 Have to go in and out of tools to move– get from the last thing the user checked, to validate (i.e. checked situational interventions), to the threshold settings

3.4 Do not have built-in communication connections to organizational units to see if new thresholds have been instituted

3.5 Do not have a single virtual workspace in which to integrate a display of alarms, log data and interactive analysis

He sees scores of fired alarms from different applications and wants to correlate them. The tool does not correlate alarms so it takes time to do this. The troubleshooter looks for his reference sheet on alarm thresholds to compare to the screen display but can't find it. His desk is too cluttered with other reports. His aims are thwarted. He relies on memory.

Finally, on the threshold screen, he scrolls to different alarm thresholds, but his alarm screen does not automatically move to corresponding alarms with him. He writes notes to remember, and they merge with the other papers on his desk.

Thresholds are not the problem but to discover this the troubleshooter did not take his desired route or achieve the accuracy that he likes.

In Figure 5.1, positive conditions in each context, those that keep opportunities open for troubleshooters to take the validating actions they need, are marked by yellow balls. Blue balls represent threatening conditions or constraints, those that have a strong potential for interacting with other conditions to close these opportunities. In the figure, the red dotted lines show these conflicts as they obstruct the action of "analyzing and checking alarm thresholds." Often, IT specialists do this action right after they finish validating that situational interventions are not the reason for the problem.

The VizAppManager team sees from its interactive context diagram that certain incompatibilities between conditions severely deter troubleshooters from working most effectively and efficiently. For example, to identify which thresholds to check, IT specialists need to see at a glance the alarms that have fired. If, in the technology context, tools do not automatically correlate or group alarms, it is taxing for troubleshooters to either do so themselves or mentally try to organize a disordered display. In this instance, this technology condition interacts adversely with the work domain condition of time pressures and the subjective constraints of human cognition, memory, and perception.

In assessing interactive conditions and their effects, the VizAppManager team members see that some incompatibilities and detrimental effects on problem solving actions are outside the scope of their intended tool. For example, they cannot build anything into VizAppManager to help troubleshooters like Benkei get to an alarm screen when a system in crisis prevents them from opening other monitoring software. The benefit of the model, however, is that it reveals incompatibilities that may not seem directly related to the VizAppManager tool's purpose and functionality but that give team members ideas about how they may design VizAppManager so it integrates better with the diverse set of fault management and monitoring tools troubleshooters use. For example, the team discusses, but temporarily tables, the possibility of including in VizAppManager a means for troubleshooters to contact their internal customers in administrative units who own various applications because at times IT specialists have to reach these customers speedily to validate the accuracy of threshold settings. Finally, team members target the few issues they see that do pertain directly to the VizAppManager tool. They note, for example, that their design concept has to accommodate troubleshooters' need for simultaneously viewing alarm screens and analysis workspaces. They need to provide such integrated workspaces in their new design.

The well-structured quality of the "validating a problem" subpattern keeps the number of obstructions the visualization team can potentially overcome through useful VizAppManager designs relatively small. However, some do exist, which the team did not realize in its first attempt in the last chapter because team members assumed that familiar and well-structured aspects of troubleshooting were exempt from complexity. The team now turns to a more open-ended subpattern to analyze and model.

ANALYZING WHAT TROUBLESHOOTERS DO TO BOUND AND FORMULATE A PROBLEM

Tier-two analysts often bound and formulate a problem many times during a single investigation. They frequently discover unexpected conditions, rethink cause and effect relationships, and reconsider what the problem may be. The VizAppManager team explores and describes this fairly complex subpattern of detection.

Describing Bounding and Formulating a Problem

IT specialists bound and formulate a problem to clarify the type of trouble going on, its severity, and its complexity. More than they do in validation, IT analysts proceed in nonlinear directions. They start with at least a vague idea of the type of problem they are facing, gleaned either from validating it or from getting unexpected outcomes in diagnoses or repair that send them back to square one. They then clarify this vague idea by surveying relevant conditions and connecting them to workplace practices that may account for disturbances.

When the visualization team looks more closely at how IT users get "from here to there" in bounding and formulating a problem, team members see from their initial descriptions that users start from one of four vantage points: Users, applications, databases, or an overview. They now realize that these descriptions, though accurate, are incomplete. Troubleshooters take two other important approaches for the purpose of discovering a problem's boundaries.

First, troubleshooters use the following methods of investigation to examine system conditions according to different slices of time and severity:

- **Relating trouble and trouble-free parts in a snapshot of the overall system:** This view of conditions enables IT users to survey everything going on in a slice of time in the network (affected and unaffected users, applications, servers, response times at each hop or processing point), and it allows them to compare different areas to find trouble spots.

- **Focusing only on trouble spots in a snapshot view:** This entry point shows performance measures for problem components, packet traffic, and processing, and it helps uncover unrealized problems.

- **Relating trouble and trouble-free parts in an over-time view:** This view allows investigations into the duration of a problem, events preceding a disturbance, and unfolding events after a problem occurs.

- **Focusing only on trouble spots in an over-time view:** This display shows trends and patterns, comparing disturbances at the time alarms fired to the same (disturbed) components at other times.

IT specialists cannot grasp what a problem is until they explore all these points of view. Seeing differences between snapshots and over-time views allows IT specialists to figure out the nature of the problem. IT specialists differ in how many interpretive perspectives they explore, when, to what depth, and in what combinations. They adapt to emerging questions and insights and make investigative choices accordingly.

The second approach the team originally overlooked is that IT specialists continually turn quantitative data into *qualitative* knowledge as they cumulatively gather evidence about system conditions. This is a central means by which these problem solvers manage large amounts of data and gauge the severity and complexity of a problem (Hutchins, 1995; Goodwin, 1997; Trafton et al., 2000). Unquestionably, hard data—quantitative performance measurements—are crucial for accuracy. Benkei, for example, modifies the scale on a line graph's axis so that he can see the small effects of his various fixes more precisely. But in bounding and formulating a problem, IT specialists come away with more than numbers and measures. From trends, deviations, and durations, they infer what type of problem they are looking at and relate new quantitative data to these cumulative, qualitative judgments.

The VizAppManager team realizes its problem solving models must capture this seamless transforming of quantitative measures into qualitative interpretations. IT users move from numbers to judgments by "seeding" their information environments. For example, they arrange data to highlight and remind themselves about certain relationships of interest on noteworthy insights. Clearly, the design team must support enabling tasks just as prodigiously as mainline tasks.

As the team sees it, all combined, IT specialists' mainline and enabling tasks for bounding and formulating a problem comprise a long list of actions:

- Accessing all relevant data

- Deciding on the appropriate graphic perspective

- Setting up and displaying the right combined graphics from either a snapshot or over-time view and either an overview or part-by-part view

- Understanding the meaning that a chosen perspective conveys for investigation purposes
- Accessing complementary data on alarms and log messages and relating them to the graphic perspective
- Selecting data of interest
- Keeping data contexts visible or filtering irrelevant data, as needed
- Arranging and transforming data to highlight and interpret relationships
- Coding by color, size, and the like
- Panning and zooming the views
- Monitoring and managing progress through a line of questioning
- Backtracking and reassessing earlier assumptions, as needed
- Saving, commenting on, and recalling views
- Moving to a new perspective by time and system location
- Keeping track of insights gained from current and prior perspectives
- Resuming after an interruption, at the right spot and with the right understanding
- Looking at two different perspectives and comparing them side-by-side
- Navigating within and between data displays
- Accessing details of value about data of interest
- Assessing the severity and location of a problem from interrelated data displays

This is an unwieldy and discrete list. Practically problem solvers integrate these activities but they can only do so effectively and smoothly if conditions in the technology, work domain, subjective traits of troubleshooters, and problem solving patterns line up compatibly. In the technology, for example, all relevant system-performance data must be available, accessible, formatted correctly, color-coded, and time-stamped compatibly across tools; tools must provide the necessary functionality and interactivity for the problem solving actions relevant to "bounding and formulating a problem." Similarly, work domains must offer minimal complications—no conflict, for example, between IT and the administrative units it serves about whether accountability for system performance lies mainly with IT's service or with the unit's appropriate uses of its applications. In best cases, subjective conditions and problem solving patterns also are in sync with each other and with technology and work domain conditions.

Rarely do such best cases occur. Therefore, the VizAppManager team turns to describing the realities of practical cases and then to modeling the interactive conditions and constraints affecting how users go about bounding and formulating a problem, just as the team did for validation.

Creating Models of Users' Work

The visualization team members describe the interactions among multi-contextual conditions that affect troubleshooters' actions for "bounding and formulating a problem" as they did for "validating alarms." (See Table 5.1.) They distinguish positive conditions (yellow balls), which facilitate users' desired patterns of inquiry, and threatening conditions (blue balls), which are those susceptible to incompatibilities that will thwart users' pattern-based intentions. Table 5.1 presents these conditions as they relate to the action of setting up and displaying the right combined graphics for a snapshot look at one part of the system. Troubleshooters do this action right after deciding on the right perspective for the given system conditions.

The VizAppManager designers see a number of incompatibilities looming in interactions between conditions likely to obstruct users from straightforwardly performing this single action of displaying and setting up the right perspective. For example, when IT troubleshooters display a snapshot view focusing on one part of the system, they set it up for analysis based on what they anticipate in this portion of the investigation. Due to problem and work domain conditions, tier-two and tier-three analysts often multitask and troubleshoot a couple of problems at once, and their investigations are frequently interrupted by competing demands of another problem. Therefore, in the set up of this snapshot view of a system component, one of their objectives is to create memorable markers in the view to remind them what it means for their purpose should they have to leave it quickly and resume later. Unfortunately, technology conditions in the tools these users have interact adversely with these problem and work domain conditions. The tools do not offer ways to highlight and otherwise create "seeded" markers or to quickly save and comment on views. As a result, troubleshooters have to divert from their desired approach of setting up a view that anticipates interruptions. Instead they have to regularly capture and print screen shots to keep a record of their moves and insights, spending time and effort making notes on them and keeping them organized on a cluttered desk.

Technology context

○ Graphic tools give users abilities to color, sort, and position data, and to change axes and view details

● Little integration across diverse tools; little ability to read/write across them

● Tools do not make it easy to save or comment on views for later use

● Tools do not allow highlighting of data views and other "seeding" interactions

Subjective context

○ Domain knowledge—know right questions to ask for system conditions

○ Experienced with graphics— know right views for right questions when given options

● No prior experience with this type of problem

Work domain context

○ Adequate staffing—specialists cover for each other when hectic

● Two areas of troubleshooting occur at once—requiring multi-tasking

● A new application just went into the production context that some higher ups objected to

Problem context

○ Patterns of inquiry involve multiple perspectives

○ Inquiry patterns require a number of discretionary choices for data set-ups based on given system conditions

○ Domain conventions for viewing certain data together in certain ways

TABLE 5.1
Interactive contextual conditions for displaying and setting up the right combined graphics.
○ positive conditions
● threatening conditions

Tools that offer no highlighting capabilities also obstruct troubleshooting actions when IT specialists have to be responsive to such politically charged workplace conditions as a controversial application running poorly and decision-makers disagreeing about who is responsible and what to do about it. If troubleshooters cannot arrange a data display to highlight this application, they cannot adequately maintain their subsequent analysis with a top-priority view of this application's performance.

The tools' numerous capabilities for arranging a view seem as if they would keep open the opportunities that troubleshooters need to set up views for analysis. Yet problem-based conditions introduce demands that are not met solely by these sorting, color-coding, and data positioning capabilities. Troubleshooters' problem solving patterns involve analyzing several sets of data at once, such as alarm data or log messages plus snapshot perspectives of system conditions. When the tools cannot read data from diverse sources, troubleshooters find that the perspective they display and verify is incomplete for their investigative goals.

Problem solvers cannot reach satisfying judgments in defining a problem if the available data and technology allow some actions but not others. Piecemeal support thwarts users from comprehensively carrying out their bound-and-formulate pattern. Unlike the validation action that the team modeled earlier, these insights are all relevant to creating a useful VizAppManager tool.

After completing and analyzing this interactive contexts model, the VizAppManger team creates visual representations of users' task landscapes and choice points (similar to those depicted for optimizing decisions in Figures 6.17-6.20). Then teammates go through the same processes of analysis and modeling for the rest of troubleshooters' detection, diagnosis, and repair patterns. When finished, team members unanimously conclude they should start conceptualizing support by creating useful designs for two of troubleshooters' particularly important wayfinding activities. These activities, recurring in detection, diagnosis, and repair, are saving, commenting on, and recalling views of interest and finding effective entry points for investigations that vary from time to time depending on the problem, its severity, and the prevailing priorities in the organization. These two areas of support are the team's first forays this go around into conceptualizing designs for usefulness.

CONCEPTUALIZING DESIGNS FOR SAVING, COMMENTING ON, AND RECALLING VIEWS

The team sees from its models of users' work that one aspect of troubleshooting crucial to effective inquiries and solutions is saving, commenting on, and recalling views. IT specialists have various reasons for conducting this activity. Sometimes they use prior, saved, and annotated views for personal reference and sometimes for collaboration. In addition, they often compare current active views to saved prior ones, and they use saved views as documentation to validate their judgments and decisions. The VizAppTeam realizes from its models of users' work that the actions in this chunked task may seem generically interchangeable, but they are not. The support users require for the same action at different points of investigation varies because each action serves a distinct function in a specific pattern of inquiry.

Setting the Scope

From models of users' work, the designers see that IT specialists have different practices for saving, commenting on, and recalling data displays of interest. One user may write shorthand comments as personal reminders, which are meaningful only to this individual as a memory jog. Another user may write more extensive comments for the different purpose of bringing a collaborator on board mid-stream. Halfway through an investigation, this user may realize a problem is thornier than it first appeared and bring in another database administrator (DBA) for help. In this instance, comments and highlights on saved views serve the purpose of bringing the co-worker up to speed quickly on the problem. Still other users may forego saving and commenting on views electronically and instead print views and use hard copies as reminders and cumulative evidence. They prefer writing comments on print outs rather than inserting notes electronically because the physical act of writing serve as a memory aid.

The design team sets its scope on supporting the wide-ranging functions associated with this wayfinding activity. The group's goal is to develop useful, robust designs so IT users can achieve varied objectives. The designs must also be approachable so that, for any given purpose, IT troubleshooters can easily do only the actions they deem relevant. The team begins to abstract the functions served by saving, commenting, and recalling views in various investigative landscapes.

In detection, they note, a prime function of saving, commenting on, and recalling views for troubleshooters is to reinforce or redirect their confidence in an evolving definition of a disturbance. IT specialists will recall a saved view, for example, if outcomes during their unfolding analysis of the system cause them to question and rethink their original definition of a problem. They will review the earlier display and its comments and try to figure out what they may have missed in their original survey.

Tier-two analysts know that during detection, their definitions are usually provisional. Capturing and commenting on views of conditions contribute to their confidence. Moreover, a saved and annotated view helps shore up faltering confidence later should an initial problem definition prove wanting. In this situation, a recalled view will help to point troubleshooters in a new direction.

During diagnosis, by contrast, IT users save and comment on views as ideas-in-the-making, not as records of judgment or barometers of confidence. The saved views and comments, highlights, and annotations stand as incomplete insights, waiting to be reactivated later and related to future views of system conditions for a more complete picture of causes.

Moreover, in diagnosis, IT users' activities in saving and recalling a view function in connection with other tasks in ways they do not in such detection patterns as "bounding and formulating a problem." For example, in diagnosis, IT users do not solely recall a view to re-examine it statically. They want to reactivate it and dynamically link it to currently active displays so they can interactively relate past and present conditions. When the tasks of saving, commenting on, and recalling a view serve this function of analyzing factors over time, they trigger and intertwine with other sets of actions, as well, for example, making sense of and coordinating color-coding that may not be consistent between prior saved and current views.

Saved views and comments assume other functions and roles during diagnosis, as well. They often double as reports to higher-ups or as work orders for corrections, a function irrelevant to "bounding and formulating a problem." After exploring various functions of this activity, the team is ready to conceptualize designs.

Highlighting Relevant Design Strategies, Criteria, and Choices

In creating support for saving, commenting on, and recalling views of data, the VizAppManager team intends to alter its design strategies and criteria from those that directed the development of its first prototype. Team members know if they were to stick with their previous orientation, they would immediately jump to "obvious candidates" for discrete, unit-level actions.

Some obvious candidates for saving and recalling a view are some combination of "Save View As...," "Insert→Comment" wizards, and directories dedicated to managing saved views. Such features are often layered with options that cover as many different things as users may want to do with the feature as possible, but the features do not call forth the functions and roles these interrelated activities play in users' inquiry experiences.

Obvious candidates, the VizAppManager team agrees, consist of a series of disconnected features and options, and the team wants to avoid such design approaches. When users encounter piece-by-piece support for their integrated investigations, they often are unsure how to combine the discrete parts to match their intentions and goals, or they frequently overlook many pertinent, yet obscure, features altogether (Borland, 2001). Paraphrasing a well-know technology analyst, the VizAppManager interaction designer quips that adding more and more features to meet individual parts of users' integrated needs is like doing drugs—you start small and end up shooting up (Latour, 1995).

To support troubleshooters more usefully, the VizAppManager designers decide on the following strategies to direct their conceptual designing:

- **Focus on the functional roles of the chunked task:** The group concentrates on supporting the different roles recurring sets of actions play in various aspects of the problem solving. These are not generic actions software can support without taking into account ICV conditions.

- **Treat saved views as active problem solving resources:** The designers' strategy is to treat saved views as active resources, not archived artifacts. These resources need to be readily available for analysts to integrate into investigations and workspaces as needed.

- **Think visually, beyond a desktop metaphor:** The VizAppManager team realizes it has to move beyond conventional UI metaphors, such as desktop displays. IT analysts need to save, comment on, and recall *graphic* views and work with them visually for various investigative purposes. Consequently, they need support in the form of visual cues, structures, annotations, and manipulations. They also need a sense of time and place in regards to prior saved and current views to orient them to where they are in their dramatic struggle with a belligerent or opaque infrastructure.

Given these strategies, the VizAppManager team agrees that its focus should be to identify criteria for usefulness in various integrated parts of this multifunctional wayfinding activity. Team members suspend considerations of technical feasibility and effort because they want to be sure they explore wide-ranging possibilities for pragmatic support and usefulness before bringing in technical constraints. Unquestionably, these constraints play a major role in final design decisions, but the team strives to construct a vision of usefulness without censoring possibilities first. Even if the vision is only partially realized in this software version, the team will have produced a concrete and holistic model of useful support, which it can push the larger development group to include in the technology roadmap for the future. The team concurs that success in designing for usefulness comes from persistence rather than expedience, from running marathons rather than sprints. Teammates now turn to brainstorming design choices.

Exploring Criteria and Choices for Saving Relevant Views for Later Use

Teammates determine that saved and commented-on views must act as visible information resources, not components of administrative filing or storage. Team members explore visual, spatial design concepts and discuss such options as Microsoft's "Data Mountains," which places saved views on a pictured mountain range and groups them thematically on various peaks. The team also considers concepts related to XeroxPARC's 3D "rooms" for storing and retrieving information according to tasks (Card et al., 1996; Czerwinski et al., 1999). Both of these options stay true to the inventive metaphor strategy, but they fall short in terms of treating views as active problem solving resources. Both have too strong an administrative and off-screen archiving bent.

A few other choices better satisfy spatial and visual approaches, while still treating saved views as active and *visible* resources. For example, saved views could be shown on the toolbar, as thumbnail sketches, and re-opened in a click of the mouse. Or designs could follow the strategy of Spring's User Creations and present collected, relevant items as icons users can visibly link with others (Figure 5.2).

The notion of visible icons is appealing to the team, but this concept must be robust enough to accommodate other pragmatic functions of users' activity of saving, commenting on, and recalling views, as well. Some other possibilities the team considers are some adaptations of Scopeware's lifestreams concept in its Vision 1.2 and a combination of the MAYAViz CoMotion 2.1 workspace and its "time travel" concept. The team withholds judgment and waits to examine these options in detail when they discuss other functions in upcoming sections.

Exploring Criteria and Choices for Commenting and Reminding

When IT users troubleshoot, they want to use their domain-specific techniques for parsing information and arranging views. In their comments, IT specialists note that they expect to be able to note important inferences, perhaps derived from aggregating values on the fly. Overall, users need to construct or highlight comments by directly manipulating the "marked view" as an object. That way they can fit comments with their intentions,

FIGURE 5.2
Icons of items that can be linked and integrated with each other (courtesy of Spring's User Creations, *www.usercreations.com/spring/*).

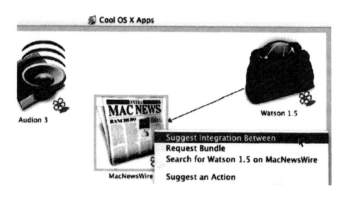

reasoning, displayed value, and data relationships. The marked view is an active problem resource that troubleshooters need to directly annotate, highlight, see, and access, not an archived file. As one design option, the "lifestreams" concept enables users to write comments directly and arrange saved items thematically according to these comments. As another option, CoMotion 2.1 and "time travel" provide workspaces in which users can annotate graphic displays and write and attach notes to views before saving them. Neither thumbnails, nor linked icons, afford such on-the-fly commenting. It is time to turn to these options.

Exploring Criteria and Choices for Being Reminded About a Saved View

Views need to be visible to users as valuable pieces of information in the larger information workspace. Sometimes these views are needed right away and sometimes later, but IT specialists need to be aware of their presence so they are reminded to recall them in some later investigative phase.

A "lifestream" visualization presents saved information as chronological "narratives" or diaries that can be thematically sub-grouped, aggregated, and summarized (Fertig, Freeman, and Gelernter, 1996). This option emphasizes time and theme so IT specialists can quickly and easily see and rearrange saved views according to events that have meaning to them in the "storyline"

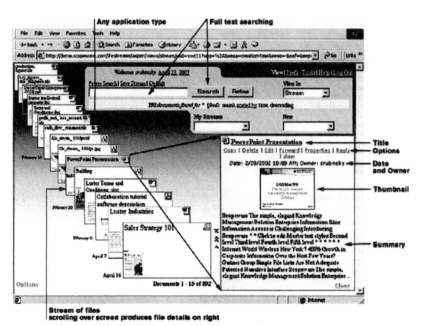

FIGURE 5.3

A "lifestream" interface. In this concept, saved items are displayed visibly and organized chronologically with visual cues in the right-hand corner indicating reminders of what they are. Mousing over an item displays its details. Search capabilities let users find items quickly (courtesy of Scopeware Vision™ 1.2, *www.scopeware.com*).

of their investigation. Such a design, for example, would give Benkei an easy way to find the time-span record he wants to replay (Figure 5.3).

The VizApp Manager designers like the idea of adapting the "lifestream" concept to saved views of data but wish they could incorporate into it some version of a fisheye-lens strategy, as well. This technique would let users view groups of saved items based on their hierarchical proximity to each other and relevance to a line of questioning (Furnas, 1986). A fisheye approach would be powerful because in addition to users seeing a single saved view for later consideration, the fisheye technique would show them other views related to it that may be relevant to this later purpose. Based on the focus and context algorithms of a fisheye lens, troubleshooters, for example, would click on a saved view of interest among a large set of saved views. Others in the set that were close to the one selected both in space and in degree of interest would also come into focus. Degree of interest would be based on an *a priori* principle such as time saved, title, theme, or topic.

Jef Raskin (2000) calls focus-plus-context visualization technique a "zooming interface paradigm." Working outside a desktop metaphor, it is a powerful alternative to linear links. Methods exist for creating a fisheye, focus-plus-context interface. Development methods are also available for achieving similar effects to a fisheye view through different approaches such as semantic (thematic) clustering. Figure 5.4 shows semantically related items displayed and retrieved together, with perceptual cues,

FIGURE 5.4
Example of grouping saved views thematically. The "islands" of items in this Visislands view are clustered by theme and sized by volume (Andrews et al., 2001).

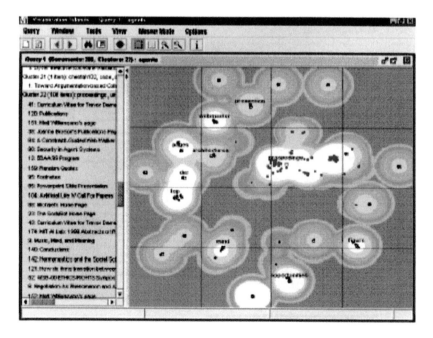

such as size and placement, signaling numbers, and categories of items. Other designs for interactive visualizations of semantic clusters have been developed, as well, such as the Pacific Northwest National Laboratory's project on Spatial Paradigm for Information Retrieval and Exploration (SPIRE) (http://www.pnl.gov/infoviz/index.html).

Exploring Criteria and Choices for Recalling a View

Treating saved views as active information resources means they must be flexible and transportable. The VizAppManager examines the MAYAViz CoMotion 2.1 workspace and "time travel" approach in relation to these needs (Derthick and Roth, 1999). The workspace gives users access to saved views (Figure 5.5) and they can drag and drop them to the workspace. A saved view opens as an active view, ready to compare or otherwise relate to other open, active views. Moreover, features are available for writing "sticky notes" and affixing them to views before saving them.

"Time travel" is an approach specifically aimed at reusing views for comparisons between prior views and a current display, with a good deal of user adaptability and control (Figure 5.6). "Time travel" is exemplary in uniting architecture, functionality, and user interface (UI) design in the cause of usefulness. It treats a user's exploration process as a dataset itself. The program structures each new line of questioning as a new branch of a user's investigation, called a *scenario* or *context*. Databases in the application are structured to capture the state of an interface (graphic view) and

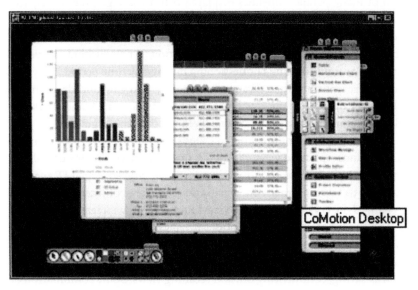

FIGURE 5.5
A workspace with saved items, which are accessible from a vertical toolbar (on the right side). Users recall and open active versions by dragging and dropping them to the workspace (courtesy of MAYAViz, CoMotion 2.1, *www.mayaviz.com*).

FIGURE 5.6

A "time travel" concept. Users can drag and drop events on the timeline to current or prior times in the investigation. The display of the selected events opens as an active view, and users can compare data from the different events (Derthick and Roth, 1999).

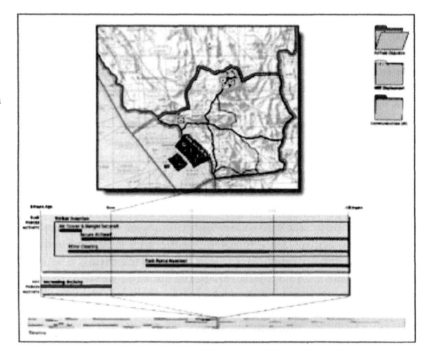

associate it with its context. To maintain the original state of the marked view, the program recreates the view instead of calling up the original.

The "time travel" UI represents the structure of a user's exploration in the form of many parallel timelines displayed beneath the graphic workspace. Each parallel line represents a distinct line of questioning (scenario) and, for each, composite interaction events and timestamps are designated through labels. Users can re-label events and, by pointing to and clicking on events, can jump around to a line of questioning during any time period. They can move any event onto the current workspace by dragging and dropping it. When they drop an event, its "replica" becomes reactivated, and users can relate or compare its data to data displayed in other linked graphics.

This design is groundbreaking in terms of support. It gives users control in fairly uncomplicated ways. It satisfies many of the criteria for usefulness for the multifunctional and unified set of actions and strategies IT analysts carry out to save, comment on, recall, and reuse views of interest. However, it changes the concept of a saved view to an event in a stream of events.

The VizAppManager team is not sure if troubleshooters are ready to leap to this conceptual change, in addition to the other leaps they will have to take for visual querying and novel spatial support for activities such as saving, commenting on, and recalling views. Some combination of the CoMotion 2.1 interface and the Vision™ 1.2 lifestream's functionality might be a better bridge. In addition, the team would like to combine the MAYAViz group's drag-and-drop and reactivated view concepts with designs that show more visibly the saved views and that bring relevant ones together and into focus. Team members sketch some designs that combine all these concepts and hold onto them for later, knowing they must tailor them to other VizAppManager screens for IT troubleshooting patterns.

Design Concepts	Criteria	Strategies
• Visible thumbnail sketches and Linkable icons	• Be able to see saved views on a current screen and access them • Be reminded of what a saved view is at a glance	• Treat saved views as active problem solving resources • Go beyond a desktop metaphor
• Fisheye lens focus plus context • Semantic groupings	• Be able to see in a meaningful focal area other saved views related to the one a user is considering reusing	• Treat saved views as active problem solving resources • Focus on the functional roles of a task for a pattern-based goal • Go beyond a desktop metaphor
• Scopeware Vision™ 1.2 lifestreams concept	• Be able to see views according to when they were saved, plus their themes	• Treat saved views as active problem solving resources • Focus on the functional roles of a task for a pattern-based goal • Go beyond a desktop metaphor

Design Concepts	Criteria	Strategies
• MAYAViz CoMotion 2.1 workspace	• Be able to recall views in an active workspace and reactivate and reuse them in analysis	• Treat saved views as active problem-solving resources • Focus on the functional roles of a task for a pattern-based goal • Go beyond a desktop metaphor
• MAYAViz Time travel concept	• Be able to recall inquiry events in an active workspace and reactivate and reuse them in analysis	• Treat saved views as active problem-solving resources • Focus on the functional roles of a task for a pattern-based goal • Go beyond a desktop metaphor

To review, the team considers and strives to innovatively integrate the following choices for various usefulness criteria and strategies.

As it turns out, team members' designs for holistically supporting IT specialists' integrated patterns of inquiry require functionality that is missing in the core graphics. Therefore, the team makes realistic design choices in keeping with available functionality. Despite compromises, redesign sessions have led the team to construct a truly useful vision of support for IT problem solvers. The team makes sure various hooks and dependencies get built in now to accommodate many enhancements for future versions.

Tradeoffs and technical feasibility deter the visualization team from realizing some, but not all, improvements in usefulness. One thing they can design is an interface for structuring effective entry points into these investigations. The visualization designers now create UIs that allow IT specialists to construct their own way into a line of questioning.

CONCEPTUALIZING DESIGNS FOR FINDING AN ENTRY POINT

In the original VizAppManager prototype, one main shortcoming in usefulness was the design of entry points. The team looks into each of these carefully to decide where to direct efforts in supporting users' needs for appropriate entry points.

Setting the Scope

When the VizAppManager team tested the original prototype in users' everyday work contexts they found that IT troubleshooters value three types of entry points: (1) Entry into triggered alarms to judge the magnitude of the troubleshooting and fault analysis that awaits them; (2) entry into a view of the available data to choose, prepare, and load only data of interest into the graphics; and (3) entry into analytical investigations. The team examines improvements needed for each.

Improving Entry into Alarms

The original prototype provided an ample overview of fired alarms, their severity, and their status. This alarm perspective still needs improvements for other requirements, including more efficiently deleting inconsequential alarms, understanding correlations, creating and verifying nested sorts, and getting details on threshold settings. Despite these shortcomings, as an entry point, the perspective is effective. The other two types of entry points are more problematic.

Improving Entry into Data Preparation

In its first round of design, the VizAppManager team thought very little about IT users' needs for preparing and filtering data before seeing and working with the visualizations. Problem solvers want to see available data and filter out irrelevant data before loading and running the graphic displays.

The visualization team now needs to create an entry point for data previews and preparation. They design an interface for perusing and filtering data by choosing an obvious candidate instead of one of the visualization techniques that are available for query previews. They choose an interactive dialogue in which the dialogue box tells users the size of the dataset, its fields, and its time and date ranges. It allows users to select the fields and time periods relevant to their inquiry and use these parameters to limit the data loaded into the graphics. This quick and straightforward design gives the team more time to spend on entry points into users' analyses.

Improving Entry into Analytical Investigations

The original prototype provided pre-defined perspectives intended as entry points for data analysis. It gave an overview of alarms, snapshots, and over-time views of conditions. These pre-defined views treated IT users' decisions about what perspective best fits their lines of questioning as a keystroke "procedure." Unfortunately, this decision has too many considerations and too much variability to be reduced to a preset procedure.

Canned perspectives as entry points limit IT analysts' problem solving range and depth. In the prototype, the design team mistakenly presumed that as long as the tool offered a view on alarms, this view would cover for all occasions requiring the use of alarm data in an inquiry. In fact, it did not. To IT users, combining views of alarms and system conditions is an integral part of setting up their workspaces. It also supports them in turning quantitative data into qualitative judgments.

Highlighting Relevant Design Strategies, Criteria, and Choices

To redesign more flexible and adaptable entry points, members of the VizAppManager team start by critiquing their original prototype's entry points for monitoring system conditions. They look at the intended entry points into detecting a problem. The first, the snapshot overview, represents the physical network—with machines perceptually coded as squares and applications as circles (see Figure 4.4A). The graphs provide details through histograms, data tables, bar charts, with color-coding bringing in the additional dimension of response time. The second perspective, the over-time view, shows all alarms for a color-coded time-series graph (see Figure 4.4B).

In the prototype trials, both of these options for entry points satisfied IT users for some types of problems. However, the perspectives were not supple enough to reflect the "just-so" conditions that occurred when an abnormality took place. Users could combine views with other views, but that resulted in a cluttered workspace. It also slowed troubleshooters down as they hassled with resizing and positioning windows.

As soon as the team finishes its critique, one member proposes a design solution, and several others become immediately committed to it. The solution is for users to create their own analytical graphics from scratch using such visualization techniques as Visualization Assistant or the Delaunay Visualization System (Ignatius et al., 1994; Cruz and Leveille, 2001). In these techniques users specify the logical, context-free tasks they want to perform—tasks such as "correlate x and y"—and automated graphing "assistants" refer to rules about graphic principles and perceptual theory to construct relevant data displays.

Other team members worry that their teammates are focusing too quickly on design solutions. They succeed in getting the team to first analyze models of work and the results of the original prototype trials to thoroughly identify the different ways IT specialists approach entering various lines of investigation. During one of these sessions, the system engineer expresses her exasperation with this method of redesign, saying, "Do we really have to do this? Let's design the view first and think of the questions afterward."

The design team finds that IT users want the flexibility to create entry points, but they do not want to create graphics from scratch. They want to use a semi-structured, "build your own" approach. As a safety net, they like having a few canned possibilities available, but only if they are accompanied by semi-structured options to create their own, with guidance as needed. The team also finds that, regardless of the situation, IT users fundamentally examine a common set of data. The team realizes these data can be captured in a dozen or so views.

Having analyzed these user needs and identified corresponding criteria, the team is able to articulate a new design strategy—to provide semi-structured choices based on users' domain-specific practices and knowledge. This strategy leads the designers to reject the earlier option of users creating graphics from scratch.

They now brainstorm possible choices and decide on one that involves offering users a separate screen for creating entry points into their investigations. On the screen are several graphic options for IT users to combine as they like to create a single perspective. Based on team members' expertise in graphics and aided by IT experts' counsel in detailing their analytical needs, the team composes graphics for core analyses in troubleshooting and fault analysis. In an entry point interface, IT users drag and drop whatever graph they choose into blank panes of what will become the perspective window. They can also preview and revise the graphs and change aspects such as fields, axis measures, color-coding, and data arrangements once they decide on a perspective. The VizAppManager team, at first, categorizes the graph options by problem type (e.g., database locks), but they learn from their user contacts in IT organizations that users simply want the entry point interface to label graphs according to the data they display and their time scale. This scheme lets users readily choose over-time and snapshot views to match their intentions and circumstances. The resulting conceptual sketch for these create-your-own entry points is depicted in Figure 5.7.

The design team asks IT users to work with a mock-up of this conceptual design. The effect is considerably better than the original prototype, in which IT users spent several minutes struggling to make meaning of a canned entry-point perspective. In the redesign, IT users know exactly

FIGURE 5.7
Design concept for creating an entry point. The prototype displays actual thumbnail graphics for each view in the boxes in this sketch.

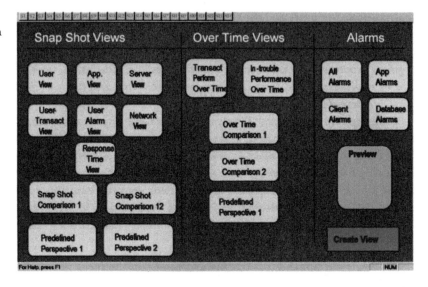

what they are looking at because the graphics show data as they think about it for specific tasks. Moreover, choosing graphs instead of defining each one from scratch keeps investigative costs low.

The original prototype and its canned views underestimated the flexibility IT specialists need. The prototype also underestimated IT specialists' facility

Design Concept	Criteria	Strategy
• Mix and match graphs from which to construct a perspective suited to inquiry needs	• Identify graphs most relevant to a desired line of questioning • Efficiently create or find an entry point without requiring training in graphic literacy • Recognize or configure the group of graphs best suited to inquiry intentions Preview the configured perspective to see if it matches intentions	• Create semi-structured choices that give users freedom to choose according to their domain expertise, pattern-based practices, and understanding of situational conditions

in mapping their inquiry intentions to graphic displays. These problem solvers want power, not simplified and overly determined inquiry workspaces, as follows.

Giving IT users a separate screen for creating entry points accommodates expert problem solvers' needs. Introducing a separate screen for this purpose is somewhat akin to the frame-by-frame filmmaking strategies discussed in the book's introduction—the technique that made the final release of *Casablanca* work with audiences. Just as *Casablanca*'s film editors revised the initial draft of the movie by adding two "pausing" frames for greater effect, the entry point screen better blends action and reflection. This seemingly slight alteration structurally shifts users' points of view dramatically. They now become involved in interacting with the application from a first-person perspective or initiative. In controlling the setup of their view they direct the plot of their own exploration. The prototype's pre-defined screens, by contrast, structured them into a generic role—a third-person perspective ("they") in which one storyline fits all. Designing the space for constructing entry points in this new way recognizes that problem solvers must interweave plans and actions from a perspective that puts them in the center of the action.

CONCLUSIONS

The VizAppManager team seeks to support IT troubleshooters in complexities that typify familiar problem solving situations as well as wicked ones. In both, users work in a highly complex infrastructure examining huge amounts of diverse data, and they draw inferences from incomplete information. In piecing together partial pictures from numerous individual tools and in integrating evidence from multiple perspectives, IT specialists often are obstructed from their desired investigative approaches by incompatibilities among interacting contextual conditions.

In this round of designing the VizAppManager, the team realizes that if this IT monitoring and problem solving tool is to mesh with the dynamic work tier-two and tier-three analysts do to keep systems up and running, it needs to offer integrated support for IT users' integrated activities. Team members, therefore, analyze and model users' patterns of inquiry in relation to the ways in which multiple contextual forces shape IT users' actions as they proceed through semi- or unstructured inquiry paths. From this analysis and modeling, team members identify wayfinding tasks that software for complex problem solving often overlooks in terms of useful support. They strive to do otherwise.

For the wayfinding activity of saving, commenting on, and recalling views of interest, the team does not think about or implement "solutions" for separate actions. Rather, they treat the actions within this wayfinding activity as an integrated whole and highlight the functional role of these actions in relation to users' pattern-based purposes. Moreover, to design holistically, they treat saved views as active resources and emphasize visual and spatial support.

For the wayfinding activity of finding an appropriate entry point for inquiry, the team pursues the strategy of giving users semi-structured choices that still leave a great deal of leeway for troubleshooters to structure an appropriate view for their domain-based priorities and situational conditions. In conceptual designs for both of these wayfinding activities, the VizAppManager designers strive for visualizations that are powerful, flexible, approachable, and forgiving.

The areas of support the team targets are often underdeveloped in current IT monitoring and troubleshooting tools and are also common usefulness flaws in software for complex problem solving in other domains. The IT case in this chapter did not address all of them. However, many not examined here surface in different forms in the design stories in the next three chapters.

As the IT case in this and the previous chapter shows, subpatterns and chunked tasks in need of support do not occur in isolation but as part of a contextually determined activity. The case in the next chapter continues to explore useful support for underemphasized areas of problem solving, this time in the domain of category management in merchandising. It focuses on the complex problem of figuring out the best mix of products to sell for the greatest competitive advantage. Like the IT case, the next one also deals with designing interactive data visualizations to support open-ended data explorations and analyses.

The product mix case, however, gives new insights into a different type of problem, system of work, and application. It explores merchandisers' inquiries into problems in complex adaptive social systems—volatile markets—not sophisticated technological systems. The software that category managers use to investigate these problems functions differently from IT specialists' tools, which are an intrinsic part of the troubleshooters' larger, technical "centrally scheduled system." Product mix problem solving applications, by contrast, are stand-alone "information service" systems, or desktop applications that provide users with analytical support for and links to historical data on product performance, market trends, and customer behaviors.

REFERENCES

Borland, Russell. Personal communication, 2001.

Andrews, Keith, Christian Gütl, Joseph Moser, Vedran Sobol, and Wilfried Lackner. Search "Result Visualization With XFind," *Proceedings of Second International Workshop on User Interfaces to Data Intensive Systems.* (UIDIS) 50-59, Zurich; IEEE, 2001.

Card, Stuart, George Robertson, and William York. "The Web-Book and the Web Forager: An Information Workspace for the World Wide Web." *Proceedings of CHI 96,* ACM Conference on Human Factors in Computing Systems, 111-117. Vancouver: ACM, 1996.

Cruz, Isabel and Peter Leveille. "As You Like It; Personalized Database Visualization Using a Visual Language." *Journal of Visual Languages and Computing* 12, no. 5 (2001): 525-549.

Czerwinski, May, Susan Dumais, George Robertson, Susan Dziadosz, Scott Tiernan, and Maarten van Dantzich. "Visualizing Implicit Queries for Information Management and Retrieval." *Proceedings of CHI 99,* ACM Conference on Human Factors and Computing Systems 560-567. Pittsburgh: ACM, 1999.

Derthick, Mark and Steven Roth. "Enhancing Data Exploration with a Branching History of User Operations." *Knowledge Based Systems* 14, nos. 1-2 (1999): 65-74.

Fertig, Scott, Eric Freeman, and David Gelernter. "An Alternative to the Desktop Metaphor." *SIGCHI Conference on Human Factors in Computing Systems Conference Companion,* 410-411. Vancouver: ACM, 1996.

Furnas, George. "Generalized Fisheye Views." *Proceedings of CHI 86,* ACM Conference on Human Factors and Computing Systems 16-23. Boston: ACM.

Goodwin, Charles. "The Blackness of Black: Color Categories as Situated Practice." In *Discourse, Tools and Reasoning: Essays on Situated Cognition,* edited by Lauren B. Resnick, Roger Säljö, Clotilde Pontecorvo, and Barbara Burge. Berlin: Springer, 111-140, 1997,

Hutchins, Edwin. *Cognition in the Wild.* Cambridge, MA: MIT Press, 1995.

Ignatius, Eve, Hikmet Senay, and Jean Favre. "An Intelligent System for Task-specific Visualization Assistance." *Journal of Visual Languages and Computing* 5, no. 4 (1994): 321-338.

Kulak, Daryl and Eamonn Guiney. *Use Cases: Requirements in Context.* Reading, MA: Addison-Wesley, 2000.

Latour, Bruno. 1995. "Mixing Humans and Nonhumans Together: The Sociology of a Door Closer." In *Ecologies of Knowledge: Work and Politics in Science and Technology,* edited by Susan Leigh Star, 257-277. Albany: SUNY Press, 1995.

Raskin, Jef. *The Humane Interface: New Directions for Designing Interactive Systems.* Reading, MA: Addison-Wesley, 2000.

Trafton, J. Gregory, Susan Kirschenbaum, Ted Tsui, Rober Miyamoto, James Ballas, and Paula Raymond. "Turning Pictures Into Numbers: Extracting and Generating Information From Complex Visualizations." *International Journal of Human-Computer Studies* 53, no. 5 (2000): 827-850.

6

Criteria, Constraints, and Choices: Optimizing the Mix in Merchandising

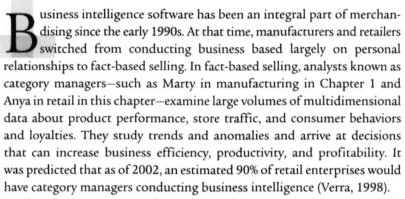

usiness intelligence software has been an integral part of merchandising since the early 1990s. At that time, manufacturers and retailers switched from conducting business based largely on personal relationships to fact-based selling. In fact-based selling, analysts known as category managers—such as Marty in manufacturing in Chapter 1 and Anya in retail in this chapter—examine large volumes of multidimensional data about product performance, store traffic, and consumer behaviors and loyalties. They study trends and anomalies and arrive at decisions that can increase business efficiency, productivity, and profitability. It was predicted that as of 2002, an estimated 90% of retail enterprises would have category managers conducting business intelligence (Verra, 1998).

This chapter examines the patterns of inquiry and decision-making that software needs to support to be useful for solving one of the main problems that confronts retail category managers: Deciding what mix of products they should sell for the greatest success. In this chapter's scenario, Anya, a grocery chain analyst, concentrates on putting together the best assortment of products for increased sales, profits, and market share without undercutting her stores' image of having the largest variety in town or her relationships with preferred suppliers. This problem differs from those tackled by category managers in manufacturing, as exemplified by Marty's inquiry into whether to introduce a new product into a growing market niche (see Chapter 1).

Anya's problem and the support she needs for it reflect a type of exploratory analysis common to many domains. Across the work world, analysts who choose a select set of items to achieve a projected outcome share Anya's patterns of inquiry. To select the optimal items, analysts evaluate which ones best satisfy numerous criteria and constraints involving multiple attributes in various combinations. For example, analysts make such optimizing decisions when they invest financially, allocate resources, manage inventory and project portfolios, select sites, plan capacity, and design product components. Like Anya, these problem solvers consider a wide range of metrics, correlate them in complicated ways and strive to balance competing criteria and priorities with anticipated future variability. Consumers also go through optimizing inquiries in Websites and application when buying homes or cars and when deciding about healthcare, insurance policies, or scores of other quality of life issues.

Software and web applications that support optimizing decisions are widely used in management, but Anya does not use them. Her situated problem solving suggests that such software would not suffice for the subjective intelligence and expert intuition she brings to bear in her work. Her emerging insights, shifting strategies, and on-the-fly judgments cannot be accounted for in advance. Moreover, as her exploratory patterns show, it is unlikely that she would be able to specify ahead of time many of the inputs required by optimizing applications, such as complete and exact mathematical detail about what she is looking for, what all the relevant parameters are, and how parameters should be weighed or traded-off in relation to one another. Therefore, for this type of inquiry, whether in category management or another domain, useful software that gives problem solvers control over critically exploring and evaluating possible choices and trade-offs is vital.

Anya's problem is at the top of the scale in terms of complexity. It has all the traits of complexity described in Chapter 1. It is a problem grounded and solved in one of the most highly variable social systems we have: The marketplace. This complex adaptive system is driven by complicated human behaviors. Retailers may apply economic formulas and analyze hard figures such as dollar sales, volume, profits, return on investment, geographic reach, traffic patterns, and market share, but the decisions they make about product mix are best guesses. Nothing similar to troubleshooting diagnostics exists to validate solutions conclusively in merchandising. Instead, in analyses of social systems such as markets, even if people seem to behave predictably based on dependable conventions and rules, the cumulative effects inevitably produce surprises. Even the most sophisticated of retailers' probabilistic models cannot foretell the unexpected.

In this chapter, I highlight the design thinking and the modeling of users' patterns of inquiry and task landscapes that are prerequisites for designing usefulness into applications for these complex optimizing problems. I present Anya's scenario and then explore her patterns of problem solving, their landscapes of mainline and enabling tasks, and their choice points. All of these need to be supported but often are not, as we will see with Anya.

In the discussion of Benkei's scenario (see Chapters 4 and 5), the emphasis in modeling IT users' work was on capturing the interactive conditions and constraints within and across contexts that shape problem solving options. Anya's case adds to the models of work relevant to complex problem solving. It provides detailed representations of pattern-based task landscapes and core interconnected inquiry activities relevant to her optimizing problem. The next chapter applies these models to conceptual designing and explores design strategies and choices for usefulness relevant to Anya's best product mix inquiry.

In thinking about these complex problems and in modeling users' work, design teams need to recognize that representing inquiry patterns at a practical (application) level is necessary for useful software. As discussed previously inquiry patterns are crucial for capturing the following:

- The structures of users' problem solving that need to frame design choices (even in inquiries fraught with variability and multiplicity)

- The leeway problem solvers require to configure landscapes of mainline and enabling tasks that accord with situational idiosyncrasies

- The cumulative quality of investigations that needs to be supported in design

- The regularity and variability that merge in choice points and the freedom users need for choosing

SOLVING PRODUCT MIX PROBLEMS

Product mix problems, deciding the best assortment of products to stock and sell, are one of four complex "p" questions that merchandise tackle. The other three are determining the best placement (what to keep in inventory and where to shelve items), price (how much to charge), and promotions (which items to push and through what means). Though Anya's scenario does not focus on these other "ps", in everyday practice, analysts like her connect product mix investigations with in-depth analyses of placement, price, and promotions.

When dealing with the product mix part of the four "ps," category managers go through multi-phased investigations. Because of limited time and space, I present only the first phase of product mix decision-making in this scenario, a phase known in the industry as efficient assortment assessment. Category managers conduct this first phase with a constant anticipation of the questions they will ask in later phases. Moreover, as we see with Anya, sometimes analysts skip ahead to preview later phases before finishing an earlier one. To provide the full context of Anya's interrelated concerns, I detail all the phases of product mix investigations in Table 6.1.

As with the information technology (IT) problem solving scenario in Chapters 4 and 5, Anya's efficient assortment assessment is a composite derived from many different field studies and design projects I have worked on in category management. The two software programs Anya uses are also composites that represent typical, though not actual, data visualization applications for these types of problems in the market.

SCENARIO: DECIDING THE BEST MIX OF SHORTENING AND OILS FOR A WESTERN CHAIN

Anya, a category manager for a large Western grocery chain, is in charge of the shortening and oils category. Lately, consumer concerns about health have been causing sales in this category to fluctuate wildly. Anya and her supervisor want to get on top of the problem and make this category

Phase of Inquiry	Investigations That Analysts Conduct
Efficient assortment assessment	Classifying products as high and low movers and as winners, losers, sleepers, or opportunities in anticipation of later decisions about items to keep, add, or drop. This includes answering such questions as: ■ What segments of products best reflect buyers' purchasing patterns, uses, and intents? ■ Nationwide, which segments and subcategories are sleepers, winners, losers, and opportunities based on sales, growth, profits, traffic, and the like? ■ How would I classify the same nationwide products in my store based on performance? ■ What items should be doing better and if I keep them in the mix what enhancements in assortment, pricing, promotions, or placement may be needed? ■ How do my provisional judgments about products to keep, drop, or enhance stack up against the nationwide findings? Are there some products I don't carry but should?
Effective assortment assessment	Evaluating the competitive strengths and weaknesses of various projected mixes of products, which might include products not currently stocked. This involves answering such questions as: ■ How are these products doing in my store versus competitors' stores in my market? ■ Where am I threatened competitively? ■ What items and segments do competitors carry that I don't?

TABLE 6.1
Different phases of investigating the best product mix.

TABLE 6.1
Continued

Phase of Inquiry	Investigations That Analysts Conduct
	What opportunity dollars am I losing by not carrying them?
	■ What new products are entering the market and what segments do they fill? What is the potential contribution of each?
	■ Based on the competition, which subcategories and segments in my store require fewer or more items? Where should I grow? What should I introduce, and what should I discontinue?
Item optimization	Judging various mixes against numerous constraints, including space, labor, inventory, strategic role of a category, and other business strategies. This involves answering such questions as:
	■ How should I rank products, considering performance, competition, resources, store image, manufacturers' incentives, and other business strategies?
	■ Should I invest more resources in pursuing opportunities or in bolstering hot items?
	■ Which items in a segment are duplicates and which are unique? Of the duplicates, which will customers be willing to switch to? Which items should I add and delete and in what amounts to balance variety and duplication?
	■ What proportion of the gross does each product in my current mix generate? What other products have similar percentages? Can I add some of these others to maintain traffic and increase profits?

TABLE 6.1
Continued

Phase of Inquiry	Investigations That Analysts Conduct
Category profit analysis	Evaluating the profitability of tentative decisions about items to drop, keep, and enhance (e.g., through promotion). This includes answering such questions as: ■ What percent of products in each segment offset their losses and what are these items? ■ What are the true costs of products, considering direct and indirect activity-driven costs? ■ What are the costs of products that do not make much money and how much do they nibble away at profits? If they should be in the mix for strategic reasons (e.g., if cutting them will reduce traffic), then should I price or promote them better?

profitable again. To assess the best product mix, she uses two different data visualization applications. Each is good for a different part of her inquiry; neither is good for both parts. One visualization application helps her analyze her category nationwide; the other is better for investigating her proprietary store data together with the national data for a close look at trends and aberrations in her own region and market.

Both visualization applications let Anya query and analyze data directly on the graphics, saving her the bother of having to flip back and forth between reports and visual displays. The graphics, perceptual coding, dynamic linking, and visual querying help her to discover relationships in the data that would take hours to find in strictly tabular displays.

Some of Anya's analysis may have a familiar ring to it. Marty in Chapter 1 looks at many similar issues in the course of his work. Despite the similarities, Anya's investigations have a different emphasis because her questions serve different ends.

Anya's Goals and Intentions

For Anya's efficient assortment assessment, her goals are to make some preliminary judgments about items she should keep, drop, and enhance, perhaps through promotions, in her stores. She concentrates on an overview of how shortening and oils are doing nationwide and a detailed view of how they are doing in her markets. First she intends to take a brief look at syndicated national data on the performance of products in the food channel. If time permits, she will analyze her category in the mass merchandising channel, as well, because she directly competes with super centers such as Wal-Mart in her region. Then she intends to delve into her own stores' proprietary data combined with syndicated data and evaluate product performance in just her markets and region. In all geographic categories (nationwide, region, markets, and her stores), she will apply baseline measures to identify products that are winners, losers, sleepers, and opportunities. She then will assess their strengths and weaknesses for the projected mix. From these findings, she will make some provisional choices about products to include or not in her stores.

Nationwide: Getting an Overall Sense of Product Performance

Anya opens the first data visualization program and calls up a perspective analogous to a 30,000 foot view of shortenings and oils. She color-codes it by subcategory. Blue represents cooking oil, green microwave and pan sprays, yellow olive oil, and red shortening (Figure 6.1). At the top left, the perspective displays a bar chart of each vendor's dollar sales, and next to this is a bar chart on dollar sales for brands. Both bar charts are ordered from high sales to low sales. In the lower left of the perspective is a third bar chart of dollar sales for each subcategory. Each type of oil or shortening is color-coded by its corresponding shade. Adjacent to it, a data table gives detailed measures and descriptions for each stock keeping unit (SKU)—a unique number identifying a product for inventory purposes. The perspective combines details and overview.

The color-coding of the view by type (subcategory) of shortening or oil never fails to give Anya pause when she looks at the vendor and brand bar charts. She knows the length of each bar represents the total dollar sales for all products belonging to a particular vendor or brand. She also knows from experience that the "striped" color-coding in any one bar shows how these total dollar sales are distributed across each subcategory of the vendor or brand's products. Vendors with blue and green stripes, for example, manufacture cooking oils (blue) and microwave and pan sprays (green). Even though Anya conceptually understands the stripes, it always takes her a moment to study and process the meaning of the coloring. Mentally, she evaluates how valid the graphics are by gauging the length of different color stripes in vendor and brand bars against what she knows

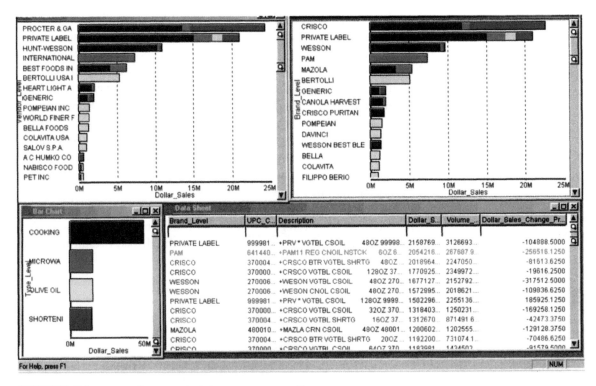

FIGURE 6.1 "30,000-foot view" of the category overall.

to be true about a particular vendor or brand's diversity in the actual market.

Anya now studies what the interrelated graphics are telling her. She sees that private labels are doing great and jots down their performance figures. Later, in another phase of this product mix investigation, she will compare these figures to her own chain's private brand. She writes down figures on private labels by hand rather than bookmarking the view for a couple of reasons. From experience she knows that she accumulates so many bookmarks during an inquiry session that the sheer number of them becomes prohibitive. She also does not bookmark because she cannot circle the private label data or otherwise call it out in this program. Without such reminders she worries she will forget why she saved the view when she turns to it later.

Nationwide: Identifying High and Low Sellers

Anya now wants to know what SKUs contribute the most to sales in each subcategory. She changes the color-coding to dollar sales to help her in analyzing. In the new color-coding, reds stand for high sellers, and colors descend through the spectrum to blue as dollar sales decrease (Figure 6.2). The new color-coding changes the stripes on the bars. These new stripes are harder to decipher because they represent ranges of numeric values. Anya calls up a legend, which shows the value ranges assigned to each color, but this information does not help much in grasping exact color-based proportions in any one bar or, harder yet, comparing proportions across bars of different lengths. The program offers little support for this sensemaking.

Anya could discern these proportions better if she standardized the bar charts, but she believes she has spent too much time studying the coloring already and moves on.

Anya is now ready to examine high and low movers in each subcategory. She selects each subcategory's bar, one by one, from the graphic in the lower left of the screen. Figure 6.2 shows the displays resulting from

FIGURE 6.2
High sellers in each subcategory nationwide: (1) cooking oil only, (2) olive oil, (3) microwave and pan sprays, and (4) shortening.

progressively selecting (1) cooking oil only, (2) olive oil, (3) microwave and pan sprays, and (4) shortening. When Anya chooses a category, its data alone stay highlighted; the rest turn gray. In this way, Anya sees the focus of her attention within the context of the rest of the data.

As Anya examines each subcategory, she cross-references the data table for details. She readily sees the high movers and their performance figures because they are highlighted in red and orange. An exception is the olive oil subcategory (see Figure 6.2.3). It has no eye-grabbing reds or oranges because the color-coding represents dollar sales in the whole category, and the olive oil group makes a relatively small contribution to total category sales. Yet in Anya's markets, olive oils are more important than their relative nationwide sales would suggest. Unlike in the rest of the nation, they are the high sellers in the West, with its health-conscious consumers. Olive oil is Anya's strongest subcategory and home to some of her most influential preferred suppliers.

Anya wishes she could custom-color the spread of data separately for each subcategory while still keeping the context visible so she could more precisely discern the distinguishing performance values for olive oils. Unable to do what she wants, Anya squints, moves in on the screen, and does anything else she can think of to discriminate between the shades of blues and greens to find the highest-selling olive oils. When she finishes with this subcategory, she moves to the next subcategory and finishes this overview inquiry into high and low performers.

Nationwide: Setting up Views of Winners, Losers, Sleepers, and Opportunities

Anya next investigates which products and brands belonging to the top vendors do best in terms of multiple performance measures. For example, are the highest selling items growing, staying flat, or shrinking in sales? Even high-selling products worry Anya if they show little growth compared to competing products. Ultimately, Anya will assess products' performances for pairs of measures and, based on outcomes, will divide products into winners, losers, sleepers, and opportunities. From the results of this "quadrant analysis," which is the stock in trade of category managers, Anya will begin to decide which items to keep, drop, or enhance.

Anya introduces a scatterplot into the graphic view that relates sales to growth (Figure 6.3). On this graphic, she can change an axis in a keystroke to a different measure, for example, to market share. Anya likes that she can create her own graphics as needed, including creating and concurrently displaying different scatterplots for various correlations. Though she could, she rarely displays numerous scatterplots at once. She opts instead to change axes, knowing from experience that too many graphics on the screen overwhelm and confuse her.

Displaying a scatterplot that relates sales to growth, Anya now intends to divide the scatterplot into quadrants and look at one subcategory at a time to see which products from top vendors fall into the sleepers (Figure 6.3a), winners (Figure 6.3b), losers (Figure 6.3c), and opportunity quadrants (Figure 6.3d).

She focuses first on cooking oils and filters to just this subcategory by sweeping the cooking oil bar in Figure 6.3, in the lower left bar chart (the top and longest bar). She then clicks a button to exclude all but the selected data. For now, context is not relevant so she excludes it. She gets the display shown in Figure 6.4A. The unselected data disappear from the display and from any calculations.

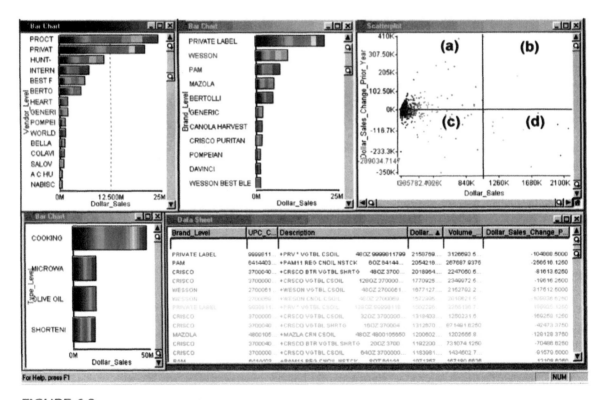

FIGURE 6.3
All subcategories' products by sales and growth. Quadrants in the scatterplot divide products into (a) sleepers, (b) winners, (c) losers, and (d) opportunities.

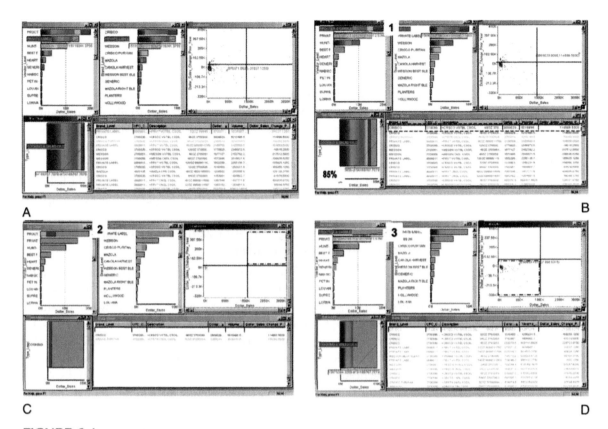

FIGURE 6.4
Identifying winners and losers in cooking oils only in a situation requiring varied selection modes. (A) An overview of sales to growth for all cooking oil products. (B) A view of sales to growth for only the top vendors' cooking oils. (C) A view of winners (high sales and high growth) in top vendors' cooking oils. (D) A view of losers (low sales and low growth) in top vendors' cooking oils.

This method of selecting one subcategory and deleting all others works fine for Anya until she needs to be reminded about how products are clustered in another subcategory—a frequent need in her investigations. If Anya has bookmarked the other view, she can flip to it, but she first has to bookmark her present view or she cannot get back to it. If she were to bookmark all views to which she might return, she would have too many bookmarks to manage. If she does not bookmark the other view, she has to re-execute all the steps for drilling down to the other subcategory and excluding the other data. In the process, she would lose her current view. In either case, she cannot keep both the current and other views visible.

Once Anya generates the cooking oil view, she sets the values for the boundaries of the quadrants based on what she knows from her category expertise to be the spread of the market values in cooking oils. The program displays the dividing lines for the quadrant analysis (Figure 6.4A). Next she further prepares for analysis by selecting and narrowing in on only the top vendors in cooking oils (Figure 6.4B). She also calls up a table that displays automatically calculated combined market shares for the data she selects. Anya is now ready to analyze and evaluate details about products falling into each quadrant by cross-referencing the data table and scatterplot.

Anya intends to pay particular attention to lite oils, which she thinks will take off soon due to consumers' health concerns. Her supervisor has told her to consider abandoning this pet strategy of hers, but she believes strongly in it and wants to discover whether the data will back her up.

Nationwide: Selecting and Analyzing Top Cooking Oil Vendors' Winners and Losers

Anya is now heading into complicated query territory. She is ready to analyze just the winners' (top right-hand) quadrant for cooking oils with a focus on only the leading vendors' products. These vendors' products are currently highlighted in all quadrants, but Anya wants them highlighted only in the winners' quadrant so when she cross-references the data table for details she will see only top vendors' winners highlighted. What she needs is a subset (winners) of a subset (top vendors) displayed against the backdrop of all the other cooking oil data for comparison. She does this querying visually, by pressing down the left button on her mouse and sweeping the mouse across the winner's quadrant. First, however, she has to change the selection mode. Different modes for mouse-based selection are built into the program for just such purposes.

Anya switches to intersect-mode so when she sweeps the winners' quadrant only the top vendors' winners stay highlighted in all the graphs on the screen (see Figure 6.4C). From this selection, Anya sees that only two of the three top vendors' items have high sales and high growth (winners), and she bookmarks the view. She also saves the data behind the view into a spreadsheet. Later she will feed the spreadsheet data into her item list. Her item list is the document in which she keeps a running record of what she will keep, drop, or enhance as she moves along in her investigation. It is located in another program, and Anya has no direct access to it from this one.

Anya now recalls the sales and growth view that highlights top vendors' products in all quadrants. Ready to investigate losers, she repeats the same querying process but this time focusing on the loser quadrant (Figure 6.4D). She concentrates hard to keep track of what selection mode she is in. Aside from some slight confusion with the selection mode, the investigations so far have been fairly straightforward.

Nationwide: Selecting Top Cooking Oil Vendors' Sleepers and Opportunities

Sleepers and opportunities present more complicated analytical demands. These products are iffy. Anya has to relate more factors to see whether they are good candidates for keeping or dropping and to see how their performance might be boosted if she decides to keep them.

Before looking separately first at sleepers and then opportunities, Anya wants to see what kind of overall assortment and performance record she is looking at in these two categories combined. To examine the two quadrants together, Anya has to once again switch in and out of different selection modes. In intersect mode, she first sweeps the opportunity quadrant to highlight top vendors' opportunity products. To add top vendors' sleepers to this subset, she switches to add mode and sweeps the sleepers quadrant. Though she does not realize it at first, she does not get the data display she intends from these moves.

When she conducts the last move—sweeping in add mode—she gets data from all vendors highlighted, not solely those from the subset of top vendors. But she does not immediately catch this mistake. The other vendors' bars are so small, and the consequent highlighting so indiscernible, that Anya does not see these other vendors' data light up after she sweeps the sleeper quadrant in add mode. She only catches her error when she scans the data table descriptions and recognizes products from minor vendors that should not be there. She tries different methods, and each fails. Finally she searches the online help, and it jolts her memory. She now recalls that she has tried this querying before and the program does not support this type of nested selection. She kicks herself for forgetting and moves on.

Nationwide: Analyzing Sleepers

Anya does not analyze items that are sleepers the same way she investigates winners and losers. Anya's supervisor is a strong proponent of promoting sleepers heavily, and following his lead, Anya gives more weight to the potential effects of promotions than to other enhancements. Unfortunately, she has to do this weighting mentally because, short of revising the raw data tables, Anya has no way to weight data on-the-fly in her program.

Next, she adds new columns to the data table, anticipating the data she wants to present in the bookmarked view and spreadsheet data when she saves this analysis. She re-sorts the table by promotions and color-codes by the same measure. The result is Figure 6.5.

Once more the bars in the bar charts change stripes and take on yet another meaning. This time Anya can make very little sense of the colors and does not have the patience to study them closely. Believing them to be

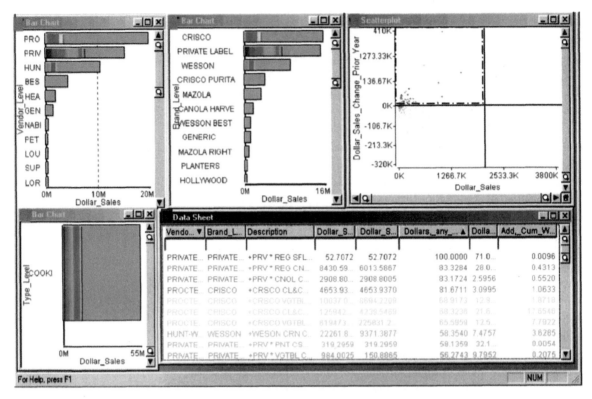

FIGURE 6.5
Top vendors' sleepers in cooking oil nationwide (color-coded by dollars brought in through promotions with red standing for high dollars and moving down through the spectrum to blue for low dollars) Red and orange items show sleepers that depend heavily on promotions for their sales.

irrelevant to her current line of questioning, Anya disregards the many-colored bars and turns directly to finding items that look like poor and good candidates for promotion. She will probably drop poor candidates for promotion—the reds and oranges—from the product mix.

When Anya is done mentally assessing the unprofitable sleepers, she turns to the blues and greens in the data table: The items that have not yet been heavily promoted and that might improve with the right promotional campaign. Anya itemizes these good candidates and saves the views.

Anya's investigation into "sleeper-keepers" and "sleeper-rejects" is not yet done. All things being equal, if several sleepers in the same segment are contending for promotional resources and Anya can only afford to keep some of them, she will go with her preferred suppliers' products and the slotting she gets from these suppliers. Slotting is when preferred suppliers give stores monetary incentives to keep their products in the mix.

Anya's next order of business is to evaluate her preferred suppliers' sleepers. Unfortunately, she cannot group together rows of all her preferred suppliers to easily view and analyze them. Sorting by vendor only works alphabetically, and these suppliers are dispersed throughout the alphabet.

Therefore, Anya tediously scrolls one-by-one to each supplier and studies its products and their figures. One product she sees has been heavily promoted already, and its sales are unimpressive (Figure 6.6). However, it demonstrates considerable growth, which might make it worth keeping. Because she cannot sort the data table to group her preferred suppliers together, Anya writes notes by hand. This is easier than saving the view and trying later to sort through an ungrouped running display of these items.

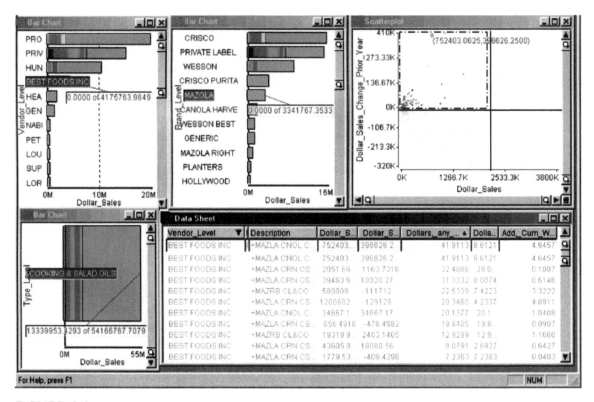

FIGURE 6.6
Preferred suppliers' cooking oils that are sleepers.
Note: All are in gray because none is a top vendor, the highlighted set of data. A heavily promoted Mazola oil with high growth is singled out (a preferred supplier's product), with figures for it displayed.

When finished analyzing preferred suppliers' sleepers, Anya runs through another analysis of top vendors' sleepers, this time evaluating good and bad candidates for price reductions. She concentrates intensely to be sure she redisplays the right view and reselects data in the appropriate modes.

After analyzing sleepers, Anya looks briefly at opportunities. She typically analyzes them more in-depth during the item optimization phase of her inquiry. Her focus now is to preview which opportunities bring in a good deal of store traffic for other items, even if they themselves do not sell or grow well. She is likely to keep such loss leaders if she sees that, in addition to traffic, they are instrumental in generating profits in these connected areas.

Anya hoped for a quick nationwide assessment, yet she still needs to run the same quadrant analysis for the other three subcategories of oils and shortenings. She is determined to finish by lunchtime, but she will have to abandon her intention to analyze mass merchandising, as well.

Organizing the Morning's Work

Lunch comes, and Anya is finished with the gist of what she had hoped would be a brief nationwide analysis. The only tasks left in this part are to export the bookmarked views to a presentation program and read data from the new spreadsheets into the program where her item list resides. To prepare, Anya has to compose annotations and arrange views and data so that important issues stand out. Then, through scripting, she will feed the spreadsheet data into several different running lists. She conducts these makeshift exports because the data visualization program does not have item list or presentation functions of its own. The preparation and export processes consume another hour and a half of Anya's time.

Anya's Region: Getting an Overall Sense of Product Performance

After lunch, Anya examines her stores' products and those of her regional competitors. For the regional assessment, she combines her store data with syndicated data. Because of the mix of data, she has to use a different data visualization program that accommodates it.

This second visualization application differs from the previous one in that it offers only pre-defined perspectives designed for product mix problems. The pre-scripted views make the program simpler to use—its deliberate marketing aim—but it is less powerful for carrying out Anya's inquiry and for understanding relationships comprehensively.

With this second visualization program, Anya displays data for the West in the perspective pictured in Figure 6.7.

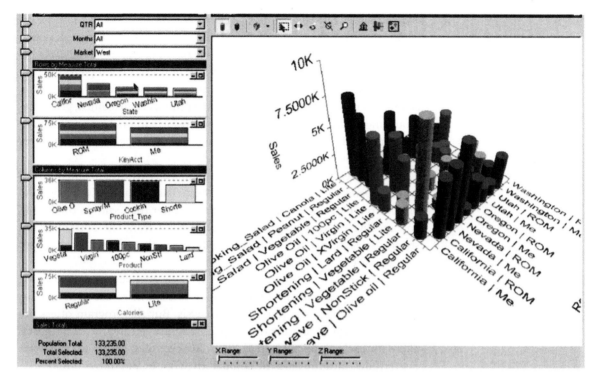

FIGURE 6.7
Sales of all shortening and cooking oils in the West (color-coded by subcategory with green standing for olive oil, red for microwave and pan sprays, blue for cooking oil, and yellow for shortening).

In the 3D view in the center of the perspective, Anya sees the dollar sales (height of the bars) for each product segment (such as Virgin Lite Olive Oil) by each state, separated into Anya's stores and the rest of the markets' (respectively labeled the Me and ROM accounts in the data set). On the left are five bar charts. Top to bottom, the bar charts display total dollar sales for each state, for Me and the ROM, for each subcategory, for different products, and for the two groups in the liteness segment (regular and lite). Under the bar charts, a table of totals displays the sums and percentages for whatever items Anya selects based on the measure shown in the bar charts, in this case dollar sales.

The center view draws Anya's eye to a red bar towering above the rest. It belongs to her stores in Nevada and represents microwave and pan sprays. The microwave and pan spray subcategory is one of the most volatile types of shortenings and oils in terms of sales, and getting its mix right has been tricky for Anya.

She focuses on the account bar chart (second from the top in the left column of bar charts in Figure 6.7) and sweeps the Me bar to discover whether her share of sales has improved this month. From the table of totals she sees it has (a 44.3% share) but only by 0.2 of a point (Figure 6.8A). She is worried that her manager will now press even harder for drastic changes in the lite assortment, which Anya thinks is misguided, given the mounting evidence. Anya strengthens her resolve to uncover an alternate explanation about what may be causing this under-performance and to find other solutions besides cutting lites.

Next in the account bar chart, Anya standardizes the ROM and Me bars and compares them (Figure 6.8B). She sees that in standardized cooking oil (bottom blue stripe) her sales are much lower than sales in the ROM, and in olive oil they are much higher (second from the bottom green stripe). Sales for her stores and the ROM are fairly even in the other two subcategories.

At this point, Anya wants to see a single textual chart displaying comparative figures behind these stripes. She wants to use such a chart as a framework for the rest of this analysis. But the program offers no quick means for generating this display, and just getting the exact figures alone for each stripe takes more than 20 keystrokes and a lot of hassle. Regretfully, Anya foregoes the comparative figures and moves on.

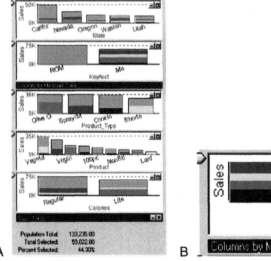

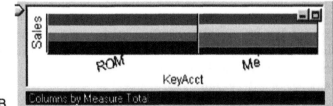

FIGURE 6.8
General (A) and standardized (B) comparisons between Me and the ROM (color-coded by subcategory, with green standing for olive oil, red for microwave and pan sprays, blue for cooking oil, and yellow for shortening).

Anya's Stores: Getting an Overall Sense of Product Performance

Anya calls up a view of just her stores in the West (Figure 6.9).

This Me-only view displays high sales in olive oil, unlike the trend nationally. The red bar of microwave and pan sprays in Nevada still looms large. Anya sees that for her stores, California trails third in sales; although they are first in the West as a whole. She begins to believe that a more lucrative strategy than reducing the number of lites in the product mix may be to build up California markets. To test this strategy and gather enough evidence to convince her manager, she will have to change her usual paths of investigation. She wonders what she may have missed so far because she did not have her eye on this strategy from the start.

Concerned about profits, Anya changes the axis measure in all the charts from sales to profits by picking profits from a drop down list under the tool bar (Figure 6.10).

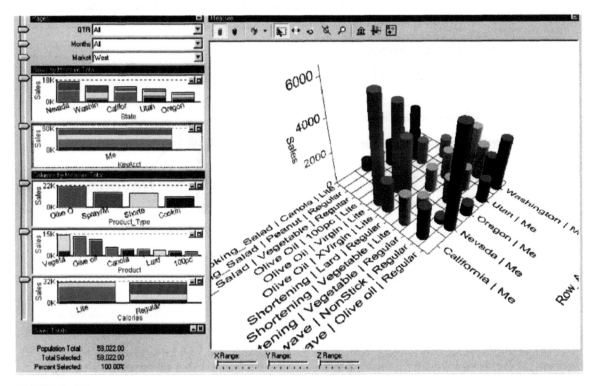

FIGURE 6.9

Sales for Me (Anya's stores) only in the West (color-coded by subcategory with green standing for olive oil, red for microwave and pay sprays, blue for cooking oil, and yellow for shortening).

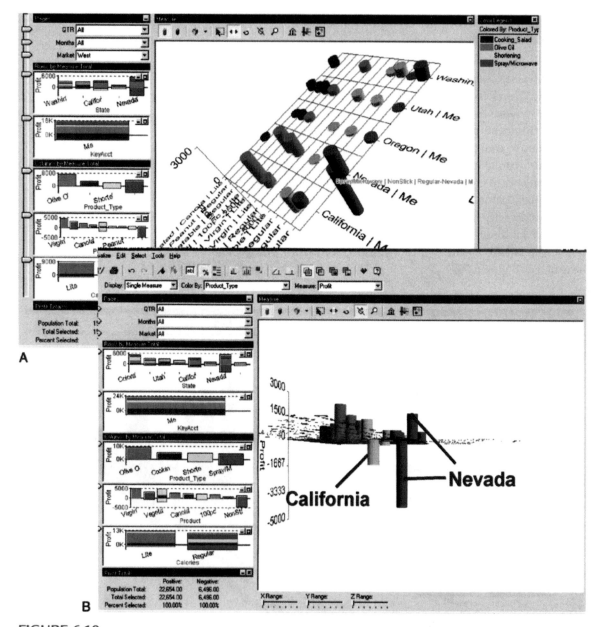

FIGURE 6.10
Two views of profits for Me only category in the West. (A) The default view, with losses extending below the baselines. (B) The 3D view rotated for a sharper view of the losses (color-coded by subcategory with green standing for olive oil, red for microwave and pan sprays, blue for cooking oil, and yellow for shortening).

The red bar (microwave and pan sprays in Nevada) is the first thing to catch Anya's eye. It is below the baseline, dipping far into the stratum of losses (Figure 6.10A). Anya rotates the 3D view to see the losses more clearly (Figure 6.10B). From this overview, she is struck by the need to re-cast her assortment in pan sprays. She sees bright possibilities for some types of pan sprays in the product bar chart (fourth down from the top in Figure 6.10). Those with an olive-oil base (the second highest bar, colored red) are turning a profit in Nevada. These are good data to bring to her boss to persuade him that customers are moving toward more health-conscious purchases. Anya cannot now remember trends for pan sprays in her nationwide assessment and would like to compare the nationwide and regional views in this subcategory. However, she drops the idea because she cannot compare views across the visualization programs without going through numerous set-up steps and having too much window clutter to think straight.

Again, Anya wants to put views side-by-side for comparison's sake—this time sales and profits. She is frustrated by the program's lack of cooperation. Her company makes product judgments on profits, not sales, and she needs to compare views of the two. She especially needs to visibly weight profits more heavily when comparing them to reflect her chain's priorities. For this weighting, she is willing to go out of the program to her data source. There she calculates weightings for profits and reads the new metrics into the visualizations.

After this, Anya is ready to do the same types of analysis she did with the nationwide data alone. She goes through similar steps to set up views and identify the high- and low-moving vendors and products in her stores. As she goes, she saves and comments on views. Then she repeats the processes of her nationwide assessment to set up a quadrant analysis for winners, losers, sleepers, and opportunities in her stores. This quadrant analysis, however, involves new sequences of steps, new concerns, and additional strategies and accumulated insights.

Anya's Stores: Selecting and Analyzing Winners and Losers

In the quadrant view Anya has set up, she plots sales against profits and sees products clustered as shown in Figure 6.11.

This time Anya starts by analyzing the microwave and pan spray sub-category. She selects just the products in this subcategory, and only they become highlighted on the screen (Figure 6.12A). She then color-codes by state and sees the same top and bottom pan sprays in Nevada (aqua) she saw earlier, now located in the winner and loser quadrants, respectively. Anya wonders what her numbers would be without the non-stick pan

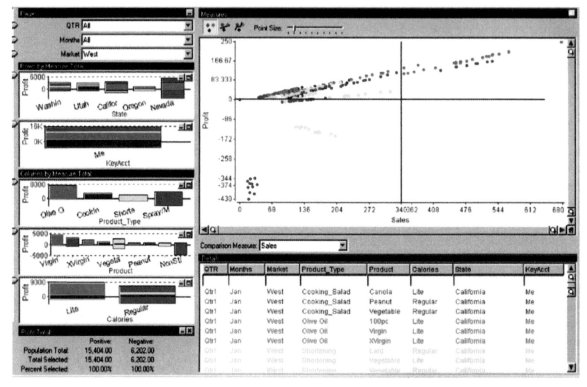

FIGURE 6.11
Sales plotted against profits for Me (Anya's stores) only in the West (color-coded by subcategory with green standing for olive oil, red for microwaves and pan sprays, blue for cooking oil, and yellow for shortening).

spray losers from Nevada. With a sweep of the mouse, she subtracts the pan sprays from the view. The values of the whole recalculate to reflect this deletion (Figure 6.12B). The automatic calculations in the lower left table tell Anya that without these products in the mix, her losses shrink from 73% to only 1% of her total. She bookmarks and saves both views.

Last month, Anya gave the non-stick pan sprays in her Nevada stores a chance by intensely promoting them. She checks now to see how badly this strategy failed. She brings back the entire microwave and pan spray set of data and switches the sales axis of the scatterplot to marketing expenses. The outcome is dismal (Figure 6.13). The non-stick Nevada losers shift to the bottom right quadrant: High expenses and high losses. These products ate up the most money and lost the most, too. She flags them as items to drop.

The rest of the microwave and pan spray products—aside from the winning olive oil pan sprays in Nevada—fall into the sleeper category. These

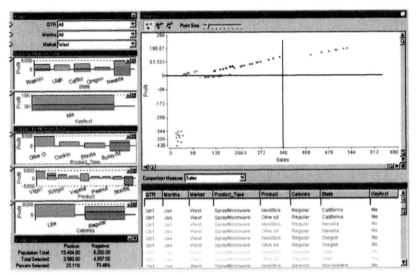

A

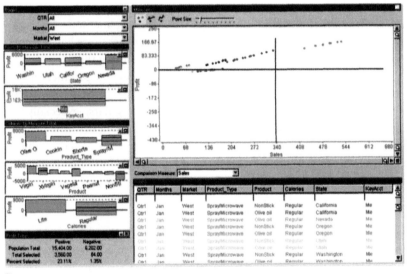

B

FIGURE 6.12
Sales plotted against profits for Anya's stores' microwave and pan spray oils only. (A) The subcategory as a whole. (B) Losers subtracted from the whole (color-coded by state with blue standing for CA, aqua for NV, green for OR, orange for UT, and red for WA).

products' sales might improve if marketing efforts are re-directed to them. This is Anya's next focus.

Anya's Stores: Examining Sleepers and Opportunities

Again, Anya repeats the analysis of sleepers she did nationwide. She evaluates which sleepers might be good to keep and enhance through promotions. She then saves the views and the underlying data from these drill downs

FIGURE 6.13

Marketing dollars plotted against profits for Anya's stores' microwave and pan spray oils (color-coded by state with blue standing for CA, aqua for NV, green for OR, orange for UT, and red for WA).

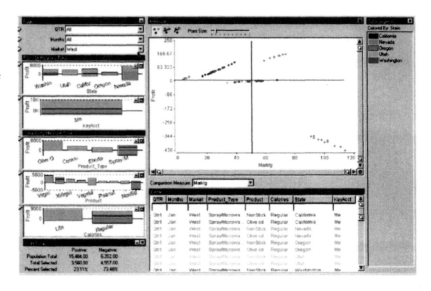

into the microwave and pan spray subcategory. Anya moves on and assesses the other three subcategories, using similar methods for each. Unlike microwave and pan sprays, however, these other types have opportunity products so Anya previews the loss leaders among them.

In all these assessments, she explores lite and regular products more extensively than others and digs into what is driving California. She finds that lites are bringing in higher profits than regulars, especially in California. Lite losses, when they occur, are limited to a new line of "lite shortenings," not oils. The "lite shortening" label does not fool consumers into thinking fats can be light. This trend reinforces Anya's intuition that health consciousness is on the rise.

Making Provisional Choices

So far Anya has made provisional decisions to drop non-stick oils in Nevada and reduce them in other markets. She will boost olive oil-based pan sprays in all of her Western stores and try to gain greater market share in California by launching a health campaign. This campaign may involve heavy promotions and price cuts for a wide variety of lites, select olive oils, and such low cholesterol, high antioxidant products as safflower and canola oil.

Anya's Stores and the ROM: Making Preliminary Competitive Comparisons

Before ending her efficient assortment assessment for the day, Anya takes a glimpse of what will later be a more extensive effective assortment assessment. For now, she wants a quick look at how her products compare to the ROM. Still using the same visualization program, Anya restores the excluded ROM data and selects everything. She color codes by account so that items related to her stores turn blue and those for the ROM become red (Figure 6.14A).

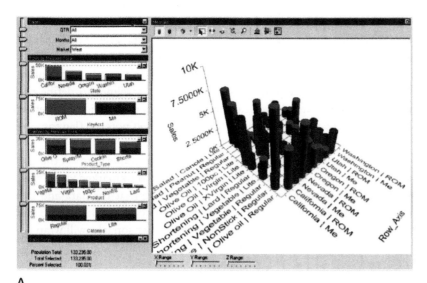

A

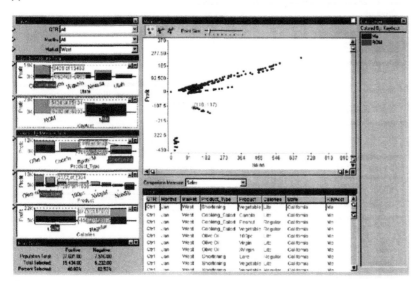

B

FIGURE 6.14
Aggregated sales and profits for Me (Anya's stores) and the ROM. (A) West region as a whole. (B) Anya's stores (Me) only selected and highlighted, with the lower left table automatically displaying her share of the West region profits (40.88) (color-coded by account so that Me is blue and the ROM is red).

First she selects only her stores, leaving the context visible (see Figure 6.14B). In this overview, she runs what-if analyses on products she is considering dropping to see the effects on her profits and market share. Keeping track of the data included in and excluded from what-if calculations is a headache. It is a minor headache now, but it will verge on a migraine later in the saved displays and spreadsheets. Anya has to carefully distinguish which data calculations are based on excluded (filtered out) data and which are based on the full West region data set.

Anya does a preliminary quadrant analysis comparing her stores with the ROM. She emphasizes lite and regular products. Figure 6.15 gives a sample of the screens she examines for these comparative analyses. Each segment has a different spread of values characterizing its sales and profits; therefore Anya needs repeatedly to set different baselines to define the quadrants. She bookmarks and captures the data for these various Me versus ROM analyses by product segment. She writes herself notes to flag some of the most crucial insights.

It has been a long analysis. Anya leaves herself a couple hours at the end of the day to organize, print, and export all of her bookmarked views, read spreadsheet data into her item lists, and validate that the data and the list are in sync. Tomorrow she will be ready to compare the lists to the nationwide findings. With this nationwide comparison, she will wrap up her efficient assortment assessment.

FIGURE 6.15
Segment-based quadrant analysis of Me (Anya's stores) versus the ROM by product attributes, investigating (clockwise) the regular segment of olive oil, the canola segment of cooking oil, and the lite segment (color-coded by account so that Me is blue and the ROM is red).

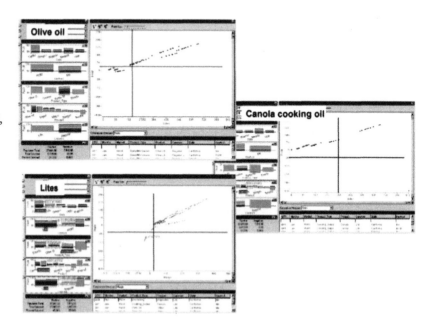

What Support Does Anya Need and What Does She Get?

Anya's investigation is filled with multiple methods and strategies, diverse and variously scaled data, numerous composing and communication intentions, and many domain-specific analytical conventions. Her programs facilitate some of her task interactions and intentions, but they block a good many more. The scenario reveals five core activities for which Anya needs software support. The summary in Table 6.2 details these needs for support and identifies whether Anya's programs amply provide it.

Anya Needs Support For	Does She Get it?	
	Yes	No
Making comparisons		
Comparing the percent each subcatergory contributes to sales in my stores (Me) and the ROM		✓
Comparing prior and current views for pan sprays nationwide and regionally		✓
Comparing preferred suppliers' sleepers to other sleepers		✓
Comparing 3D views of sales and profits, side by side		✓
"What do I see and what does it mean?"		
Seeing a legend that explains the color coding	✓	
Seeing labels of axes	✓	
Seeing labels for data points (mouse-over information)	✓	
Quickly determining the meaning of "striped" color-coded bars		✓
Viewing color-coding that reflects true market spreads		✓
Discriminating between slight differences in shade that might be meaningful		✓
Easily seeing that a complex visual query based on a faulty model of the program is wrong		✓
Getting from here to there		
Getting totals and shares of all selected data combined in a single keystroke	✓	

TABLE 6.2
What support Anya needs and what she gets.

TABLE 6.2
Continued

Anya Needs Support For	Does She Get it?	
	Yes	No
Changing the axis of a scatterplot in a keystroke	✓	
Setting user-defined dividing lines for quadrant analysis	✓	
Creating weightings on-the-fly		✓
Creating a textual chart with each subcategory's percent of sales for Me and the ROM		✓
Performing complex queries visually		
Drilling down to one subcategory and excluding data on the rest		
Bringing back only a part of the excluded data		✓
Drilling down to a subset of vendors, selecting their sleepers *and* opportunities, and seeing the results against the whole data context		✓
Composing in tandem with data analysis		
Saving views	✓	
Being able to do all the annotations, comments, and reminders needed in a saved view for later reference		✓
Easily finding and calling back saved views and comments relevant to a question at hand		✓
Quickly and easily moving selected data in winners, losers, sleepers, and opportunities into the right places in the running item list		✓

Chapter 7 examines in depth a number of strategies and conceptual designs that lead to better support and improved usefulness. The reason for noting these shortcomings here is that they convey that Anya's software was built on an incomplete and nonintegrated model of the work that category managers actually do when they decide on best product mix. To represent this work adequately, models should capture the regularities, variability, and choice points in users' patterns of inquiry and highlight the task landscapes users configure based on interactive contextual conditions. Modeling the problem solving terrain in this way represents the integrated workings of many of these user activities, needs, and contextual conditions. Such models can help guide design teams toward creating better support than Anya received.

CREATING MODELS OF WORK THAT CAPTURE SUPPORT FOR PROBLEM SOLVING NEEDS

Abstracted, the regularities in Anya's efficient assortment assessment—typical of the way analysts conduct this assessment across retail contexts—chunk into several subpatterns. For example, Anya organized her investigation into such subpatterns as assessing products nationwide, assessing only her products, organizing findings into item lists and persuasive evidence, and taking a first run at comparing her stores and the ROM. Within any one subpattern, she pursues a number of objectives, such as identifying winners and losers and deciding on sleepers or opportunities that are worth keeping. The chunked tasks she performs to satisfy these objectives have some regularity to them and some variability.

If design teams were to look only at the mainline tasks for a subpattern of Anya's inquiry—for example, the subpattern of assessing products nationwide—they would likely come up with the chart shown in Figure 6.16.

Subpattern—Assessing Products Nationwide

Context and goal: Problem solvers need a sense of broad category trends and patterns nationwide to use as a framework for assessing their stores and the ROM.

Example: A category manager wants to know the top movers, dominant brands, and segments, and growth leaders in oils to gauge trends in her own market and store.

Tasks
- Create segments reflecting customer purchasing decisions and use (e.g. flavor, size). Validate them.
- Create a view for evaluating high and low performers.
- Identify high and low performers and their combined shares in each product branch. Verify.
- Analyze and compare items on important measures, including change over time. Verify.
- Create a view for evaluating winners, losers, sleepers, and opportunities.
- Set accurate and valid quadrant dividers. Validate.
- Distinguish winners and losers. Verify.
- Analyze winner and loser performances and decide which to keep and drop.
- Distinguish sleepers and opportunities. Verify.
- Disqualify sleepers that are not worth keeping any longer (e.g., analyze effects of promotions and price cuts).
- Identify good sleepers for keeping (e.g., analyze promotions and price cuts, match against preferred supplier duplicates).
- Glance at opportunities for a sense of those worth keeping or not (e.g., analyze traffic generation).
- Use findings for an item list of what to keep or drop and why.
- Save important displays and their underlying data for later comparisons to one's own stores and other stores in the market and for presentations to stakeholders.

FIGURE 6.16
Mainline tasks in a subpattern of the efficient assortment assessment pattern.

However, as we have seen several times, mainline tasks tell only a part of any problem solving story. As in IT investigations, Anya moves through landscapes of mainline *and* enabling tasks.

Highlighting Mainline and Enabling Tasks in Practical Cases

Mainline and enabling tasks shape and constrain each other. Designing software without an ample emphasis on both is a recipe for inutility and user frustration. In modeling product-mix inquiries, therefore, design teams need to move beyond obvious task sequences for subgoals and subpatterns and represent the way category managers put together landscapes for all aspects of the open-ended wayfinding, sensemaking, and data ordeals that characterize their complex problem solving processes for a particular subgoal.

As seen in IT troubleshooting, problem solvers have the easiest time constructing and moving through these task landscapes when the interactive contextual conditions during their investigations give rise to actions that line up compatibly for their goals and desired actions. That is, in a best-case scenario such influences as problem solving expertise, pressures from preferred suppliers and supervisors, domain knowledge, professional practices, organizational priorities, and visual literacy converge in ways that leave open all the choices for action that merchandising experts value. With the right fit between conditions, these problem solvers can work with the relevant information for their purposes based on approaches they value.

But best cases are rare in product mix problems, even more scarce than in the IT world. Too many factors impinge against them. Even if software companies succeeded in developing one integrated *and* useful program for all the phases of product mix decisions, or better yet for analyzing all retail ps together, best cases would still be atypical. Practically, they do not occur because of unavoidable variability and serendipity. In cases such as Anya's—common throughout the merchandising world—idiosyncratic work-related pressures, such as supervisors' biases or preferred suppliers' incentives, may lead one problem solver down a path that which another may not need to tread. In addition, different companies have distinct priorities that need to be weighed into the analysis in certain ways, and different analysts have varying levels of visual literacy and memory. Moreover, actual market values often are not distributed in the same way they are visually encoded and displayed by programs. Finally, uncertainty due to incomplete information hovers over all product mix investigations. Because of these variations and uncertainty, actions made possible by contextual conditions often do not line up compatibly.

In marketing and sales, interactive contextual forces can never be tamed into obedience, but if software teams understand and represent them well enough, they can address them structurally in their applications through cues, signposts, strategic user control, and adaptability. Chapter 7 explores these strategies. Here I examine ways to represent the task landscapes of merchandisers' patterns of inquiry to capture the regularity and variability of their dynamic problem solving.

Anya's story shows that as she concentrates on relevant data, the meanings she draws and practical uses she makes of them are highly attuned to and shaped by a mix of predictable and variable influences. Predictable or regularly occurring forces include domain-based conventions and interpretations, patterns of inquiry, and shared business rules. Variable influences include fluctuating markets, debates with supervisors, Anya's own strategic biases, and time. Because of time, merchandising analysts may decide to forego some aspects of their analysis. Trapped in a Catch-22 situation, the more time merchandisers devote to preparing data, the less time they have for strategic planning and analysis. However, if they shortchange data preparation, they do not have the information they need to explore relationships, which is a must for competitive advantage.

The range of factors affecting analysts' approaches is huge. Other variables that recur and shape inquiries differently across problem solving situations include the type of store (mom and pop, chain, super center), store image and branding, manufacturer collaborations, organizational culture, and individual expertise. Each of these conditions influences analysts' choices about the data, scope of analysis, relationships of interest, weighting of factors, and actions.

Capturing Users' Patterns of Inquiry, Task Landscapes, and Choice Points

As in other scenarios in this book, usefulness in software for complex problem solving involves modeling and designing for regularities with a readiness for user adaptability. For practical product-mix problems, category managers vary in the tasks, emphasis, and sequences they use for a specific investigative goal. But the options from which they choose are bounded.

Creating Task-Landscape Diagrams for Specific Goals

Figure 6.17 illustrates the task landscape that Anya puts together to assess winners and losers in her stores, which leads her to decide, respectively, the items to keep and drop. From a complex array of possible routes, she configures a path that involves six chunked tasks (basically classes of

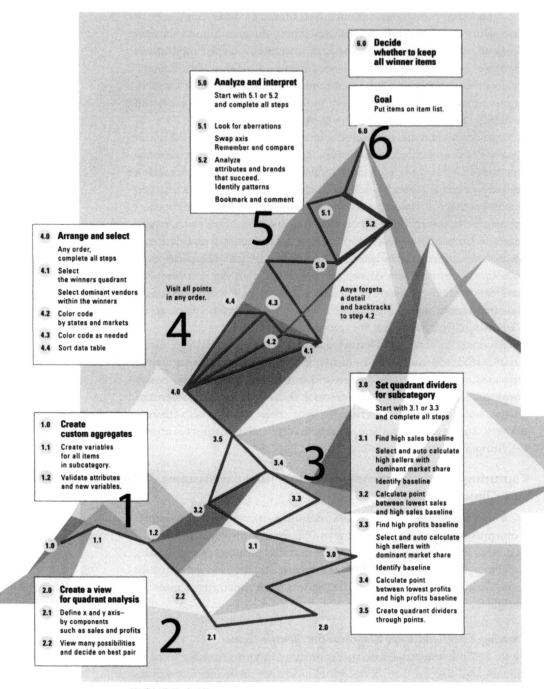

6.0 Decide whether to keep all winner items

5.0 Analyze and interpret
Start with 5.1 or 5.2 and complete all steps

5.1 Look for aberrations
Swap axis
Remember and compare

5.2 Analyze attributes and brands that succeed.
Identify patterns
Bookmark and comment

Goal
Put items on item list.

4.0 Arrange and select
Any order, complete all steps

4.1 Select the winners quadrant
Select dominant vendors within the winners

4.2 Color code by states and markets

4.3 Color code as needed

4.4 Sort data table

Visit all points in any order.

Anya forgets a detail and backtracks to step 4.2

1.0 Create custom aggregates

1.1 Create variables for all items in subcategory.

1.2 Validate attributes and new variables.

3.0 Set quadrant dividers for subcategory
Start with 3.1 or 3.3 and complete all steps

3.1 Find high sales baseline
Select and auto calculate high sellers with dominant market share
Identify baseline

3.2 Calculate point between lowest sales and high sales baseline

3.3 Find high profits baseline
Select and auto calculate high sellers with dominant market share
Identify baseline

3.4 Calculate point between lowest profits and high profits baseline

3.5 Create quadrant dividers through points.

2.0 Create a view for quadrant analysis

2.1 Define x and y axis— by components such as sales and profits

2.2 View many possibilities and decide on best pair

FIGURE 6.17
Task landscape for finding the winners to keep and losers to drop.

In this part of Anya's pattern of inquiry, her goal is to find winners and losers in her stores only and decide which to keep and drop, respectively. She creates a view, sets it up, creates custom aggregates, and arranges and selects relevant data.

From there, she analyzes and interprets relationships. This includes cross-referencing the quadrant graph and the data table to check details on attributes and performance measures. She saves views that show data of interest that will be relevant to later aspects of her investigation. When she forgets facts or figures about various items she backtracks to earlier views and then comes back and resumes her analysis. Finally she arrives at provisional judgments of what to keep and drop.

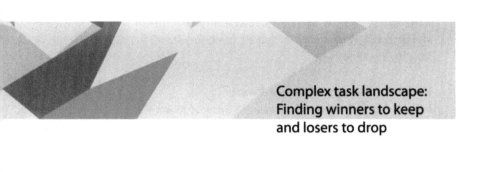

Complex task landscape:
Finding winners to keep
and losers to drop

Main path
Backtracking

problem solving interactions) with many prongs of action within them. Actions within chunked tasks vary based on what are often the unpredictable outcomes of preceding moves or other interdependent actions. In addition, before reaching her subgoal of identifying items to keep, Anya may backtrack to compare a current view with an earlier one of other correlated measures.

Even with these tasks' variability and multi-faceted set ups and interpretations, this subpattern of identifying winners to keep and losers to drop is less complex than many of Anya's subsequent subpatterns of inquiry. The boundaries for acceptable choices are more well-defined with fewer contending criteria and idiosyncratic considerations.

A more complicated task landscape is illustrated in the Figure 6.18: The landscape for examining sleepers and determining which ones to drop. Some of the initial steps in the sleeper task are familiar and well-charted based on Anya's earlier winner and loser assessments (Tasks 1 and 2 in Figures 6.17 and 6.18). Soon after starting, however, problem solvers such as Anya encounter new and greater complexities.

For example, they have to create custom aggregates for whatever particular work domain issues may shape their decisions about this iffy group of items, issues such as preferred suppliers and slotting. They regularly bring in, compare, and evaluate more correlated factors than they do with winners. They backtrack and go off on tangents more frequently and with increased activity for saving and commenting as they go. The work is structured but with more unpredictability in terms of how to configure and direct its course and with more compounded and conditional criteria shaping their decisions.

What are Conceptual Choice Points?

For a closer look at users' choices, Figure 6.19 magnifies one chunked task from Figure 6.18: Identify poor performers (Task 7). It shows in more detail the mainline and enabling tasks and choice points that engage Anya for this objective.

This close view shows places at which Anya's path can take any number of directions depending on the decision she makes at crossroads of conceptual choices. For HCI specialists and software designers, these choices in the middle of specific classes of problem solving interactions (users' chunked tasks) signal the need to support types of interaction trajectories. When design teams know various conceptual choices associated with category managers' domain-based patterns of inquiry, they can move beyond feature-based designing and identify sets of interactions that have to be ready for users to adapt to their discretionary decisions.

In Anya's case, she comes to numerous conceptual crossroads, such as "What data should I examine?" and "What should I refer back to?" These conceptual choice points are related to but different from choices that problem solvers make in regard to using or operating program functionality. Program choices involve "How do I sort columns most efficiently?" or more difficult "How do I select subsets of subsets?" To support such program choices design teams rightly look closely at ease of use and other usability design choices. By contrast, for users' conceptual choices, ("Is selecting subsets of subsets the right thing to do in the first place?") designers need to help problem solvers identify and choose responses and corresponding programmatic actions at a higher level.

Software designers can anticipate and design for some, but never all of the varied directions problem solvers actually pursue. Choices users make at conceptual crossroads are shaped by a combination of predictable constraints, domain-based conventions, contingency, and other variable conditions. The following three sample choice points illustrate the blend of stability and variability affecting category managers' decisions (stable factors software teams can anticipate are noted with green squares, variable ones with yellow circles).

- ■ Stable factors
- ◦ Variable factors

Do I need to save this view for my later use or communications with others, and if so what should I highlight?
This decision depends on the following:

- ■ Existing utilities for turning data into information in another workspace
- ■ Highlight and comment capabilities in the software
- ◦ Supervisor and manufacturer pressures
- ◦ Intended audience for presentations
- ◦ Gap size between my actual market share and my industry-designated fair share
- ◦ Market realities and trends
- ◦ Extent of need based on prior saves
- ◦ Progress in judgments about the mix

What factors should I weight more heavily than others to decide whether it is better to keep a sleeper with low sales, high growth, and flat profits or a sleeper with high sales, low growth, and low profits?
This decision depends on the following:

- ■ Domain conventions and business rules

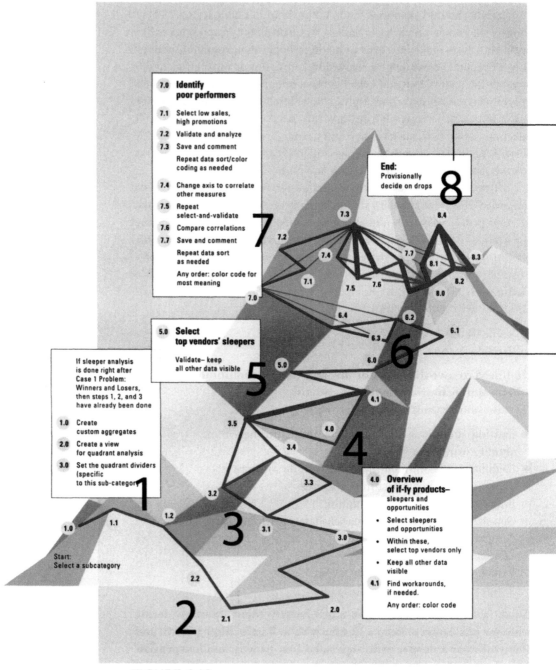

FIGURE 6.18
Task landscape for finding the sleepers to drop.

Anya now analyzes sleepers in her stores. She puts together this landscape to decide which ones to drop. The first three tasks that Anya performs are similar to those she conducts to analyze winners and losers.

After that, the inquiry gets more complex. She gets an overview of sleepers and opportunities together— all combined, the if-fiest products in the stores— but this requires complex queries and workarounds.

Next she studies more factors than in the winner and loser analysis. For example, she looks at sales and growth for sleepers that her stores promoted heavily this past quarter. It these products did poorly, she would be throwing good money after bad to keep them in the mix much longer. She looks also at price cuts but gives more weight to promotions.

She identifies poor performers and checks if they perform poorly based on sales and growth, sales and profits, market share and growth, and so on. These successive comparisons require her to either save or remember a lot of data and their meanings. In another path of analysis, she runs what-if questions to see how her bottom line would be without some items. When these do not give the outcomes she expects she goes back to earlier tasks in the landscape. Finally, she reaches a tentative decision about which poor performers to drop from the mix.

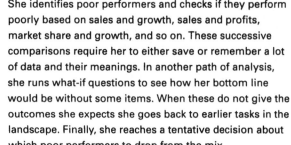

8.0 Analyze 'what-if's'

8.1 Subtract out
poor performer(s)

8.2 Calculate outcomes

8.3 Save and comment

Repeat axis
change as needed

Repeat data sort
as needed

Any order: color code

8.4 Compare what-ifs:
current and saved views

**6.0 Arrange to find
poor performers**

6.1 Add data: Promotions,
price cuts, penetration

6.2 Weight promotions
more heavily

6.3 Sort data table
by top criteria

6.4 Make sense
of sorted view

Repeat sort as needed

Any order: color code
for most meaning

 Main path
━━━━━ Backtracking

**Getting more complex:
Finding sleepers to drop**

Complexity writ small:
Tasks and choice points for one activity

This close-in view shows just the part of the task landscape for finding sleepers to drop that involves "Identifying Poor Performers" (Task 7 in Figure 6.18). This magnified view of Anya's moves and choice points reveals the multiple paths and backtracking that she takes for what to her is one basic task in an integrated whole. Green lines show that she moves back and forward again between steps within just this one activity. The backtracking and tangents lead in from and extend to other surrounding activities, as well.

Anya encounters several choice points. For example, she decides what view to use as an entry point in 7.1 and determines whether to examine more correlations in 7.7. A decision that she makes at any crossroad prompts her to configure subsequent portions of her task landscape in ways that are distinct from what she would do if she had chosen an alternative.

7.1 Select low sales, high promotions

Choice: What's my entry point— which one of 2 options?

7.11 Quick view of quadrant

  a Color by promotions

  b Eye goes to high promo/low corner of quadrant

  c Sweep where eye is

7.12 Quick view of table

  a Sort by promo- high to low

  b Sweep high promo

  c Recolor by sales

  d I.D. low sales in high promo group

7.13 Choose Quadrant as entry– trade off details for accurate selection

7.14 Undo to go to quadrant view in 7.11a

7.15 Sweep as in 7.11c, but more precisely

Main path

Backtracking

FIGURE 6.19
Task landscape of one chunked task: Identify poor performers.

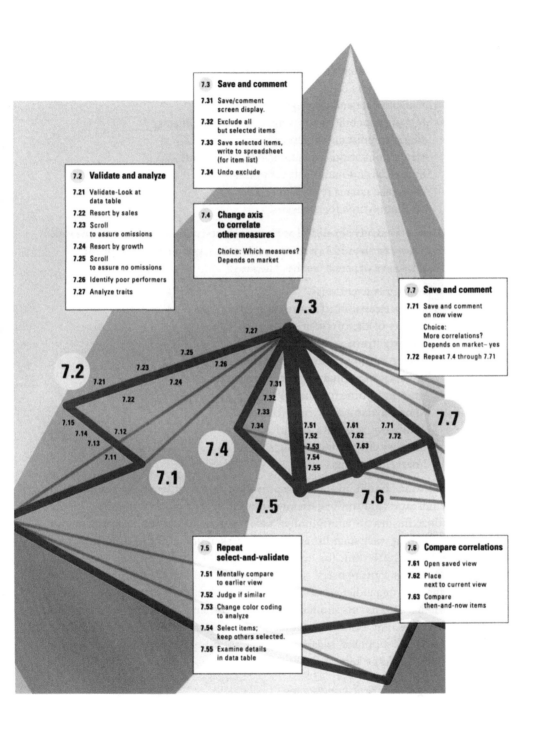

7.3 Save and comment

7.31 Save/comment
screen display.

7.32 Exclude all
but selected items

7.33 Save selected items,
write to spreadsheet
(for item list)

7.34 Undo exclude

7.2 Validate and analyze

7.21 Validate-Look at
data table

7.22 Resort by sales

7.23 Scroll
to assure omissions

7.24 Resort by growth

7.25 Scroll
to assure no omissions

7.26 Identify poor performers

7.27 Analyze traits

**7.4 Change axis
to correlate
other measures**

Choice: Which measures?
Depends on market

7.7 Save and comment

7.71 Save and comment
on now view

Choice:
More correlations?
Depends on market– yes

7.72 Repeat 7.4 through 7.71

**7.5 Repeat
select-and-validate**

7.51 Mentally compare
to earlier view

7.52 Judge if similar

7.53 Change color coding
to analyze

7.54 Select items;
keep others selected.

7.55 Examine details
in data table

7.6 Compare correlations

7.61 Open saved view

7.62 Place
next to current view

7.63 Compare
then-and-now items

- Stable factors
- Variable factors

- Heuristic strategies dictated by organizational precedent and priorities
- Available data and displays
- Software capabilities for weighting and comparing
- Market trends and dynamics
- Strength of various consumer-based segments
- Supervisor and manufacturer pressures
- Workplace norms regarding risk
- Amount of time for analysis

How extensively should I look at products, markets, and time periods and how far should I drill down? Is this a good stopping point?
This decision depends on the following:

- Domain conventions
- Software capabilities for manipulating data
- Severity of the problem
- Findings from earlier analyses
- Trigger for the product mix analysis
- Supervisor and manufacturer pressures
- Amount of time for analysis
- Market dynamics of competition
- Number of relevant categories
- Category churn and products' history
- Emergent findings

Software should give users the freedom to put different faces on similar landscapes and traverse them without interrupting their inquiry. To reinforce the idea of "configurable" task landscapes, software teams may start designing with such broadly outlined sketches as those seen in Figures 6.17 and 6.18. But, for design purposes, they have to create representations that capture users' subgoals and task landscapes along with choices and interdependencies at the level of Figure 6.19. Software teams need to model dozens of similar subgoal-based landscapes for product mix inquiries. For example, another challenging subgoal is discovering which preferred suppliers' sleepers might respond to promotions and whether they should be kept in the mix.

Integrating Task Landscapes
In practice, users integrate task landscapes with one another across subpatterns and across patterns of inquiry. For example, Figure 6.20 captures

category analysts' preliminary forays into a competitive analysis, as we saw with Anya after she examined the performance of her own stores' products. In such preliminary competitive analyses, problem solvers often dynamically traverse patterns of inquiry. As the figure depicts, in their patterns for comparing their stores and the rest of the market (Task B) problem solvers' unfolding results might prompt them to question items (Task C) they provisionally dropped as losers in their earlier "my stores only" pattern of analysis (Task A). They then return to a point in that earlier pattern (Task D) but now pursue some new moves due to their discoveries in the competitive analysis. Unifying insights and demands from their prior and current investigations, they now run more complicated analyses of loser products. The outcome—the products they now intend to drop—are often different from the end-goal they reached in their earlier pattern of inquiry (Task E). Software teams need to be sure they give users support for traveling smoothly within and across many task landscapes for interconnected goals and not just for any one discrete task or task chunk.

Combined, the task landscapes sketched in Figures 6.17, 6.18, and 6.20 and the close-up version represented in Figure 6.19 emphasize how category managers' experiences are constrained by a mix of regularity and idiosyncrasy. As discussed for IT troubleshooting, constraints, in general, are positive because they reduce uncertainties and unchecked freedoms. But constraints stop being positive when they thwart retail specialists from conducting complete analysis. In retail problem solving, many program designs have this negative impact largely because they do not adequately model category managers' practical patterns of inquiry. The next chapter examines design strategies and choices for usefulness that strive to stay true to these integrated models of these problem solvers' work in context.

CONCLUSIONS

Anya's product mix case shows one of many analyses category managers conduct when making decisions about the best assortment of items to sell. Anya's inquiry is multi-phased. Its task landscapes are integrated and cross-referential. Her investigation and findings are cumulative; and she needs sufficient control over analysis to configure her landscape of tasks around the predictable *and* unpredictable forces shaping her moves and choices. Her case shows that design teams often overlook the design of adequate support for many of the core activities related to these complexities because their models of work fail to capture them.

Software designers can support such inquiries by modeling the complicated terrains of domain-based patterns of inquiry. Visualization

After analyzing only her stores (step A), Anya moves to step B for a preliminary look at the losers in her stores compared to the rest of the market. She comes up with a surprising finding– the losers she first thought of dropping may need to be changed because of competitors' likely moves. That sends her between peaks.

In step D she figures out what happens when she subtracts out losers in her stores compared to when her competitors hypothetically subtract some of their worst losers. She runs these 'what if', comparison-subtractions until she comes up with the optimal set of losers to omit from her stores.

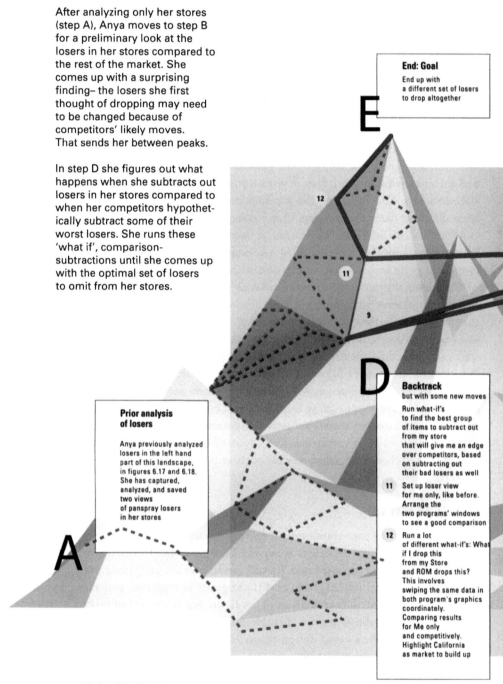

End: Goal

End up with
a different set of losers
to drop altogether

E

12

11

9

D

Backtrack
but with some new moves

Run what-if's
to find the best group
of items to subtract out
from my store
that will give me an edge
over competitors, based
on subtracting out
their bad losers as well

11 Set up loser view
for me only, like before.
Arrange the
two programs' windows
to see a good comparison

12 Run a lot
of different what-if's: What
if I drop this
from my Store
and ROM drops this?
This involves
swiping the same data in
both program's graphics
coordinately.
Comparing results
for Me only
and competitively.
Highlight California
as market to build up

**Prior analysis
of losers**

Anya previously analyzed
losers in the left hand
part of this landscape,
in figures 6.17 and 6.18.
She has captured,
analyzed, and saved
two views
of panspray losers
in her stores

A

FIGURE 6.20
A competitive analysis.

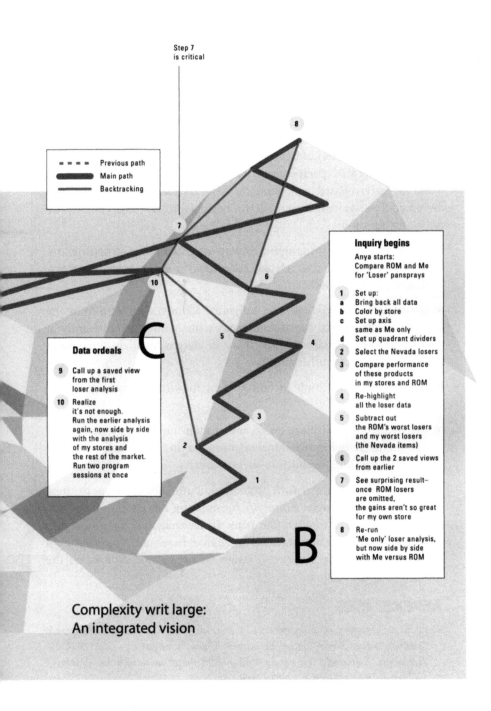

Step 7
is critical

- - - - Previous path
━━━ Main path
─── Backtracking

Inquiry begins

Anya starts:
Compare ROM and Me
for 'Loser' pansprays

1 Set up:
a Bring back all data
b Color by store
c Set up axis
   same as Me only
d Set up quadrant dividers

2 Select the Nevada losers

3 Compare performance
   of these products
   in my stores and ROM

4 Re-highlight
   all the loser data

5 Subtract out
   the ROM's worst losers
   and my worst losers
   (the Nevada items)

6 Call up the 2 saved views
   from earlier

7 See surprising result—
   once ROM losers
   are omitted,
   the gains aren't so great
   for my own store

8 Re-run
   'Me only' loser analysis,
   but now side by side
   with Me versus ROM

Data ordeals

9 Call up a saved view
   from the first
   loser analysis

10 Realize
   it's not enough.
   Run the earlier analysis
   again, now side by side
   with the analysis
   of my stores and
   the rest of the market.
   Run two program
   sessions at once

Complexity writ large:
An integrated vision

programs must be able to support straightforward inquiries like winners and losers and, at the same time, support uncertainty and expanded complexity as soon as category managers need it—sometimes predictably and sometimes not.

Anya's story shows five core activities that need better-integrated designs for useful support. Support for any one of these activities has to be connected with the other areas to ensure that users can construct and traverse pattern-based landscapes coherently, completely, and efficiently. For this integrated perspective, design teams need to model users' work as pattern-based task landscapes and choice points and judge design choices against these models. They need to ask, for example, the following questions:

- Do design choices for graphic displays offer users clear structures and moves to get from one related task chunk to another and from one landscape to another?

- Do actions (chunked tasks or individual actions) that seem to be the same on the surface across landscapes actually function differently in relation to particular subgoals? If so, do designs highlight these functional differences sufficiently?

- Are opportunities built in and evident for users to vary recurrent moves as needed?

- Do visualization displays evoke and sustain inquiry experiences that users value in their professional identities, or do they, by contrast, meet the letter but not the spirit of various tasks?

Had apt models of users' work been created and had responses to these questions driven design choices in formulating Anya's programs, she might not have had to abandon many of her analytical intentions and instead could have related data and integrated moves and strategies more easily and completely. Improved design strategies and choices are the focus of the next chapter.

REFERENCES

Verra, G. J. Category Management: A Matter of Joint Optimisation. *Nijenrode Research Papers Series-Center for Supply Chain Management.* No. 1998-01. Breukelen: Nijenrode University Press, 1998. *http://www.nijenrode.nl/library/ publications/nijrep/1998-01/1998-01.html*

7

Design Strategies and Choices for Optimizing the Mix

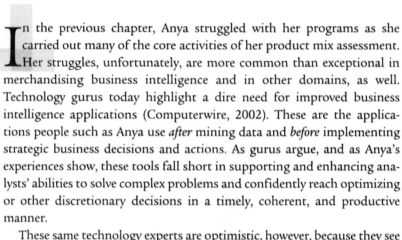

In the previous chapter, Anya struggled with her programs as she carried out many of the core activities of her product mix assessment. Her struggles, unfortunately, are more common than exceptional in merchandising business intelligence and in other domains, as well. Technology gurus today highlight a dire need for improved business intelligence applications (Computerwire, 2002). These are the applications people such as Anya use *after* mining data and *before* implementing strategic business decisions and actions. As gurus argue, and as Anya's experiences show, these tools fall short in supporting and enhancing analysts' abilities to solve complex problems and confidently reach optimizing or other discretionary decisions in a timely, coherent, and productive manner.

These same technology experts are optimistic, however, because they see three promising trends toward improvement: (1) A growing adoption in applications of data visualizations, (2) integrated solutions, and (3) domain content for vertical industries. As we saw in the last chapter, these trends match the electronic support Anya needed for her strategic inquiries. They also create urgency for software design teams to get problem solvers' work right and build in usefulness from the beginning.

Incorporating innovative improvements such as data visualizations into problem solving applications is not enough to get the work right. As we have seen before, data visualizations alone do not guarantee adequate, and therefore truly useful, support and enhancement. For usefulness, software teams need to start with models of the interactive contextual conditions that shape problem solvers' options and, as described in Chapter 6, with appropriate models of their inquiry patterns, task landscapes, and choice points. These models need to be integrated and consolidated to capture problem solvers' situated patterns of open-ended inquiry. With such representations in hand, teams are then better equipped to apply the needed design strategies and choices to conceptualize useful and elegant software designs.

We have already explored some of these high-level design strategies for usefulness in the information technology (IT) troubleshooting case (see Chapters 4 and 5). These strategies require software teams to shift from the usual primary concern with discrete features and functions and procedural support and instead emphasize integrated support for integrated tasks and designs that communicate to users the *structure* of problem solving workspaces and information environments. Teams need to build in domain content and move beyond a desktop metaphor. In this chapter, I examine the practical forms these high-level strategies take when applied to finding design solutions for specific activities in complex product mix assessments, activities that are notoriously ill-supported in most complex problem solving software today.

Chapter 6 highlighted five core activities that are difficult for Anya to perform as coherently and completely as she would like due to insufficient support (see Table 6.2). This chapter focuses on design strategies and choices for supporting these activities. Specifically, I examine strategies and choices for the following activities and corresponding areas of support.

Core activities	Area of relevant support
Making comparisons	Integrating data Controlling analysis
"What do I see and what does it mean?"	Controlling the meaning of views
Getting from here to there in task landscapes	Controlling analysis Navigating inquiry
Performing complex queries visually with uncomplicated interactions	Controlling analysis
Composing in tandem with cumulative analysis	Saving and noting important insights Collaborating

The design strategies and choices in this chapter are not "The Answer" to Anya's usefulness problems, either for a core activity alone or in combination with other aspects of her inquiry. But they do point design teams in the right direction. In these strategies and choices, I explore and apply some of the most recent innovations and commercial breakthroughs in visualizations and other technological support for specific activities in complex optimizing decisions, activities that currently go unsupported in many applications. I describe separate strategies and choices, but interaction designers, usability specialists, and their teammates must not apply them in a piecemeal fashion. Rather, from this "toolkit" of choices, they need to inventively combine and craft elegant and integrated designs for the constraints, opportunities, and task landscapes of their own projects.

Beyond category management, this toolkit of strategies and choices is relevant to software applications in any domain or area of deliberation involving optimizing decisions. With this in mind, I present the design strategies and choices with enough domain-neutral dimensions to be relevant to design experts who may be working on any number of software projects for complex problem solving.

In examining each of the five previously listed activities, I first analyze the shortcomings in current visualization software, such as Anya's, and then propose strategies and choices that can help interaction designers, usability specialists, and their teammates compose more useful designs. When relevant, I bring in examples of recent visualization designs that apply many of these strategies and options.

MAKING COMPARISONS

Anya's investigations clearly show that retail analysis would not be strategic or competitive without comparisons and weightings. Two types of comparisons are critical:

- Comparing similarities and differences within a visible set of graphics

- Making cumulative comparisons between prior and current views

Anya routinely performs the first type of comparisons, and her visualization programs partially meet her needs for them. For example, the displays support comparative quadrant assessments through scatterplots (also called starfield displays by information visualization specialists). The program also provides ready means to compare many correlations simply by changing the graph axes, standardizing values, and sorting data. In fact, through axes, color, shape, orientation, texture, motion coding, and blink coding, Anya can bring in and display as many as eight variables at once (Ware, 2000).

In the second type of comparison, Anya cumulatively compares the many graphic perspectives she uses throughout her inquiry session— largely relying on visual memory. Commonly, when analysts inquire into multivariate and differently scaled data to speculate about such matters as the effects of dropping losers, they go through the following process of comparison:

- They turn quantitative data into qualitative judgments ("Is this sleeper with its performance metrics worth keeping if promoted?").

- In light of these judgments and framed by their expertise, they mentally compare progressive displays.

- During these comparisons, they incrementally construct models of the competitive situation to guide their decisions.

This process of mentally integrating information during cumulative analyses and comparing insights from different displays helps problem solvers simplify complexity. Anya mentally compares clusters in quadrants when she changes the axis variables and mentally notes any changes in clustering. She also stores in her head impressions about how lite products look across views and about where product performances on difficult measures show opportunities for enhancing her California markets.

Examining Current Shortcomings

Anya's visualization programs support some aspects of both types of comparison, but they fall short, as well. Anya often does not get the outcomes she needs. At one point, she wants figures combined and formatted in a comparison chart. At another, she wants to compare the performance patterns in subcategories. The programs, however, offer no pre-structured support for such isomorphic comparisons. Nor can Anya compare views across programs to customize colors or compare subcategories based on their distinct spread of values. Moreover, because of workplace influences she wants to give more weight to some elements than others. However, to do this, she has to go back to the data source, calculate, generate a new weighted field, and re-create the visualization perspective.

Another shortcoming is that Anya cannot get a perspective that shows side-by-side comparisons of prior and current views. Nor can she display two versions of the same view color-coded differently without launching the program again in another window. Admittedly, if she wanted to take advantage of the power offered by her first visualization program, she could create such comparisons. Anya, however, prefers not to display and manipulate such side-by-side comparisons. She is cowed by the prospect of perceptual overload. In part, this avoidance of overload is tied to the program's support: There is a large gap between what the program can do—side-by-side scatterplots—and what it cannot do—ease comparative analysis. For example, the program does not provide support for finding an entry into multiple side-by-side scatterplots for comparison purposes or for staying oriented within them in meaning and place, especially when, due to distinct program launches, interactions in one window do not update to the other.

Because of this lack of integrated support, Anya never analyzes side-by-side views. Therefore, neither she nor field teams who observe her actually know whether side-by-side views are truly what she needs for her purposes. Problem solvers usually benefit most from side-by-side comparisons when they conduct descriptive but not causal analysis (Bertin, 1983; Burns, 2000; Trafton et al., 2000). For "why?" questions, they are more likely to succeed if relevant data are integrated and compressed into a single, rich visualization.

For the second type of comparisons, progressive ones across perspectives, Anya's programs do not provide a way to make remarks on or otherwise annotate the graphs. Nor do the programs support visual memory. They do not, for example, offer ways to increase the accuracy of mentally remembering an earlier graphic display to compare to a visible one. Such a reliance on visual memory would not be necessary if, at propitious points, the applications offered rich representations of data in single, compressed, multipurpose visualizations instead of several singularly focused graphics.

Focusing on Design Strategies and Choices for Usefulness

Anya's experiences show that the first type of comparison—comparing views of data within a perspective—involves a number of connected subgoals and moves: Extracting figures to generate charts, making isomorphic or cross-program comparisons, weighting factors, and arranging graphics differently for distinct purposes. At present, few commercial products offer integrated support for all these interwoven moves, but some do provide strategies for part of them that interaction designers and usability specialists can draw on to fashion coherent and complete solutions. For example, some visualization applications are beginning to include weighting through scoring tools (e.g., IBM ScorCat based on multi-attribute utility theory, the Emptoris Sourcing Portfolio 1.0 *[www.emptoris.com]*, or Perfect Supply Manager Suite 1.0 *[www.perfect.com]*). Others offer dialogue-based mechanisms in which users specify measures of interest, designate items to be weighted, and compute weights that the program then applies and displays. Additional comparison needs, such as side-by-side comparisons of current and prior graphs or of replica graphs, require architectural improvements, such as structuring and creating data vectors appropriately for such displays.

Useful designs also need to structure interface-workspaces for comparisons in ways that match users' notions of their chunked investigations. For example, programs may let users define templates for recurrent comparisons and highlighted relationships that can be recalled with ease. Another strategy is for programs to replicate part of a graphic in a display-within-a-display scheme, what the Tioga group at the University of California-Berkeley calls a "DataSplash" window (Figure 7.1). Users can select and call out just a portion of a currently displayed graphic, create from the portion a new graphic within the larger view, and color-code this replicated part in a different way to compare it to the larger, alternately colored view.

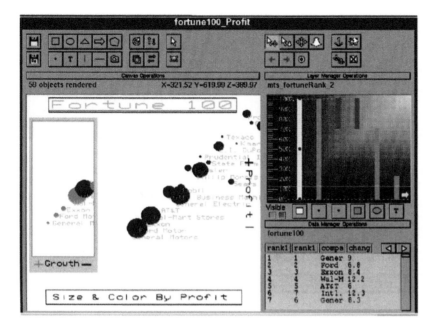

FIGURE 7.1

A DataSplash display-within-a-display. In this example, a user has selected only a portion of the "Growth" data and this narrowed in view is displayed within the larger view of Fortune 100 companies. For comparison purposes, users can perceptually code the narrowed-in display differently from the larger picture. Unlike the larger display, which is color-coded by profit, the replica is color-coded by growth (Woodruff et al., 2001).

Strategies that offer users even more power and flexibility, while still remaining approachable and forgiving, include the MAYAViz development group's approach of offering workspaces users can populate with pre-programmed frames, each structured to support users' common, domain-specific questions (part of the group's Visage system). Users choose the frames relevant to their questions, bring them into the workspace, and drag and drop data of interest into them (Figure 7.2). Each workspace holds any number of frames that users can activate for comparison purposes. Developers customize the frames ahead of time by conducting extensive user studies to discover the problem solving patterns in users' area of specialization. As long as frame-clutter does not get in the way, these designs give problem solvers a "structured freedom" to pursue idiosyncratic paths within bounded patterns of inquiry and to control the display of data of interest.

By applying this strategy to product mix investigations in category management, for example, design teams could pre-program a frame to display graphic *and* textual standardized comparisons for each subcategory's sales, as Anya desired, for a retailer's own stores and the rest of the market (ROM). Another frame might be structured to display side-by-side comparisons, enabling users to drag, drop, and view data on preferred suppliers' sleepers grouped by product segment next to a view of the sleepers

FIGURE 7.2

Workspace of frames filled with drag-and-drop data. Once dropped, the data are displayed in the graphic format pre-programmed into the given frame, in this case "Plot" (courtesy of Visage). (*www-2cs.cmu.edu/Groups/sage/visagedd.html*)

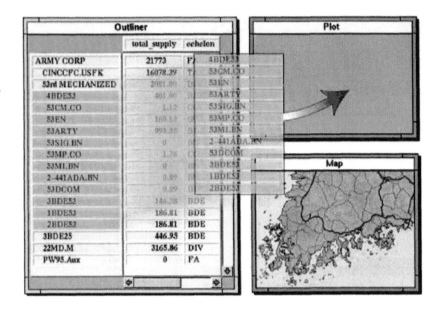

that are good candidates to keep, similarly grouped by product segment. Even better than side-by-side comparisons may be graphs users can move and overlay for comparisons (Figure 7.3).

The flexibility of DataSplash or Visage system designs gives problem solvers a good deal of leeway for making concrete comparisons that, in turn, reduce the strain on their visual memory. Yet these strategies alone do not address users' needs for multipurpose, rich graphics that help them answer several questions at once. Developers have to explicitly create and pre-program such graphics into views in the first place. Such graphics are especially useful in answering such "why" questions as "why are losses

FIGURE 7.3

Overlay graphs to compare data. In this prototype, users can move one scatterplot over another to make comparisons (Acharya et al., 2002).

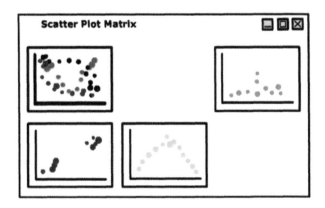

in a specific market far greater than the regional average?" These rich, compressed visualizations are vital to problem solving because, when designed well, they foster the probing of sophisticated interpretive questions (Bertin, 1983; Tufte, 1990). Rich, purposefully constructed data in a single view—for example, small multiples—relieve users of the burden of holding prior views in visual memory. Figure 7.4 provides four examples of such rich, compressed visualizations, three of which pertain directly to optimizing decisions (see Figures 7.4B, 7.4C and 7.4D).

In designing compressed visualizations, interaction designers, usability specialists, and visualization experts need to be aware of the usability drawbacks. It is challenging to invent appropriate visualizations customized to problem types and domain-based inquiry practices that are powerful *and* approachable. As a quick glance at the graphics in Figure 7.4 suggests, problem solvers are likely to have a hard time initially finding effective entry points and figuring out how to "read" and interpret meanings. They will probably need some training, perhaps electronic performance support, which software teams will need to create in conjunction with the visualizations. Once users grasp the meaning and analytical uses of such graphics, however, they are likely to explore complex questions better with compressed visualizations than with side-by-side or serially displayed (and visually remembered) graphs (Burns, 2000).

In summary, for comparisons, the following problems occur, which designers can address by experimenting with various combinations of the strategies and choices in this table. In the Toolkit of Choices, items in parentheses refer to implemented examples discussed in this section.

Making Comparisons

Usefulness problems

- Coding that does not validly reflect true market distributions
- Difficult-to-discern entry points
- Inability to see a current and prior view within or across programs at once
- Inability to see the same view, colored two or more different ways
- Cognitive overload when comparisons rely on visual memory

Toolkit of choices from which to create integrated solutions

- Scoring tools for weighting (such as IBM ScorCat, Emptoris, or Perfect)

FIGURE 7.4
Rich, compressed visualizations. (A) A classic trellis example showing f barley production over time in different regions. Small multiples show several variables at once and enable users to see at a glance when patterns diverge from normal, as they do in the Morris graph (third down from top) (Becker et al., 1996).

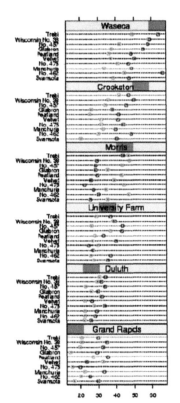

A   Barley Yield (bushels/acre)

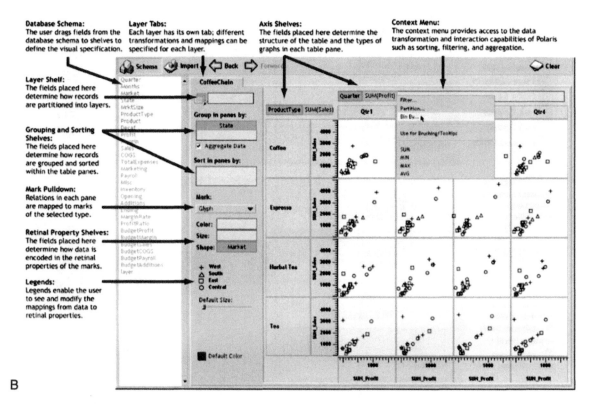

Database Schema:
The user drags fields from the database schema to shelves to define the visual specification.

Layer Tabs:
Each layer has its own tab; different transformations and mappings can be specified for each layer.

Axis Shelves:
The fields placed here determine the structure of the table and the types of graphs in each table pane.

Context Menu:
The context menu provides access to the data transformation and interaction capabilities of Polaris such as sorting, filtering, and aggregation.

Layer Shelf:
The fields placed here determine how records are partitioned into layers.

Grouping and Sorting Shelves:
The fields placed here determine how records are grouped and sorted within the table panes.

Mark Pulldown:
Relations in each pane are mapped to marks of the selected type.

Retinal Property Shelves:
The fields placed here determine how data is encoded in the retinal properties of the marks.

Legends:
Legends enable the user to see and modify the mappings from data to retinal properties.

B

FIGURE 7.4 *(cont'd)*
(B) A scatterplot matrix (small multiples) displaying marketing data for making retail decisions. Dynamically linked to the matrix are numerous attribute filters, changeable axes, and tabs for different views (Stolte et al., 2002).

"WHAT DO I SEE AND WHAT DOES IT MEAN?"

Throughout their assessments of best product mixes, category managers ask "What do I see?" and "What does it mean?" Visualization teams conventionally address these user questions by offering support based on graphic theory and perceptual principles. For example, they design algorithms and screen interactions for data placement, layout, arrangement, perceptual codings, the mapping of information to graphs, resolution of displays, and the labeling of data and graphic components. They exploit people's pre-attentive and attentive perceptual processing and comprehension abilities and use well-crafted graphics to express difficult concepts. They also mix mouse-rollover information, legends, online help, and other instructional information to explain various graphics.

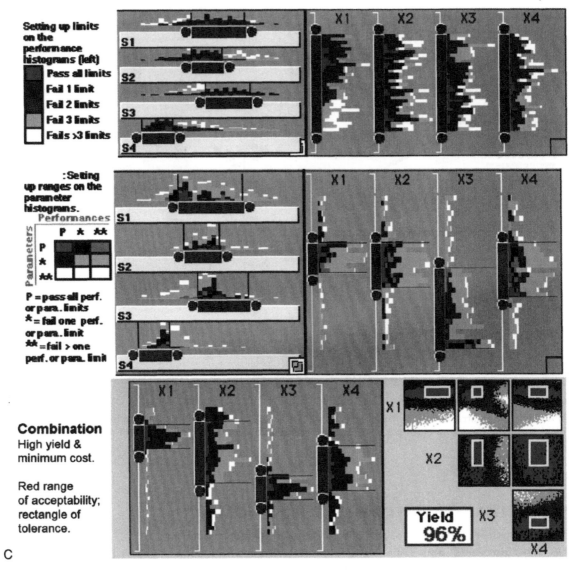

FIGURE 7.4 (*cont'd*)

(C) Influence Explorer for making optimizing decisions in product design. As depicted in this example, designers find the best ways to produce long-lasting, inexpensive light bulbs by manipulating sliders and histograms that stand for performance measures and production parameters. They combine these criteria in different mixes to find the combination of factors that provides the greatest yield. The legend for color-coding shows that this program lets users set values for color-coding that correspond to their evaluative judgments (Spence, 2001).

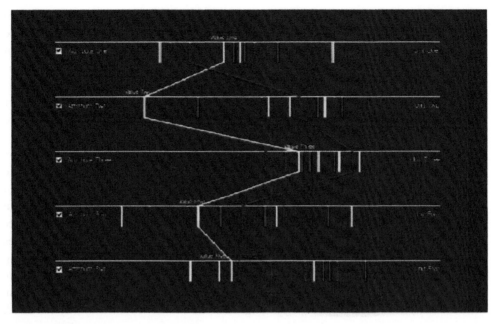

FIGURE 7.4 (*cont'd*)

(D) Parallel coordinates for selecting optimally performing products in online merchandising. In this example, each color tic across the rows represents a different product. The graphic is color-coded by product so that analysts can pick out the same product in each row by its color. Each row represents an attribute of this product group, ranging along the scale from left to right from lesser to greater desirability. (Attribute values are arranged in each row according to whether a high or low value for that metric is more desirable.) Attribute rows are arranged top to bottom from most to least important attributes. Analysts can draw lines down the rows to see how any one product (tick) performs on all attributes and, as shown in the graphic, how two products (yellow and blue) compare (Lee et al., 2001).

These and other "visual science" design strategies are well developed and explained elsewhere in a number of excellent sources (Tufte, 1990; Cleveland, 1993; Ware, 2000). In addition, many of these principles have been captured in automated graphics generators that can aid design teams in pre-defining the best graphics to display for different tasks in the applications they develop. Some visualization teams even include automated graphics generators in the application itself, offering end-users a guided opportunity to create and shape graphics to their own purposes. These generators ask users to specify data ranges, types of problems, data content, and analysis tasks, and from these inputs the program generates the right graphs with the appropriate visual properties (Ignatius et al., 1994; Foltz and Davis, 2001).

When visualization teams focus on creating pre-defined graphics or pre-formatted frames to help users see data and relationships that mean something to their inquiries, one of their main design deliberations typically centers on how much screen space to devote to data versus text, signposts, legends, affordances, and other "non-data" cues for sensemaking and wayfinding. Design debates often are so intense about how to apportion screen real estate that teams lose sight of larger issues. They devote more energy to deciding the *amount of space* to allot to the information markers and cues that address the "what do I see?" question than to devising the best content and form for answering it.

Programs are not usable without "visual science" design strategies, including the principles about data-to-ink ratios that underlie these debates about apportioning screen space. However, these strategies alone do not address all of analysts' "What do I see and what does it mean?" questions usefully. Many times these questions demand more than aids for decoding, discriminating, and offloading cognitive burdens. In fact, sometimes sensemaking difficulties occur because principle-based visualization designs collide with users' preferred methods of analysis. For example, such a collision occurs when category managers can only make data of interest stand out perceptually by getting rid of the data context, which they also need.

Examining Current Shortcomings

Anya's experiences show many variations of the "What do I see and what does it mean?" question. In each, as the following sections show, she needs support that she does not get.

"Is what I see relevant to what I'm looking for?"

In bar charts, Anya has trouble deciphering "striped" bars, especially when stripes stand for numeric measures such as dollar sales rather than categorical dimensions such as brands. Typically, people understand categorical coding more easily than numeric coding. Moreover decoding at times holds little *practical* meaning or value. In one instance in Anya's case, market distributions of sales are different from the color spans encoding them, and it is the market reality that Anya must understand. Because the visualization programs do not give Anya control over defining cut-off points for the spread of colors, the graphics are less than useful for her strategic purposes and competitive needs.

Another difficulty Anya experiences with multicolor aggregates is that sometimes she cannot tell what they signify. When she color-codes a multigraph perspective by promotions, she cannot make sense of what any individual color-coded bar is telling her. In this instance, Anya moves on. However, in others she, like most analysts, may impose a meaning that is not there, and often an unwarranted one that leads to inappropriate decisions.

"Can I see what I want to see?"

When Anya searches nationally for high and low selling products, she first drills down to olive oils and then, within olive oils, to the products of vendors that dominate the market, keeping the rest of the shortening and oils visible, though grayed out. Within the olive oils, she cannot readily discern the data of interest. For this small set of the whole, the colors distinguishing top sellers from the other olive oils show only shades of difference. One solution is for Anya to exclude all but the data on olive oil, thereby triggering the program to recolor the display so it reflects only the spread of values in the olive oil data. But in doing this Anya would lose her view of part-to-whole relationships, an important analytical need. "Exclude-and-recolor" solves the visual discrimination problem, but it is not useful. In this instance, a solution to remedy perceptual difficulties clashes with practical goals, and it adds to other "What do I see?" burdens, as well. If Anya excludes data, she needs additional program support for sensemaking as she continues through her inquiry and asks, "What data have been filtered out and omitted in calculated totals or percentages of the whole. How can omitted data be cued as such in presentations created from captured views?"

"Is what I see what I ought to see?"

In addition to problem solvers gauging what they see against market realities, they also continuously validate the integrity of their data. Category managers want to make sure their analysis does not rest on flawed data. Sometimes it is easy for them to catch faulty data in a view because they know the market realities and how graphed structures should look because of them. Other times, however, invalid data are hard to detect, and problem solvers need cues from the graphs themselves. From them, they need to read indications of duplicate data, format inconsistencies, and missing data. Anya's programs do not offer this support.

"What did I see before interruptions and what did it mean?"

Anya's program also does not support interrupted and resumed investigations. When interruptions occur, users need reminders about the questions they were asking, their place in a task landscape, and the current program state. Displaying such signposts in the graphics is as important as applying perceptual principles for differentiation, emphasis, unity, and integrity.

"Are seeing and believing the same thing?"

Finally, a less obvious support for "What do I see and what does it mean?" involves anticipating users' common misconceptions and guarding against users making inappropriate moves and interpretations because of them. Users often impose assumptions on visualizations based on perceiving familiar images or calling up standard interactions that actually run counter to the logic of the application.

Anya makes errors based on familiarity when she does not remember and lacks adequate cues about the program's dynamic query logic. She assumes that her simple, familiar drill-down routines and selection modes will work even though the query she makes is complex. Moreover, she fails to catch her mistake because it is hard to discern that the query results do not match her intentions. Only later, when she searches online help and experiences déjà vu, does she realize that relying on familiar query moves that do not concur with actual program constraints caused the problem.

Another common misconception based on familiarity in product mix problem solving involves retailers falling back on the familiarity of pie charts—a commonly used graph in this domain—when they interact with similar-looking displays such as circular networks of a product hierarchy (Figure 7.5). Without realizing their misconceptions, they often superimpose notions of pie slices and proportionality on this network diagram and draw wrong conclusions.

FIGURE 7.5
Network graph of a product hierarchy. From the center out, the levels of the network represent the product category, subcategories, vendors, brands, and stock keeping unit (SKU) of various products. These are color-coded by dollar sales, moving through the spectrum from low sales (blue) to high sales (red).

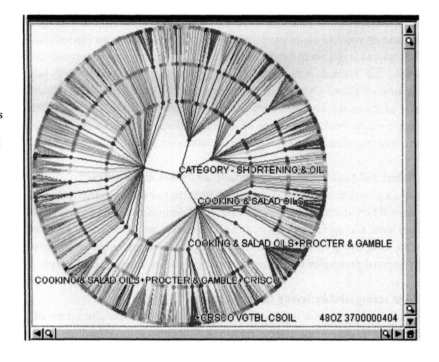

Focusing on Design Strategies and Choices for Usefulness

Adequately supporting users in answering, "What do I see and what does it mean?" is an open design problem in visualization today. Some design strategies emphasize operational support to give users control over various aspects of color-coding, such as allowing customized color distributions by setting a midpoint in a quadrant analysis and letting users choose their own chromatic scales and degrees of luminance (red-green, blue-yellow, or grayscale) (Ware, 2000). Intactix's Intercept applies this strategy (*www.intactix.com*).

Despite these "visual science" solutions, problem solvers invariably conduct some analyses, as Anya does, in which gradations of color are still too indiscriminate for their purposes. These situations may be further confounded if problem solving is collaborative and analysts are accustomed to socially negotiating meaning. They now find themselves jointly negotiating whether a shade is "dark enough" to warrant a go-ahead decision (Goodwin, 1997). Strategies used by Influence Explorer (displayed previously in Figure 7.4C) offer a sophisticated solution to such problems. The program allows users to control color-coding by specifying how many colors to use in coding and what each should represent in terms of a value judgment (e.g., acceptable, borderline, unacceptable) or in terms of criteria satisfied.

Other design strategies aimed at increasing problem solvers' understanding of a graphic display take the approach of drawing users' attention to the "signature of algorithms" in an interface display (Noy and Schroeder, 2001). Based on the premise that people understand what they see better when they understand why it appears, a "signature explorer" strategy strives to cue users about the algorithmic results of their program interactions. For example, in Anya's case, she would have benefited if a perceptible "signature" had highlighted the connection between her having excluded data and the automatic redistribution of the color spread reflecting the consequently reduced data pool.

This "What do I see?" signature strategy is limited to one-by-one programmatic actions. Users also need to make sense of what they see in terms of a view's relevance to particular product mix questions and goals. Toward this end, design teams may draw on strategies developed by XeroxPARC that highlight information scents. Perceptual codings and highlighted markings in the graphics give users "proximal cues to assess distal content" (Pirolli et al., 2000). The goal is to help problem solvers readily see content in the larger information space that is relevant to the data in focus for their specific information goals. Displays based on this strategy help analysts understand the data of interest in relation to its context by highlighting thematically associated data and indicating the strength of the relevance. Such cues, however, have proved to be unsupportive when analysts know little about the information displayed (Pirolli et al., 2000).

Design teams also need to address problem solvers' tendencies to impose the familiar on a display to answer "What do I see?" when no suggestive cues are apparent. Software can build in rules to reduce human errors but can never be foolproof in eliminating them in complex tasks. Therefore, the goal is to help users catch errors resulting from familiarity before the errors become entangled and damaging to practical decisions. Such support has challenged software designers for years, especially in regard to complex tasks. No matter how self-evident a graph may be or how informative an algorithm signature explorer is, problem solvers will always rely on familiarity. It is an inevitable adaptive strategy in open-ended, multiphase inquiries (Payne et al., 2001). Because problem solvers like Anya fall back on the familiar when they cannot rely on more informed knowledge about program displays or modes, visualization designs must help them recollect this knowledge or, barring that, guide their attention toward sharper verification after they interact with screens based on familiarity.

Design solutions may require a focus on advanced support that includes built-in domain knowledge. Gearing users toward better verification through software intelligence and domain content would involve a built-in knowledge base of moves for typical category management patterns of inquiry. The software could compare this knowledge to the moves users take in their inquiries to identify users' likely lines of questioning. Based again on intelligence and stored knowledge, the software could target points at which increasing complexities are apt to cause misdirection. When users' actual moves arrive at these points, the visualizations could anticipate potential mistakes and draw an outline around perspectives. The outline would cue users to verify the outcomes of their interactions against their expectations. In this way, users could read from a display whether what they see is what they should see.

Moreover, to help users recollect their knowledge of displays, and thereby divert them from resorting to the familiar, software teams can implement strategies based on intelligence in user profiling. A program could capture repeated interaction patterns from one month to the next, including likely errors and error corrections. When errors seem imminent, the program could alert users that they have been over this ground before, perhaps even showing previous results. To pursue such intelligence-based design strategies and probabilistic modeling, software teams need to gather a great deal of observational data on category managers' various lines of questioning and related patterns. They then need to use these findings to define interaction events appropriately for marking and predicting impasses in interaction log data.

Overall, in supporting category managers in "What do I see and what does it mean?" questions, visualization teams need to address the following usefulness problems. For them, they should put together, as needed, the following design strategies and choices. Examples are given parenthetically.

What Do I See and What Does It Mean?

Usefulness problems

- Perceptual coding that lacks face validity
- Difficult-to-comprehend color-coded aggregates, such as bar charts colored by numeric variables
- Color gradations and spreads that are hard to discriminate
- Displays that do not make corrupt or missing data apparent
- Difficulty in resuming after interruptions
- Inappropriate uses of familiar methods and assumptions
- Socially negotiated meanings about shades of color

Toolkit of choices from which to create integrated and elegant solutions

- Visual science principles shaped by practical task intentions and strategic angles
- User control over the spread of colors in color-coding (as in Intercept)
- Ability to set the number and value range of colors and tie them to judgments or criteria satisfied (as in Influence Explorer)
- Interface cues indicating what the program does algorithmically in response to users' interactions (as in Signature Explorer)
- Information scents and path tracking (for example, XeroxPARC)
- Time travel doubling as reminders after interruptions (as in Scopeware)
- Built-in domain knowledge, intelligent agents, and user profiling to signal inappropriate reliance on familiarity

---

GETTING FROM HERE TO THERE IN TASK LANDSCAPES

Because problem solvers in any one domain put together task landscapes differently due to distinct conditions, they need adaptable yet pattern-based support to get from here to there in configuring and navigating these landscapes. For Anya, one form of support she receives from her visualization programs is the table of totals. In a single keystroke, Anya selects data of interest such as top vendors, and combined sales totals and market shares for them are displayed in the table. Because the program automatically calculates and gives access to these values vital to Anya's lines of inquiry, she is not slowed down in her investigations. Design strategies such as these improve usefulness by transforming higher-level recurrent inquiry routines into analysis in-a-keystroke.

Examining Current Shortcomings

Unfortunately, Anya's programs also hinder her. They lack a means for replaying groups of repeated moves. They do not support her in saving and replaying customized baselines, and her second visualization program undercuts continuity by requiring an inordinate number of steps to get the figures she wants when comparing the two standardized bar charts for her stores and the rest of the market. Steps are so time-consuming that she abandons her intention altogether. Moreover, Anya's smooth-flowing, here-to-there movements are hampered dramatically when she has to go out of the program to create weightings. Finally, Anya finds she cannot easily put together a landscape for grouping data into custom aggregates on-the-fly, as she wants to do with her preferred suppliers.

Focusing on Design Strategies and Choices for Usefulness

To help users expediently get from here to there within and across task landscapes, visualization teams need to design for users' full range of actions based on typical patterns. Microsoft's Data Analyzer 1.0 lets users, in a keystroke, call up an Excel spreadsheet of figures behind the selected graphics, something Anya would have appreciated (Figure 7.6). Unfortunately, it does not display the spreadsheet and graphic versions of the data simultaneously, as Anya needs.

To more usefully display charts and textual data at once, visualization teams often use the strategy of presenting dynamically linked data tables and graphics in the same perspective. Or, unlike Anya's second visualization program, they allow users to create a table or spreadsheet, as needed,

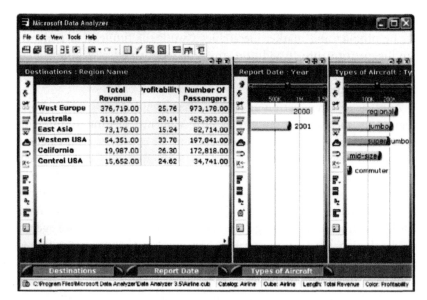

FIGURE 7.6
Microsoft DataAnalyzer 1.0. This program replaces the bar chart in the left column with the spreadsheet of data behind the chart in a keystroke. (Courtesy of *www.Microsoft.com/office/dataanalyzer/default.asp.*)

and "snap" it together with other relevant visualizations to create a single perspective (North and Shneiderman, 2000).

These solutions all result in fewer keystrokes and improved continuity of investigations, but they skirt the real issue important for usefulness: Addressing users' domain-based analytical and integrated moves with holistic support. Anya, for example, needs more than access to a spreadsheet or data table. In the two standardized bar charts situation, the figures Anya wants are derived values for groups of data, the shares and totals of the "stripes," which are probably not part of the raw data table displayed in a keystroke. She also needs these figures formatted into a chart for continuous reference. Analysis in-a-keystroke for automatically deriving such values as offered by Anya's program's table of totals, is a start, but it must mesh with the other objectives of problem solvers' pattern of inquiry, in this case the creation of a reference chart. A possible structural approach, discussed previously in regard to comparisons, is for design teams to pre-format a MAYAViz-type frame into a reference table of derived values, as Anya needs, and let users drag and drop the relevant data into it.

In designing for getting from here to there, visualization teams need to strike just the right balance between supporting recurrent tasks and overly determining users' work. For example, analysis in-a-keystroke is probably a good solution for many repeated lines of questioning associated with "what?" questions category managers ask as they traverse each level of the product and market hierarchies ("work the funnel") to evaluate product performance. In addition, Anya and retail experts welcome a table of totals in-a-keystroke, provided they have the leeway to choose the calculated values.

Another recurrent action in category management is creating custom aggregates, such as grouping items into segments relevant to different market niches. Merchandisers do not foresee or construct all the aggregates they need ahead of time, and, as with Anya and her preferred supplier data, they often need to create them *ad hoc*. Several strategies and choices for aggregate managers exist at present for visualization applications (Bhavnani and John, 1997; Chuah, 1998; Tang and Shneiderman, 2001). As an alternate strategy, specialists in the area of software agents are developing interfaces to give users easy ways to program aggregate creation themselves without having to become programmers. In one approach, users would specify examples and identify text strings in a desired grouping (such as all preferred suppliers' names) and automatically the program would generate an aggregate (Lieberman et al., 1998). Figure 7.7 shows an interface for this "programming by example," enabling users to drag examples and texts into boxes, and from them, the program infers the coding for the desired set of activities (in this case, making travel reservations).

In contrast, for other, less systematic repetitions, such as replaying certain sets of actions for exploratory "why?" and "what-if?" questions, merchandisers need more freedom than pre-structured analysis in a keystroke provides. One design strategy that gives this control to users is to provide timelines of their inquiry events and allow users to manipulate them (Figure 7.8) (Derthick and Roth, 2001a). As users move along in their inquiry, they may find they want to run the same analysis they conducted earlier on different data. For example, Anya uses the same steps to get an overall sense of product performance nationwide and regionally. Using manipulable timelines, users can copy the portion of the timeline representing their current event and move it to the earlier portion in which they first applied these desired methods. The program then lets users click through the same methods with the new data. This strategy demands that development groups do front-end analysis to determine the sets of moves that stand for meaningful inquiry events from users' perspectives, and it requires incorporating this event tracking and timeline display into the program. Figure 7.8B illustrates another visual presentation for replayable events on a timeline developed at the University of Maryland Human-Computer Interaction Laboratory.

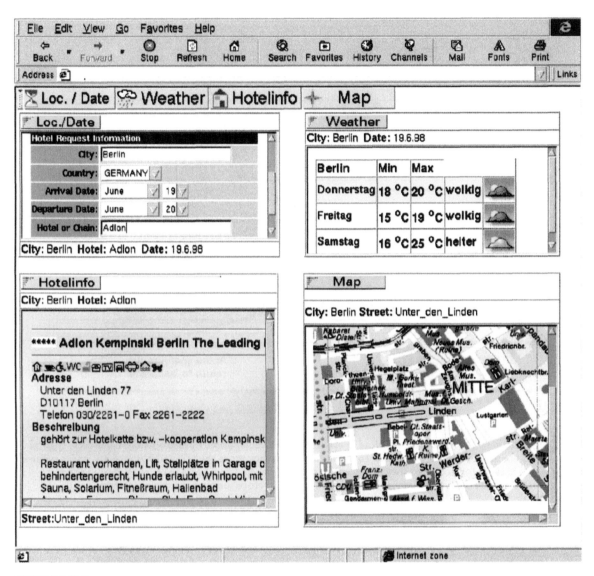

FIGURE 7.7
Interface for programming by example. Users provide the content in each of the predefined boxes and the program infers the desired coding (Lieberman et al., 1998).

Another way for users to replay moves is through "macro-building" (Derthick and Roth, 2001b). Similar in strategy to the manipulable timeline, this approach gives users more power and is akin to guided end-user programming. In this approach, users visually see past operations, drag and

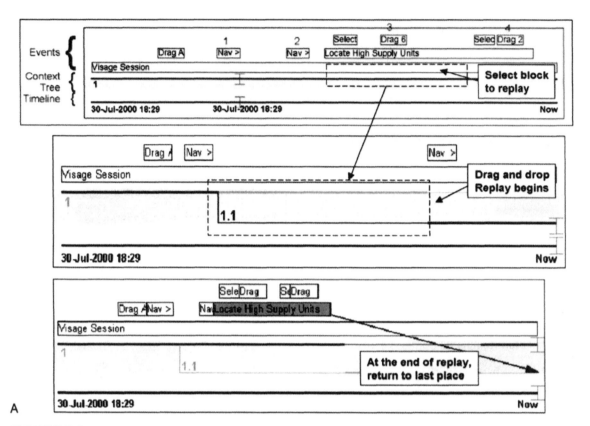

FIGURE 7.8
Replaying of actions. (A) A movable timeline of events for replayed actions. In the top view, users copy data of interest that are part of a block of actions. In the middle view, they move the selected block to an earlier event—one in which they performed steps they now want to repeat. In the bottom view, users click through the repeated actions and finish by returning to where they started before running the replay (Derthick and Roth, 2001a).

drop them to a space in which they first define the automated replay, then edit or refine the representation and trigger the replay when they want it. This strategy serves other wayfinding ends, as well. It helps users know where they are and how they got there. This design strategy is integrative, approachable, and attuned to the flexibility users value in composing actions for replay. As seen in strategies for creating aggregates, as techniques make it increasingly easier for non-technical users to "program by example," to drag and drop indicators, and to use program-assisted dialogue boxes, design teams may use such strategies to offer the control and customized support users need for complex problem solving.

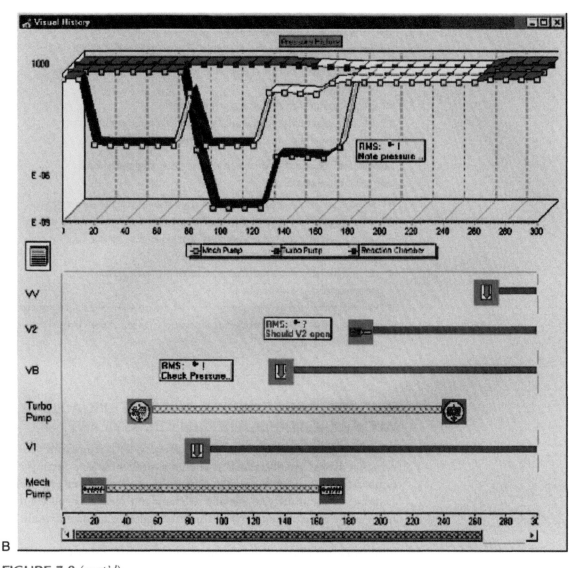

FIGURE 7.8 (*cont'd*)
(B) The "Learning Historian." This tool records and displays the history of interactions and allows users to replay them (Plaisant et al., 1999).

Helping users get from here to there in task landscapes involves addressing the problems in the following table by creating integrated support that takes advantage of the listed choices. Examples are provided in parentheses.

PERFORMING COMPLEX QUERIES VISUALLY WITH UNCOMPLICATED INTERACTIONS

In product mix investigations, a special category for getting from here to there that deserves to be treated separately is problem solvers' attempts to conduct complex queries visually. This task is central to emergent and dynamic work and involves visually selecting and retrieving subsets that are logically related through what, in written query statements, would be compound, nested uses of the terms *and, or,* and *not*.

In data visualizations, the common design mantra for visual querying is "overview first, zoom and filter, then details on demand" (Shneiderman, 1996). But this mantra does not distinguish between simple and complex queries. As a result, design teams often presume that support is sufficient for all of users' visual querying as long it offers the basic functionality for overview-zoom-filter-and-details. Such support includes: Panning, zooming, and rotating; showing a contextual view; selecting, hiding, excluding, and restoring data; undoing, and saving; and viewing selected relationships and their details.

Examining Current Shortcomings

On the face of it, this support seems to cover users' needs. Yet Anya's experiences reveal shortcomings. For example, Anya cannot drill down to sleepers *and* opportunities of only the top vendors. She has trouble, as well, in testing her pet strategy of dropping pan sprays in Nevada by mixing standard drill-downs into winners and losers with a more pointed drill-down to a specific subcategory, all the while keeping the data context visible. In these instances, discrete operations for selecting the data of interest actually work against each other.

Data visualizations commonly lack the power to carry out the visual equivalent of complex, nested query statements while keeping contexts intact and visible. For her business goals, Anya needs both of these conditions satisfied. Such query situations push the dynamic querying typically found in applications beyond problem solvers' notions of acceptable trade-offs. They reveal other deficiencies, as well. In drill-downs, for example, Anya has to change selection modes and would benefit from salient reminders about the current selection mode, something she does not get from her current applications. She also needs help verifying that the selected data are, in fact, her intended data (an enabling task omitted in features associated with the visual querying mantra). Finally, like other category managers, she needs to look at two things at once: What data look like for analysis and what they need to look like for presentation. This issue of composing in tandem with analysis is discussed in detail in a later section.

Focusing on Design Strategies and Choices for Usefulness

An issue that often preoccupies visualization designers is devising strategies and choices for the best visual query mechanism. Different visualization groups have their favorite mechanisms, among them selection by sweeping with the mouse (brushing), dynamic sliders, movable lenses, buttons, and drop-down lists. Visualization teams often test the usability of various mechanisms, and their findings prompt continual improvements. For example, findings show that selecting data of interest through sweeping is more powerful for complex questions but less approachable than using dynamic query sliders (Stone et al., 1994). As a result, visualization designers such as those at Spotfire are now creating more powerful sliders (see *www.spotfire.com*).

In Anya's visualization applications, the mechanisms of sweeping and multiple selection modes offer flexibility and power, but they are still too brittle for complex queries in which users need to keep the data context visible. Overall, query paradigms for complex problem solving need to offer users the following types of flexibility:

- Seeing selected data in the context of the whole, as needed

- Filtering out (excluding) non-selected data, as needed

- Restoring only part of the data filtered out during a multiphased inquiry session

The strategy of "nested sorting" is another way besides selection mechanisms to answer some of users' complex visual querying needs. (Nested sorting involves sorting first on a primary factor and then, within that factor, sorting again on others.) The table lens tool, for example, lets users easily and visually create whatever nested sorting and matrix permutations they want by dragging and dropping columns (*www.inxight.com*).

Other design teams seek to address the demands of complex querying more comprehensively. The Influence Explorer developers, for example (see Figure 7.4C), have devised ways to keep data contexts visible while drilling down in complex ways into multiple parameters and performance criteria, including those related to users' organizational priorities and market demands (Tweedie et al., 1996). This dynamic query design, however, is labor intensive for users at the front end. It requires them to prepare data and pre-calculate parameters based on the standards of their domain-based analysis (Tweedie et al., 1996).

MAYAViz and the Sage Visulization Group have a less labor-intensive approach for facilitating complex querying without overly determining or simplifying users' work. As we have seen exemplified in Figures 5.5 and 7.2, these groups' applications, such as Visage and CoMotion, have drag-and-drop capabilities built into the data rather than using selection modes (*www.mayaviz.com*). Users conduct complex queries by dragging selected data, grouping intricate subsets, moving them to the foreground for attention, and contracting or expanding them, as needed. All the while, the context persists so users can relate the data in focus to it.

In summary, support for complex querying often falls short in regard to usefulness and requires design strategies as detailed in the following table, with examples provided in parentheses.

Conducting Complex Queries Visually

Usefulness problems

- Difficulty getting results from complex, nested queries and seeing them in the context of all the data

- Uncertainty about what data are excluded at any given moment and difficulty in bringing back only part of the excluded data

Toolkit of choices from which to create integrated and elegant solutions

- Powerful query mechanisms that are uncomplicated and allow users to see part-to-whole relationships, as needed (for example, multiple selection modes; Tablelens; Influence and Attribute Explorer; Visage and CoMotion)

COMPOSING IN TANDEM WITH CUMULATIVE DATA ANALYSIS

In product mix investigations, category managers first turn facts about product performance into judgments about winners, losers, sleepers, and opportunities; then into decisions about items to keep, add, drop, and enhance; and finally into persuasive justifications. These processes involve conducting investigations from two *concurrent* perspectives: Analyzing and composing. Category managers analyze data to relate facts and make judgments and, at the same time, they compose communications about their analytical insights. These communications include lists for their own uses and presentations to stakeholders.

Examining Current Shortcomings

Category managers' composing goals for item lists or presentations continuously shape their analytical methods. Because Anya progressively composes in tandem with analysis, she is willing to make extra efforts, such as moving out of the visualization program and back again to weight variables elsewhere. She knows she needs such a weighted view for a persuasive presentation to her supervisor. In addition, she adds extra columns to the data table in the visualization perspective because she wants to be sure all these data are captured for later use in communication and list making.

Moreover, for communications—to herself and to her manager—Anya creates a large number of bookmarks and needs a system for managing these functionally different marked views. She relies on a bookmarking system in the first place because her visualization programs do not adequately support analyzing and composing in tandem. In these bookmarks, Anya and other category managers need to quickly find the views that are relevant to a current line of questioning. They need reminders to signal what a saved view is about, what other associated views may be relevant, and what thoughts they had when they first saved the view. Finally, they need to freely annotate saved views. As we saw in Anya's case, these activities cannot be too diverting because they occur simultaneously with analysts' investigative lines of thought.

Anya faces many sensemaking difficulties, as well, due to the overlap of analysis and communication. Multicolored bars in bar charts are just as confusing to audiences in presentations as they are to Anya during analysis, and she needs to create easy-to-grasp displays for presentation purposes. Moreover, the color-coding of views is not always distinct enough to draw an audience's attention immediately to the data of interest. Anya needs other ways to direct her viewer's gaze. In addition to tweaking views for presentations, Anya needs to manage the notes she leaves to herself as she examines data so that she can use them effectively to inform her item list and presentations. Currently, the only "system" she has is to keep track of these numerous notes mentally and cross-reference them with her electronic workspace and lists.

On a more conceptual level, composing in tandem with analysis involves a demanding blend of reasoning about data and planning communications. For this blend of reasoning and planning, category managers need two types of program support. First, in the midst of analysis, they need to manipulate data for communication purposes. Second, they have to choose the right graphics, arrangements, and lay-outs in the first place for the communications implicit in their intended item lists and presentations. Category managers' initial choices about graphics and layout shape their subsequent notions about what they can communicate.

At base, software teams' design strategies need to account for the ways in which domain experts turn facts into judgments and judgments into communications. Teams need to recognize that these joined cognitive processes are paradoxical. To analyze numbers, interpret relationships, and draw provisional judgments, problem solvers look beneath the surface striving to discover deep structural patterns. They examine a great deal of raw data, draw on several sources of knowledge, and make detailed notes (Davies, 1993). Yet when analysts translate these insights to goals and communications, they shift from thinking in low-level detail to high-level concepts. Having grasped the deep structure of a problem and its potential solutions, they now produce comments and highlight relationships that reveal the conceptual aspects of their particular claims, narratives, potential options, and decisions. Experienced experts take a long time composing these high-level notes and highlights (Davies, 1993). Very little in Anya's visualization programs reflects a sensitivity to these divergent yet concurrent intellectual needs.

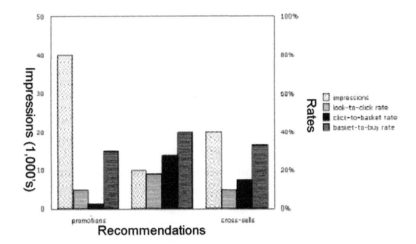

FIGURE 7.9
A second y axis for a
visualization of online
merchandising cues, effective
for analysis and
communication
(Lee et al., 1999).

Focusing on Design Strategies and Choices for Usefulness

Visualization teams face the challenge of providing functions and displays that support category experts when focusing on low-level, multi-source details and in communicating them through careful notes and readily apparent conceptual relationships. To do so, they need to know the main questions and patterns that drive these problem solvers' specialized inquiries *and* strategic communications, and they need to match them to the most appropriate graphics, signposts, functions, and workspaces. At times, the same graphic displays may serve both ends, such as making comparisons in data analysis and showing these comparisons in communications. To support both types of comparison adequately, visualization teams must evaluate design possibilities in terms of how well they serve both ends. For example, numerous side-by-side graphics do not translate well to communications in which it is critical to direct viewers' attention to insights of interest. A more useful choice may be to add a second y-axis to a scatterplot graph so that it shows two types of data at once (Figure 7.9) (Lee et al., 1999).

In addition to these needs, complete and coherent support must address other critical complex problem solving requirements related to interwoven analysis and composing, such as the following:

- Turning data into another form, such as item lists, and easily transferring it

- Working with the data in an analytical view for communication purposes while keeping the original view intact and in sight

- Highlighting important relationships

- Getting adequate reminders about relevant views

- Writing notes to viewers about unseen data

- Generating aggregates

Because category managers move back and forth between analyzing and composing, designs that separate these needs into unconnected modes do not fit seamlessly with merchandisers' integrated patterns of inquiry. Microsoft's Data Analyzer 1.0, mentioned previously in the Getting From Here to There section (see Figure 7.6), is one such example (*www.Microsoft. com/office/dataanalyzer/default.asp*). This program allows users to readily transfer Analyzer graphs to presentation and Web-display programs in the Microsoft Office suite, but they must work with each in separate applications.

Given Anya's current disjointed save-and-compose efforts, she is likely at first to experience this integration as a welcome improvement. Yet program capabilities and interoperable back-end servers and front-end office suites drive this improvement more than users' practical inquiry patterns. Eventually the efficiency Anya and others like her gain from such programmatically based enhancements will plateau, and they will still not have experienced truly useful support. Data Analyzer, for example, does not give problem solvers, in its composing functionality, the ability to manipulate analytical graphics for communication purposes: To annotate them, highlight insights, transform and rearrange data, or write comments while still maintaining the original analytical view. Data Analyzer facilitates inquiry by reducing the number of keystrokes for composing and analyzing but problem solvers such as Anya never receive the power they need to compose while analyzing for decision-making and persuasive purposes. Moreover as mentioned earlier, with Data Analyzer, users still need to move in and out of separate programs in the Office suite.

More robust strategies for finding-and-reminding may be found in the Scopeware Vision™ 1.2 design (see Figure 5.3) concepts described in the section on the redesign of the IT troubleshooting tool (see *www.-scopeware.com*). Another more integrated strategy is the MAYAViz and SAGE Visualization group's Visage workspace with its drag-and-drop "briefer frame" (*www.2cs.cmu.edu/Groups/sage/visagedd.html*). In Visage, while problem solvers explore and analyze data, they can move whatever views they want in the workspace to a briefer frame. This frame is designed for reporting, publishing, and collaborative purposes and offers composing and annotating capabilities (Figure 7.10).

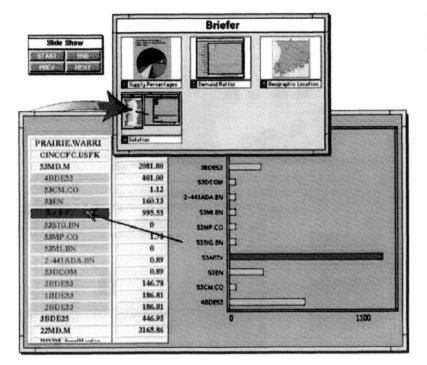

FIGURE 7.10
The Visage briefer frame for analyzing and composing in tandem (courtesy of *www.-2cs.cum.edu/ Groups/ sage/visagedd.html*).

Similar capabilities are offered in a suite of analysis tools produced by Spotfire that are customized to specific domains and problem types (*www.spotfire.com*). Figure 7.11 shows samples of the Spotfire Decision Site Posters that problem solvers can compose by dragging views of interest from their analytical workspaces onto a presentation work board.

Like Spotfire Decision Site Posters, collaborative analytical tools such as IBM's MerBoard for scientific analysis provide annotating capabilities. Though a different type of tool from the applications discussed so far, MerBoard offers some instructive approaches for designers of software like Anya's (Russell et al., 2002). MerBoard gives problem solvers the ability to compare and annotate images freehand with drawing tools or by voice (Figure 7.12). One downside, especially for analysts such as Anya, is that its annotation workspace is separate from the space in which problem solvers view and analyze data. In addition, as findings on the usability of MerBoard suggest, design teams must be aware that once analysts have an ability to annotate, many of them expect and want more. They expect associated support for tracking and identifying individual annotations so they can find and apply earlier insights to subsequent analyses. They also want to access and edit annotations and track changes in the annotations for analytical purposes (Russell et al., 2002).

FIGURE 7.11
Spotfire's Decision Site Posters. Users can quickly communicate analysis with collaborators by dragging views of interest onto the Decision Site Posters. Posters include an annotation board for collaborative commenting (courtesy of *www.spotfire.com*).

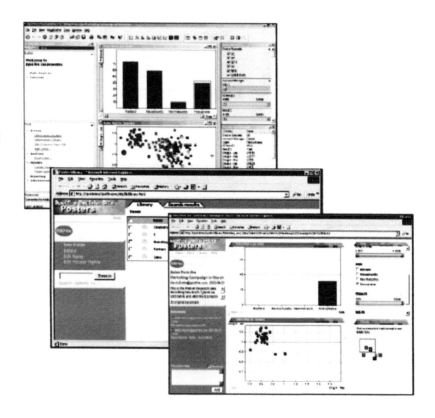

FIGURE 7.12
MerBoard annotation capabilities (courtesy of *www.space.com/businesstechnology/ technology/merboard_rover_0208 21.html*).

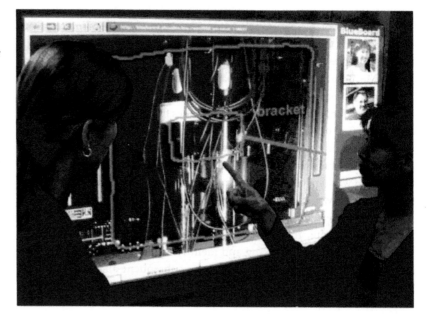

The following table first summarizes usefulness problems related to concurrent analysis and composing, and then details design choices visualization teams may creatively join with other strategies and options to develop useful support. Examples of such support are included parenthetically.

Composing in Tandem with Data Analysis

Usefulness problems

- High overhead in recognizing, organizing, and working with large numbers of functionally different bookmarks or otherwise saved views
- Labor-intensive composing steps or preparations that interfere with ongoing analysis
- Difficulty in changing in-progress analytical views when trying to make salient issues apparent in presentations and then shifting back to analysis
- Difficult shifts between high- and low-levels of analysis for composing and exploring
- Time consuming steps to format, transfer data, and go in and out of separate programs to move from analysis to item lists (in decision-making)
- Missing mechanisms for integrating users' notes into item lists and presentations

Toolkit of choices from which to create integrated and elegant solutions

- Graphic displays that serve both analysis and composition (such as the second Y axis)
- Workspaces for creating annotations (such as Visage, Spotfire Decision Site Poster, and MerBoard)
- Integrated modules or workspaces for analysis and composing that are seamless from users' points of view, including coordinating color-coding, axes, scales, and attributes (for example, Visage and CoMotion)
- Item lists embedded in a data visualization analysis program with easy formatting and transferring of data
- Finding and reminding built into bookmarked or saved views integrated with the other activities of joint analysis and composition (as in Scopeware Vision™)

CONCLUSIONS

Anya's story shows five areas of software support that need better designs to be useful. Design teams need to ensure that category managers can carry out the full range of comparisons crucial for maximizing their competitive advantage and that screen displays combine graphics or compress data into a rich graphic display appropriate for particular types of questions. Interaction designers need to move beyond single-focus visual science principles and give problem solvers control over and cues about aspects of perceptual coding critical to their analytical intentions. They need to help problem solvers recognize when familiar methods will lead to inaccurate results, and they should build in analysis in-a-keystroke for recurrent, high-level lines of questioning. Designers need to structure workspaces and provide functionality for problem solvers to conduct complex queries visually and accurately. Finally, design teams need to support the data manipulations, annotations, saved views, findings-and-reminders, and conceptual shifts that category managers perform when, in the midst of exploring and investigating data, they turn an analytical view into a persuasive communication and then continue analyzing.

Combined, these strategies and choices suggest high level design guidelines for usefulness, including the following:

- Provide different views and give users ample control for distinct, though often concurrent, intellectual needs (such as descriptive and explanatory analyses, composing and analyzing, high- and low-level details)

- Create workspaces, frames or graphics, and keystrokes structured by patterns of inquiry with enough functional flexibility for users to construct their own paths and content through the pattern-based landscape

- Ensure that users can conduct complex, nested queries and can keep data contexts visible and understand their content, as needed

- Provide a great amount of adaptability in color-coding and other perceptual coding for a wide range of user purposes (for example, comparison, "what do I see?", and getting from here to there)

- Create in a single visualization display unified support for mainline analysis tasks and such enabling tasks as finding *and* reminding, and preparing the replay of prior actions

- Exploit software agents, user profiling, and programming by example to trace and cue important patterns and information scents and to put customization and control in the hands of users without technical burden

■ Exploit the power of rich and compressed visualizations

Most importantly, none of the strategies or choices discussed in this chapter should be piled on piecemeal for discrete user tasks. If they are, applications may end up providing monolithic solutions to individual parts of a complex inquiry without giving problem solvers integrated frameworks. Problem solvers need these frameworks to move seamlessly and recursively within and across different processes and objectives of dynamic problem solving (Goebel et al., 2002). Therefore, design teams must combine and integrate different selections from the toolkit for specific and related patterns in users' open-ended investigations, which brings us back to the need to create valid models of users' situated, complex work as a prerequisite for designing useful support.

As part of these models interaction designers, usability specialists, and others on design teams should compose diagrams of task landscapes and choice points accounting for the connections and discretion that shape users' work. Based on these diagrams team members need to create provisional designs, perhaps in the form of prototypes. As Chapter 6 emphasizes, teams then need to evaluate whether a potential design is the most coherent choice. For example, they need to ask if a potential "solution" implies the need for users to create countless bookmarks, which in the long run will adversely affect their efforts to manage their inquiry. Ideally, walkthroughs that evaluate design choices and prototypes against diagrammed landscapes and models of interactive contextual conditions lead to more elegant designs. Elegance may be difficult to achieve, but if integrated support is absent, analysts will opt for workarounds, often to the detriment of their work.

Visualization teams have no pre-determined formula or fixed principles for composing integrated and elegant designs for situated patterns of complex inquiry that are powerful, flexible, approachable, and forgiving. Unfortunately, short of a handful of commercial products, integrative designs such as those produced by MAYAViz, are not yet well established in the market. To create them, designers need to be aware of and target the activities for which problem solvers receive too little support at present, such as those described here. Designers' judgments also depend on other support they have created and how coherence and completeness are best served. For example, "What do I see and what does it mean?" occurs in a wide range of users' task landscapes, and visualization designers must integrate support for a variety of inquiry patterns.

Anya's story shows usefulness shortcomings and design strategies for software-supported problem solving in which large volumes of data are available and in which effective analysis depends on problem solvers being able to retrieve the right data for their purposes and manipulate them advantageously for the questions they need to answer. Usefulness becomes even more complicated when problem solvers analyze data that are shared and constantly changing because the information along with its diverse users is part of a large, multi-application computerized record system, such as a hospital healthcare systems. The scenario in the next chapter explores usefulness for such systems. It examines nurses as they interact with an electronic medication-administration program for the complex problem of figuring out the right dosage for patients who are on a sliding scale for their medication. For these problems, nurses have to consider factors and values that reside in dynamically interactive and interdependent applications. Though users predominantly work in an electronic medication-administration application, the success and safety of their dosage decisions depend, as well, on interactions with under-the-hood interdependencies of the computerized patient record system, the medication ordering modules within them, and the in-patient pharmacy application.

REFERENCES

Acharya, Arti, Erik Dahl, Jason George, Kelly Krout, and Salena Malik. "ProQuest: An Information Visualization Approach." Unpublished course paper. University of Michigan, Ann Arbor, 2002.

Becker, Richard, William Cleveland, Ming-Jen Shyu, and Stephen Kaluzny. *A Tour of Trellis Graphics.* Technical report. Murray Hill, New Jersey: Bell Labs, 1996.

Bertin, Jacques. *Semiology of Graphics.* Madison, WI: University of Wisconsin Press, 1983.

Bhavnani, Suresh and Bonnie John. "From Sufficient to Efficient Usage: An Analysis of Strategic Knowledge." In *Proceedings of CHI '97, ACM Conference on Computer-Human Interaction,* 91-98. Atlanta: ACM, 1997.

Burns, Catherine. "Putting It All Together: Improving Display Integration in Ecological Displays." *Human Factors* 42, no. 2 (2000): 226-241.

Chuah, Mei. "Dynamic Aggregation with Circular Visual Designs." In *Proceedings of the IEEE Symposium on Information Visualization,* 35-43. Triangle Park, NC: IEEE, 1998.

Cleveland, William. *Visualizing Data.* Summit, NJ: Hobart Press, 1993.

Davies, Simon. "Externalising Information During Coding Activities: Effects of Expertise, Environment, and Task." In *Empirical Studies of Programmers: Fifth Workshop,* edited by Curtis R. Cook, Jean C. Scholtz, and James C. Spohrer, 42-61. Palo Alto, CA: Ablex Publishing Corporation, 1993.

Derthick, Mark and Steven F. Roth. "Enhancing Data Exploration with a Branching History of User Operations." *Knowledge Based Systems* 14, nos. 1-2 (2001a): 65-74.

Derthick, Mark and Steven F. Roth. "Example-based Generation of Custom Data Appliances." In *Proceedings of Fifth ACM Conference on Intelligent User Interfaces*, (IUI 2001) 57-64. Santa Fe, NM: ACM, 2001b.

Editors of Computerwire. "What's in Store for Business Intelligence in 2002?" *Computerwire*, January 29, 2002 (www.computerwire.com).

Foltz, Mark and Randall Davis. "Query by Attention: Visually Searchable Information Maps." In *Proceedings of Fifth International Conference on Information Visualisation* (InfoVis 2001), 85-92. London: IEEE, 2001.

Goebel, Stephen, Joerg Haist, Claudia Kares, and Uwe Jasnoch. "INVISIP: Establishment of a Context Repository to Support the Site Planning Process." In *Integrated Assessment and Decision Support, Proceedings of the first Biennial Meeting of the International Environmental Modeling and Software Society*, edited by Andrea Rizzoli and Anthony Jakeman, Vol. 3, 336-341 IEMSS, Manno, Switzerland, June, 2002.

Goodwin, Charles. "The Blackness of Black: Color Categories as Situated Practice." In *Discourse, Tools and Reasoning: Essays on Situated Cognition*, edited by Lauren B. Resnick, Roger Säljö, Clotilde Pontecorvo, and Barbara Burge, 111-140. Berlin: Springer, 1997.

Ignatius, Eve, Hikmet Senay, and Jean Favre. "An Intelligent System for Task-Specific Visualization Assistance." *Journal of Visual Languages and Computing* 5 (1994): 321-338.

Lee, Juhnyoung, Mark Podlaseek, Edith Schonberg, Robert Hoch, and Stephan Gomory. *Analysis and Visualization of Metrics for Online Merchandising*. Technical Report. IBM Institute of Advanced Commerce, November, 1999 (www.research.ibm.com/iac/tech-paper.html).

Lee, Juhnyoung, Ho Soo Lee, and Priscilla Wang. *Analytical Product Selection Using a Highly Dense Interface for Online Product Catalogs*. Technical Report. IBM Institute of Advanced Commerce, January 2001 (*www.research.ibm.com/iac/tech-paper. html*).

Lieberman, Henry, Bonnie Nardi, and David Wright. "Grammex: Defining Grammars by Example." In *CHI '98 ACM Conference Summary on Computer-Human Interaction*, 11-12. Los Angeles: ACM, 1998.

North, Chris and Ben Shneiderman. "Snap Together Visualization: A User Interface for Coordinating Visualizations vs. Relational Schemata." In *Proceedings of the Fifth International Conference on Advanced Visual Interfaces*, (AVI 2000), 128-135. Palermo, Italy: ACM, 2000.

Noy, Penny and Michael Schroeder. "Introducing Signature Explorer: A Means to Aid the Comprehension and Choice of Visualization Algorithms." In *Proceedings of the International Workshop on Visual Datamining*, 18-57. Freiburg, Germany: ECML, 2001.

Payne, Stephen, Andre Howes, and William Reader. "Adaptively Distributing Cognition: A Decision-Making Perspective on Human-Computer Interaction." *Behaviour and Information Technology* 20, no. 5 (2001): 339-346.

Pirolli, Peter, Stuart Card, and Mija M. Van Der Wege. "The Effect of Information Scent on Searching Information Visualizations of Large Tree Structures." In *Proceedings of the Fifth International Working Conference on Advanced Visual Interfaces,* (AVI 2000) 161-172. Palermo, Italy: ACM, 2000.

Plaisant, Catherine, Anne Rose, Gary Rubloff, Richard Salter, and Ben Shneiderman. "The Design of History Mechanisms and Their Use in Collaborative Educational Simulations." In *Proceedings of the Computer Support for Collaborative Learning (CSCL) Conference,* edited by Christopher Hoadley and Jeremy Roschelle, 12-15. Palo Alto, CA.: Lawrence Erlbaum Associates, 1999.

Russell, Daniel, Jay Trimble, and Roxana Wales. "Two Paths From the Same Place: Task-Driven and Human-Centered Evolution of a Group Information Surface." IBM Sixth Make it Easy Conference, San Jose, CA, June 3-6, 2002, *(www-3.ibm.com/ibm/easy/eou_ext.nsf/Publish/2778.)*

Shneiderman, Ben. "The Eyes Have It: A Task Data Type Taxonomy for Information Visualizations." In *Proceedings of 1996 IEEE Conference on Visual Languages,* 336-343. Boulder, CO: IEEE, 1996.

Spence, Robert. *Information Visualization.* Harlow, England: Addison-Wesley, 2001.

Stolte, Chris, Diane Tang, and Pat Hanrahan. "Polaris: A System for Query, Analysis, and Visualization of Multidimensional Relational Databases." *IEEE Transactions on Visualization and Computer Graphics* 8, no. 1 (2002): 52-65.

Stone, Maureen, Ken Fishkin, and Eric Bier. "The Movable Filter as a User Interface Tool." In *Proceedings of CHI '94 ACM Conference on Computer-Human Interaction,* 306-312. Boston: ACM, 1994.

Tang, Lisa and Ben Shneiderman. "Dynamic Aggregation to Support Pattern Discovery: A Case Study with Web Logs." In *Proceedings of Discovery Science: 4th International Conference 2001,* edited by Klaus P. Jantke and Ayumi Shinohara, 464-469. Berlin: Springer-Verlag, 2001.

Trafton, J. Gregory, Susan Kirschenbaum, Ted Tsui, Robert Miyamoto, James Ballas, and Paula Raymond. "Turning Pictures Into Numbers: Extracting and Generating Information From Complex Visualizations." *International Journal of Human-Computer Studies* 53, no. 5 (2000): 827-850.

Tufte, Edward. *Envisioning Information.* Cheshire, England: Graphics Press, 1990.

Tweedie, Lisa, Robert Spence, Huw Dawkes, and Hus Su. "Externalising Abstract Mathematical Models. In *Proceedings of CHI '96 ACM Conference on Computer-Human Interaction,* 406-412. Vancouver: ACM, 1996.

Ware, Colin. *Information Visualization: Perception for Design.* San Francisco: Morgan Kaufmann, 2000.

Woodruff, Allison, Chris Olston, Alexander Aiken, Michael Chu, Vuk Ercegovac, Mark Lin, Mybrid Spalding, and Michael Stonebraker. "Datasplash: A Direct Manipulation Environment for Programming Semantic Zoom Visualizations of Tabular Data." *Journal of Visual Languages and Computing* 12 (2001): 551-571.

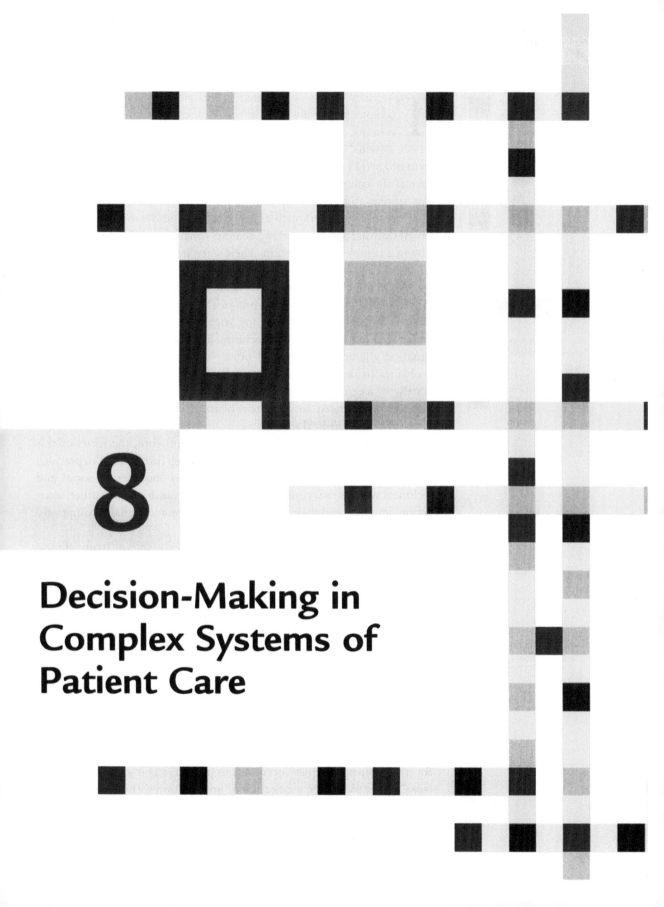

8

Decision-Making in Complex Systems of Patient Care

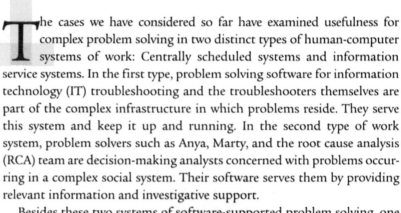

The cases we have considered so far have examined usefulness for complex problem solving in two distinct types of human-computer systems of work: Centrally scheduled systems and information service systems. In the first type, problem solving software for information technology (IT) troubleshooting and the troubleshooters themselves are part of the complex infrastructure in which problems reside. They serve this system and keep it up and running. In the second type of work system, problem solvers such as Anya, Marty, and the root cause analysis (RCA) team are decision-making analysts concerned with problems occurring in a complex social system. Their software serves them by providing relevant information and investigative support.

Besides these two systems of software-supported problem solving, one other is left to explore. In this one—a flexible operations and administration system—problems and investigations occur in converged and dynamically adaptive complex technical and social systems of work. This situation characterizes hospital nurses who solve patients' medication problems. In large medical centers, their analytical activities are shaped equally by a centralized system of computerized records and data and a complex coordinated social system of medication processes within and across different medical services.

This type of problem solving and system of work, the focus of this chapter, pushes designing for usefulness one step further than in previous cases. To design for problem solvers' complex inquiries in social and technical systems that constantly adapt to and transform each other, interaction designers and their teams need to employ additional assumptions, methods, and conceptual design strategies.

Solving problems about medication dosages is one of many clinical practices in hospitals that is centrally planned and administered by a technological core but equally governed by organizational and professional dynamics. Like troubleshooters, nurses carry out medication work looking inward to the technological processing of patient care data, but their problems and solutions also face outward to care-giving and patient safety and to a complex adaptive social system coordinating nurses, doctors, pharmacists, and specialists in other units.

When nurses use software applications to facilitate administering medications and solving dosage problems, this software is central to their merged technical and social system of patient care. Software is not solely a part of the complicated and problematic technical system, as it was in Benkei's case (see Chapter 4). Nor is it a standalone "information service" for investigating complex social-system problems as it was in Anya's case (see Chapter 6). Rather, medication-administration software at once feeds into nurses' central computerized system of work and the myriad social aspects of their activities: Bedside interactions with patients, administrative responsibilities, patient care planning, coordination, and communication. In ways we have not seen before, problem solving software for dosage problems must mesh with the intertwined and co-emerging social and technical systems of nurses' work.

For these situations, designing for usefulness must start with designing for integration, that is for the coordination of people and technologies in large scale organizations. Many software teams that develop applications for flexible operations and administration systems of work already place a high value on integration. In fact, usability specialists often take the title of Integration Analyst. But this attention to integrated technical and social systems of work usually falls short in terms of usefulness in two ways. First, analysts often mistake designs that succeed in *interfacing* different systems and functions for designs that succeed in *integrating* them. Second, they treat technical and social systems separately. On one hand, they find technical means for technical systems to work to together, and on the other, they train people in the social system to operate new applications and to avoid unsafe or unacceptable organizational practices. By contrast, I explore design approaches that maintain a focus on integration with usefulness as a primary goal.

This chapter starts with a scenario of Katherine, a nurse, who makes dosage judgments while she administers drugs to patients during her regularly scheduled medication pass. The scenario emphasizes the social coordination that structures medication activities by bringing in a pharmacist and physician, as well. Katherine's case serves as a springboard for examining assumptions, methods, and strategies that interaction designers and their teammates should employ to create software useful for integrated technical and social systems of work. These approaches include the following:

- Adopting new assumptions about designing for socio-technical systems of work, including assumptions about the politics of design

- Contextually analyzing multifaceted coordination and communication

- Modeling patterns of inquiry to capture the effects of combined computerized patient record and medication systems and social systems of medication administration

- Conceptualizing designs for two predominant user needs in convergent technical and social systems of patient care, which are:

  - Integrating diverse information and analyzing it in a single workspace

  - Working in an electronic "place," not just a space

These aspects of designing for usefulness pertain to a wide range of complex socio-technical systems of work beyond hospitals, such as problem solving in the military and air traffic control. In any of these systems, if software developers do not enhance the meshing of social and technical systems of work, users are likely to experience their applications as a layer of imposed rules and control, not as an aid to work. Moreover, when insufficiently interwoven with their social system of work, the technology is often a layer that breeds resentment. As the scenario below shows, it undercuts users' professional identities and deters them from their specialized patterns of inquiry. The approaches proposed in this chapter seek to avoid such effects.

The medication scenario is drawn from numerous user experiences I have observed and analyzed and design projects I have participated in. The software applications in the scenario are fictitious. Yet these applications—the bar code medication-administration program, pharmacy software, and computerized patient-record system—are representative of actual programs.

SCENARIO: MAKING DECISIONS IN A MEDICATION PASS

Katherine, a registered nurse (RN) on the acute care floor, is ready to start her morning medication pass and anticipates a time-consuming round of drug administration. Time often runs short in her drug passes because a couple of months ago, due to staffing shortages, the psychiatric ward began boarding patients on Katherine's ward. These patients have all fallen under Katherine's care, in addition to her usual load. For most of the day, the boarders go back to the psych ward for counseling and activities, but in the mornings, Katherine is in charge of giving them their medications.

Katherine begins by printing her regular set of lists and reports including drugs due on this round for each patient and a report noting the effectiveness of any medications given to each patient on an as-needed basis. For safety's sake, Katherine double-checks the information on these reports against the content displayed on the medication administration computer screens when she gives each patient his or her drugs.

Using a Bar Code Medication-Administration Program

As Katherine begins her round, she glances at the bar-code scanner and laptop computer perched atop the rolling medication cart. She is pleased to be one of a growing number of nurses trying to make bar-code medication technologies work in their hospitals.

Developed by her hospital's corporate IT group for all member medical centers the e-Bar medication administrative program ensures that the right patient gets the right drugs at the right time and place. To use it Katherine scans the bar code on a patient's identification bracelet, and in response, e-Bar displays the patient's prescribed drugs for that scheduled medication pass. Katherine then scans the bar code of each drug stored for the patient in the medication cart. When a scanned drug matches the patient's order, e-Bar "bings" positively and enters a "G" in the status column to designate that the drug has been given (Figure 8.1). In addition, e-Bar lets Katherine access centralized data records and pre-defined reports, and it gives her immediate email access to pharmacists so she can investigate and solve problems that may arise during her medication round.

Administering Medications to a Detoxification Patient

Katherine wheels the medication cart into her first patient's room: A new boarder from the psychiatric ward who is near the end of a detoxification regimen. Because this regimen includes some drugs with tapered dosages, Katherine has to clinically judge how much of these drugs to give the patient at this scheduled administration. Before Katherine began working with recovering detox boarders, she had only a textbook familiarity with this regimen of drug therapies. Now she is more experienced and facile in deciding the right dosages based on numerous factors about a patient's

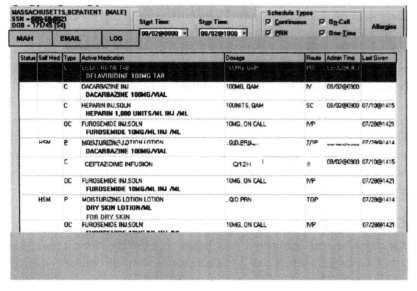

FIGURE 8.1
Bar code medication-administration program showing drugs due for a patient in this medication pass.

current and past conditions and dosages. Making a judgment about a detox patient, however, still takes a long time—not for want of knowledge but because the relevant information is scattered in diverse sources and formatted inconsistently.

Katherine greets the patient, scans her ID bracelet, and looks at the e-Bar record. She notes that this patient is to receive vitamins along with detox drugs. Katherine pulls out the patient's medication drawer in the cart and takes out all the drugs but finds none of the vitamins. She quickly clicks a tab on the e-Bar screen to bring up an email request directed to the pharmacy. She writes a message notifying the pharmacist about the missing vitamins and sends it.

Handling the Request for Vitamins

In the pharmacy, a dedicated printer for nurses' messages flashes, indicating that a note has arrived. Amir, the pharmacist, picks up Katherine's request and begins looking for the missing vitamins. He opens the in-patient pharmacy application (IP-Pharm) and calls up the patient's record to inquire into the medication orders. Amir wonders if the patient's physician might have cancelled the vitamins for some reason. He opens the computerized patient record (CPR) system through which physicians order prescriptions. He sees that, far from having cancelled the vitamins, the doctor renewed them last night.

Amir returns to the IP-Pharm program to check whether the finished order includes the vitamins. It does. On closer look, he sees that the renewed vitamins were finished shortly after midnight by the night pharmacist at a sister hospital that covers for Amir's medical center at night. Now Amir has an idea of what must have gone wrong. Pharmacists at the sister hospital do not know about this medical center's relatively new practice of boarding psych patients on the acute care ward. The pharmacist who finished the order probably assumed the vitamins should be dispensed to the psych ward.

To check this hunch, Amir runs a drug file inquiry in IP-Pharm and gets a display of the information affixed to the dispensed vitamin packages. Finally after tracing the vitamin order in three different modules across programs he sees that the destination, indeed, was the psych ward. Amir asks a technician to bring the vitamins to Katherine's floor immediately and to retrieve the misdirected ones from the psych floor.

Gathering Data for Decisions About Detox Drugs

Katherine, in the meantime, has begun her deliberations about this patient's drug therapies. For some medications in the regimen, she has ranges from which to choose—such as 20–100 mg of methadone. For other medications, she needs to make more significant dosage adjustments based on the patient's evolving conditions. For these decisions, Katherine examines numerous relationships, including the following:

- Medications given to the patient in the past 72 hours, their unit doses and concentrations (both alone and in relation to each other for each prior med pass), and, lastly, the totals for the day

- Side effects from cumulative doses and joint therapies, including changes in blood pressure, other vital signs, and pain levels

- Other expected and unexpected symptoms and outcomes, such as hyperactivity

- Correlations between medication amounts and dosages and side effects or symptoms

- The patient's subjective assessments, such as feeling in control emotionally

- Nurses' comments from earlier shifts about the effectiveness of each drug given so far

Unfortunately, none of this information is currently displayed on the e-Bar screen, and getting it is a hassle. To see an overview of the doses and combinations the detox patient has received in the past three days, Katherine clicks on a tab that takes her to the patient's medication history screen. This history is read in from the CPR system and appears in that system's character-based form (Figure 8.2).

This screen gives the individual but not total medication dosages for each day. Katherine once asked the help desk staff why e-Bar could not generate these totals, and they told her the data are fed in from IP-Pharm, and the pharmacy program does not yet include totaling capabilities, though it may do so in later versions.

Using a calculator that adds clutter to her already crowed medication cart, Katherine figures out the totals and writes them on a sheet of paper. A pile of papers begins to form on top of the printed reports. Next she goes out of e-Bar and into CPR to access the patient's vital sign data and pain level scores. These data are not accessible directly from e-Bar. Therefore, Katherine has to flip back and forth between the screens of the two systems, first checking CPR for vital sign data, then cross-referencing nurses' comments in e-Bar for times and drugs corresponding to the vital sign measures. The comments help Katherine expand the meaning of the vital sign data by describing nurses' assessments of the effectiveness of each detox drug after it was administered.

```
----------------------------------------------------------------------------------------------------
Continuing/PRN/Stat/One Time Medication/Treatment Record (VAF 10 -2970 B, C, D)
Run Date: JUL 26, 2002@10:53

Page: 1

Patient:  ASHLEY, BRETT          SSN:       408-XX-8777        DOB:    JAN 2,1961
Sex:      FEMALE                 Ht/Wt:     */*                Ward:   PSYCH A427-02
Dx :      DETOX                  Last Mvmt: APR 8,1999@14:07:51 Type:   SPECIALTY BOARD

Reactions:  STRAWBERRIES
====================================================================================================
Start        Stop         | Admin |          |            |           |           |           |
Date         Date         | Times | 04/11/2002 | 04/12/200 2 | 04/13/2002 | 04/14/2002 | 04/15/2002 |
04/16/2002 | 04/17/2002
----------------------------------------------------------------------------------------------------
04/14/1999 05/14/2002  24.00    0500                        0519 N2     0515 N2
METHADONE  20-100MG              1100                                    R1130 N2    H1146 N2

    METHADONE 20-100            1700                                    1729 N3     1746 N3

Give: 20 MG PRN BID             2300                                    2255 N3     2310 N3

 RPH: P2  RN: N2
----------------------------------------------------------------------------------------------------
04/13/1999 04/23/1999  24:00    0500                        1324 N2                 1400 N2

NALTREXONE ORAL                 1300

    NALTREXONE 50-100MG         2100

Given: 50  PRN Q26

 Spec Inst: FOR 10 DAYS ONLY

RPH: P2  RN: N2
----------------------------------------------------------------------------------------------------
```

FIGURE 8.2
Medication history screen in e-Bar.

Frustratingly, Katherine cannot rearrange the comments in e-Bar into meaningful groupings. She has to couple the flipping of views with a lot of scrolling, causing her to lose her place frequently.

Analyzing Data and Making Dosage Decisions

Katherine jots down data on vital signs, drug dosages, administration times, and effectiveness on the same paper she used to calculate daily totals. She is now ready to graphically format and analyze all the data she has accumulated. As she works on paper, she keeps the medication history open on screen to check individual dosages. She spends five minutes drawing multiple correlation plots and flow diagrams. Every nurse for detox patients does the same thing, agreeing that graphic representations of the data are best for making dosage decisions. They are the tools of the trade. Katherine compares her plots and diagrams to the previous graphs other nurses have left affixed to the patient's paper medication administration record (MAR). These cumulative graphics are indispensable to nurses' decisions.

Katherine, absorbed in composing the flowcharts and correlation plots, temporarily loses contact with her patient. She has not yet figured out a way to do her offline analysis for dosage decisions and still keep up good bedside communication with her patient, enlisting her as a partner in the medication process. The best Katherine has come up with is to interact with her patient before she creates the graphics and analyzes the data. Earlier, before this analysis and while gathering data and waiting for the screens to come up, Katherine chatted with the patient and found out the patient's own assessment of her progress and drug reactions.

Now finished with the analysis, Katherine concludes that one of the patient's detox drugs should be modified. Instead of the usual injected 1.2 mg dosage twice a day, Katherine decides to switch the patient to 0.8 mg given orally three times a day. However, to administer this new dosage Katherine has to get the pharmacy to send it as soon as possible. She sends an email request and writes herself a note to remember this oral medication and the vitamins still due from the pharmacy.

Reacting to the Dosage Change

Amir receives Katherine's request for the orally administered detox drug. Though the amounts are comparable, e-Bar is exacting and will not allow such substitutions. The doctor will have to write another order, specifying the new dosage and oral form. Amir wonders if this may lead the doctor to change more of the order. The pharmacist begins what is often a drawn-out effort to track the doctor down to discuss a modified order. Katherine is unaware of Amir's difficulty in finding the doctor and, as the morning moves on, she cannot imagine what is taking him so long to finish a simple request.

Communicating Reasons for Decisions to Future Shifts

Katherine now needs to enter comments into e-Bar. These notes are optional and are designed as pick-lists of pre-defined comments in controlled terminology. Nurses are free to override the system and enter free-text comments, but organizationally the hospital frowns on such overrides. Free text entries cannot be aggregated for other analysis.

Many of the nurses on the psychiatric ward neglect to enter canned or free-text comments. They assume that their diagrams afixed to the paper MAR are more explanatory than the pre-defined options in the e-Bar program's "comments" field. Other nurses choose only the most cursory of the pre-defined comments, and these do not particularly help Katherine. Katherine often wishes for more illuminating notes to guide her assessments. One psychiatric nurse, a "resident expert," enters the best combination of comments, and Katherine always seeks them out first. However, manipulating the program or flipping through the report to do so is a hassle. Katherine, in turn, is diligent about entering comments, even though it takes extra time. When she adjusts a dosage, she writes free-text comments, despite hospital administrators' objections.

The system requires a separate entry for each drug, and it takes Katherine another five minutes to move through the composing comments for each medication.

Making One More Dosage Decision

Katherine is finally done with this patient and moves on to give the rest of her patients their medications. Twenty minutes—almost a quarter of this morning's medication pass—have elapsed with just this one patient. Katherine knows she will not finish this morning's pass on time. Since the boarders came, this has happened several times.

Katherine has one more patient requiring a discretionary judgment. This time the dosage decision relates to a sliding scale insulin prescription. In this instance, Katherine's judgments rest on prior data about blood sugar levels and nurses' comments on the effectiveness of prior dosages. She is frustrated by omissions in other nurses' comments. Many nurses presume that lab results tell the story, and they leave the comments section blank. But this omission means Katherine now has to leave e-Bar and go to a different program for lab tests and outcomes .

Katherine also is uncertain whether nurses actually administered the insulin amounts listed in the electronic record. Sometimes, due to a patient's condition, a nurse gives only part of the contents in a vial, but e-Bar's automatic G function records the full amount as given. Most nurses note this discrepancy in the comments field. However, e-Bar provides no cues to signal to nurses on subsequent shifts that comments exist.

Encountering Other Medication-Administration Difficulties

After these dosage decisions, many of Katherine's other patients are also time consuming, but for other reasons. One patient, for example, cannot swallow easily so Katherine crushes his 13 prescribed pills, mixes them with apple sauce, and feeds them to him. The patient is able to swallow only a quarter of the mixture, but the program has automatically entered a G for all 13 scanned drugs, implying that the patient successfully took the whole dose. To revise the documentation, Katherine has to go outside e-Bar to the CPR system. e-Bar automatically documents medication actions in the electronic MAR, which resides in the CPR system. For safety purposes, this documentation resides solely in this one place, and it is not in e-Bar. Once Katherine accesses the CPR system, she has to undo each G, override the pre-defined system comments because none is relevant, and write a comment for each drug explaining the reason for revising the entry.

In another instance, Katherine has a patient who takes a drug once every 18 hours—what is called an odd schedule order. It is odd because it is not divisible by 24 and does not readily fall into a two, three, four, or five times a day category. Such orders are tricky for pharmacists to finish and are prone to errors.

Katherine remembers giving this patient the medication yesterday during this same 8 AM medication pass, and she presumes the patient got another dose 18 hours later. If Katherine gave one now, it could be too early and could damage the patient's kidneys. Therefore, even though the medication pass is getting lengthy and may not be completed in the allotted time span, Katherine wants to resolve the discrepancy between what she remembers and what the screen shows. Within e-Bar, she accesses the patient's medication administration history. She sees that the patient received a dose at 2:00 AM and, therefore, should not receive another dose at 8:00 AM.

Katherine wants to find out the cause of the problem, but she leaves this issue for now and jots a reminder to call the pharmacist later. In the meantime, she marks the medication H (for Held) and adds an explanatory note in the comment field. Unfortunately, this field is not linked to anyone in pharmacy. Indeed, nothing in e-Bar automatically alerts pharmacists, doctors, or other nurses that a comment about this near-miss incident exists.

Running Over Deadline

As she anticipated, Katherine runs out of time before she can give all her patients their scheduled drugs. The program has a pre-programmed deadline for each medication pass. Upper-level management decides on the deadline, and IT specialists program it in. Changing the time span (for instance, to accommodate to the extra work caused by boarders) is a multi-step, bureaucratic process. Nurses on Katherine's floor have requested this change but are having trouble cutting through the red tape. In the meantime, the deadline has arrived, and the program automatically removes all medication information for this scheduled medication pass, including drugs that Katherine has yet to give. Katherine has the remaining drugs in the cart, but she now has no screen on which to process them.

Ironically, Katherine has to invest more time to bring these entries back, which delays the drug pass longer. She first has to pick from a list of reasons the one that comes closest to explaining why she ran late. None mentions boarders. She then must tinker across programs to regain the ability to document the given medications. Her deadline overrun gets recorded in the program log, which Katherine's nursing manager uses for her performance evaluation.

WHAT SUPPORT DOES KATHERINE NEED AND WHAT DOES SHE GET?

Katherine's dosage decisions embody many of the traits of complex problem-solving. She has to make sense of relevant information that is dispersed across diverse sources. Her decisions depend on the actions and prior judgments of many stakeholders, including nurses from other shifts, pharmacists, and physicians. She deals with problems that have no one right answer. Finally, she is never 100% sure of the accuracy of data due to the workarounds people have used to get the program to conform to actual events, such as pharmacists with odd schedule orders. Adding pressure to her deliberations, Katherine knows high stakes ride on accurate judgments—the safety and well being of her patient.

Later sections in this chapter go into more detail on the support that nurses like Katherine need from their bar-code medication applications for them to be truly useful for their drug-giving responsibilities and complex investigations. Here I briefly summarize a part of what went wrong in Katherine's software-supported medication pass to give closure to her story and to highlight the ways her needs for more useful support are intricately tied to core aspects of her social system of work. This summary sets the stage for the discussion that follows about how design teams should view the dynamic relationship between social and technical systems and how they should examine the many interactive socio-technical factors and patterns of inquiry that shape Katherine and other nurses' task interactions and dependencies. To be useful, medication-administration programs need to account for these factors and patterns of inquiry better than e-Bar does.

Some of the gaps between what Katherine needs and what she gets include the following:

Analyzing Data and Making Dosage Decisions

- **The need for graphic representations and analysis:** Despite nurses' central need to analyze data for detox dosages by accessing, integrating, and graphing differently formatted data that reside in different places, none of the hospital's applications provides an easy way to do these core problem solving activities.

- **Patient rapport:** Extensive analytical efforts cut into quality time with patients at the bedside.

Communicating Reasons for Decisions to Future Shifts and Making One More Dosage Decision

- **Shared comments**: Pre-defined comments in controlled vocabulary often do not adequately express assessments of effectiveness or situational conditions. Overriding them with free text entries is organizationally frowned on and time consuming.

- **Completed communication**: Communications through comments is incomplete because it is not readily visible to others, and the program does not alert users when comments await.

Encountering Other Medication-Administration Difficulties

- **Core activities at point of care:** Needing to go outside of the medication-administration system to edit the documentation on ongoing medication passes severs the connection between point-of-care responsibilities and point-of-care support.

- **Common occurrences that do not conform to formalized task sequences:** Although such situations as patients not ingesting all of their medication are common, the program offers no pre-set explanation that covers it, requiring separate entries instead (in this case, 13 separate entries).

Running Over Deadline

- **Extra time due to extenuating circumstances:** The program permits no leeway to shape the deadline to prevailing circumstances.

- **Best work leads to punitive consequences:** Nurses fear that log-recorded deadline overruns may be used punitively.

As the scenario suggests, the model of work in the software is too rigid. It is ill-matched to nurses' actual work experiences and poorly represents relevant coordinated medication processes. To address these flaws and create more useful software for problem solving in complex mutually adaptive technical and social systems, interaction designers, usability specialists, and their teammates must take a new look at what is required for usefulness when people's work resides in these co-emergent systems.

ADOPTING DESIGN ASSUMPTIONS ABOUT SOCIO-TECHNICAL SYSTEMS OF WORK

When software teams design applications for large, integrated record systems such as patient care, they often separate users' work practices and software interactions into two categories with distinct properties. The design goal—misguidedly—is to make them equivalent (Berg, 1997; Agre, 2001).

Katherine's case shows that, far from being separate systems, organizational practices and technology tools dynamically fashion each other. Medication applications are "active participants" in hospital medication practices, and the two—applications and practices—co-evolve as nurses handle unpredictable events daily in patient care. Mutually dependent, the interactions between tools and practices cannot be thoroughly predefined. For instance, work and programs change each other in even the seemingly small event of Katherine sending an email request to the pharmacist for a modified detox drug for her patient. The email message introduces speedier cross-service coordination than occurred before e-Bar was implemented, but it also gives rise to uncertain boundaries between roles. Removed from direct physical contact, the email permits a "space for suspended accountability," that is, for the nurse, pharmacist, and doctor to pass this request around until they gain clarity about who has the authority to change the order. The participants approach work in new ways and, in the process, the technology becomes complicit in negotiating new role boundaries and relationships.

Acknowledging an Inevitable Gap and Designing for It

When design team members assume that practice and software converge and mutually transform each other, they shift from trying for a fit between the two as separate phenomena to designing for the *interrelation* of the two. Software teams need to understand this interrelation and realize there will always be a gap between what is technically feasible and what the situated requirements are for actual work (Ackerman, 2000). To cope, Katherine shapes her work around what the medication programs let her do. For example, because e-Bar lacks a workspace for integrating and graphing dosage-related data, she works offline to create trend diagrams and correlation plots. One result is that this work practice keeps the important data of her findings out of the system. In turn, this omission often adversely affects other medical professionals who want to access the graphic correlations electronically for other unrelated purposes.

Co-practices require design teams to create work models and conceptual designs that represent when and how people's social practices and software strengthen each other and when and how they do not. This view holds with the perspective presented in this book that designs for usefulness must strive to enhance compatibilities and reduce incompatibilities between interactive contextual conditions that open or close problem solvers' actions and outcomes.

When these interactive conditions and constraints occur in co-emergent social and technical systems of work, certain dimensions of design take on greater importance. One is shaping design to users' organizational and professional roles. If applications are to integrate with users' co-emerging socio-technical practices, they must support and evoke the role-based behaviors, responsibilities, and coordinated connections that, to users, constitute clear and acceptable boundaries of their work.

Concentrating on Role Clarity in Converged Socio-Technical Systems

Nurses do best when they work within boundaries that define the roles, knowledge, work, and interactions that give their work meaning. As professionals, nurses pride themselves in situational awareness, task performance, work planning and management, and specialized know-how. They expect that any software-supported tasks they perform should reinforce, manifest, and extend these roles.

For example, nurses' professional identities, in part, rest on being acutely aware of the multiple conditions and events going on in a situation and in passing that knowledge on to other clinicians. Because nurses perform their work and problem solving with this ever-present situational awareness, they risk distraction. Acceptable situational awareness, consequently, demands combining "eyes in the back of their head" with a consistent focus on goals. Nurses also need to constantly organize their running mental list of information and events flowing into and out of their work and to keep track of what information pertains to other medical professionals and to members of patients' families.

In this and other role-based aspects of their work, nurses have boundaries for acceptable behavior. This scenario, for example, reveals threats to Katherine's need to maintain a consistent focus on goals as she performs her work attuned to ongoing situational activities. The numerous interactions in and out of e-Bar she must take to gather data, compare across screens, and graph figures are not just clunky inconveniences to task performance. They also are distractions from her goal, and they add unnecessary details to the others to which she attends. They are threats to her sense of identity and role. These extraneous details introduce numerous degrees of separation between her actions and her goal.

Programs should not push users to the edge of their role boundaries in such ways.

Software interference with users' work roles is not unique to converged socio-technical systems of work. However, in these systems of work, it has an extra layer of importance because users' software-supported problem solving is just one part of a larger role-based activity in which they are engaged. Deciding on a drug dosage for any one patient, for example, is part of a nurse's larger activity of administering a patient's whole set of medications, which is a piece of passing medications to a whole floor of patients, and in turn, a component of the larger, in-patient medication process of coordinating doctors, pharmacists, nurses, patients, and their families. With all these functional layers of work, nurses in this system are more prone to disruptions of their role clarity than users who work on more self-contained software-supported inquiries.

Nurses' needs for role clarity and control in their software support are tricky design issues. When design teams assume that social and technical systems of work are mutually adaptive and when they assume that these systems cannot be made equivalent through design, the goal of software support becomes helping nurses harness the complexity of their medication-related inquiries. Nurses harness complexity when they fill in and work with the gap between tool constraints and actual circumstances. Designing for this goal is different from trying logically to erase this gap (Cohen and Axelrod, 1999).

For example, on occasions in which tools and role-related practices clash, users need the leeway "to digress from the tool's prescribed steps, to skip or skew input, or to sometimes avoid the tool altogether" (Berg, 1997). Rather than trying to enforce certain behaviors, such as commenting in a controlled vocabulary, software designs need to anticipate nurses' needs for leeway, based on multilayered role considerations, and inventively achieve both the goals of standardized entries and of localized comments.

To design for roles appropriately, interaction designers, usability specialists, and other team members need to investigate such questions as the following:

- How may the software alter and not just facilitate the practices of it targets?

- What are the local needs of nurses, pharmacists, and physicians that prompt them to tinker with the software in an effort to make it more useful?

- When do medical professionals transform tools by *not* affording them certain roles and functions designers intended for them?

Overall, design teams must examine the ways in which coordinated processes in nurses' socio-technical system of work affect their medication passes and complex decisions.

CONTEXTUALLY ANALYZING IN-PATIENT MEDICATION PROCESSES

Prior scenarios have emphasized that designing for usefulness involves understanding, analyzing, and modeling problem solvers' patterns of inquiry, as these patterns are shaped by interactive conditions within and across multiple contexts of work. This case is no different. However, because designing for usefulness starts with designing for integration, teams need to begin examining interactive contextual conditions that shape nurses' actions and choices at a higher level. User-experience analysts, interaction designers, and usability specialists need to set their sights on the whole picture of in-patient medication processes in a hospital. I purposely left out many parts of this whole picture in Katherine's scenario so the story would focus on her immediate software-supported problem solving and decision-making. Yet to design for the realities of actual medication-administration situations, it is important for HCI specialists to recognize the full array of conditions and dynamics of the hospital-wide medication process that affect drug-giving and decision-making.

The technical side of the process involves a distributed computing environment, data that are continuously updated by users across services, and dozens of software programs, some integrated with each other and some not. The intertwined social side involves interactions among doctors, nurses, and pharmacists, all of whom design teams' must study in contextual inquiries and analysis.

The following discussion highlights what design teams should examine and consider during contextual inquiries, analysis, and work modeling. Because of the integration demands of designing for usefulness when applications target converged social and technical systems of work, the contextual descriptions are necessarily more extensive than in previous cases.

Getting an Overview of Cross-Service Coordination

Supporting nurses usefully in their medication activities and problem solving involves fitting activities into the larger medication processes in the hospital. As outlined in Figure 8.3, coordinated medication processes start with physicians ordering prescriptions for patients, usually through an electronic ordering system. Doctors fill in the drug information and special instructions, and they check for allergies and drug interactions. The information feeds into the pharmacy application (IP-Pharm in the scenario) and is available to nurses through the computerized patient record system (CPR in the scenario).

FIGURE 8.3
Coordinated medication processes (Cousins, 1998).

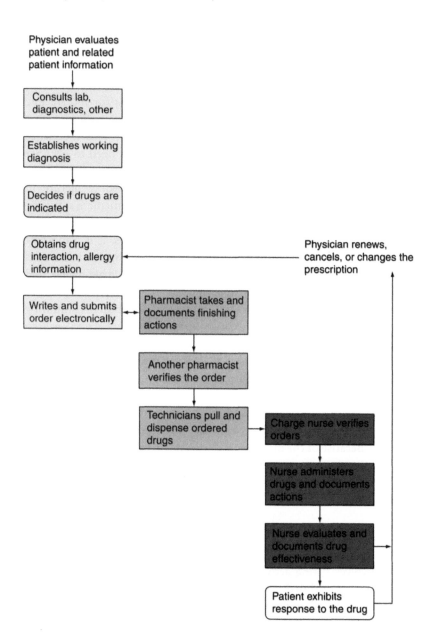

Using the pharmacy software, a pharmacist processes (finishes) the physician's order, which includes scheduling administration times and entering unit doses that match the inventory stock and drug database entries. A different pharmacist verifies the order. After verification, technicians package and dispense drugs to the patients' floors. They can only dispense exactly what a finished order specifies because most electronic medication systems are exacting. Technicians, for example, cannot substitute two 20 mg tablets for an order specifying one 40 mg tablet. In an average day, 5000 orders may flow in and out of the pharmacy.

Finished and verified orders automatically feed into the medication-administration software and update the CPR system. In the nursing unit, a nurse verifies the drug orders in either the CPR system or in the pharmacy program (if he or she understands it), then other nurses administer the medications to patients and document their actions—often handling more than 100 doses in a medication pass. Increasingly, nurses administer medications with electronic bar code medication-administration programs, which link to and update the CPR system during medication rounds.

This medication process repeats itself whenever physicians change their patients' prescriptions. For this medication process to run smoothly, technical and social systems of work need to provide complementary support. As with other cases we have seen, best-case visions often fall short of practical realities.

Distinguishing Best From Practical Cases

A number of medical oversight groups dedicate themselves to defining criteria for effective social structures and processes for safe and efficient medication procedures. They envision physicians, pharmacists, and nurses communicating 24 hours a day about orders, drug information, and questions on charts. They assume adequate staffing levels, reasonable workloads, and professional and technical competence. They campaign for non-punitive approaches to performance problems, and they stress such organizational arrangements as cross-functional teams that make decisions consultatively, visible managerial support for new computerized processes, and reliable infrastructure performance and integration with around-the-clock IT support (Bogner, 1994; Reason, 1997; Hunt et al., 1998; Helmreich and Merritt, 1998; Leape et al., 1998; Croteau and Schyve, 1999; Spath, 1999; Bates et al., 1999; Institute for Safe Medication Practices editors, 2001).

It would be nice if software teams could count on such ideal conditions. But more often than not, hospitals fall short for several reasons.

Typically many hospital workflows and processes require a tight coupling between events and procedures for dealing with them so personnel can respond to risks of medical errors with rapid decision-making, scheduling, clear status and power boundaries, and immediate awareness of deviations. Other workflows and processes, by contrast, must be flexible to respond to unpredictable illnesses and other variable events. For these situations, loosely coupled, decentralized structures and processes are best. Hospitals are organized with complicated combinations of loose and tight couplings, but software teams frequently gravitate only to the tightly coupled practices of medication work. They represent this tight coupling in applications but, on some occasions, decentralized, user-controlled approaches are more appropriate. The effect is an imposed layer of rules and constraints when in fact, flexibility is in order.

Gaps between medication realities and ideals are large and, at times, overwhelming. Dynamic conditions and constraints in the technology, work domain, subjective, and problem contexts challenge the clear-cut outlines, flows, and role boundaries of the medication process in Figure 8.3. If design teams are to improve usefulness, they must observe and analyze actual cases of medication work and use findings to model users' patterns of inquiry and to conceptualize design. Teams must know the boundaries that define each group's responsibilities, access to information, and acceptable behaviors, and they must know those that give the groups a place and identity in their work.

The following sections describe the realities of technical and social systems of work that affect nurses' medication and problem solving activities and that design teams need to include in their task analysis and work models.

Analyzing Technologies of Work Affecting Medication Processes

Many technological conditions that design teams need to analyze and account for in their models of nurses' work are similar to the multi-component and distributed computing issues described in Benkei's case (see Chapter 4). Risking some repetition, I present these technical conditions for this case to remind design teams about technological conditions and to show that they are now more intricately intertwined with social dimensions of problem solvers' work than in Benkei's situation.

Every year new technology systems and standards for hospitals proliferate. Medical centers are always in the process of putting together up-to-date, unified applications for every phase of the medication process, and combining them with integrated clinical information systems, other decision-support software, infrastructure standards, and architecture strategies. In their contextual analyses, design teams must highlight how these technologies interact with each other and with users' practices.

Examining Infrastructure and Architecture Conditions Affecting Nurses' Work

The effects of infrastructure and architecture on nurses' medication activities and problem solving cannot be over-emphasized. Information in physician orders, pharmacy-finished orders, patient records, medication histories, logs, and administration screens are vital for making sure the right patient gets the right drug in the right time, route, and amount. Success in realizing these five "rights" depends, in part, on how medical centers set up their infrastructures.

Interaction designers and usability specialists need to know the aspects of their users' infrastructure conditions, as detailed in Table 8.1. The table presents the issues and questions to investigate. Immediately after, I note the implications of these issues for design.

By identifying the prevailing conditions in these areas of the infrastructure, design teams discover the following insights crucial to designing for usefulness.

Infrastructure issue	Questions to ask in analysis
Data transfer	What message standards for transferring diverse data are implemented in the hospital? What data incompatibilities exist? What messaging and direction of messaging between programs does *not* yet exist?
Data access	What programs give access to what data? What redundant interactions does access require?
Data integration	**Data conversion:** How well do processing formats coincide with formats required for end-user tasks? **Data terminology:** What data are modeled as shared information? What standardized terminology is implemented on what data?

TABLE 8.1
Infrastructure issues to examine in contextual inquiries and analysis.

- **From data transfer:** The extent to which users have to go in and out of programs to get data and the redundant steps that might be eliminated through design

- **From data access:** An anticipation of the effects of time-consuming moves on other aspects of problem solving

- **From data integration:**

  - The difference between the formats of stored data and the formats users need for problem solving and exploring ways to improve compatibilities or consistencies

  - The standardized vocabularies that structure the data and the extent to which a controlled terminology furthers or obstructs clinicians' coordination and communication

Examining Software and IT Support Conditions Affecting Nurses' Work

In hospital contexts, two conditions that often adversely affect nurses' medication practices and inquiries are detailed in Table 8.2.

TABLE 8.2
Software and IT support issues to examine in contextual inquiries and analysis.

Software issue	Questions to ask in analysis
Heterogeneous and incompatible software	What interrelated software runs on different operating systems?
	What is the blend of new and legacy software; and which interfaces are graphical and which are character-based?
	What in-house and contracting groups develop what software and to what extent do they interact with each other and with users?
Insufficient IT support	Does IT have a technology roadmap, and are resources allocated equitably for it?
	To what extent is funding lagging behind needs and how does that affect priorities?
	What support exists for newly implemented systems, especially in intensive care units, and for Web access and Portable Digital Assistants (PDA)?
	How adequate are resources for ensuring appropriate upgrades and equipment?

By identifying the prevailing conditions in these software and support areas, design teams discover the following insights crucial to designing for usefulness:

- **From heterogeneous and incompatible software:**

  - Whether clinicians across services can solve problems consultatively online by pulling up compatible software and finding ways to facilitate their related investigations

  - Whether the fields in which a physician enters an order in a graphical user interface (GUI) show up and in what ways if the pharmacy order-finishing software is character-based, and how users coordinate if the interfaces are different

  - Whether the logic behind related systems developed by different groups is cohesive

- **From analyzing insufficient IT support, design teams know:**

  - The extent to which users have adequate and reliable hardware, connectivity, and capacity to conduct the required work and cross-program accessing

  - The safety issues that underlie various design choices, given the technology support and set-up users have

These technological issues strongly influence the approaches to medication administration nurses take. When possible, design teams need to improve nurses' abilities to take critical action. The conditions in the linked social part of nurses' socio-technical work are equally important for design teams to analyze.

Analyzing Social Systems of Work Affecting Medication Processes

In hospitals, physicians, pharmacists, and nurses divide the labor of coordinated medication processes. Computerized systems codify a good number of these groups' practices, making it necessary for the three groups to learn what the others do in their parts of the medication process. To use new tools for medication processes effectively, these medical professionals must be able to "walk in each other's shoes." They need to understand program displays that present data drawn from other services' programs. They have to know how to compose their own entries so the data will be useful when shared by other specialists.

"Walking in each other's shoes" is a tall order for professionals who ordinarily know the surface, but not intricate workings, of each other's trades. To facilitate this sharing of coordinated practices as part of effective drug giving and dosage judgments, software designers must analyze each service's responsibilities and the interactive conditions shaping each group's approach. In the next three subsections, I highlight and explain conditions that design teams should look for during their contextual inquiries and analysis for each service: Physicians, pharmacists, and nurses. These conditions often obstruct professionals in their medication work and, consequently, have implications for software designs.

What Conditions Complicate Physicians' Ordering Medications?

Physicians' work styles, positions in the hospital hierarchy, and geographically dispersed workloads introduce conditions and constraints that subtly confound coordinated medication processes, both online and off. These influential factors include those in Table 8.3.

TABLE 8.3
Conditions in physicians' systems of work affecting medication practices.

Conditions and effects	Explanations and problems arising from conditions
Doctors work in several hospitals at once and cannot keep track of varying administration times and formulary stock.	Wards within and across hospitals vary widely in scheduled medication administration times, and formularies in different medical centers often stock distinct drugs and drug dosages. Pharmacists need to see this information in the electronic orders, but doctors often do not provide it.
Doctors travel from hospital to hospital to see patients, and they cannot always enter orders electronically from dedicated workstations.	If doctors prescribe drugs while driving, they may call in orders. They typically call nurses because, before computerization, they ordered medications from them. When doctors order drugs remotely, they may use Web-based interfaces, PDAs, or send faxes—usually to nurses. IT specialists play a crucial role in medication processes at this point. They must support remote access.
Physicians may order medications through	In many hospitals, only select nurses have privileges to enter doctors' orders into a

TABLE 8.3
Continued

Conditions and effects	Explanations and problems arising from conditions
nurses, but hospitals often have no procedures in place for this exception, and these orders slip through the cracks.	pharmacy or CPR system. If too much time elapses between a doctor ordering via a nurse who lacks privileges and a nurse with privileges entering it, a patient may miss an intended dose of medication for want of an official entry in the e-Bar program.
Rotating residents do not know the physician ordering system well enough to create complete and accurate orders.	Because of their transience and high status, residents and other doctors are often exempt from training for new medication-related technologies and are given leeway not to participate in teams dedicated to helping users smoothly adopt recently implemented technologies (teams largely composed of nurses, pharmacists, and IT specialists). But residents often use physician ordering programs inaccurately. Two hundred or more new residents may rotate in each month from different facilities that often use dissimilar physician ordering programs. These doctors no longer turn to nurses to mentor them in the medication practices and policies of this new hospital. Instead they focus on mastering the software, and they work alone. With the former one-on-one consulting gone, doctors and nurses lose some of their shared knowledge about patients and their close professional bonds.
Doctors cannot check electronic MARs on-the-fly because they lack permission to access the program.	Nurses do not want physicians to have privileges to the medication administration program loaded on their laptops because doctors then might continually interrupt them to get information on patients. Nurses fear that doctors would end up monopolizing the laptops and disrupt nurses' already tightly paced medication passes.

TABLE 8.3
Continued

Conditions and effects	Explanations and problems arising from conditions
Many doctors prefer paper over electronic MARs for comprehensive information about patients.	For expedience and from habit, doctors like paper MARs because they can see a week's worth of data on a patient at a glance. In the midst of hurried rounds or a crisis, doctors want this quick-scan information. Doctors also like to retrieve comments from targeted caregivers quickly by recognizing their handwriting.

What Conditions Complicate Pharmacists' Finishing, Verifying, and Dispensing?

Pharmacists similarly face work domain constraints that deflect them from best-case approaches to their portion of the medication process. These include those listed in Table 8.4.

TABLE 8.4
Conditions in pharmacists' systems of work affecting medication practices.

Conditions and effects	Explanations and problems arising from conditions
Pharmacist and technician shortages create heavy workloads that put a strain on medication processes.	When new bar code medication-administration programs are introduced, it is not unusual for pharmacies to require one or two additional full time technicians to package, label, and check inventory. Hospitals, however, often fail to budget for this need.
Economics force many pharmacies to outsource night time coverage, which raises the risk of medication errors.	Sister hospitals across town often cover for pharmacies that cannot afford to staff 24-hour coverage. These "sister" pharmacists, however, typically do not know the idiosyncratic administration times of wards in the home institution. Wards within and across hospitals vary widely in their scheduled administration times. Pharmacists must know each ward schedule inside out so that when they

TABLE 8.4
Continued

Conditions and effects	Explanations and problems arising from conditions
	finish orders they specify administration times correctly. For example, for the same "every four hour" (q4h) drug, the morning administration time may be 6 AM in intensive care, 8 AM in acute care, and 9 AM in the psychiatric ward.
Hospital mergers adversely affect medication processes and increase risks.	Merged facilities typically spend months making their drug databases and administration time codes consistent. During the transition time, pharmacists in one merger site may finish medication orders for patients who have transferred from the other site without administration realizing that the medication application is not yet primed to accept certain codes. The orders consequently will never appear in the electronic medication-administration program, and patients will not receive needed medications.
Different models of work influence how pharmacists and nurses coordinate their work and jointly solve problems.	In a traditional work model, pharmacists reside in the pharmacy, distant from nurses and patients, making it hard to rapidly resolve some confusions or problems. By contrast, in a decentralized, zone model, pharmacists are stationed on nursing floors. On the floor, they can expediently finish orders that nurses receive from doctors and keep nurses apprised of progress in resolving problems. Computerization introduces this opportunity for pharmacists to be free-floating.
Greater workloads due to physician ordering systems and bar code medication programs.	Before computerization—when doctors ordered medications through nurses—pharmacists spent a relatively short time finishing orders. Now they often have to inventively create codes that

TABLE 8.4
Continued

Conditions and effects	Explanations and problems arising from conditions
	can "trick" the exacting pharmacy and medication-administration applications into accepting unusual cases. In addition, pharmacists spend hours tracking down doctors when orders come in specifying drugs that are not in the formulary, or when the orders include puzzling information about renewals, faulty administration times, or unit doses without dosages.
Pharmacists fear, and often have experienced, reprisals due to metrics collected by medication software.	Managers have been known to give pharmacists poor performance evaluations based on software log data showing they have a high number of missed doses or wrongly finished orders.

What Conditions Complicate Nurses' Verifying, Administering, and Documenting?

Nurses' approaches for verifying, administering, and documenting medications vary widely based on such factors as their ward's level of acuity, census, workloads, staffing, funding, models of nursing, uses of transient registry nurses, and the existence and influence of unions. These and other factors affect nurses' medication practices in ways included in Table 8.5.

TABLE 8.5
Conditions in nurses' systems of work affecting medication practices.

Conditions and effects	Explanations and problems arising from conditions
Strongly unionized nurses often resist electronic medication-administration processes.	Unionized nurses—frequently surrounded at work by non-union colleagues—object to the surveillance functions of the software. The program automatically logs their drug passing times and provides data that managers may use against a nurse in performance reviews, running counter to contract stipulations.

TABLE 8.5
Continued

Conditions and effects	Explanations and problems arising from conditions
Insufficient equipment strains medication-passing efficiencies.	When hospitals lack funding for sufficient laptops, medication carts, scanners, back-up batteries, or upgraded servers and wireless networks, nurses' tasks related to medication passes take longer. When a ward has too few medication carts, nurses often double up on a cart, which leads them to overrun the deadline of the scheduled medication pass. For safety purposes, when time is up, unpassed medications are likely to drop off the screen of the medication administration program. Nurses who still need to finish their drug pass cannot access electronic displays of remaining patients' medications without extensive effort, often requiring the aid of pharmacists.
Staffing shortages diminish medication-administration efficiencies and erode nurses' acceptance of their e-Bar programs.	In understaffed wards, nurses frequently have to devote an unexpectedly long time to a patient during a medication pass and if "extra" nurses are not available to cover for them, they are unlikely to finish the medication pass on time. To explain running over deadline they can record a comment in the program, but they resent that exacting programs make them appear disorganized when, in fact, they are not.
New learning, greater workloads, and increased risks to patient safety may be caused by newly introduced software systems.	Many nurse managers cite bar code medication-administration programs and rigid time constraints as the main reason for changing their units from a primary care model of work (a single nurse responsible for all aspects of care for an assigned set of patients) to a team model (each nurse responsible for a specific nursing duty for all patients, such as passing drugs).

TABLE 8.5
Continued

Conditions and effects	Explanations and problems arising from conditions
	This new program also introduces new record-keeping burdens. To ease nurses through the transition to an electronic MAR—and a paperless system—many hospital administrators designate the electronic MAR as the official documentation (for liability purposes) but informally allow nurses to use both the paper and electronic MARs until they get used to the new system. In many sites, this transition lasts well over a year. Maintaining a dual documentation system takes far more work. It also disperses information across both sources and increases the chances that neither system will be complete on all counts. In addition, in some programs nurses write comments about as-needed drugs and other medication incidents in a free-text field, but the application does not cue other nurses that comments exist.
Lower motivation and productivity result from time spent with the tool.	Nurses in many sites report that the time they spend working a bar code medication-administration program diminishes the time they have for tending to patients. They are distressed because it is bedside care that motivated them to go into nursing in the first place.

In summary, diverse circumstances in co-emergent social and technical systems of work frequently direct physicians, pharmacists, and nurses toward approaches to their parts of the medication process that are incompatible with each other and out of sync with many technological processes and constraints. Faced with these incompatibilities, medical professionals make accommodations, and in many ways, they succeed.

Nurses, for example, become skilled in keeping precise dual documentation systems and in working around clunky barcode and computing apparatus to maintain a close connection with their patients. However, better than having medical professionals rely on workarounds would be if design teams could describe, model, and design for nurses' patterns of work in relation to socio-technical influences with the aim of helping them harness these adaptive complexities.

MODELING PATTERNS OF INQUIRY AND TASK LANDSCAPES

An abstraction of Katherine's pattern for her dosage decisions involves the mainline tasks shown in the following chart.

Mainline Tasks for Deciding on Dosages for Tapered Orders

Conduct standard preliminary steps in bar coded medication passes. These include: Print reports to guide administration, log onto the medication-administration program, scan a patient's bar-coded identification bracelet to open his or her record, set the right filters on the medication-due screen to display the patient's drugs as desired, remove the drugs from the patient's drawer in the medication cart, and check that all drugs are there and that the drugs dispensed are the drugs on the screen.

Take care of any missing dose problems. Notify the pharmacy through an email request.

Examine a patient's history: Based on professional conventions, analyze relationships among 72 hours of medications, vital signs, pain scales, and other care and conditions to determine the dosage to give in tapered orders. This task includes searching for and retrieving relevant quantitative and qualitative data within and across programs, putting them in formats conducive to analysis, transforming measures and deriving values as needed, and creating displays that facilitate analysis and inferences.

Consult with the patient. Elicit a patient's subjective experiences and comments, such as increased anxiety or hypertension in detox cases.

Interpret data, draw conclusions, and decide on dosages. Apply conventional protocols to the outcomes and explore what-if drug combinations and dosages.

As with complex problem solving in other domains, these mainline inquiry tasks are incomplete without the many enabling tasks and choice points that combine with them in complex medication-administration work and problem solving. The enabling tasks and choice points reveal the leeway nurses must have in their patterns of inquiry for dosage decisions. Examples of these enabling tasks and choice points appear in the following table.

A number of these medication actions are tied to coordinated work practices ("Why didn't the doctor renew this part of the drug regimen?"), to electronic data processing ("Where are the comments from the morning-shift psychiatric nurse, and can I group just these together from the past 72 hours?"), and to the unity of both ("What should I say about

Remember what data have been reconfigured, transformed, and placed in various locations and why.
Sample choice point: What should I look at next, and have I laid out those relationships yet?

Highlight and remark on insights relevant to an immediate decision. Underscore and make comments in ways that serve other nurses', pharmacists', and doctors' later purposes for the data, as well.
Sample choice point: What should I say about this insight? For the sake of others should I say it in the program's controlled vocabulary, elaborate on it, or both?

Decide on the best graphic display of data for the circumstances.
Sample choice point: Given that this patient has an unexpected infection, do I need to create a different graph from the usual ones to account for it?

Look for comments by specific caregivers who inspire confidence.
Sample choice point: Where are the comments from the morning-shift psychiatric nurse, and can I group just these together from the past 72 hours?

Consult with other nurses, doctors, or pharmacists.
Sample choice point: I don't know why the doctor didn't renew this part of the drug regimen. It could be that the patient is improving in ways I don't realize, or maybe the pharmacist made a mistake in finishing. Should I interrupt my work now and follow up or wait until later?
Sample choice point: If I don't hear from the pharmacist about the new dosage in the next hour should I give the patient the original order? Is it better to give a "good enough" dose or skip a dose?

Maintain interactions in which patients are partners in care-giving.
Sample choice point: How might I bring communication with the patient into some of the analysis I am doing?

Relate differently scaled quantitative data and draw relationships between quantitative and qualitative data.
Sample choice point: How do I measure and communicate to others the trends I see in nurses' comments about the patient's agitation? In two contradictory opinions from different nurses, which one has more credibility?

this insight? For the sake of others should I say it in the program's controlled vocabulary, elaborate on it, or both?"). Nurses need programs that help them take the initiatives they need across this complex work system.

PREPARING FOR CONCEPTUAL DESIGN: RECOGNIZING THE POLITICS OF CHOICES

Design teams may implement many design strategies and choices to improve the usefulness of medication software for nurses' pattern-based needs, but usefulness in programs such as e-Bar cannot be achieved solely through software design. To some degree, this qualification pertains to all software because usefulness is a result of interactions between situated work and technical design, but it is especially true for applications that facilitate problem solving in complex socio-technical systems of work. In these systems of work, doing work well requires complementary social *and* technological adaptations to professionals' requirements. If the necessary organizational innovations are not instituted in users' work environments along with useful software, even the most useful software may not succeed.

An extensive discussion of the ways in which organizational choices in medical centers affect the diffusion of software innovations is outside the scope of this chapter, but such discussion can be found in numerous other sources (Massaro, 1993; Strauss et al., 1995; Engestrom, 1999; Berg, 1997; Berg and Goorman, 1999). Concrete organizational changes in users' workplaces may fall outside the direct control of development groups, but software teams indirectly participate in them through the politics of their design choices.

Making design choices for programs such as e-Bar is political because these applications serve numerous competing goals in users' workplaces. For example, with medication-administration software, hospital decision makers aim for reduced operational costs; improved quality in patient care; maximized efficiency; increased patient safety; an equitable distribution of responsibility, authority, and resources; and easier maintenance of records. Organizational realities make it difficult to satisfy all these goals and interests at once. Hence, software design teams play an important role in the competing trade-offs in users' organizations. These teams choose an application design and, in doing so, craft a program that serves some medical center aims better than others. Through their choices, designers take a position on which interests take precedence over others. Their software design embodies these biases, and the implemented product embeds them in users' workplaces.

Politics are forever present in design choices, but they are not always acknowledged by software teams. When software teams maintain conventional assumptions—emphasizing design as a logic for making the separate entities of practice and tools equivalent—it may appear that designing is neutral in regard to competing interests in users' workplaces. However, when designers regard medication work as a process of tools and practices that co-produce each other, it is much harder to ignore the political side of design. From this vantage point, even benign, logical design choices such as data formats or methods to access data take on a dimension of power in users' workplaces. These choices affect nurses' analysis, the distance of information from the point of care, the clarity of nurses' roles, and their communication channels.

In many cases, users' acceptance of software hinges on the extent to which they find their roles, as structured by the software, to be politically acceptable. In some hospitals, for example, nursing unions have staged boycotts of medication-administration software for fear that the software puts them under surveillance. In other medical centers, older nurses have left hospital nursing in favor of home care because they find that working with bar code programs changes their roles from caregivers to "tool operators."

In most of the following strategies and choices for usefulness, I do not explain the political aspects of design because they vary by situation and software project. Each design team must explicitly discuss the specific political implications of their designs on their users' work and environments and use these discussions to inform their strategies and choices.

CONCEPTUALLY DESIGNING SUPPORT FOR INTEGRATING DIVERSE INFORMATION

In thinking about what it would take to make Katherine's e-Bar program more useful, human-computer interaction specialists cannot help but focus on glaring interface problems, such as the need to make relevant information stand out in dense displays of medication history. These user interface (UI) problems may tempt interaction designers and usability specialists to jump right into interface improvements. Indeed, usability for interfaces in clinical applications is a major issue, covered extensively in the medical informatics literature (Ramey et al., 1992; Kushniruk et al., 1996; Hayes and Bainbridge, 1997; Coble et al., 1997; Bridger and Poluta, 1998; Powsner et al., 1998; Rosenbaum et al., 1999; van Ginneken, 2002).

Giving priority to many of these UI issues, however, is not the focus of this chapter. In the e-Bar case, many UI choices for improving use of ease, navigation, and the like hinge on first determining conceptual designs for usefulness. For example, Katherine needs easier and quicker ways to access data from other sources. She also needs places to record notes with localized comments and a way to make the comments readily visible to other clinicians. But these issues, at base, cannot be resolved adequately by adding a few more tabs to display data from other sources or by piling more options into the comments field. Before making UI choices, design teams need to conceptualize holistically the integrated sets of program interactions and electronic workspaces nurses need for administering medications and for deciding on dosages effectively, all the while staying true to their roles and patterns of work. Adding piece-by-piece tabs or other UI fixes as discussed later is likely the wrong answer for nurses' needs.

With an emphasis on conceptual designs that foster a productive intermeshing of nurses' social and technical systems of medication work, I explore in this section design strategies and choices for supporting nurses in integrating diverse information for dosage decisions and analyzing it in a single workspace. As Katherine's case reveals, e-Bar fails to offer this support in the numerous ways detailed in Table 8.6.

One main need nurses have for analytical medication work and clinical judgment is a virtual information environment in which they can expediently access, integrate, graph, manipulate, and analyze data and

TABLE 8.6
Support for integrating diverse information.

Katherine needs support for Integrating Diverse Information	Does she get it?	
	Yes	No
Accessing relevant information easily and quickly		✓
Accessing complete comment and dosage totals information		✓
Arranging comment information as needed for analysis purposes		✓
Having a workspace for gathering all relevant information		✓
Having a workspace for creating compatible data formatting		✓
Having a workspace for composing graphic displays of the data		✓
Making sure all important data get electronically documented, including correlation plots and diagrams		✓
Facilitating the multitasking involved in analyzing data and giving care		✓

communicate findings. e-Bar gives access to some data in other systems through hot buttons and tabbed windows but does not enable nurses to complete all the data interactions and interpretations required for dosage decisions.

Improving upon the e-Bar model, many interfaces today for other types of systems enable users to see diverse sources of data on a single screen and from them select data of interest, as illustrated in Figure 8.4.

This access and display of all relevant data and data sources may be coupled with giving users a way to filter to data of interest and display them in analytical screens, as in the two examples in Figure 8.5.

Figure 8.6 picks up on the "small multiples" design of Figure 8.5B, and presents a more complete and coherent example of an analysis workspace designed by Seth Powsner and Edward Tufte (1994). The "legend" to the display in Figure 8.6A shows that the scatterplot graphics in the small multiples displayed in the interface (Figure 8.6B) have been scaled to allow a common vertical axis so clinicians can readily compare the multiple graphics. In addition to the scatterplot matrix in Figure 8.6B the interface also includes visible textual comments along the right-hand side of the screen.

Alternately, designs may integrate *all* nurses' activities in a single workspace: Data access and filtering, graphing, and communication. We have

FIGURE 8.4
Pathfinder program interface for displaying data from diverse sources (courtesy of *www.cocoatech.com/*).

FIGURE 8.5

Displaying relevant data and graphics for dosage decisions. (A) Different perspectives of relevant medical data on a single screen (courtesy of *www.cooper.com/content/services/shs.asp*). (B) Small multiples in the form of a line graph matrix showing various readings of vital signs at different times of day (courtesy of *www.Belmont.com/ belweb2/ software/cg/ cg_about. html*).

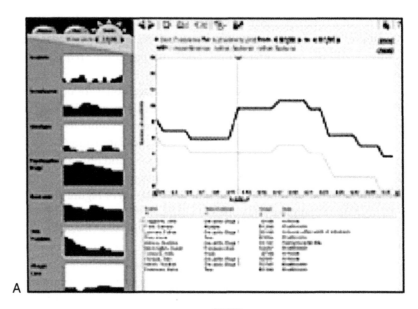

A

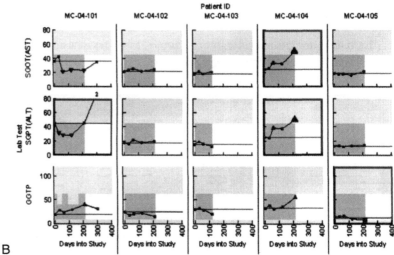

B

seen this design concept in the other scenarios in the Sage Visualization Group and MAYAViz frame-based workspaces *(www.mayaviz.com)*. As displayed in Figure 8.7, this workspace design could enable nurses to access and display data from diverse sources. They could drag and drop data of interest from any source into a frame pre-formatted to display graphics appropriate for analyzing and interpreting correlations over time among vital signs, patient conditions, and drug dosages.

The Sage Visualization Group and MAYAViz approach is one of the most powerful design strategies in the market today for complex problem solving. It provides structured openness, domain-specific frames of analysis, and interactions in sync with the mainline and enabling tasks in domain specialists' patterns of inquiry. As mentioned in previous cases, however, this approach requires restructuring data in fundamental ways so that they have the functionality typically built into other software at the application level. Consequently, this approach may be too costly or infeasible for many design teams' situations.

Designers, however, should not give up the notion of an elegantly crafted single workspace for the whole sweep of nurses' analytical needs. The design pictured in Figure 8.8 gives a single workspace that does not require the custom data-structuring associated with the Sage Visualization Group and MAYAViz option. Alan Cooper conceptualized and implemented this design for St. Jude Medical Center in order to represent the full task landscape of medical users' exploratory and analytical activities on a single screen. In actual use, this interface and its complexity proved to be accessible to domain specialists who were highly familiar with the content.

As these examples show, even if design teams do not start from scratch with new data and data repository structures, they still can adopt many of

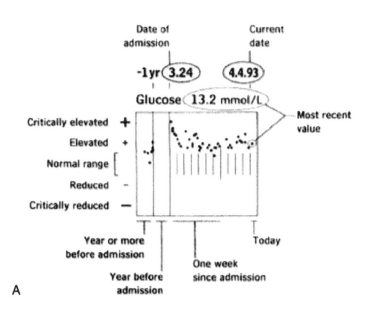

FIGURE 8.6
A comprehensive workspace for analyzing data for dosage judgments (Powsner and Tufte, 1994). (A) Legend for interpreting the small multiples displayed in the interface design in part B.

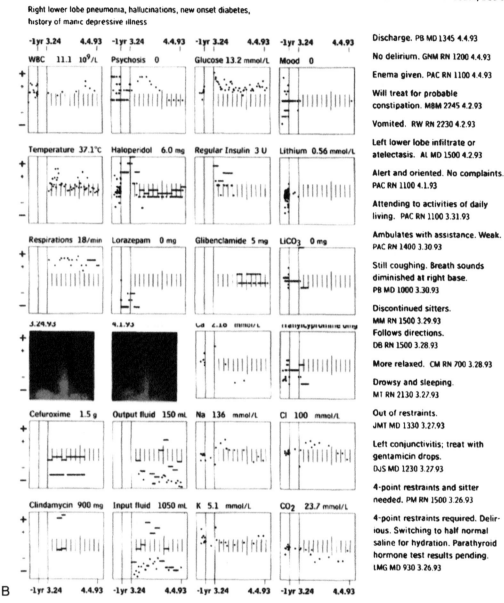

Surname, forename   Admitted 3.24.93   4.4.93   7-South, Bed 5

Right lower lobe pneumonia, hallucinations, new onset diabetes, history of manic depressive illness

Discharge. PB MD 1345 4.4.93

No delirium. GNM RN 1200 4.4.93

Enema given. PAC RN 1100 4.4.93

Will treat for probable constipation. MBM 2245 4.2.93

Vomited. RW RN 2230 4.2.93

Left lower lobe infiltrate or atelectasis. AL MD 1500 4.2.93

Alert and oriented. No complaints. PAC RN 1100 4.1.93

Attending to activities of daily living. PAC RN 1100 3.31.93

Ambulates with assistance. Weak. PAC RN 1400 3.30.93

Still coughing. Breath sounds diminished at right base. PB MD 1000 3.30.93

Discontinued sitters. MM RN 1500 3.29.93
Follows directions. DB RN 1500 3.28.93

More relaxed. CM RN 700 3.28.93

Drowsy and sleeping. MT RN 2130 3.27.93

Out of restraints. JMT MD 1330 3.27.93

Left conjunctivitis; treat with gentamicin drops. DJS MD 1230 3.27.93

4-point restraints and sitter needed. PM RN 1500 3.26.93

4-point restraints required. Delirious. Switching to half normal saline for hydration. Parathyroid hormone test results pending. LMG MD 930 3.26.93

B

FIGURE 8.6 *(cont'd)*
(B) A multidimensional and multi-model display of data relevant to clinical analysis and judgment.

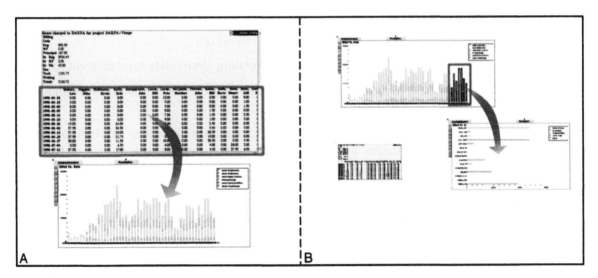

FIGURE 8.7
Dragging and dropping data into different pre-formatted frames in a workspace. (A) Selected data get dragged, dropped, and formatted into a bar chart frame. (B) Users drill down further by selecting only a portion of the bar chart and dragging and dropping it into another differently formatted frame in the workspace (courtesy of *www.mayaviz.com*).

FIGURE 8.8
User interface for a cardiac rhythm management device. "Users work with this interface all day long and become familiar with its complexity. All the essential information [is] on the initial summary screen. Rich visual feedback on this screen gives the user clues about information in need of deeper investigation. For instance, the boxes outlined in alert orange indicate states that could have health consequences for the patient.... [Before this] users had to move through multiple screens in order to find all the information needed." (Courtesy of *www.cooper.com/content/services/shs.asp*)

the Sage Visualization Group and MAYAViz ideas into their programs. For example, they can do the following:

- Create workspaces for integrating diverse data from different sources
- Generate graphic and tabular displays relevant to nurses' diagnoses of dosages
- Design interactive data visualizations and query capabilities that fit nurses' purposes, with the richness and density of data matched to nurses' patterns of inquiry
- Provide necessary user control over judgments and communication
- Create seamless interfaces between data and workspaces

Design teams must work with the systems development groups on such issues as standards for terminology, data formats, and conversion; data models and database structures; and data transfer and interfaces across applications. These collaborations are crucial. If nurses cannot retrieve the information they need or bring data together, even the most useful workspace is of little value to them.

Such design improvements largely target the creation of better information spaces, but nurses also need a place, not just a space, for their work.

CONCEPTUALLY DESIGNING SUPPORT FOR WORKING IN AN ELECTRONIC "PLACE"

The difference between electronic *places* and *spaces* for nurses' medication work is that in a *place* they see their social roles, relationships, and identities represented in the program. A *space*, by contrast, is neutral and generic. Nurses are at home socially and cognitively in an electronic workplace when its design includes the vital contextual and subjective reminders, cues, structures, resources, constraints, and focal practices that call forth the qualities of their profession that make them irreplaceable institutionally. Place is diminished when the generic neutrality of an electronic space suggests that the work can be assigned to any cog in the system. Admittedly, nurses perform generic functions in an electronic workplace, but the sense of place is maintained by framing these functions in nurses' multidimensional roles and task landscapes.

One way for programs to provide nurses with a workplace when they analyze data for clinical judgments is to offer support for coupling analysis with time spent with patients. One of the biggest flaws in current medication-administration applications is that in serving administrative, regulatory, financial, legal, and clinical needs, they become largely a device for storage and are not designed with patient care in mind (Poswner and Tufte, 1994). To evoke a sense of place, software designers need to highlight and enhance patient care and a nurse's coordination with pharmacists and doctors. Because these activities are central to dosage decision- making, designing for place is a usefulness issue.

Nurses develop a sense of place in their virtual workspace from their cumulative impressions about who the program structures them to be compared to, who in fact, they are. As Katherine's scenario reveals, the program supports very few of her needs for a workplace, as detailed in Table 8.7.

Designers can strive to approximate a match between nurses' real and virtual identities by targeting three areas in which usefulness problems are tied to an insufficient creation of place:

- Communicating through notes in controlled vocabulary and free-text entries

- Strengthening communication processes

- Controlling the timing of crucial aspects of work

Communicating Through Notes in Controlled Vocabulary and Free-Text Entries

For medication safety, accuracy, and efficiency, nurses need to write and receive communications with the right content, level of detail, and structure. In e-Bar and many other medication administration applications a comments field takes care of the bulk of a nurse's electronic remarks related to a patient's care and condition. The use of this single field for wide-ranging communication functions raises two design questions relevant to improving the usefulness of applications such as e-Bar:

- For nurses' comment entries (whether in a comments field or some other design), to what extent should software pre-supply standardized (formal) messages and to what extent should it allow for looser, natural-language entries (informal)?

- Do users need more than a single field for their varied purposes in communicating comments?

Deliberating About Standardization vs. Looseness in Entries

Questions about standardized or free-text entries are part of a larger design issue related to how much control over communication nurses

TABLE 8.7
Support for working in an electronic place.

Katherine needs support for	Does she get it?	
	Yes	No
Working in an Electronic Place, not Just a Space		
Communicating Through Notes		
Leaving comments for others based on insights from integrated information	✓	
Being able to enter the right content for the right purposes		✓
Ensuring that others know about and see the comments		✓
Strengthening Communication Processes		
Closing the loop on a decision by bringing in pharmacists and doctors (e.g., via emails)	✓	
Being aware that pharmacists receive and act on email		✓
Being aware of outcomes of communication about decisions		✓
Controlling the Timing of Crucial Aspects of Work		
Adjusting time clocks to contextual demands		✓
Efficiently keeping accurate electronic documentation		✓

should have in regard to the content and organization of their remarks about patient conditions and care. The positive side of giving nurses a great deal of control over the content of comments is that they can express and share with nurses on other shifts local details relevant to a patient's ongoing story. The downside is that loose and informal comments cannot be easily aggregated and used for later analysis by medical professionals who need them for other purposes. For design teams, negotiating this tension effectively is crucial for usefulness and for evoking a sense of place. As socio-technical specialists have found in studies of patient care systems, when systems validate the formal and ignore the informal (or vice versa), they are doomed to fail (Star and Strauss, 1994).

Design teams can only make informed decisions about when and how much to standardize by knowing a great deal about both the *instrumental* and *expressive* purposes and effects of medication professionals' communications (Timpka et al., 1994; Thomas et al., 2001; Timmerman and Berg, 1997). They need to know when nurses find it acceptable to use controlled terminologies and when they need more control over what they say and how they say it. To discover these conventions, designers must come to know the functions that clinical information plays under various circumstances and conditions.

Another consideration in designing for standardized versus loose entries is medical professionals' uses of qualifiers when they exchange information. Qualifiers are terms such as *severe, acute,* or *recurrent.* They are relative terms whose meanings rest on the surrounding content in the context of their use. Standardized terms—even if terms include these qualifiers—cannot fully express meanings without the elaborations needed for making these meanings clear. Similarly, if entries are formalized as set measures of symptoms, pain levels, reactions, and so on, they will capture some aspects of observed care but include no intermediating qualifiers. Studies have shown that when clinicians make diagnoses from only measures and signs of conditions, they have a 10–15% chance of getting the diagnosis correct. By contrast when they couple measures with qualifiers surrounded by elaborations, their chances shoot up to 90% (Bordage et al., 1997). Clearly, the right balance of standardization and elaboration is vital in supporting and enhancing medical judgments.

To be useful for judgments, and to "speak" to nurses as insiders in a community of practice, designs must build on nurses' conventions for passing and receiving knowledge through notes. Katherine's scenario exemplifies some of these conventions related to content brevity, omissions, and the ordering of ideas. For example, in nursing cursory comments are often intentionally brief. In certain situations, brevity is a means to convey that a patient is progressing as expected. Relatively new to psychiatric patient care, Katherine may not have been enough of an insider to detox therapies yet to appreciate that the sparse comments she encountered may have been conveying this meaning. Similarly, the omission of comments on blood sugar levels signals the nursing convention of not duplicating lab reports. The signs are in the reports, why re-write them? To nurses, giving more information than is needed actually signifies deviant professional communication in many circumstances. Detailed comments are important for troublesome cases, and the comments nurses need are elaborations and qualifiers, not reiterated measures.

Trade-offs in design are inevitable. If, for example, designers choose a controlled vocabulary in comments or fixed requirements for measures to enter, nurses cannot enter observations, precautions, and context-rich qualifiers. If free-text entries are allowed, medical professionals cannot work with aggregated comments. Both are vital to good healthcare, and they are, to some extent, contradictory.

In Katherine's case, designers may try to build rules that require nurses to enter blood sugar readings in a fixed syntax and standardized level of detail before moving on in the program. Nurses, however, already pressed for time in completing their medication rounds, may see this program constraint as redundant data entry. They may bristle that it runs counter to both their usual reliance on lab reports and their desire to control the pacing of their work. Telling nurses this choice makes information available to wide numbers of hospital professionals and relieves them from having to traverse applications to retrieve lab results is not likely to counteract what they perceive as a lack of "place" in the program. What they would rather have is keystroke access to the lab reports or one of the designs detailed previously for integrating information from diverse sources (see Figures 8.6-8.8). As yet another alternative, designers could build data-transfer methods into the architecture to let nurses, without effort, selectively move information from sources such as lab reports to the electronic MAR.

Figuring out the appropriate degree of formality or informality is one of the most under-explored areas in designing useful support for complex work, and it is especially significant as a gap in medication software where safety depends on effective coordination and communication. Therefore, when designers decide about trade-offs they must base their choices on users' demonstrated needs as observed through cases such as Katherine's, not on pet theories, assumptions, or even subject experts' notions about the nature of the work.

Deliberating About Adequate Comment Designs for Varied Purposes

"Comments" in e-Bar stands as the only available field for notes that serve a wide range of functions. Katherine, for example, uses this field to document the effectiveness of an administered drug, to note the exact amount given for a drug that has a range such as 20–100 mg, to give reasons for running over deadline, and to communicate a close call with an overdose.

In terms of nursing roles, the danger of having a single comments field is that it tacitly conveys to nurses that their knowledge, insights, and exchange of them warrant only one small field in an electronic record used by numerous professionals across the hospital. Nurses take pride in and base their identities on their situational awareness, problem solving skills, "backstage" work in planning and carrying out patient care, and their abilities to exercise just the right discretion at the right time and place. A program that gives scant place for nurses to record and pass these insights on to others subtly undercuts these traits by omission. The electronic workspace becomes a generic administrative environment of record-keeping, separated from the nuanced insights relevant to bedside patient care, even though, to nurses, the two are integrated. In short, when designs focus on generic information processes instead of the varied functions and conventions of nursing communications with co-workers, space trumps place.

Moreover, without appropriate channels for diverse information, important knowledge may get lost. Before fixing "comments," designers have to question whether "comments" itself is the right design in the first place. They have to decide if usefulness is best served by improving "comments" or by designing a more integrated and elegant approach to nurses' information-sharing needs. The numerous usefulness flaws associated with the lack of "place" in e-Bar suggest that elegant designs are preferable.

Strengthening Communication Within and Across Services

In addition to adequate content and channels for information exchange, design teams also must support users in *strengthening* communications. Designs are needed that guard against messages going unheeded and against users being uncertain about the reception and effects of their communications. e-Bar, for example, offers nurses a comments field but does nothing to signal to pharmacists, doctors, and other nurses that a colleague's comment is waiting for them, possibly requiring action.

The email pharmacy request is another aspect of e-Bar that does not adequately strengthen communication and often evokes only a partial sense of place to nurses. The email request positively provides a place in terms of making nurses' roles in relationship to pharmacists apparent. As long as pharmacists quickly respond, the email request is useful, but if nurses are not notified that a pharmacist has received their request, has a problem with it, or is waiting for a doctor to respond, the program fails to support one of the major issues in coordinated work: Knowing where everyone is in his or her part of patient care. For example, Katherine is left hanging about her request for the new detox drug dosage. If nothing happens before her shift ends, the next nurse on duty inherits an unfinished communication that she knows little about.

Nurses and pharmacists can and do use the telephone to resolve such issues. But the program nonetheless falls short in the communications it promises. Addressed to a nameless, faceless "pharmacy," the email function has a "send" button, but no "reply" button, and no personal connection until an actual phone call is made. The request fulfills the letter, but not the spirit, of coordinated processes. If designers are to build support for communication, strengthen coordinated practices, and solidify a sense of place, they must develop fuller and richer support than "comments" or email requests.

Controlling the Timing of Crucial Aspects of Work

In Katherine's scenario, two usefulness problems related to time are rigid deadlines imposed electronically for medication passes and lengthy processes required for editing entries when documenting their medication pass. For improved support, software design teams need to tie their choices for deadlines and editing to nurses' roles and identities.

Deliberating About Timed Medication Passes

In the e-Bar example, the clock ticking for medications passing is inconspicuously designed and displayed as a benign start and stop time, but it looms large in a nurse's consciousness (Figure 8.9). When the allotted amount of time is reached, the medications immediately drop off the screen, whether the nurse has administered them or not. Nurses lack autonomy over the timing of their medication passes, which often leads to diminished quality of care. It also results in a blow to nurses' professional identity.

Redesigns for timed deadlines in medication-administration schedules depend on other strategies a design team enacts for other usefulness flaws. For example, if workspaces for better data integration and analysis are implemented, running over a deadline may become less of a problem. Similarly, nursing units may institute team models of nursing to make it easier and faster to administer medications. Observations show, however, that even team nurses run over deadline.

Such improvements are helpful, but deadlines will continue to be an issue because unforeseen events inescapably crop up in nursing care and

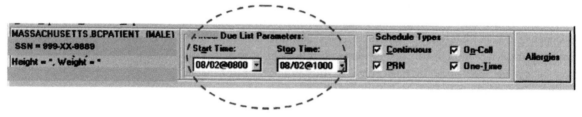

FIGURE 8.9
Display in e-Bar of the allotted time for a current medication pass.

countermand assembly line processes and speed. Katherine, for example, knew early in her medication pass she was going to be late. She would have liked to adapt the program to her needs by resetting the stop time or by suspending the countdown while she caught up in her medication activities. Design choices need to be made for balancing the institutional need for standardized timing with nurses' need to adapt to circumstances.

Deliberating About Editing at Point of Care

Medication administration software may threaten nurses' roles and hamper the quality of care they deliver when it forces nurses to edit documentation for ongoing medication passes outside the program.

Katherine's need to edit the automatic Gs that e-Bar entered for the drugs the "applesauce" patient could not swallow is not unusual and may occur frequently in the course of a single medication pass. Nurses expect to be in control of documentation and have it on hand at the point of care. They do not feel "at home" in their work if this required resource is not readily within reach. Moreover, the need to go into another program to edit the electronic MAR takes time, a scarce commodity in drug passes.

Improvements for editing are obviously possible. Designers and developers can build hooks to other programs and editing capabilities into electronic medication programs. The issue, however, is that these functions for core activities are omitted in the first place in finished products such as e-Bar. Human-computer interaction specialists may say this example of omission is just a cautionary tale about letting core features slide. But more importantly, it underscores what happens when software designers think primarily in terms of features in the first place.

Categorizing support as "editing" and matching it to a feature is far different from thinking about classes of program interactions that serve users' problem solving and time management initiatives. For "place" and greater usefulness, design teams need to first think in terms of classes of program interactions. Nurses' initiatives for program interactions they want to take are motivated by their role-related sense of ownership of patient charts, including the electronic MAR. Being able to edit the results of their actions on such charts at the point of care is a professional and organizational role issue. By identifying this need to assure electronic "places," designers can create more elegant designs that unify numerous low-level actions into high-level, situated patterns of work.

CONCLUSIONS

In medication administration and problem solving, patient safety, quality of care, and efficiency depend on accurate and reliable technical systems that centrally store and process enterprise-wide data, that manage diverse records, and that keep numerous decision-support applications up and running. Equally important is the social system of interpersonal caregiving and collaboration within and across services. Software support for medication administration must fit into these intertwined social and technical systems of work.

Compared to the problem solving in other scenarios, the scope of nurses' complex investigations for dosage decisions is somewhat narrower, but the design implications are considerably more complicated. Complications are tied to evolving and unpredictably emerging local conditions; to a mix of tightly and loosely coordinated interactions; and to shared, constantly updated data used, at times, for contradictory purposes.

To improve usefulness, design teams need to start by assuming that medication processes reside in an environment in which highly complex technical and social systems of work dynamically transform each other and are never altogether compatible. This assumption implies that interaction designers and their teammates need to direct their efforts toward helping users harness their social practices and technical tools to each other rather than attempting to eliminate a gap between the two.

When software teams frame design around the *interrelation* of practices and tools rather than trying to make them equivalent, they focus on the interactive social and technical work affecting medication activities. In their contextual analysis, they aim to discover interactive and multifaceted conditions in the technology and in the medication work of physicians, pharmacists, and nurses that affect coordinated medication processes. From findings, they can compose patterns of inquiry for administering drugs and deciding on dosages and use them to conceptualize designs.

Two important aspects of conceptual designs useful for dosage problems include helping nurses access, integrate, and analyze heterogeneous data from diverse sources and giving nurses electronic workplaces to experience a unity in such multifunctional roles as caring for patients, documenting medications, recording insights for other medical professionals, and retrieving others' comments. To evoke a place and not just a space, design teams need to strike the right balance between free-text entries and controlled vocabulary, strengthen and close the loops in communications, and give nurses optimal control over timing.

Improvements at a feature-by-feature level will not address the many intertwined demands nurses face. Designs, for example, fall short if they focus on improving existing fields in a program by adding a new feature to it for an individual shortcoming instead of exploring elegant redesigns for combined usefulness needs.

In addition, design teams' choices affect the politics and work structures of users' medical centers. Interaction designers and usability specialists must explicitly discuss the political implications of design choices within their design teams and with hospital decision makers, nurses, and other services. Usefulness hinges on interaction designers and usability specialists having direct and trusting relationships with hospital users and customers.

The major emphasis in this book has been on new ways of thinking about complex work and innovative methods, strategies, and design choices. Politics is also important. In this chapter we have seen some of the issues related to the politics of design choices. Human-computer interaction specialists also must do a good deal of political positioning in their own workplace to get the support and resources required to design for usefulness. For example, getting access to hospital decision makers and nurses takes political maneuvering.

The politics of usefulness requires a book of its own. However, I cannot conclude this one without devoting at least a chapter to it. Therefore, after closing part two with a synthesis of the cases in it and what they reveal about necessary design frameworks, methods, and choices for usefulness, I conclude the book with a chapter that explores the necessary next steps for realizing usefulness approaches politically.

REFERENCES

Ackerman, Mark. "The Intellectual Challenge of CSCW: The Gap Between Social Requirements and Technical Feasibility." *Human-Computer Interaction* 15, nos. 2-3 (2000), 181-205.

Agre, Philip. "Changing Places: Contexts of Awareness in Computing." *Human-Computer Interaction* 16 (2001): 177-192.

Bates, W. David, Jonathan Teich, Joshua Lee, Diane Seger, Gilad Kuperman, Nell Ma'Luf, Deborah Boyle, and Lucian Leape. "The Impact of Computerized Physician Order Entry on Medication Error Prevention." *Journal of American Medical Association* 6, no. 4 (1999): 313-21.

Berg, Marc and Els Goorman. "The Contextual Nature of Medical Information." *International Journal of Medical Informatics* 6, nos. 1-3 (1999): 51-60.

Berg, Marc. *Rationalizing Medical Work: Decision Support Techniques and Medical Practices.* Cambridge, MA: MIT Press, 1997.

Bogner, Marilyn Sue, ed. *Human Error in Medicine.* Hillsdale, NJ: Lawrence Erlbaum Associates, 1994.

Bordage, George, K. Connell, R. Chang, M. Gecht, and J. Sinacore. "Assessing the Semantic Content of Clinical Case Presentations: Studies of Reliability and Concurrent Validity." *Academic Medicine* 72 (1997): S37-S39.

Bridger, Robert and Mladen Poluta. "Ergonomics: Introducing the Human Factor into the Clinical Setting." *Journal of Clinical Engineering* 23, no. 3 (1998): 180-188.

Coble, Janette, John Karat, and Michael Kahn. "Maintaining a Focus on User Requirements Throughout the Development of Clinical Workstation Software." In *Proceedings of CHI '97 Conference on Computer Human Interaction*, 163-164. Atlanta: ACM, 1997.

Cohen, Michael and Robert Axelrod. *Harnessing Complexity: Organizational Implications of a Scientific Frontier.* New York: Free Press, 1999.

Cousins, Diane DiMichele, ed. *Medication Use: A Systems Approach to Reducing Errors.* Oakbrook Terrace, IL: Joint Commission on Accreditation of Healthcare Organizations, 1998.

Croteau, Richard and Paul Schyve. "Proactively Error-Proofing Health Care Processes." In *Error Reduction in Health Care*, edited by Spath, Patrice, 179-198. San Francisco: Jossey-Bass, 1999.

Engestrom, Yrjo. "Expansive Visibilization of Work: An Activity-Theoretical Perspective." *Computer Supported Cooperative Work* 8 (1999): 63-93.

Hayes, Glyn and Michael Bainbridge. "The Benefits of Different Ways of Displaying Patient-based Data." In *Healthcare Computing '97*, edited by Richards, Bernard. Harrogate: British Journal of Healthcare Computing, Ltd, 1997, 274-280.

Helmreich, Robert and Ashleigh Merritt. *Culture at Work in Aviation and Medicine.* Aldershot, UK: Ashgate, 1998.

Hunt, Dereck, R. Brian Haynes, Steven Hanna, and Kristina Smith. "Effects of Computer-Based Clinical Decision Support Systems on Physician Performance and Patient Outcomes." *Journal of the American Medical Association (JAMA)* 280, no. 15 (1998): 1339-1346.

Institute for Safe Medication Practices (ISMP) editors. "ISMP Survey on Perceptions of a Nonpunitive Culture Produces Some Surprising Results." *ISMP Medical Safety Alert Newsletter®.* August 22, 2001 *(www.ismp.org/ MSAarticles/nonpunitive.html).*

Kushniruk, Andre, David Kaufman, Vimla Patel, Y. Levesque, and P. Lottin. "Assessment of a Computerized Patient Record System: A Cognitive Approach to Evaluating Medical Technology." *MD Computing* 13 (1996): 406-415.

Leape, Lucien, L. Wood, and M. Hatlie. "Promoting Patient Safety by Preventing Medical Error." *Journal of the American Medical Association (JAMA)* 280 (1998): 1444-1447.

Massaro, Thomas. "Introducing Physician Order Entry at a Major Academic Medical Center: Impact on Organizational Culture and Behavior." *Academic Medicine* 68 (1993): 20-25.

Powsner, Seth, and Edward Tufte. "Graphical Summary of Patient Status." *The Lancet* 344, no. 8919 (1994): 386-389.

Powsner, Seth, Jeremy Wyatt, and Patricia Wright. "Opportunities for and Challenges of Computerisation." *The Lancet* 353, no. 9140 (1998): 1617-1622.

Ramey, Judith, Carol Robinson, Denise Carlevato, and Ruth Hansing. "Communicating User Needs to Designers: Hypermedia-Supported Requirements Documents." *IEEE International Professional Communication Conference (IPCC '92) Conference Record*, 241-247. Santa Fe: IEEE, 1992.

Reason, James. *Managing the Risks of Organizational Accidents*. Aldershot, UK: Ashgate, 1997.

Rosenbaum, Stephanie, Deborah Hinderer, and Philip Scarborough. "How Usability Engineering Can Improve Clinical Information Systems." In *Proceedings of the Eighth Annual Usability Professional's Association Conference*, 135-149. Scottsdale, Arizona: UPA 1999.

Spath, Patrice, ed. *Error Reduction in Health Care*. San Francisco: Jossey-Bass, 1999.

Star, Susan Leigh and Anselm Strauss. "Layers of Silence, Arenas of Voice." *Computer Supported Cooperative Work* 8, nos. 1 and 2 (1999): 9-30.

Strauss, Anselm, Shizuko Fagerhaugh, Barbara Suczek, and Carolyn Wieder. *Social Organization of Medical Work*. Chicago: University of Chicago, 1995.

Thomas, C. John, Wendy Kellogg, Thomas Erickson. "The Knowledge Management Puzzle: Human and Social Factors in Knowledge Management." *IBM Systems Journal* 40, no. 4 (2001): 863-884.

Timka, Toomas, Ewa Rauch, and James Nyce. "Toward Productive Knowledge-Based systems in Clinical Organizations: A Methods Perspective. *Artificial Intelligence in Medicine* 6, no. 6 (1994): 501-519.

Timmermans, Stefan and Marc Berg. "Standardization in Action: Achieving Local Universality Through Medical Protocols." *Social Studies of Science* 27, no. 2 (1997): 273-305.

van Ginneken, Astrid M. "The Computerized Patient Record: Balancing Effort and Benefit." *International Journal of Medical Informatics* 65, no. 2 (2002): 97-119.

9

Designing for Usefulness
Across Cases

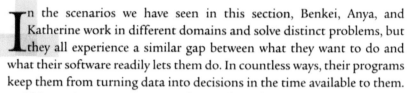

In the scenarios we have seen in this section, Benkei, Anya, and Katherine work in different domains and solve distinct problems, but they all experience a similar gap between what they want to do and what their software readily lets them do. In countless ways, their programs keep them from turning data into decisions in the time available to them.

This gap is no surprise to professionals in the computing industry. In a recent report from Forrester Research, a firm that assesses the impact of technology trends on business, analysts disparaged as "shovelware" applications "that may be technically appropriate for a task but [practically] of little value to people who actually end up using the application" (Dalton, 2002). Customers, they claim, must demand greater usefulness to break the cycle of software firms rushing to market with applications, selling them "on technical merits as opposed to usability metrics," and "load[ing] them with features" but not with the capabilities "that actually perform for what users really need" (Dalton, 2002).

Software firms acknowledge this problem, and many industry leaders publicly call for software designers to build better tools for complex problem-solving. They urge development groups to de-emphasize functions like delete and sort and "all the things you can do on a keyboard" (Lohr, 2002). Instead designers target the complex work processes that animate users' work and make it creative and meaningful. Findings from many studies support this direction. In one study, for example, results show that when software falls short in "task fit," as it does in the scenarios, that is when it only partially models users' work, lacks functionality for what they want to do, and offers poor support for existing functionality, no amount of additional experience or training with the program helps users do their work effectively (Sutcliffe et al., 2000).

Awareness of less-than-useful software for complex work is an important start. Next, as the scenarios in Part Two showed, interaction designers, usability specialists, and their teams must move from this awareness to tackling many usefulness challenges implicit in creating products problem solvers will truly value. Toward this end, the cases in this section presented relevant orientations for design thinking, methods, and choices.

As they adopt new orientations, many designers and developers often wonder whether their teams can actually create useful designs for complex problem solving. After all, as the medication scenario in Chapter 8 shows, the distance between users and applications—that is, between social and technological systems—can never be fully erased. Yet accepting that we cannot eliminate the socio-technical gap is not the same as believing that we cannot *improve* useful interactions between people and technologies. HCI specialists can achieve improvements for complex problem solving but to do so they must highlight the implications of socio-technical dynamics for specific types of complex problems, help users harness these dynamics, and make software more adaptable to users' domain-based patterns of inquiry.

As Forrester Research analysts note, supporting complex work is more difficult than many software companies have been prepared to admit, let alone tackle, but it is possible and the gains will be groundbreaking. Synthesized from the scenarios in Part Two, three design steps are necessary for making such improvements:

- Orienting design thinking toward usefulness

- Identifying and describing core activities in need of support

- Conceptualizing design for useful support

This chapter succinctly describes these three steps. It aims to provide HCI specialists with a relatively compact overview that they can bring to their teams to motivate new directions for better products.

STEP 1: ORIENTING DESIGN THINKING TOWARD USEFULNESS

Throughout the scenarios in this section, we have seen several conventional orientations to design that lead software teams to create less-than-useful products for complex problem solving. To improve usefulness, design teams need to guard against such orientations and instead adopt more appropriate assumptions. One is that dynamic work is synergistic and cannot be completely formalized. Another is that structural and spatial design strategies are equally, if not more, important than procedural support. Earlier chapters elaborate on these positive assumptions and also expand on productive methods for designing for usefulness in regard to gathering and analyzing contextual data, modeling users' work, and conceptually designing (see Chapters 2 and 3). In this chapter the focus is on additional positive orientations the scenarios revealed, but that have not yet been synthesized. It highlights specific techniques to avoid, as well.

Adopting Appropriate Perspectives and a Shared Vocabulary for Usefulness

Designers need to adopt the view that *open-ended inquiries are coherent, even if not formalizable, and integrated even though indeterminate.* As we have seen in the scenarios, human-computer interaction specialists need to promote design processes with the following orientations:

- Conceptually designing integrated support for integrated models of users' work without leaping to formalistic, object-oriented methods and feature lists

- Helping users work with the socio-technical gap by designing for user adaptability rather than trying to eliminate the gap by formalizing and subsuming discrete parts of problem solving into program tasks

- Encouraging software and user adaptability by including critical domain knowledge and competence and by providing opportunities for users to seed the workspace

- Creating software that gives users a space and place, signposts, and cues to connect knowledge and moves as needed, rather than thinking the software can anticipate and capture all possible approaches in controlled procedures, terminology, and views

- Stressing structural support equally if not more than procedural support so problem solvers see multiple possibilities for proceeding through their work

These orientations are often difficult for software teams to sustain. Teams may lack a shared vocabulary for discussing and coming to agreement about the special requirements of dynamic, open-ended inquiries. As a result, designers resort to discussing users' work and the support it requires in their familiar design terms, leading them, not surprisingly, into old, inappropriate design habits.

The scenarios and discussions in this section presented ways for design teams to converse about software in terms that reinforce the orientations discussed previously. Relevant vocabulary and concepts include the following:

- Interactivity, context, and variability (ICV)

- Patterns of inquiry, task landscapes, enabling tasks, mainline tasks, and choice points

- Domain specificity

- Core data ordeals, wayfinding, and sensemaking for problem solving

- Complex problem solving objectives and processes (such as preparing, planning, querying, analyzing, organizing, and communicating)

- Power, flexibility, and approachability

- Integration, coherence, and completeness

- User adaptability

- Complex problem solving as drama

Shifting to these terms and frameworks is a vital way for design teams to refrain from leaping prematurely to object-oriented design before conceptualizing integrated support for users' practical patterns of inquiry.

Watching For and Resisting "Don't Do's"

As mentioned before, the scenarios in this section have depicted many positive methods and approaches, and these were summarized in earlier chapters, especially Chapter 3. Equally important are the methods and orientations the scenarios depicted that undercut designing for usefulness. Interaction designers and usability specialists need to watch for these "red flag" practices on their teams and actively resist them. These "Don't Do's" include the following:

- Centering primarily on data or even on the main *individual* analytical questions that users investigate instead of practical patterns of inquiry

- Building support primarily for mainline tasks and neglecting many core enabling tasks and choice points that get problem solvers from "here to there"

- Emphasizing a fit between cognitive processing at a unit task and program task level instead of looking at classes of program interactions governed by users' initiatives and problem solving trajectories that can be made ready for users' adaptive moves

- Building consolidated but not *integrated* models of users and their work

- Formalizing models of work without regard to *ad hoc*, opportunistic, or emergent inquiries; work systems in flux; or users' applied expertise

- Treating practice and tools as separate, disconnected entities

- Building in rigid rules and processes without giving users ample leeway to adapt interactions to variability and uncertainty

- Jumping immediately to feature lists, with ranked priorities for discrete items instead of creating models and conceptual designs for integrated open-ended inquiries

- Designing for procedures more than for structures of inquiry patterns

- Focusing on usability and visualization principles without giving priority to usefulness criteria, including users' time constraints

- Designing first for standard aspects of complex problem solving and only later tacking on what is needed for more confounding inquiries

- Deciding that support that is hard to build is outside the "business case" the program addresses

- Avoiding discussions about the political implications of design choices and how certain choices give preference to some interests in users' workplaces over others

Overall, the processes design teams must avoid are those that take a "rational agent" view of problem solving without a sense of its drama and contingency, or those that emphasize logical over situated goals. These inappropriate processes typically take a piece-by-piece approach to support instead of designing for integrated task landscapes within patterns of inquiry shaped by interactivity, contexts, and variability. Moreover, as the troubleshooting and design scenarios in Chapter 4 showed, design teams can be contextually oriented and still take these approaches. None of these approaches is adequate for designing the core support users need for complex problem solving.

STEP 2: IDENTIFYING AND DESCRIBING CORE INQUIRY ACTIVITIES IN NEED OF SUPPORT

Approaching design for usefulness by focusing on users' core inquiry activities involves a range of design tasks. First, design teams must differentiate between types of complex problems and then distinguish which aspects of users' patterns of inquiry are similar across problem types and which vary. From these resemblances and differences, design teams then should identify areas of support problem solvers need in any situation and areas of support that are local to certain problem types and domains. Based on this array of necessary support, design teams can then decide on the core areas to target in their own products, ideally striving to create effective designs for core activities that are inadequately supported in most current applications for complex problem solving.

Differentiating Between Types of Complex Problems

In the scenarios in Part Two, we have seen three distinct classes of complex problems. They are:

- **Divide and conquer or process of elimination:** Troubleshooting complicated problems within highly complex technical systems is an "intervention to an elusive error" problem. Problems are often compounded, entangled, or intermittent. Tier-two and tier-three information technology (IT) analysts reach solutions by eliminating first one potential source of trouble, then another until they locate the origin. Often, in the midst of detecting and locating faults, they quickly assess causes and institute temporary fixes to buy time for more intensive root cause analysis later and longer-term solutions. (See Chapters 4 and 5.)

■ **Constraint optimization**: Merchandisers face a "best option out of many" problem when they investigate and make decisions about an optimal product mix in relation to a fluid and adaptive-market system. They compare numerous attributes and evaluate them against several criteria, which at times may be competing. Mathematical approaches to constraint optimization do not work for these inquiries because analysts do not know from the start all the considerations that will factor into their decisions. As they explore the data they discover insights and strategies and rethink priorities. (See Chapters 6 and 7.)

■ **Clinical intervention**: Dosage decisions are interventions in the workings of the human body, influenced by a complex co-emerging social and technical system of work. Nurses make clinical judgments about medication dosages by correlating and trending multiple drug factors (such as drug interactions, side effects, and therapeutic response over time) and patient variables (including disease state, physiological state, vital sign history, medication history, and absorption and metabolization of drug). They also integrate into these interpretations prior nursing assessments, care plans, lab results, and patients' comments. (See Chapter 8.)

Distinguishing Similar Aspects of Inquiries Across Problems

At a high level, complex inquiries for troubleshooting, product mix decisions, and dosage judgments are similar in terms of sharing uncertainty and the defining traits of complex problem solving as described in Chapter 1. Because they share these general traits, the three different types of problems in the scenarios reveal many common problem solving needs and expectations for support. These similarities in users' needs and approaches to problem solving are listed in Table 9.1.

Given the user experiences described in Table 9.1, designers clearly must support more than the logics of analysis or procedures for mainline tasks. They must also support users' fairly universal tendencies to seed problem and information spaces to account for situational idiosyncrasies; carry out *ad hoc* pursuits; note, find, remind, and communicate insights; and control such resources as time and data. By highlighting similarities across problem

TABLE 9.1
Similar user experiences across problems and domains.

Similarities Across Problems

Reliance on patterns of inquiry: Problem solvers structure problem solving around patterns of inquiry and expect to see these patterns represented in their software.

Inescapable variability: Inquiries are tinged with variability and competing choices due to dynamic environments or the discovery of new strategies mid-stream, with the need for cues and seeding that indicate situational issues.

Nonlinear methods: Problem solvers follow nonlinear investigative paths with varied entry points.

Analysis of diverse information: For open-ended inquiries, problem solvers regard diverse information as an intrinsic good, and they need to manipulate it in numerous ways for thorough and valid judgments.

Chunked tasks as "basic units of work": Practically, people perform their dynamic work at the "basic level" of chunked actions, sometimes requiring parallel efforts such as diagnosis and prognosis or analysis and composition.

"*Adhocracy*": Problem solvers do a great deal of analysis and data transformation on-the-fly, even in straightforward problem cases.

Interlocking issues and incompatible conditions: Inquiries involve networks of issues, the combination of which often results in incompatible conditions that require problem solvers to adapt data and workspaces to the demands of a situation.

Cumulative insights threaten to be unwieldy: Accumulated inquiry results often build to a critical state unless managed and monitored well.

Progressive analyses: Analysis is progressive, and problem solvers persistently turn quantitative data cumulatively into qualitative judgments and communications.

Collaboration and communication: Collaboration and communication are intrinsic parts of complex exploratory analyses.

High stakes: People's success in problem solving is directly tied to their workplace performance reviews. Their problem solving also leads to decisions with significant consequences for people's health, safety, profits, infrastructure of work, and the like.

situations, design teams can maintain a constant awareness of these vital, wide-ranging activities and their consequent areas to support. To determine the content for this support, designers must turn to problem variations, that is, to the user experiences in complex inquiries that are specific to a type of problem and domain.

Distinguishing Varied Aspects of Inquiries Across Problems

Design teams must thoroughly know the domain, patterns, and users of their targeted problem area so they can discriminate between support that can be "vanilla" and support that must be "flavored." Distinct classes of domain-based problems require different types of support. The scenarios have revealed problem- and domain-specific conditions that lead users toward varied approaches to problem solving. These are reviewed in Table 9.2.

These variations require designers to customize support. Yet programs rarely provide such customized support. For example, software commonly omits workspaces for conditioning data or for integrating information based on domain-specific correlations between certain data types, formats, and sources. The result is extensive frustration for users.

Having a thorough understanding of domain-based patterns is an ongoing theme of this book, and it leads to designing for ICV. Central to an ICV approach is recognizing core activities that arise from the interplay of regularity (generalized features) and variability (localized features) and designing to support them.

Identifying Core Support for Core Complex Problem Solving Activities

At present, available software for complex problem solving supports some, even if not all, of users' complex problem solving needs. Many applications are useful, for example, for the following analytical tasks: Seeing overviews and details at the same time, analyzing some data of interest against a larger information context, zooming in and out of views, drilling down, rolling up, analyzing multiple relationships, perceptually encoding data, and arranging them as needed in existing displays.

However, as seen time and again in the scenarios, many aspects of problem solvers' data ordeals, wayfinding, and sensemaking are ignored or underemphasized in software for complex inquiries. The list in Table 9.3 presents the support problem solvers need for their complex inquiries but rarely get. These are core areas of support because they target activities essential to resolving complex problems productively. The support in Table 9.3 is described generally in order to apply to diverse types of problems

TABLE 9.2
Varied user experiences across problems and domains.

Variations Across Problems and Examples

The Locus of a Problem

- In *troubleshooting*, the problem resides in the adaptive complexity of the technical system.
- In *product mix choices*, it resides primarily in the adaptive complexity of the social (market) system.
- In *dosage decisions*, it resides in the convergence of mutually adaptive social and technical systems.

Degree of Complexity in Terms of the Number of Complexity Traits

- *Troubleshooting* lacks the "complexity traits" of no clear stopping point and only provisional solutions because of the underlying physics and electronics of distributed computing.
- *Product mix* and *dosage decisions* have all the traits of complexity.

Degree of Complexity in Terms of Methods, Multifactor Interactions, and Data

- In *troubleshooting* and *dosage decisions*, some inquiries require fairly straightforward, structured methods and multifactor interactions for resolving them end-to-end. These types of problems, however, are still complex because of prevailing uncertainties, ordeals bringing data together, and the number of dimensions considered, and they cannot be solved formulaically.
- *Product mix decisions* have portions of inquiry that are standard, but end-to-end they always involve open, variant approaches due to situational idiosyncrasies and market volatility. Data have numerous dimensions and more varied levels of detail than in dosage decisions.

Dynamic Data Dispersion and Data Integration

- In *troubleshooting*, IT specialists have to look at real-time and historical data, with little control over the format of the real-time data, and they draw on data from numerous network components, often with timestamps out of synch and with some data missing.
- In *troubleshooting* and *dosage decisions*, problem solvers must integrate and correlate data from different tools and databases that are often incompatible because data are shared in a centralized system and co-configured by other tools or by users from different services.

TABLE 9.2
Continued

- In *product mix decisions*, retailers work with far less dynamic data. They download syndicated data and integrate them with proprietary and perhaps enterprise-wide data. They can control formatting and incompatibilities, but such data preparation takes tremendous time and effort.

Risks and Costs and the Time Users Have to Make Decisions

In all cases but with some variation risks are high, and timing influences decisions.

- *Troubleshooting* risks infrastructure collapse and a shut down of company operations. Built-in system redundancy gives analysts some leeway in timing, but the longer troubleshooters spend in analysis without resolving a problem, the more degraded system performance becomes.
- *Product mix choices* risk profitability and competitive advantage. Analysts have more time for resolution than IT specialists or nurses and more leeway to make amends for poor decisions.
- *Dosage decisions* risk patient safety, perhaps even life and death. In crises, nurses have little time to make decisions.

Accountability and Justification for Choices

- In *troubleshooting*, IT specialists' accountability is automatically registered when they investigate an escalated problem or claim a trouble ticket. As they explore trouble spots, they justify their hunches and choices largely for the benefit of collaborators and themselves.
- In *product mix decisions*, analysts deliberately create records of their accountability and justifications. They compose and analyze in tandem to justify their judgments.
- In *dosage decisions*, nurses' accountability is automatically registered through their entries on the electronic and paper medication administration record (MAR). They leave explanations of their decisions and actions through comments.

Success Measures and Extent to Which They Are Contradictory

- *Troubleshooting* is measured by the recovered health of the system and by a reliable performance that meets or exceeds service level agreement. Costs and efficiency factor into evaluations of success as well, as does tacit preferential treatment of certain people or divisions.

TABLE 9.2
Continued

Variations Across Problems and Examples

- *Product mix decisions* have a large variety of success measures, in part because of numerous stakeholders and unpredictable competitor actions. Often outcomes have to satisfy contending criteria and interests.
- *Dosage* success is measured by the patient's health and ongoing care. Efficiency, clarity in record-keeping, and role-appropriate coordination also factor into success.

---

and domains. The exact content and form of the support depends on the distinct function they serve in the inquiry patterns of a specific type of problem and domain.

No one area of this support is sufficient for usefulness if isolated from the other areas. In everyday practice, users' core inquiry activities are

TABLE 9.3
Areas of core support.

Core Support for Complex Problem Solving

Integrating Data

- Easily retrieving and integrating data from different views within and across tools or data sources and making them compatible for analysis
- Easily putting data into the right set of interrelated graphic displays for an inquiry purpose and pattern

Saving and Noting Insights of Interest

- Saving, commenting on, finding and reminding, recalling, and reactivating views of interest
- Reformatting captured views of interest for later personal reference, reporting, or other communication purposes
- Interweaving analysis and composing

Controlling the Meaning of Views

- Controlling the values on which colors are distributed (binned) in color-coding so they accord with investigative intentions and have face validity with external circumstances
- Transforming data on-the-fly by deriving values and creating new groupings and fields
- Creating entry points for new lines of questioning
- Controlling arrangements to highlight complex data relationships

---

TABLE 9.3
Continued

- Keeping the data context visible during complex queries or comparisons

Controlling Analysis

- Conducting complex (nested) queries visually
- Comparing prior and current views side-by-side or making cumulative comparisons at high, low, and mixed levels of granularity
- Knowing what a display means on its own and in relation to cumulative lines of questioning
- Seeing and setting cues, signposts, flags, or weighting for situational issues that influence the problem and its solution processes
- Having the program automatically control some of the higher-order reasoning or calculations that recur in domain-based patterns
- Having leeway to adapt items and events in workspaces and "places" to the demands of work roles, situational factors, and constraints

Navigating Through Inquiry

- Monitoring inquiry progress, including the history of where investigations have been and what they have revealed so far
- Carrying out valued practices of the domain and profession coherently without having to traverse program modules, switch between many modes, or move singly through several features
- Selectively replaying sets of moves that recur in different portions of an inquiry

Collaborating

- Coordinating color-coding and other perceptual cues across tools
- Setting up collaborative workspaces that give users assurances of shared, up-to-date information status, consistency in focal points, and synchronized color-coding across workstations
- Writing data into shared data sources in ways that accommodate other people's likely uses and reconfigurations of the data.

integrated and part of a task landscape. Design teams must not represent required support as a list of separate items or features. Instead, as the scenarios have emphasized, designers need to model the interactive contexts, task landscapes, crossroads, and social and technical processes that shape users' program interactions for dynamic work.

STEP 3: CONCEPTUALIZING DESIGN FOR USEFUL SUPPORT

When design teams create conceptual designs, they must explicitly address how to distribute control between users and the applications—a central question for designing useful applications for complex problem solving. Discussions about control should go hand-in-hand with teams' efforts to brainstorm and decide on effective design choices.

Deciding on How to Distribute Control Between Users and the Application

Regarding control, the scenarios have demonstrated the importance of how users' particular moves and strategies actually *function* in inquiries. Focusing on the practical roles of users' choices, task "chunks," and strategies establishes a different set of criteria for choosing how to assign control from usual design approaches.

Often many software teams' tacit criteria for distributing control are to automate what is easy to automate, let users define preferences that are technically easy to accommodate, and ignore many other user needs that do not fit either of the first two categories. The result is that problem solvers are left to their own devices in addressing some of their core data ordeals, wayfinding, and sensemaking activities.

Clearly, specialists with problem solving and subject matter expertise need real autonomy not just preferences. As experts, they know when and how to make their actions sensitive to situations, when to seed information environments, when and how to turn quantitative data into qualitative judgments, and when the time is right to shift to new levels of detail. They need autonomy in shaping these interactions.

There are a number of tasks in problem solving that should be offloaded to a program. Unfortunately, few guidelines exist to direct designers in these choices about control. One of the biggest unknowns in HCI is how distributions of control compare when it comes to users achieving certain problem solving purposes through particular inquiry processes (Parasuraman et al., 2000). Yet no design questions are more important to usefulness than: What should the software automate or pre-structure? What should it leave for users to control? To what extent? How?

Decisions about distributing control often take the form of debates about the following issues:

- Flexibility versus forced functions

- Familiar consistency versus moving beyond conventional metaphors

- Generic features versus customization

- The "latest and greatest" versus usability improvements for existing features

As guidance, designers should draw on the similarities and variations described in Tables 9.1 and 9.2. These descriptions along with the core support detailed in Table 9.3 imply the higher-order reasoning, situational awareness, and critical judgments that require some degree of freedom on users' parts. Designers also should identify the ways in which costs, risks, accountability, and success measures shape users' approaches to their work, influence their willingness to rely on pre-structured or automated processes, and dictate the reliability and feedback software must provide if users are to trust it.

Design teams' decisions about control inevitably involve evaluating the gains and losses associated with giving users or the program more control over certain interactions. As the following questions detail, designers need to assess whether creating pre-defined methods, views, and terminology is worth users becoming unaware of critical situations. By the same token, human-computer interaction specialists also must evaluate whether too much user freedom leaves domain experts foundering in a problem space with too little coherence. Alongside the questions are examples from the previous scenarios that illustrate how gains and losses stack up for specific troubleshooting, product mix, and dosage needs. Similarities and variations relevant to these decisions are also highlighted.

Does pre-structuring for an eased workload adversely lower users' situational awareness?

In Chapter 6, Anya's visualization program relieves her mental burden by letting her bring in additional variables through color-coding. The color-coding, however, does not aptly represent actual market distributions. To bring true market realities into her analysis, Anya needs her program to give her control over the values defining the color-coding "bins." By not sharing this control with users, the program places limitations on category managers.

Similarities and variations relevant to designing control: Situational variability, locus of the problem, motivation tied to personal performance evaluations

Do automated calculations and other relief from repetitive actions diminish users' critical eye for accuracy and comprehensiveness?

Anya's program automatically calculates the combined market share for all items selected, a calculation that recurs in dozens of her questions. Because it is a straightforward mathematical calculation and computers excel at such things, she does not need a critical eye for accuracy. Thus, the program control provides useful support. (See Chapter 6.)

Katherine's experiences in Chapter 8 are different. Her program does not pre-structure the data she regularly uses, and Katherine's workload would be tremendously relieved by such automation. However, program control should not extend to some types of decision support. To have the program generate a dosage solution could diminish Katherine's accuracy and attentiveness to details.

Similarities and variations relevant to designing control: Regularities and patterns, diversity of data, risks and costs, accountability, degree of complexity in multifactor interactions

Do pre-structuring and program logic for an eased workload undermine the effectiveness and efficiency of users' performance in unintended ways?

In Chapter 8, the physician order entry module in the electronic patient record systems automatically feeds data into the pharmacy in-patient medication software and vice versa. Unintentionally, these interdependent programs increase the workload of pharmacists and doctors because the applications are poorly synchronized. These medical professionals now have to confer about shared entries they do not see compatibly. Similarly, the bar code medication program quickly updates the electronic patient record as soon as nurses scan a drug's bar code with the unintended side effect of causing nurses more work. Because nurses cannot edit the electronic MAR in e-Bar, they have to exit e-Bar and take many seemingly extraneous steps that put distance between them and their immediate nursing goals.

In Anya's case in Chapter 6, the program's automated selection logic makes querying easy for her, up a point. However, when her real world questions push the selection logic beyond the program's limits, she encounters errors and does not catch them right away. When she does, she spends a long time determining what went wrong. The program provides inadequate feedback to Anya, and when left to her own misconceived assumptions, she diverts much time from her task to the tool.

Similarities and variations relevant to designing control: Collaboration and communication, accumulation of interdependent inquiry processes, cumulative findings, personal performance evaluations, dynamism and dispersion of data, success measures

Do pre-defined views and controlled terminology make problem solving more manageable or obstruct users from nonlinear, ad hoc explorations or complete investigations?

The application-performance manager software discussed in Chapters 4 and 5 gives IT analysts fixed views of multiple graphics designed to answer their questions. Yet it does not allow them to reconstruct these views with their own choice of graphics for entry points. Without the right representations of data, they cannot explore issues suggested by emerging insights. In applications for product mix decisions, such as Anya's in Chapter 6, built-in structures obstruct category managers from analyzing and composing at the same time, as they need to do.

In addition, Anya's visualization program pre-structures the views for her analysis, which in many ways positively relieves her of having to think about which graphs are best for her data and analytical purposes. Yet one of the programs does not give her the freedom to create a data table on-the-fly to see details on data of interest, nor can she create a chart to compare sales of all four subcategories proportionally to guide a whole chunk of her inquiry.

Similarities and variations relevant to designing control: Nonlinear paths and methods, parallel efforts, *ad hoc* analysis, interlocking issues, situational variability, chunked actions, accumulation of interdependent inquiry processes, degree of complexity in multifactor interactions

Do built-in work efficiencies cause users to mistrust the program?

In Chapter 8, the bar code medication program builds in medication-delivery time limits for safety and efficiency reasons. Yet without giving nurses an ability to "stop the clock" when needed, the program forces them to cut corners and may prompt union grievances. In either case, they perceive the application as an adversary.

Similarities and variations relevant to designing control: Personal performance evaluations, accountability, success measures

Do multiple options for the sake of flexibility and user control result in inefficient or inaccurate investigations?

In the remote collaboration that Benkei in Chapter 4 plans on having with his colleague in the applications group later in the day, the two troubleshooters will spend a great deal of time making sure their screens display the same view, coloring, and layout. If the screens differ, the accuracy of their joint analysis will suffer. Also, Benkei and Anya both have at their fingertips a good number of low-level options for saving views but none makes their problem solving more efficient by corresponding to their practical, chunked approaches for saving, finding, and recalling perspectives.

Similarities and variations relevant to choices: Collaboration and communication

Similarities and variations can guide design teams in determining trade-offs effectively. They also are essential for identifying design choices for the core support that users need for their dynamic work.

BRAINSTORMING AND DECIDING ON EFFECTIVE DESIGN CHOICES

The scenarios we have examined cover many design strategies and choices for creating useful support, and Table 9.4 summarizes them. This table looks at the core support complex problem solvers need described in Table 9.3 and now categorizes it by problem solving processes. For support required within each problem solving process, Table 9.4 identifies relevant design strategies and choices. The choices detailed in Table 9.4 cross-reference pages or figures from relevant scenario relevant to them.

One benefit of organizing support, design strategies, and choices for usefulness by problem solving processes is that the approach often speaks effectively to software engineers. They recognize and appreciate the roles of problem solving processes in users' inquiries. Consequently, when HCI specialists specify support according to these processes, developers often readily respond to the criticality of this support.

TABLE 9.4
Support based on problem solving processes, related strategies, and choices.

Problem Solving Processes and Required Support	
	Preparing Data for Inquiry
Support users require:	Integrating data:
	Integrate data from diverse sources and format them compatibly.
	Display data in relevant graphics without traversing or working in multiple programs.
	Controlling the meaning of views:
	Transform data on-the-fly
Design Strategies	Create a *wholesale* solution for users to retrieve, integrate, and display data of interest, not numerous separate buttons or tabs to go to numerous data sources.
	Enable users to easily derive values and format data compatibly as shaped by domains and problem types.
	Collaborate with software architects to ensure appropriate data models, data base structures, data transfer.

TABLE 9.4
Continued

	Preparing Data for Inquiry
Design Choices	■ Workspaces and preformatted frames for domain-based data analysis that let users drag and drop data and relevant graphs, write notes, and capture and store outcomes and judgments in an electronic record. (See Figs 5.6, 7.2, 7.8, 8.7, and 8.8 p 193)
	■ User-defined calculations, e.g., through programming by example (See Ch. 7, pp 263-265 and Fig. 7.7).

Querying and verifying

Support users require:	Controlling analysis:
	Conduct complex queries visually
	Have the program automatically control some of the higher-order reasoning that recurs
	Controlling the meaning of views:
	Keep the data context visible during complex queries
	Transform data on-the-fly
	Navigating through inquiry: Selectively replay query moves

Design Strategies	In designing the query paradigm for software, make sure that it accounts for such interrelated support as seeing selected data against the data context, keeping oriented, and restoring just part of previously deleted data.
	Provide visual means for constructing and executing complex queries. Identify and design for various ad hoc transformations that users may need to make in a given pattern of inquiry as part of their querying and verifying.
	Ease users' integrated work by supporting recurrent repertoires of query moves, carefully gauging the amount of

TABLE 9.4
Continued

Querying and verifying
freedom users need. Automatically calculate values that users need regularly as they query and verify for various patterns of inquiry.

Design Choices
- Pre-programmed views specific to domain-based analyses to minimize the amount of users' complex drilling down and up, e.g., multigraph perspectives (See Chs 4 and 6 and Figs 8.5, 8.6, and 8.8)
- Automated weighting of attributes (See Ch 7, p 246)
- Aggregate makers (See Ch 7)
- Macro-building, replaying of moves, or programming by example (see Figs 7.7, 7.8, 7.9, and Ch 7, p 267)
- Pre-structured analysis in a keystroke (See Figs 6.3 and 6.8 and Ch 7, p 263)
- A unified workspace that includes composing capabilities and frames pre-programmed to display data that users drag and drop in graphs meaningful to domain-based analyses. (See Figs 5.6, 7.2, 7.8, 8.7, and 8.8 and p 193)
- Graphics specifically designed for deciding on optimal choices from a large set of possibilities (See Figs 7.4b, 7.4c, and 7.4d)

Analyzing and judging

Support users require:
Controlling analysis:
    Compare prior and current views
    Make cumulative comparisons
    Know what a display means on its
        own and in relation to cumulative
        lines of questioning
    Have the leeway to adapt items and
        events in workspaces and "places"

TABLE 9.4
Continued

Analyzing and judging

as to suit workplace roles, situational factors, and constraints

Saving and noting insights of interest: Interweave analysis and composing

Design Strategies

Provide weighting as a means for users to bring in situational priorities

Provide support for descriptive analysis through views that give side-by-side or overlay comparisons; provide support for cumulative causal analysis through rich, compressed visualizations.

Build in intelligence and user profiling to catch users' (repeated) reliance on misleading familiarity and flag potential missteps because of it.

Provide users the freedom to set the distribution of values in perceptual coding to fit the external realities of their situation.

Know users' domain-based lines of questioning well enough to *identify and create support for contradictory yet unified modes of* thinking (e.g., taking detailed notes and highlighting a high level of judgments)

Design Choices

■ Pre-formatted graphics based on domain-specific analytical patterns that can be combined in a single workspace for side-by-side comparisons. (See Figs 7.1, 7.2, and 7.3.)

■ Rich, compressed visualizations such as trellis views, graphs with an extra y axis, parallel coordinates, "magic lens" overlays, or a custom-designed graphics like for domain-specific

TABLE 9.4
Continued

Analyzing and judging

problems such as Influence Explorer (See Figs 8.6 and 8.7)

- Linked context and drill-down views that can be perceptually coded differently (See Fig 7.1)
- User control over color binning (See Ch 7, p 258)
- Visible explanations for system behaviors and the reasoning behind algorithms (See Ch 7, p 259)
- Built-in intelligence to expect and flag likely misconceptions and errors. (See Ch 7, p 260)
- Annotation mechanisms, including collaborative annotation. (See Figs 7.10, 7.11, and 7.12 and Ch 7, p 275)
- Workspaces that allow for ongoing, concurrent analysis and composing/communicating with the optimal mix of controlled vocabulary and free-text entries when relevant (See Ch 7, pp 273-278, Figs 7.9, 7.10, and 7.11; and Ch 8, pp 327-331)
- Visible prior moves and the events to which they belong (See Fig 7.8)

Managing inquiry

Support users require:

Saving and noting insights of interest: Reformat captured views for later personal reference, reporting, or other purposes.

Save, comment on, and be reminded about views of interest

Controlling the meaning of views: Keep the data context visible during complex queries

Controlling analysis:

Have the leeway to adapt items and events in workspaces and "places" to

TABLE 9.4
Continued

	Managing inquiry
	suit workplace roles, situational factors, and constraints
	See and set cues, signposts, and flags for situations that influence the problem and its solution processes
	Navigating through inquiry: Monitor inquiry progress, including the history of where investigations have been and what they have revealed so far.
Design Strategies	Create designs for saving, commenting on, and recalling that arerobust enough to cover diverse purposes yet approachable enough for users to easily do only what they need for a specific purpose.
	Treat saved views as active resources, not archived items.
	Create a design for saving, commenting on, and recalling that calls forth the functional roles the interrelated actions play in an inquiry pattern, where "obvious candidate" designs are not always best.
	Identify the autonomy vital to users' roles and create support for it, such as being able to "buy time" when needed, to discover if communications for coordinated efforts have been received.
Design Choices	▪ A presentation of saved views that highlights time and chronology, with thematic groupings for ready finding-and-reminding (See Fig. 5.3)
	▪ A fisheye lens approach to see data of interest against a context (See Ch 5, p 190, and Fig. 5.4)
	▪ An interactive time-based presentation of lines of questioning that allows jumping back to specific views,

TABLE 9.4
Continued

Managing inquiry

comparing past and current views, and structuring new data into a set of prior views. (See Figs 5.6, 7.8, and 8.7)

- Entries that fit domain conventions for local and standardized content (See Ch 8, pp 328-331)
- Support for social coordination that closes the loop on all communications (See Ch 8, pp 331-332)
- Ability to suspend time clocks (See Ch 8, pp 332-333)
- Control over notes and documentation at points of care or analysis (see Ch 8, pp 333-334)
- Interactive visualizations and visual macro-builders for user-defined replays of moves. (See Fig 6.5 and 7.8 and Ch 7, p 267).
- Visible prior moves and events to which they belong (See Figs 5.6 and 7.8).

Communicating and reporting

Support users require:

Collaborating:

Set up collaborative workspaces that give users assurances of shared, up-to-date information status, consistency in focal points, and synchronized color-coding across workstations. Coordinate color-coding and other perceptual cues across tools. Write data into shared data sources in ways that accommodate other people's likely uses and reconfigurations of the data.

Saving and noting insight of interest:

Interweave analysis and composing

Comment on views of interest

Reformat views of interest for later

· reporting or other communication purposes

TABLE 9.4
Continued

Communicating and reporting

Design Strategies	Provide quick synchronizing routines for remote collaboration.
	Create adequate cues to signal to other users that relevant data exists.
	Know users' patterns for communicating comments under various conditions to determine when to provide controlled terminology or free-text entries.
Design Choices	■ Mechanisms for synchronizing in-a-keystroke (See Ch 7, pp 263-264)
	■ Annotation mechanisms, including collaborative annotations (See Fig. 7.12)
	■ Built-in email and other mechanisms for sharing comments (see pp. 328–332)

Planning and defining goals

Support users require:	Controlling the meaning of views:
	Create entry points for new lines of questioning.
	Control the values on which colors are distributed (binned).
	Control arrangements to highlight complex data relationships.
	Integrating data: Put data into the right graphic display
	Saving and noting insights of interest later: Find, recall, and reactive views
Design strategies	Give users a space to pause, concentrate, and create their own entry point based on a bounded set of options related to a given pattern of inquiry.
	Provide users optimal control over arranging and laying out data to see relationships relevant to their goals.
	Make potentially relevant views and reminders visible and easily accessible for pursuing and moving between goals.

TABLE 9.4
Continued

	Planning and defining goals
Design choices	■ Mix and match views from which users can choose tied to categories that reflect their analytical strategies. (See Ch 5)
	■ Graphic displays designed for data types and relationships relevant to a liner of questioning (See Ch 5, pp 198-200).
	■ Graphic views that easily adapt to users' arranging and rearranging needs (e.g. tablelens' nested sorting) (See Ch 7, pp 269-271)
	■ A Scopeware Vision™ approach that facilitates finding and reminding (See Ch 5, p 191 and Fig 5.3).

As Table 9.4 shows, many areas of required support and their associated design strategies and choices occur in more than one problem solving process. For example, users need to save and note insights of interest, focus on details and context, and control the values on which colors are distributed when they plan their inquiries, analyze, and communicate or compose reports. Because these tasks function differently for distinct problem solving objectives and patterns of inquiry, design teams need to adapt their strategies and choices accordingly. They need to examine problem solvers' interconnected subpatterns and patterns of inquiry for a particular problem holistically and devise elegant solutions attuned to the diverse functional roles that tasks serve for various purposes. In elegant support, a single solution satisfies many problems. It addresses the largest number of needs with the least complicated design.

CONCLUSIONS

Generating elegant software solutions calls for what the founder of IDEO, David Kelley, and his colleague, Bradley Hartfield, refer to as "designer-engineers" (Kelley and Hartfield, 1996). The "engineering" side of this role involves following a methodology, analyzing problems, and conceiving creative fixes. The design side involves being open-ended and nonlinear, welcoming messiness or ambiguity rather than trying to do away with it, trusting creative leaps, and narrowing down only after "looking at the universe of possible solutions" (Kelley and Hartfield, 1996). Designing elegantly requires this blend of talents. When applied to usefulness issues, this designer-engineer blend of can advance software for complex problem solving considerably.

In addition, design teams need to concentrate on the whole tool—architecture and all—not just user interfaces (UIs). Making good on this requirement is no small feat as it often calls for nothing less than changing the prevailing development model in a software company. In most companies, the prevailing model is to allocate UI design to human-computer interaction specialists and delegate everything "behind" the screen to software engineers and architects. For the purpose of usefulness, however, these boundary lines must become far more permeable. In each scenario in Part Two, problem solvers needed support that exceeds interface designs alone. From the start, usability specialists and interaction designers have to influence the design of architecture, functions, and features. However, in many production contexts, when HCI specialists insist that the interface is the wrong place to begin and strive instead to focus on the whole tool, they venture into turbulent political waters (Norman, 1990). In organizations in which usefulness is not yet at the forefront of product development, attempts to put it there threaten the status quo.

In these situations, one more step is needed. Design teams must gain acceptance from their larger development groups and from their company at large to build usefulness into products from start to finish. As a fitting end to this discussion of how to create more useful software, the last chapter explores the politics of this step of strategically positioning usefulness in the production context.

REFERENCES

Dalton, John. "Packaged Applications Fail the Usability Test." *Forrester Research Technology Strategy Report*, April 2002. Streaming video/audio: *www.forrester.com/ Research/List/Date/1,3767,0,FF.html?selecteddatevalue =April:2002*

Heath, Christian, and Paul Luff. "Documents and Professional Practice: 'Bad' Organisational Reasons for 'Good' Clinical Records." *Proceedings CSCW '96 ACM Conference on Computer Supported Cooperative Work*. Boston: ACM, 1996: 354-363.

Kelley, David, and Bradley Hartfield. "The Designer's Stance." In *Bringing Design to Software*, edited by Terry Winograd, 151-169. Reading, MA: Addison-Wesley, 1996.

Lohr, Steve. "He Loves to Win. At IBM He Did." *New York Times* (March 10, 2002): BU 11.

Norman, Donald. "Why Interfaces Don't Work." In *The Art of Human-Computer Interface Design*, edited by Brenda Laurel, 209-219. Reading, MA: Addison-Wesley, 1990.

Parasuraman, Raja, Thomas Sheridan, and Christopher Wickens. "A Model for Types and Levels of Human Interaction with Automation." *IEEE Transactions on Systems, Man, and Cybernetics* 30, no. 3 (2000): 286-297.

Sutcliffe, Alistair, Mark Ennis, and Jiawei Hu. "Evaluating the Effectiveness of Visual User Interfaces for Information Retrieval." *International Journal of Human-Computer Studies* 53 (2000): 741-763.

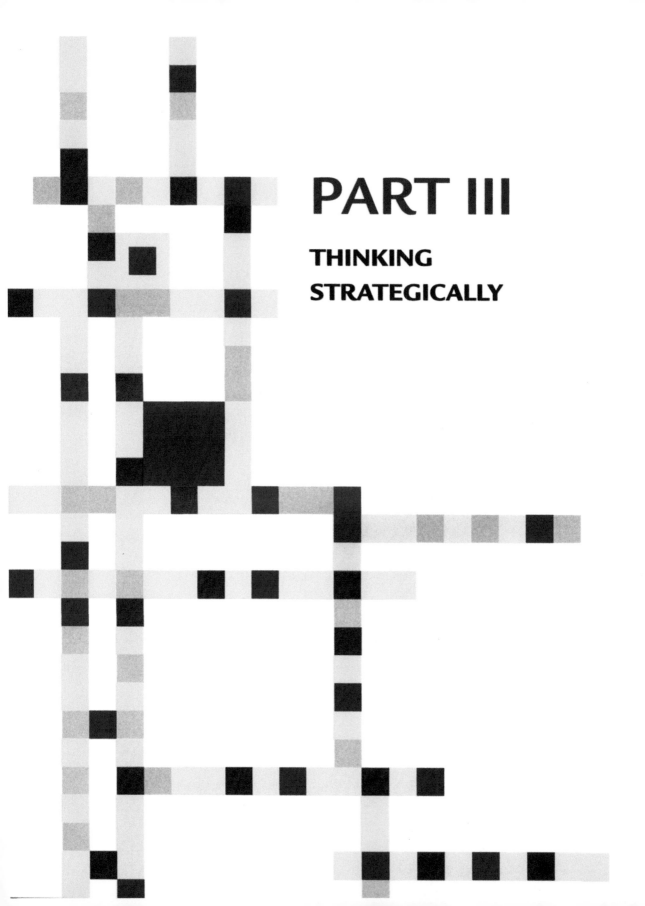

PART III

THINKING STRATEGICALLY

10

Next Steps: Politics and Positioning of Usefulness

The fortunes of usefulness depend as much on social and political maneuvering in a workplace as they do on designers' software and HCI skills and knowledge. For at least 20 years, usability specialists have recognized this political reality and have sought to incorporate usability into critical processes of the product life cycle. Ordinarily, in organizational innovations, when a change such as user-centered design reaches a certain "inflection point," it begins to get institutionalized into an organization (Stryker, 2000). User-centered design, however, has yet to reach this inflection point in most production contexts, even though it has achieved some legitimacy in many of them. Initiatives to design for usefulness continue to face obstacles, notably inadequate resources, programmer resistance, inertia, and exclusion from critical decisions.

No discussion of software for complex problem solving is complete without addressing the politics of institutionalizing usefulness in the production context. Politics refers to how people "put in place a set of relations and practices that more nearly approximate [their] view of the way things should work for themselves and for the organization as a whole" (Thomas, 1994).

As we have seen, designing for usefulness calls for changes that affect many of the structures and processes of a development organization. These changes include the following:

- Giving user-experience analysts a collaborative role with business strategists and marketing experts in defining the business case for a product

- Conducting field studies to observe users performing their actual work in context

- Using field data on users and tasks in context at the start of a project to inform decisions about architecture and functionality

- Modeling and designing for patterns of inquiry and task landscapes and ensuring the conceptual design is right before jumping to task and interface objects

- Designing for integrated tasks rather than discrete lists of features

- Including usability and usefulness assessments in prototype testing and in beta site studies

- Applying usefulness data to plans for the next version of the software

If these practices are not firmly embedded into corporate cultures, they require political moves for getting them integrated, especially when resistance is imminent. Deep structural resistance often occurs and may take many forms. Opponents of UCD changes, for example, may claim that organizational processes or abstract principles are universally accepted and, therefore, off limits to discussion. Or detractors may strive to maintain the status quo by pulling rank, formalizing communication channels, or distributing labor across groups into small, compartmentalized (assembly line) tasks.

To promote usefulness and overcome resistance, usability specialists need to implement wide-ranging strategies on diverse fronts. For example, they may implement renegade initiatives aimed at generating prototypes to prove their vision. They may capitalize on opportunities to unify their expertise with that of allies in other specialized areas to achieve status commensurate with hierarchical rank, and they may advantageously use such organizational formalisms as project schedules and plans, features databases, and requirements documents to better unite usefulness and software engineering.

In the HCI community, discussions about the politics of usability usually focus on obvious areas for promoting usability practices and stress such cardinal rules for gaining political influence as finding a champion or proving usability's return on investment (Trenner and Bawa, 1998). But discussions rarely address what it takes to embed usability practices in many less-apparent work structures in development organizations.

This chapter examines political strategies for these less-obvious areas of development. The discussion assumes that organizations have not yet fully assimilated designing for usefulness into their practices and that in these organizations technical and marketing concerns predominate over user experience. It also assumes that three prerequisite conditions for campaigning for usefulness are in place:

- **Uncertainty:** For the politics of usefulness to succeed, some organizational uncertainty must exist—uncertainty about products, processes, users, competitive advantage, markets, structures, or strategies. Without uncertainty, the changes required for usefulness are unlikely to take root; people will have little reason to depart from the status quo. Uncertainty prompts members of an organization to look for alternatives to whatever they believe is contributing to the uncertainty. Designing for usefulness can fill this role. It can offer an alternative to existing development processes when people begin to doubt whether these processes will lead to a product that users will accept.

- **Uniform vision about designing for usefulness:** To institutionalize usefulness, HCI specialists in the development group must start with a shared, uniform vision about designing for usefulness. Agreement among HCI specialists gives strength in numbers, a fundamental strategy for achieving high "exchange value" in organizations (Lovaglia, 1999). Moreover, in organizations in which HCI professionals are not in powerful positions, disunity among them can harm usefulness efforts. If HCI professionals put forth different agendas, they are likely to vie with each other for scarce resources and recognition. Some wind up getting excluded; others diminish their demands to remain included in the larger conversation. By presenting a united front, HCI specialists avoid such divide-and-conquer outcomes.

- **Strategic organizational outlooks:** The final prerequisite is for usefulness advocates to assume *strategic* outlooks and treat designing for usefulness as an organizational process that does more than institute discrete practices such as user studies or usability testing. As an organizational process, designing for usefulness redefines team compositions, tasks, responsibilities, and relationships. Bringing about such changes is often painfully slow. For example, progress can be inhibited by self-restoring patterns in organizational life that frequently undo supposed gains, and by many changes that seem to promote usefulness but actually have little effect until some threshold is reached based on activities in another dimension of work (Axelrod and Cohen, 1999). Therefore, to institutionalize design for usefulness, usability specialists must capitalize on obvious *and* subtle opportunities. They must become strategically sensitive to situations that do not seem directly relevant to usability issues. As second nature, they must ask strategically: Who controls choices? How are decisions made? Who defines the criteria for what count as valid problems and acceptable solutions? Who is closest to the information and what influence does that confer? How are conflicts resolved, and in favor of what interests?

This chapter looks at four areas of software development that are critical places for strategic, political action. For each of the four areas, I present sample cases, based on actual workplace experiences, as instructive examples. For each case, I examine associated political issues and propose strategic moves for usability specialists to take. The four areas are as follows:

- Creating long-range plans for products and markets

- Determining the scope of the software

- Creating teams, dividing tasks, and communicating

- Formally handling modification requests

CREATING LONG-RANGE PLANS FOR SOFTWARE PRODUCTS AND MARKETS

One reason why organizational leaders create a long-range strategic plan for software products is to mitigate differences that otherwise pull development teams in contrary directions (Carlson, 2000). Consequently, a long-range plan needs to be a stable document. It also, however, must be agile enough to keep pace with the speed of software advancements. Upper-level managers frequently alter company directions in response to changes in markets, customers, or intended product uses. When they do, development may get pulled in contrary directions. At such times, three perspectives increasingly compete for control over decisions and definitions: Development, marketing and sales, and finance.

> Three perspectives increasingly compete for control over Decisions and definitions: Development, marketing and sales, and finance.

- **Development:** Proponents of a development perspective typically stress production processes and quality control. They prefer running one main product line through these systematic processes.

- **Marketing and sales:** People with a marketing and sales bias, in contrast, prefer diversifying. They emphasize a mix of applications in different markets and tie organizational success to knowing how to sell products and find new markets.

- **Finance:** Leaders with a finance perspective emphasize measures of profitability and directions for investment. They think less about specific markets or industries and more about competing firms. Their goal is to increase their company's rank in relation to these large firms. They emphasize the short-term objectives and profits for elevating their company's rank (Fligstein, 1990).

As the following case demonstrates, fluid plans and the surfacing of contending perspectives often result in an opening to position usefulness into the company's processes.

Case: Product Plans and Contested Directions

A commercial visualization software company has progressively written a series of long-range product plans. The first dates back to when the company shifted from selling primarily to original equipment manufacturers (OEM) (designed for software engineers) to making applications for end-users' business intelligence. At the time of this change, the CEO wrote the first product plan to emphasize the need to transform from an engineering-driven to a market-driven company. Despite its market orientation, the plan still reflected an engineering bias in its product definition. Developers were to create two versions of a single type of application: One for non-technical knowledge workers and the other (a "pro" version) for technical experts who would customize the program, as needed. Moreover, Development was to maintain control over decisions about features, priorities, and development processes.

Four months later, the CEO hired a new vice president of product management. This VP immediately issued a broad, new product plan naming ten top projects to pursue. Reactions were mixed. The VP of development preferred the original plan with its two versions of a single product and a straightforward production process. Sensing an opening for their ideas, usability specialists pushed for user-experience studies and a greater say in current development projects.

Soon after, the VP of sales proposed a sales pipeline that gave the product management VP's top ten plan more weight. A week later, the product management VP followed with a now exceedingly detailed business plan. It consolidated the ten projects into three product lines and identified required features, priorities, and schedules.

The VP of development saw the plan as a direct affront. As he saw it, the product management VP had crossed the line between his rightful responsibility for planning and the development group's responsibilities for operational decisions and scheduling.

Ordinarily, the executive team in a closed vote decided whether to approve a product plan. This time, however, the development VP maneuvered for a larger hearing. He scheduled three discussion meetings with participants from all functional areas and made sure each participant had a decision-making vote. During the meetings, the VPs and members of their groups argued vigorously over product priorities and over such issues as who "owned" the category of "developing for interactivity." The situation became so heated that the final-vote meeting was cancelled. Consequently, no product plan was adopted, and the company went without one for eight months in an effort to give everyone time to heal and regroup.

This uncertainty gave usability specialists a chance to promote usefulness to all divisions. Some of these specialists worked through quick and informal means to get their own teams to create new support. Others tailored more formal appeals to higher ups around various development, marketing and sales, and finance perspectives.

At this point, the CEO's finance-oriented perspective led him to emulate product lines of top business intelligence software firms and to strive to turn out a product quickly to attract venture capitalists. Seizing this opportunity to merge the CEO's aims with his own marketing and sales interests, the VP of product management latched onto the CEO's goals and made yet another plan—this time a plan for a "sexier" product line.

He did not formally put the plan in writing, however. Instead, he had the CEO restructure the organization so that the systems engineering, usability, and documentation groups reported to Product Management instead of Development. Now the product management VP had within his department the technical skills and user expertise to develop a modest application for a new product line without Development resources.

In a short time, the first version of the new product was ready for market. However, the VP of development strenuously objected to launching it. It had not gone through all the established production processes and quality control standards "owned" by Development. In response, the product management VP used usability as a "bargaining chip" because both vice presidents valued it. The VP of product management asked if the development VP would agree to the launch if the usability specialists found through on-site, actual use testing that the beta version of the application was ready. The VP of development refused to be pinned down. The usability specialists went ahead anyways and conducted beta assessments for usefulness, and they found a major problem. The product was held up another month for revisions.

In the meantime, the systems engineer wrote a plan detailing the future directions of this product line. Included in this plan were processes for designing for usefulness from the start of a project onward. Usability thus became a central criterion for product release and achieved a primary position in project planning, product definition, and design. The political climate, however, had become so volatile that it was a bittersweet victory.

> The systems engineer wrote a plan detailing the future directions of this product line. Included in this plan were processes for designing for usefulness from the start of a project onward.

Commentary

Executive-level political machinations are usually outside the scope of usability specialists' everyday concerns. However, they significantly affect the role usefulness professionals assume in product development. At one time or another in this example, proponents of the development, product management, and finance perspectives each had control over product strategies and, in each, usability specialists needed to position usefulness advantageously.

During these shifts, usability specialists did not wait passively for the outcome of upper-level planning. Strategically, they presented arguments for usefulness to leaders based on development, marketing and sales, and finance rationales. They customized their appeals, realizing that no single argument would be enough. They were forthright with the various factions and clearly emphasized that, though their appeals to each were different, the objectives they sought unified the interests of all perspectives. Usability specialists amassed allies and instituted roles and development actions that would embed usefulness into product life cycles.

Profession-wide, HCI
specialists need to generate
and share more findings and
recommendations on
usefulness issues.

Usability specialists often have to make convincing cases for usefulness. When usability specialists' own products are still in the conceptual phase, as they were in this case, it helps if they can draw on findings from other similar products and situations. Profession-wide, HCI specialists need to generate and share more findings and recommendations on usefulness issues. Sharing findings across the field will advance the institutionalizing of usefulness in many sites.

Based on this case, strategies for promoting usefulness during shifts in long-range planning include those in the following chart.

STRATEGIES FOR PROMOTING USEFULNESS AMIDST FLUX IN LONG-RANGE PLANS

- Recognize when department biases vie for dominance and how they evoke changes in long-range plans and processes
- Pursue opportunities by customizing appeals and proposed actions to each perspective, gaining allies in each
- Work in parallel to make these appeals and to informally gain the needed improvements in the product
- Run usefulness assessments in parallel with other aspects of beta testing, and look for improvements required for the next version of software
- Turn allies into champions who can represent usefulness in long-term strategic planning processes and who can write usefulness practices into road maps for the next versions
- Share successes and failures so usefulness advocates in other situations can draw on them when evidence from their own project needs additional support

The planning of products and markets described in this case leads directly into defining the scope of software applications. As the next case shows, for usefulness purposes, usability specialists have many political maneuvers to conduct on the software-scope front.

DETERMINING THE SCOPE OF THE SOFTWARE

Scope setting often falls outside usability specialists' spheres of influence because, in many workplaces, user-experience analysts do not enter the development process until after the scope of a software project is defined. Usability specialists may participate in some brainstorming sessions for product scope but usually not as prime decision makers. The trouble with this lack of influence is that when user experience analysts head to the field to gather data on users and tasks, they discover significant mismatches between the pre-set scope and people's actual approaches to their work in context. Usefulness requires that the work supported by a program be in sync with users' notions of the inquiry patterns that bound their work. Usability specialists need to make sure user-experience findings figure into this definition.

In most software companies, almost anyone *other* than usability experts defines scope: Marketing specialists, business strategists, account managers, product managers, system engineers, or other technology leads. Later, should user studies uncover troubling mismatches between program and user models of work, software teams often redefine users and occasions for use to fit the scope, rather than re-conceiving the scope to fit users.

Scope is one of the most significant decisions for usefulness. Defined early, it sets the course of designing for usefulness by tacitly determining what design problems and solutions are open or closed to future consideration. To build usefulness into software, usability specialists must have a say in setting the scope during the business-case phase of a project. This seemingly slight change can have a large effect, potentially altering many habitual procedures, reconfiguring authority, and revising criteria for deciding on product definitions. In organizational politics, these are significant and contentious changes.

The following example shows usefulness advocates bringing about important changes in defining the scope of a product.

> To build usefulness into software, usability specialists must have a say in setting the scope during the business-case phase of a project. This seemingly slight change can have a large effect, potentially altering many habitual procedures, reconfiguring authority, and revising criteria for deciding on product definitions.

Case: A Champion at the Right Time and Place

In a mid-sized company that develops financial software, a project manager and usability specialist find themselves together for the fifth time now on a new application team. From their prior joint experiences, the two have come to share a vision and commitment to usefulness that few in their organization hold.

Because the application on which the two colleagues will now work is the first in a new product line, they agree that it presents a perfect opportunity for making usefulness a top priority. But processes are already in place that threaten to block this goal. Marketing requirements and the product definition and scope have already been set, without considering usefulness.

Nevertheless, the project manager and usability specialist start by making a case to the head of development to treat the already-set requirements as tentative and contingent on the application team gathering and analyzing user needs and tasks through field studies. After long discussions, the head of development agrees and takes it upon himself to obtain consent across divisions. The project manager then revises the initial schedule to build in time first for immediate user studies and then for application team discussions about findings. To follow this process, she writes into the schedule a meeting with Product Management to negotiate priorities and, if necessary, revise the product scope. Only after these steps have occurred does the new schedule make time for conceptual designing.

To gain buy-in for this approach from the rest of the software team, the project manager enlists the team's system engineer, usability specialist, lead developer, and herself for two weeks of user studies and contextual observations. The usability specialist quickly trains the group in conducting these observations, and they collaboratively gather field data, analyze them, and present findings with scenarios to the rest of the team.

> To gain buy-in for this approach from the rest of the software team, the project manager enlists the team's system engineer, usability specialist, lead developer, and herself for two weeks of user-site visits for contextual observations.

At the meeting to review findings and scenarios of use, the team as a whole specifies many high-level requirements, detailing the categories of users' work, associated tasks, and required support. This document has some overlap with the initial product scope, but it includes other needs and directions, as well. It provides the basis for the meeting with the product manager.

The project manager chairs this subsequent meeting. Through lengthy deliberations, the product manager, usability leader, and system engineer each rank the items in the requirements document based on their respective points of view. This cross-functional group then collaboratively assesses these rankings and negotiates an acceptable scope. The application team's design team can now clarify the design, create prototypes, and move to more detailed requirement specifications.

Commentary

In this case, the shared vision and experiences of the project manager and usability specialist created deep bonds that pay off for usefulness. Informally, these two teammates used scheduling, task naming, team buy-in, and influence across divisions to succeed in getting usefulness built into the product's scope.

The project manager and usability specialist drew on their prior experiences together and on their previous slow-but-steady advances in usefulness on earlier projects to make a credible case to the head of development.

When the opportunity arose, the head of development agreed to treat the pre-defined scope and marketing requirements as provisional. Politically, finding such a champion was indispensable. Innovations take hold best when someone acts as a point of passage between the organization at large and the people initiating change (Thomas, 1994). These champions must be skilled in turning friction into creative debates and finding collaborative solutions for the good of the product and the company as a whole.

The right timing was crucial, and the project manager and usability specialist negotiated effectively while the design path was still open for redirection. They brought in the right communications and coordination at a phase when the project would not get slowed down. The project manager also used her control over naming team tasks and scheduling to make room for contextual inquiry and to recast what counted as acceptable information for defining the scope of the software. In the meeting with the product manager, these criteria carried weight because usability had a vote equal to that of marketing and technology requirements.

This case suggests various strategies for making usefulness an influential force in setting the scope of an application, which are listed in the following chart.

> Innovations take hold best when someone acts as a point of passage between the organization at large and the people initiating change (Thomas, 1994).

STRATEGIES FOR PROMOTING USEFULNESS IN DECISIONS ABOUT SOFTWARE SCOPE

- Cultivate relationships that produce small incremental gains for usefulness practices

- Introduce initiatives with the right timing so change does not interfere with meeting deadlines

- Manipulate tasks and schedules to structure user-experience studies from the start and justify the investment of time and resources

- Call meetings with people to share evidence about scope problems and arrive collectively at solutions

- Create partnerships with marketing and business specialists by providing them with information about how people will use the product—information that becomes equal in weight to marketing and technical information in defining the product scope

As these past two cases stress, a vital target for usability specialists' political influence is the conceptualizing of software plans and scope. Equally important are processes for implementing these plans. As the next case shows, the direction of implementation hinges greatly on team composition, task differentiation, and communication across workgroups, all of which often become politically charged issues.

CREATING TEAMS, DIVIDING TASKS, AND COMMUNICATING

Groups must believe that improving product for greater utility depends on doing things in new ways, not just doing what they already know better.

As we saw in the product plan example, usability specialists must make compelling cases for usefulness to the *many* groups that contribute to software planning, production, and sales. Ideally, usability specialists become irreplaceable to these groups because they are closest to information on users, their practices, and requirements (Casson, 1997). In any organization, two of the most important sources of power are having such irreplaceable knowledge and being connected to the workflow of several units (Scott, 2001).

But usability specialists cannot tap these sources of power unless the various workgroups recognize user and task knowledge as invaluable to their efforts and structure usability specialists into their core processes. Valuing usefulness information depends upon workgroups attaching importance to variety. Groups must believe that improving products for greater utility depends on doing things in new ways, not just doing what they already know better. To generate this commitment to variety, usability specialists have to negotiate some of the most fundamental structures and processes of a workplace: Team composition, task differentiation, and communication practices across groups. The following case shows an example of such negotiations.

Case: Formal and Informal Routes to Usefulness

In a visualization software company that creates solutions for fraud detection and prevention in banking, insurance, and healthcare, development groups are divided into several teams. Core teams build the technologies used by all applications across industries, and custom teams adapt core technologies to the demands of specific domains. For a program currently being developed for insurance, the main teams include the following:

- The core architecture team

- The core data visualization team

- The core "platform" team that produces the generic "container" that holds the visualizations and provides data access, toolbars, menus, controls, and functions

- The custom insurance team that designs and develops the application for insurance fraud analysis

In this software company, usability specialists function as "content" specialists and are on every custom application team. Core teams, by contrast, have no usability specialists and are composed exclusively of software engineers. Members of the core teams seek usability specialists' opinions about such issues as legibility, phrasing, background colors, or cursor symbols, but they do not include them in official decisions about design and development. In this company, the unspoken rule is that core technologies drive applications rather than the other way around. The result is that more often than not invention is the mother of necessity (Arksey, 2001). Necessity becomes the mother of invention only when implemented applications prove they need user-driven improvements.

At present, however, this unspoken rule has less of a hold on the development group than it used to. Disappointing sales over the past three quarters signal that something is amiss. Seeing an opportunity for change, the usability specialist on the insurance application team begins to campaign for modifications in the core platform. User studies show that in fraud detection, insurance company users need to bring bookmarked data back "live" from an earlier phase of investigation and need to call up the bookmarked view while viewing different data. The current platform offers neither a "live" recall of bookmarks linked to current views nor a static recall that can display data and view states, content, and properties that are different from the current display. The usability specialist wants the platform team to modify bookmarking so it has these capabilities. This request is met by strong resistance from the platform's lead developer.

The usability and platform leaders meet in the insurance team's war room and discuss the issue for two hours. The platform leader allows that the user findings are important and even seems moved for a moment by evidence that fraud analysts make inaccurate assessments that adversely affect business decisions when they cannot recall bookmarks as they want. In fact, he praises the cause of usability and encourages the usability specialist to continue her efforts to improve the software. Nonetheless, he refuses to change anything. He requires more data, he says. His hunch is that once the product is launched users will make do and find a way to do what they need. Before considering changes, therefore, he wants to wait for outcomes after a couple versions of the product are already in the market, with data collected from numerous sites and hundreds of users. He justifies his caution on the grounds that the enhancements are difficult to do and require coordination with core graphics changes. They also take time because they have to be scriptable, a top priority for the platform team.

> The unspoken rule is that core technologies drive applications rather than the other way around. The result is that more often than not invention is the mother of necessity.

The meeting ends, and the platform leader has not budged in his position. The next day he formalizes it by issuing a white paper in which he justifies the rationale for the platform and claims these rationales as accepted truths in the larger world of platform technology.

Now realizing that she had better pursue alternate routes, the usability specialist turns to a developer on her team who is a strong proponent of usefulness. Having formerly worked on both the core graphics and platform teams, this developer is an expert with the code in both areas. Together the developer and usability specialist gain the approval of their team to redesign the platform themselves and to build a quick version of it for the needs of insurance company users. Their goal is to create a platform that does enough of what insurance users need but do not currently get from the existing platform to prove it can be done and is needed. They decide to risk conflict by bypassing the platform leader in an effort to generate a concrete creation that, if successful, can establish their case with the development group as a whole.

The insurance team regroups for new development processes and roles. The team meets daily in a dedicated "war room." The developer and the usability specialist lead them in quickly developing prototypes. The usability specialist takes the prototypes to the field and brings back findings that lead to revisions and new prototypes. The teammates repeat this process until they reach their goal.

The usability specialist forges alliances on other fronts, as well. She finds that the system engineer in charge of the features database and the senior developer who makes decisions about modification requests and enhancements are receptive to restructuring the features database around problem solving processes. Together, the three collaborate on this new database structure and also create new criteria for setting priorities in modification requests, criteria based on complex problem solving requirements. These new criteria make it possible for usefulness to become a prime consideration in software modifications and requirements without needing buy-in from specific team leaders.

In the meantime, the insurance team finally evolves a successful prototype with users. The team presents it to the development group and is praised for it. The platform leader, now interested due to the proven feasibility, even goes so far as to set up a meeting with the insurance developer to go over the code he used for the prototype.

Commentary

In this case, the usability specialist was closest to information about users and shared it with the platform team, but the information alone had no political clout. Exclusively composed of software engineers, the core platform team members thought in unison about their objectives and programming priorities and that unison placed a low priority on user demands. They prized scriptability for the functionality it offered to the users they knew best: Other developers in charge of local adaptations. As far as the platform leader was concerned, the usability specialist's role as "content specialist" did not extend to the platform where generic design criteria, such as scriptability, modularity, reusability, and maintainability, prevailed. Moreover, organization-wide the division of tasks into core and custom activities unintentionally led to programs that oversimplified users' complex work.

The division of tasks into core and custom activities unintentionally led to programs that oversimplified users' complex work.

The platform leader used classic political strategies to resist. He used rank to bar the gate. He gave the illusion of flexibility by praising usability as a "good," but on a deeper level he made sure his interests and control were secure by defining what should count as adequate evidence for taking action to redesign. His follow-up white paper added extra resistance. He communicated through a formal, finished document rather than through a more open document or interpersonal discussion coordinated with other groups' work. He laid claims to indisputable, long-held "objective truths" in the programming profession and emphasized their legitimacy over the demands of usefulness.

He laid claim to indisputable, long-held "objective truths" in the programming profession and emphasized their legitimacy over the demands of usefulness.

In the face of these "truths," the usability specialist recognized that in times of uncertainty, even purported truths are suspect to more people than their purveyors assume, and when they are, expert knowledge vital to production tasks often trumps rank (Bell et al., 2000). She drew on the insurance team developer's expertise in the code of the graphics and platform, and on her own expertise about user needs, and they pooled them in a renegade effort to circumvent structural barriers. Renegade efforts often launch innovations in organizations because they produce convincing proof that usability findings alone cannot provide (Thomas, 1994; Agre, 1997).

The war room gave this renegade team the negotiation space required for innovation efforts (Law and Callon, 1995). Team members established other informal structures to promote innovation, as well. They enlarged their roles, relocated control of the platform to the application team, met daily, and decentralized decision processes (Scott, 2001). These efforts showed that advances are possible when invention springs from necessity.

The usability specialist also pursued efforts through formalized routes. She worked collaboratively within established channels to organize the features database, structuring it by the functions that features played in users' complex problem solving processes. She also worked to have

The prototype became the
persuasive tool for an
alternative platform, and the
language of problem solving
became the tool for
conceptualizing projects.

problem solving needs become part of the criteria for deciding on fixes and enhancements. In stressing problem solving processes as organizing schemes, the usability specialist went beyond affecting database structures and the priorities for modification requests. She also put problem solving language in a central role in the front end processes of all projects: Product definition and scope. The prototype became the persuasive tool for an alternative platform, and the language of problem solving became the tool for conceptualizing projects.

The usability specialist and insurance developer pursued innovation in ways that risked conflict between the insurance and platform teams. They gambled that the experimental platform would prove effective and win company support. In promoting innovations for usefulness, advocates must address the potential conflicts connected to their strategic moves. To maintain stability, they need to build in checks and balances and latch innovations onto existing structures and processes, just as the usability specialist did with the features database and modification requests.

As seen in this case, strategies for promoting usefulness include those in the following chart.

STRATEGIES FOR PROMOTING USEFULNESS AMIDST UNRECEPTIVE STRUCTURES OF WORK

- Present data on users' demonstrated needs or return on investment, but also have alternative strategies if the information does not yield desired outcomes

- Recognize resistance on a specific front and mobilize resources on alternate fronts

- Counter a veneration of long-held "truths" that keep inflows of user information at bay with proof of the advantages of looking outward to other relevant sources

- Find areas where expertise and information can exert more influence than institutionalized authority

- Use working prototypes as concrete persuasion for innovation

- Secure workspaces to conduct face-to-face team activities

- Balance renegade efforts with established formalized processes

- Institute the structures and language of users' problem solving into every phase of program development

In this case, the usability specialist's strategy of collaborating with the senior developer in charge of modification requests highlights this area of change control as another realm in development critical to usefulness but often ignored in the politics of usability literature. It is also perhaps one of the most difficult areas for usability specialists to influence in terms of getting usefulness requirements elevated to a high priority.

FORMALLY HANDLING MODIFICATION REQUESTS

In software companies, systematic modification request (MR) processes help to assure the integrity of development projects and the quality of the products. When time and resources are in short supply, projects must have as few surprises as possible in anticipated development tasks, including fixes and enhancements. Systems for modification requests typically include classifying proposed fixes and enhancements by severity level and giving precedence to those that involve emergency problems, regulatory standards, industry standards, and interface conformity. Requests related to usability and usefulness usually rank lower and are often grouped with technical advancements and other less-pressing improvements. To keep MR processes stable, development groups are slow to alter criteria for deciding which requests get priority.

Despite this conservatism, usability specialists have made great strides in getting usability criteria instituted into MR decisions. Most MR committees today consider usability needs along with other criteria such as development costs, benefits to customers, conformity to conventions, and compatibility with upgrades in interdependent systems. Many MR committees also formally consult with people who submit such requests before making decisions. Together, they analyze the effects of changes and create specifications for modifications. Politically, it is often easier to get committees to institute usability criteria and such consultative practices than it is to get them to include usability specialists in the inner circle of decision makers.

MR committees are often made up of people from diverse specializations, including usability and documentation, but the main decision makers usually are technical experts with technical interests and priorities. Historically, MR decision-making has resided with software engineers, and the political force of this precedent adds to usability specialists' difficulties in getting a seat at the decision-making table.

To promote *usefulness*, usability specialists need to have decision-making roles in regard to MRs. Usability criteria—good as they are—do not necessarily serve usefulness well. Rather than focusing on integrated

To promote usefulness, usability specialists need to have decision-making roles in regard to MRs. Usability criteria—good as they are—do not necessarily serve usefulness well.

support for complex problem solving, MR decision makers typically respond to usability requests through one-by-one, low-level changes, such as adding a capability to save user settings in one particular field. To dramatically improve problem solving usefulness, however, MR committee members must either focus on daisy-chained features or more likely on an all new elegant modification. For software engineers, these shifts in design thinking and habits are significant, and the best HCI position for bringing them about is from the inside, at the decision-making table. As the following example shows, achieving this position at the table is difficult because MR decision-making is often more impenetrable than it seems.

Case: Vote Early, Vote Often, But Notice Who's Counting

In a corporate information technology (IT) division of a hospital conglomerate, application teams develop software used by member medical centers. Each software product has its own modification request committee, composed of product team members. For a medication administration application, the MR committee includes the system engineer, two developers, software architect, nursing informatics specialist, and pharmacist who helped develop it.

When this medication-administration software was designed, the nursing and pharmacy experts were practicing professionals in a member hospital and served as surrogate users and subject matter consultants to help model the application. Because they were experienced in the field, they never felt compelled to watch actual users. As development evolved, they found they gained status with developers by talking about user-centered improvements in programmatic terms. For example, instead of discussing what users wanted to do in their work, such as knowing when a patient with asthma was scheduled for treatments, they talked in terms of needing to query the scheduled patients and sort by condition. The shift may be slight but the effects were critical. The focus became program functions, and the application team specified functions before looking in an integrated way at what users really wanted to accomplish. This group has since evolved into a technically oriented team, which is reflected in the name of its MR committee: The engineering change request (ECR) committee. [Note: My thanks to James Gutierrez (2002) for providing this example.]

The nursing informatics expert and pharmacist never returned to the trenches in their medical centers and instead took full-time positions in the IT corporate division. Now they spend a good deal of time deciding on changes in the ECR committee. The committee solicits improvements from liaisons from various hospitals who represent clinical users and technical support staff at their sites. The liaisons have backgrounds in medical informatics and usability and report software problems experienced by doctors, nurses, pharmacists, and IT staff.

The ECR committee wants to convey a user-centered image and continually tells liaisons that users' needs drive decisions about changes. Committee members make decisions in private, however, and do not consult with authors of requests. They keep liaisons posted about decisions through monthly status reports.

Recently, liaisons have been growing dissatisfied with the ECR group's processes because the group has been tabling numerous requests. To assuage liaisons, the ECR committee holds a conference call with them. In it, the liaisons repeat their main requests to the ECR committee and explain their importance. Committee members respond evasively, saying the range of requests is large, resources are scarce, and not all MRs can be realized within the next version. The liaisons press further. They ask the committee for ways to get their particular users' interests heard and problems answered in this situation.

At this point, the ECR committee gives them a direct answer: Find out across hospitals which problems users share. Then join together and write the same ECR for it. "Flood us with ECRs," the committee urges. "We listen to numbers."

> "Flood us with ECRs. We listen to numbers."

Many liaisons are placated by this response; they are happy to have a strategy in hand for influencing ECR decision-making. One nursing informatics specialist, however, is still not satisfied. He wants stronger influence over usability issues. He proposes that usability specialists from each hospital send the ECR committee monthly findings from usability tests and that the committee use these findings, along with requests, to make ECR decisions. He stresses that the findings would bring the ECR committee in touch with what is actually happening in the field, an important factor for ECR decisions.

The committee members balk at this proposal. Privately, it threatens their prerogatives. In response, they justify their current criteria and processes, emphasizing that the expertise and practical experience of the two nursing and pharmacy committee members are more than sufficient for understanding users' needs.

Commentary

This case illustrates a strong organizational tendency: People in control resist change, especially in processes vital to project stability. In the ECR case, production stability was just one of many political issues involved in maintaining or changing the ECR processes and criteria. Also at stake were ECR committee members' identities, status, job design, expertise, and authority. During the conference call, to decrease liaisons' dissatisfaction and diffuse its threat to their own power, ECR members offered surface-level "participatory democracy." They advised liaisons to band together for greater representation and influence. But on a deeper level, committee members retained exclusive rights to expertise. They guarded ownership over criteria for judgments and autonomy over how to count the votes, and they held fast to closed-door decision-making.

The heterogeneous composition of the committee might suggest a good representation of users' interests. But the group had been together long enough to have grown uniformly technical, and they leaned toward "groupthink." The nursing informatics expert and pharmacist had initially joined the group to further the goals of user-centered design. In such cross-functional groups, usability specialists are influenced by the array of contending worldviews, priorities, and interests of their teammates. Potentially, this experience can advance the cause of usefulness because it enables usability specialists to frame their own ideas in the language and frameworks of alternate perspectives. In this ECR committee, however, the nursing and pharmacy specialists grew removed from users' actual work in the field. When the dissenting liaison proposed a new information process, the ECR committee gave priority to its own group processes for exchanging information. It chose to guard the decision-making process from disruption.

Modification-request procedures remain *the* procedures because people— even dissatisfied liaisons— ultimately consent to them.

This example is not a success story. Organizations hold fast to established change processes. MR procedures remain *the* procedures because people—even dissatisfied liaisons—ultimately consent to them. Social norms uphold these procedures as appropriate for the good of the product and the organization. In this case, the lone objection expressed by the remaining discontented liaison did not introduce enough doubt or inspiration to disrupt the legitimacy conferred on ECR processes. Rather, this dissenter pushed participatory democracy too far, and the ECR group resisted. Amidst these dynamics, gaining access to decision-making power becomes a long, drawn out process.

The proprietary nature of MR processes and criteria in this case are not unusual. Breaking into the inner circle frequently requires usability specialists to incrementally maneuver on numerous fronts, often in ways that are not directly tied to MR issues. To promote usefulness in MR processes, usability specialists need to implement the strategies shown in the following chart.

STRATEGIES FOR PROMOTING USEFULNESS IN MODIFICATION-REQUEST DECISIONS AND CRITERIA

- Influence MR decision makers to treat required improvements for users' integrated patterns of inquiry in unified "chunks"

- Strive for meaningful inclusion, which involves a say in decision-making criteria, access to deliberations, and recognized expertise that inspires action

- Question resistance when it rests on claims that established procedures or formalities are out of bounds for reinvention and instead shift attention to concrete realities and necessary usefulness remedies

- Work on several fronts with diverse allies—often unrelated to MRs directly—to gain the position and visibility required for assuming a role as an MR decision maker

- Become a core member of MR committees, equal in voice to marketing and engineering, or have an influential champion at the table

The lack of success in this MR case does not diminish its instructiveness for the politics of usability. As with the other cases, successful or not, it reveals how forces line up in workplaces to shape how much usability specialists can maneuver for innovation, on what diverse fronts, and with what alliances. Taken together, the four areas of development discussed in the cases bring to light important insights about the politics of usability.

POLITICAL POINTS FOR PROMOTING USEFULNESS

To effectively institutionalize usefulness, usability specialists must be skilled in reading subtexts and listening to the political timbre of a situation. These skills allow them to understand situations and apply appropriate strategies. The strategies related to the cases in this chapter are not cardinal principles for usability specialists to apply with guaranteed results. Nor are they meant to be all-inclusive. Some important issues are not addressed, such as the politics of resource allocation, return on investment, or planned improvements for next versions. What the strategies do provide, however, is a wide range of maneuvers that usability specialists should use as a situation demands.

Use varies with circumstance, but points made in the previously discussed cases provide frameworks for employing these strategies. To maneuver advantageously, usability specialists should apply the following points about the politics of institutionalizing usefulness to their situations:

- **Conceptualizing makes a difference:** How software is conceptualized early in a project influences the rest of the product's life cycle. Focusing political strategies and efforts on the early product concept is critical. When organizational structures exclude usability specialists from early planning, specialists need to find opportunities and take the initiative.

- **Conflict is inescapable:** Innovations for usefulness disrupt many workplace processes and can threaten some people's status, turf, security, and job designs. Far from being some "evil" to avoid at all costs, conflict is an inherent part of growth and improvement. It is a gamble in any initiative that introduces innovation. Usability specialists must prepare for this risk with plans for dealing with it.

- **Timing can change the character of events:** In analyzing the politics of an ongoing situation, usability specialists must be sensitive to timing. Within a sequence of events they must assess the amount of disruption that the production context and product schedule can handle and where, when, and how interventions for usefulness are most likely to be accepted. The right strategies carried out at the wrong time can cause long-term setbacks to the cause of usefulness.

- **Variation is necessary for innovation, if coupled with checks and balances:** An inescapable organizational tension exists between exploring new ways and maintaining accepted practices, many of which are crucial to stability and continuity. Efforts to design for usefulness benefit from exploration and variety, but not if strategies for institutionalizing them bring about a dysfunctional organization. To avoid such disorder, the value of some existing processes must be recognized. Systematic processes of quality assurance, for example, rarely should be tossed aside.

- **Beware of "truths" and ownership of criteria:** How objections to usefulness innovations are framed does not necessarily reveal true motives, especially when these motives involve a desire to retain identity, status, control, and resources. Frequently, the more threatened opponents feel, the more they express their objections in terms that do not directly voice resistance. Typically, they uphold standard practices and deeply held organizational beliefs as inviolate, claiming that abstract principles, rules, or precedents justify current organizational practices.

They shift conversations from content to process to deflect inquiries into any realities that may jeopardize their turf or status. They treat their positions as "truths" rather than value-laden expressions of their interests. They defend these positions by calling on some greater good, such as organizational stability or loyalty, and they lay claim to the privilege of defining what counts as a problem, a valid solution, adequate data, or acceptable grounds for action. Usability specialists must recognize these strategies and know when the results of letting them pass are worse than actively resisting them. When appropriate, usability specialists must push workmates and stakeholders to examine and reconsider such objections.

- **Opportunities call for running many strategies simultaneously:** Institutionalizing usefulness calls for political strategies that address many issues at once in varied contexts. This multiplicity is necessary because many influences contribute to the processes and interdependencies that need to change. These numerous forces can merge in complicated ways and evoke dynamics that do not neatly arrange themselves into opportunities and strategies. For the same situation, usability specialists often need reactive *and* proactive strategies, renegade *and* mainstream methods.

- **Knowledge is power:** In light of evolving markets, software companies need continuing information about the uses to which programs are put. Usability specialists provide this information. When usability specialists are skilled in collecting and communicating this information efficiently, they establish roles for themselves that can exert influence greater than rank. Many developers achieve a similar type of expert influence by virtue of being versatile in many elements of program and program library coding. For usefulness, some of the most influential alliances are those between usability specialists and these expert developers.

When usability specialists are skilled in collecting and communicating this information efficiently, they establish roles for themselves that can exert influence greater than rank.

As these points suggest, the politics of usability must be part of the initiatives described throughout this book to build usefulness into design thinking, methods, and software choices. Together, political and design efforts provide what is needed to institute usefulness into products of complex problem solving.

LOOKING AHEAD: A STRATEGIC PROGRAM FOR USEFULNESS

As established early in this book, the first step in creating more useful software for complex problem solving is for the software industry to treat these applications as a distinct development category requiring their own approaches. At present, because the demands of this class of programs get insufficient attention, many applications in the market impose support for well-structured tasks when, in fact, users want to use them for dynamic and open-ended work. When software teams recognize software for complex problem solving as a distinct class, designing for usefulness becomes primary. The challenge is to create useful support for problem solvers' patterned work in which inquiries are bounded yet emergent, and rarely repeat themselves in the exact same way twice.

HCI specialists must urge development groups to build useful software for complex problem solving. Designing usefulness into software for complex problem solving will change design practices, organizational structures, and processes. Throughout this book, I have explored the nature of these changes and the directions in which human-computer specialists and their co-workers should navigate through them.

Advocates of usefulness should motivate teammates to see the shortcomings of many conventional assumptions and models of users' work for the demands of dynamic and emergent inquiries. They must urge teammates to replace approaches relevant to well-structured tasks with those that treat users' complex work as synergistic, adaptive, nonlinear, and intellectually sophisticated. HCI specialists need to discover users' actual patterns of inquiries by observing them in the field. From observations, they need to create integrated and consolidated models of users' patterns of problem solving, models that account for the interactive conditions across contexts that shape users' actions. Interaction designers and their teammates must model tasks for the range of problem solving processes that occur in a pattern of inquiry, capturing the variability and regularity in sensemaking, wayfinding, data ordeals, and choice points that move users closer to achieving their inquiry goals.

These models must inspire teams to build integrated support in the software with the power to accommodate the complexity of users' explorations. Applications also must be adaptive, approachable, and cue relevant variables. Moreover, they must signal to users the structure of their domain-based investigative patterns while still giving them leeway to take unexpected routes. To create useful designs for complex problem solving, software teams must pursue creative approaches. They need to exploit the capabilities of advanced technologies, such as data visualizations and software agents, and seek elegant ways to support sets of core problem solving activities, many of which are inadequately addressed in current programs.

When HCI specialists initiate these design approaches, they are bound to upset existing development conventions. When they recommend useful support, they bring up troublesome design issues that teams would just as soon ignore, such as questions about reusability versus domain specificity;

low-level modularity versus integration; simplicity versus adaptability and flexibility; and formalization versus *adho*cracy. These questions have no right answers and no prescribed means of resolution. They are best handled as "both-and" issues rather than "either-or," and participants should negotiate the tensions by focusing on how much of each, when, and why.

Ideally, these debates introduce creative friction and inventive solutions that benefit the product. Realistically, they also arouse political tensions as team members strive to make their biases and interests dominant. In decision-making about design choices for usefulness, politics play a constant role. Design-specific politics, however, are outside the scope of this chapter and can be found in the literature on the politics of usability (Grudin, 1991; Poltrock and Grudin, 1996; Browne and Friend, 1998; Crear and Benyon, 1998; Nodder, 1998). The political strategies advanced here focus instead on integrating usefulness practices into organizational processes during such development activities as defining products or deciding on modification requests. These political strategies, when coupled with initiatives to direct design thinking, methods, and choices toward usefulness, can go a long way toward institutionalizing usefulness in production.

Such political strategies start with HCI specialists sharing findings across situations so usability specialists have access to convincing evidence, even when it is unavailable from their immediate contexts. HCI specialists must see or create opportunities for political action in periods of uncertainty and transition. They must not wait passively for directives to be passed down from "on high." Rather, they need to take advantage of their expertise in user-centered design and their information about product use to create communication networks and to organize efforts to improve the products.

Knowledge, however, may become ineffective if opponents succeed in using strategies that uphold the status quo at the expense of exploring concrete needs for change. Faced with this resistance and its appeals to organizational stability, HCI specialists must mobilize support on other fronts and often engage in renegade strategies while still ensuring organizational stability. They must find champions among their allies to implement the informal processes required to pursue usefulness practices. Finally, in campaigning for usefulness in any area of development—be it scope, job design, or modification requests—usability specialists must employ a multiplicity of strategies, often simultaneously. At once they may need to work at gaining a champion, manipulating scheduling, renaming tasks, bringing team members to the field, holding unprecedented cross-functional meetings, and creating user-requirements documents. Success requires both knowledge and agility.

The software industry is poised to make dramatic advances in design and development. Nowhere is this potential greater than in the area of complex tasks. Many of the pieces necessary for this change are already in place. In technical areas, such as software architecture, many developers have embarked on creating domain-specific architectures. Others have made significant advances into context-aware computing. In addition, many advanced technologies exist that can facilitate the complexities of problem solving, such as interactive data visualizations, distributed software agents, and end-user customizing through programming by example. Moreover, programmers and application designers have long been interested and engaged in pattern languages. In the area of HCI, a well-established body of knowledge and methods focus on contextually based, user-centered inquiry, design, and testing. Finally, many HCI specialists are well positioned to initiate compaigns for usefulness because usability now has a respected role in a number of production contexts.

The challenge is to fashion a visionary project for usefulness. We must take the next steps and give users the support and enhancements they need to solve complex problems productively, effectively, and efficiently in their workplaces. To do so, we must understand the usefulness practices required for getting the work right in an application. We must institute these practices in our design thinking, methods, software choices, and organizational processes.

Whether useful support evolves through incremental improvements or as a "killer app" that takes the market by storm, the need is clear. Software teams must push past the boundaries of current practices to the next great breakthrough: Useful support for dynamic work. The software industry will only make this breakthrough, however, if we approach this effort with fresh visions, varied expertise, creativity, and political know-how.

REFERENCES

Agre, Philip E. "Toward a Critical Technical Practice: Lessons Learned in Trying to Reform AI." In *Social Science, Technical Systems, and Cooperative Work: Beyond the Great Divide*, edited by Geoffrey Bowker, Susan Leigh Star, William Turner, and Les Gasser, 131-157. Mahwah, NJ: Lawrence Erlbaum Associates, 1997.

Arksey, David. Personal communication, 2001.

Axelrod, Robert and Michael Cohen. *Harnessing Complexity: Organizational Implications of a Scientific Frontier*. New York: Free Press, 1999.

Bell, Richard, Henry Walker, and David Willer. "Power, Influence, and Legitimacy in Organizations." *Research in the Sociology of Organizations* 17 (2000): 131-171.

Browne, Dermot and John Friend. "A Structured Approach to User Interface Design." In *The Politics of Usability: A Practical Guide to Designing Usable Systems in Industry*, edited by Lesley Trenner and Joanna Bawa, 61-68. London: Springer-Verlag, 1998.

Carlson, Patricia. "Information Technology and the Emergence of a Worker-Centered Organization." *Journal of Computer Documentation* 24, no. 4 (2000): 204-212.

Casson, Mark. *Information and Organization: A New Perspective on the Theory of the Firm.* Oxford: Oxford University Press, 1997.

Crear, Alison and David Benyon. "Integrating Usability Into Systems Development." In *The Politics of Usability: A Practical Guide to Designing Usable Systems in Industry*, edited by Lesley Trenner and Joanna Bawa, 49-60. London: Springer-Verlag, 1998.

Fligstein, Neil. *The Transformation of Corporate Control.* Cambridge, MA: Harvard University Press, 1990.

Frost, Peter and Carolyn Egri. "The Political Process of Innovation." *Research in Organizational Behavior* 13 (1991): 229-295.

Grudin, Jonathan. "Systematic Sources of Suboptimal Interface Design in Large Product Development Organizations." *Human-Computer Interaction* 6 (1991): 147-196.

Gutierrez, James. Personal communication, 2002.

Law, John and Michel Callon. "Engineering and Sociology in a Military Aircraft Project: A Network Analysis of Technological Change." In *Ecologies of Knowledge*, edited by Susan Leigh Star, 281-302. Albany: SUNY Press, 1995.

Lovaglia, Michael. "Understanding Network Theory." *Research in the Sociology of Organizations* 16 (1999): 31-59.

Nodder, Chris. "Making a Business Case for Usability and Beyond – the Fight for Survival." In *The Politics of Usability: A Practical Guide to Designing Usable Systems in Industry*, edited by Lesley Trenner and Joanna Bawa, 3-19. London: Springer-Verlag, 1998.

Poltrock, Steve and Jonathan Grudin. "Organizational Obstacles to Interface Design and Development: Two Participant Observer Studies." In *Human-Computer Interaction Design: Success Stories, Emerging Methods, and Real World Contexts*, edited by Marianne Rudisill, Clayton Lewis, Peter Polson, and Timothy McKay, 303-337. San Francisco: Morgan Kaufmann, 1996.

Scott, W. Richard. *Organizations: Rational, Natural, and Open Systems.* Englewood Cliffs, NJ: Prentice-Hall, 1987.

Scott, W. Richard. *Institutions and Organizations,* 2nd ed. Thousand Oaks, CA: Sage Publications, 2001.

Star, Susan Leigh. "The Politics of Formal Representations: Wizards, Gurus, and Organizational Complexity." In *Ecologies of Knowledge*, edited by Susan Leigh Star, 88-118. Albany: SUNY Press, 1995.

Stryker, Robin. "Legitimacy Processes as Institutional Politics." *Research in the Sociology of Organizations* 17 (2000): 179-223.

Thomas, Robert and Thomas Kochar. "Technology, Industrial Relations and the Problem of Organizational Transformation." In *Technology and the Future of Work,* edited by Paul Adler, 210-231. Oxford, UK: Oxford University Press, 1991.

Thomas, Robert. *What Machines Can't Do: Politics and Technology in the Industrial Enterprise.* Berkeley: University of California Press, 1994.

Trenner, Lesley and Joanna Bawa, eds. *The Politics of Usability: A Practical Guide to Designing Usable Systems in Industry.* London: Springer-Verlag, 1998.

APPENDIX
Distribution of Control in the VizAppManager Tool

Activity	Program Control Over...	User Control Over...
■ Acquiring information	■ Formatting data so it is consistent with notions of users' infrastructure configurations and processes, deriving and displaying values critical to domain-based analyses	■ Filtering data, integrating data from diverse tools or program modules (e.g., triggered alarms and alarm threshold settings)
■ Setting up entries into information	■ Making relevant options available	■ Selecting the data and graphics for entry into a line of questioning
■ Preparing for analysis and analyzing data	■ Calculating and displaying context-dependent summaries and metrics (e.g., an overall "health of the system" statistic), options for highlighting certain relationships relevant to complex analyses (such as interwoven diagnosis and prognosis)	■ Arranging data, laying out information-scapes, data encoding perceptually, customizing values for color distributions, deriving values on-the-fly, *ad hoc* aggregating and synthesizing of data, cuing of situation conditions of import, marking and recalling views, saving and resuming after

Activity	Program Control Over...	User Control Over...
		interruptions, coordinating meanings across tools
■ Deliberating about decisions and actions	■ Making relevant options available for users' possible decisions and actions and providing some recommended courses of action for common or critical types of investigations	■ Deciding, with easy reversal, whether to be responsible for trouble tickets or alarms or not; how to arrange, integrate, or correlate specific data; how to highlight analysis-specific points of interest and visual structures; what references across tools to make; how and where to designate reminders; how to integrate tools and data from diverse sources
■ Implementing actions	■ Automatically returning threshold values to original settings when cued to do so, facilitating hand-offs and escalations, providing necessary functionality for marking insights and reusing them as needed	■ Selecting, hiding, and filtering out data; arranging data, graphics and windows

FIGURE CREDITS

Figure 1.1 from "The Visual Display of Quantitative Information" by Edward Tufte (Cheshire, Connecticut: Graphics Press, 1983). Reprinted with permission.

Figure 2.1 courtesy of PPD Informatics,
http://www.Belmont.com/ belweb2/ software/cg/cg_about.html.

Figure 4.1 courtesy of *Network Magazine*, © AAPT Networks,
http://www.net.aapt.com/au/netmag/diagram2.html

Figure 5.2(a) from "Elastic Windows: A Hierarchical Multiple" by Eser Kandogan and Ben Shneiderman, Human-Computer Interaction Laboratory at the University of Maryland.
http://www.cs.umd.edu/hcil/elastic-windows/script.html.

Figure 5.2(b) courtesy of UserCreations LLC at
http://www.usercreations.com/spring.

Figure 5.3 courtesy of Lifestream, Mirror Worlds Technologies, Inc., 2003,
http://www.scopeware.com/products.

Figure 5.5, 8.7(a) and 8.7(b) courtesy of MAYA Viz CoMotion™,
http://www.mayaviz.com.

Figure 5.6 courtesy of The Sage Visualization Group,
http://www-2.cs. cmu.edu/Groups/sage/sample.html.

Figure 7.9 from "A Visual One-Page Catalog Interface for Analytical Product Selection" by Juhnyoung Lee, Ho Soo Lee, and Priscilla Wang. EC-Web, 2000. Reprinted courtesy of EC Web Technologies, Inc., http://www.ecweb.net.

Figure 7.12 from http://www.space.com/businesstechnology/technology/ merboard_rover_020821.html. Reprinted courtesy of IBM Research, Almaden Research Center. Unauthorized use not permitted.

Figure 8.4 from PathFinder 2.02 courtesy of CocoaTech, 2003.

Figure 8.6 from "Graphical Summary of Patient Status" by Seth Powsner and Edward Tufte. (*The Lancet*, 1994, ol. 344, 386-389). Reprinted with permission from Elsevier.

Figure 8.8 courtesy of St. Jude Medical, Inc. and Alan Cooper,
http://www. cooper.com/content/services/shs.asp.

INDEX

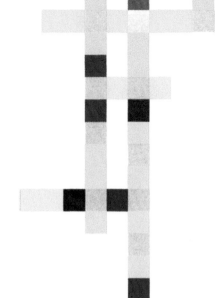

Printed and bound by CPI Group (UK) Ltd, Croydon, CR0 4YY

03/10/2024

01040325-0013